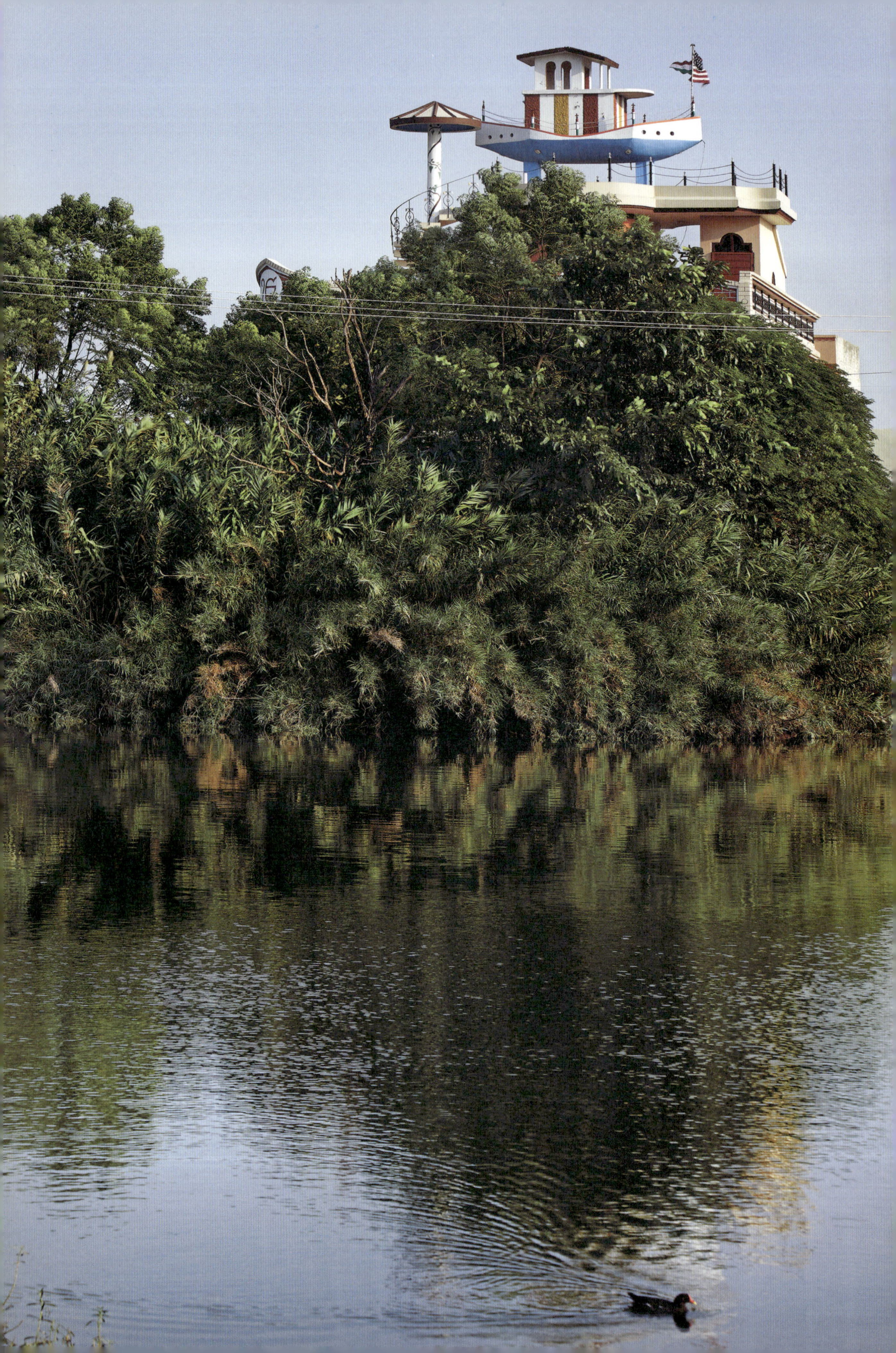

# EVERYDAY MONUMENTS

# RAJESH VORA

# EVERYDAY MONUMENTS

## The Rooftop Sculptures of Punjab

**PHOTOGRAPHS BY**
Rajesh Vora

**TEXTS BY**
Satwinder Kaur Bains, Rahul Mehrotra,
Sajdeep Soomal, Rajesh Vora, and Keith Wallace

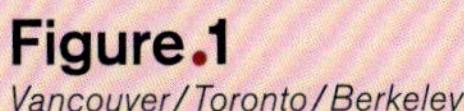


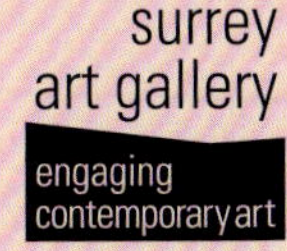

# CONTENTS

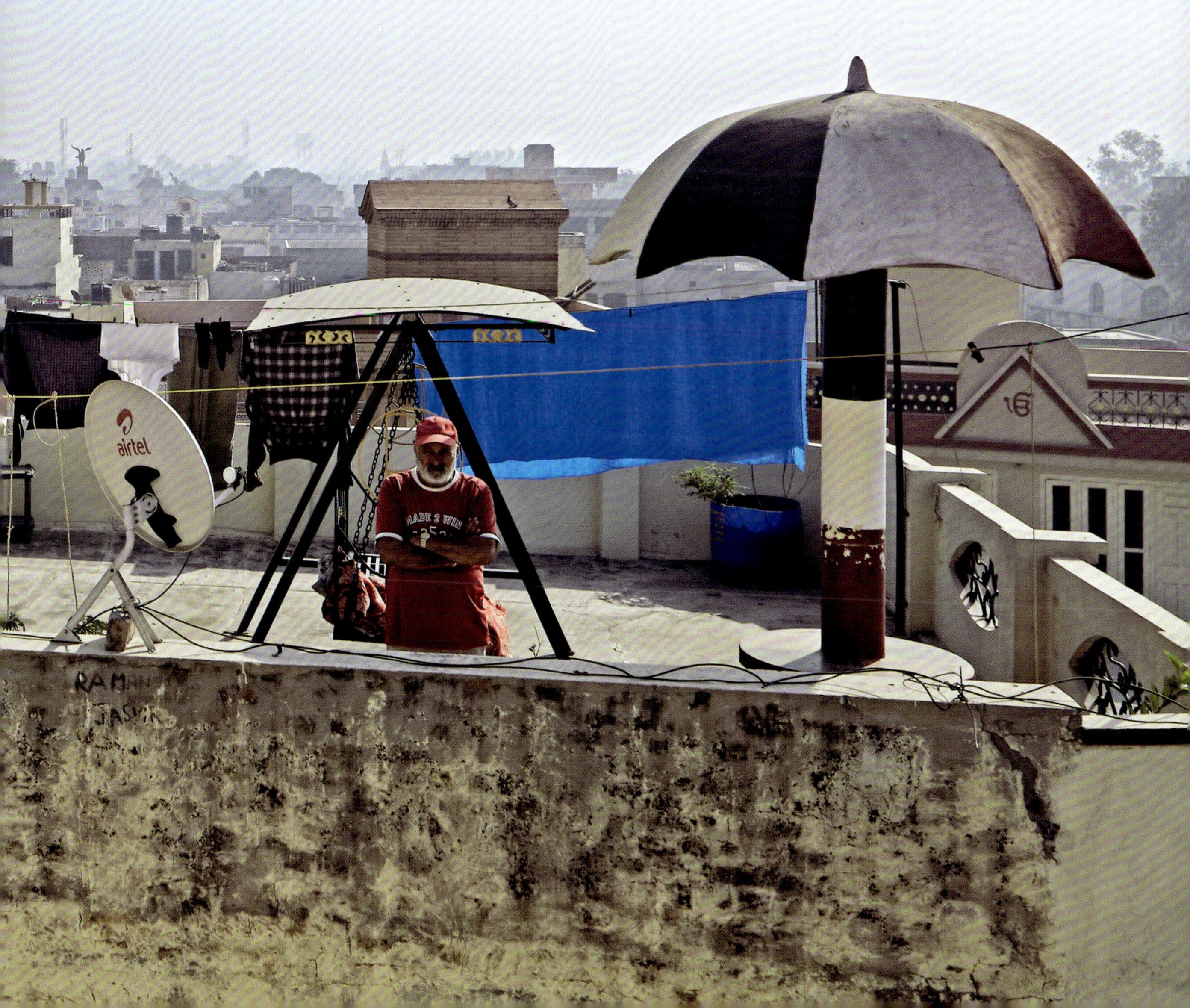

airtel

# FOREWORD

## JORDAN STROM

Curator of Exhibitions and Collections
Surrey Art Gallery

THE PHOTOGRAPHS of Rajesh Vora encompass a complexity of composition and subtle illumination. He knows at exactly which angle and perspective and in what condition of light to expose his images with respect to the challenges that the landscapes and atmospheric conditions can pose in attaining them. The pictures from Vora's Punjabi rooftop sculptures series defy any easy categorization. They are at once landscapes, architectural photographs, and portraits; they capture personal stories and architectural expressions that are also forms that serve as public art and family history.

Surrey Art Gallery hosted *Rajesh Vora: Everyday Monuments* in the spring of 2022, the first exhibition of this work outside of India. As the title suggests, through these works both art and the monumental are integrated into everyday life. The exhibition and now the book also showcase the region's rich vernacular architectural traditions, which took shape around the turn of the twentieth century.

Surrey, in Metro Vancouver, British Columbia, is home to one of the largest Punjabi diasporas in North America. Nearly 130,000 residents of the city speak Punjabi as their first language, over 20 percent of the city's population, making it the largest community outside of India to speak Punjabi—and many more members of the community have roots in Punjab. Many of Surrey's residents maintain strong ties to the region, including the villages where most of the works in the exhibition were photographed. The Punjabi village—both the actual home communities scattered across northern India and the idea of the *pind*—maintains a strong influence on the diasporic community in Surrey and British Columbia.

Surrey Art Gallery's *Rajesh Vora: Everyday Monuments* exhibition would not have taken place without the financial support of the British Columbia Arts Council, the Zheng Shengtian Art Foundation, Hari Sharma Foundation, and The Hamber Foundation. We are also deeply grateful to the South Asian Studies Institute at the University of the Fraser Valley for partnering on the exhibition and its tour. Special thanks as well to Harbhajan S. Gill, Satwinder Kaur Bains, and Rajinder Bhandari for their input into the exhibition. And thank you to the writers Satwinder Kaur Bains, Rahul Mehrotra, and Sajdeep Soomal for their thoughtful contributions to this book. We would like to sincerely thank Keith Wallace for approaching us with his concept for the exhibition and for realizing it so thoroughly in the gallery and in book form. And, of course, we are most grateful to Rajesh Vora—not only for his vision and fortitude in achieving this epic multi-year project, but also for his generosity and care in sharing it with the world. His passion for this underrecognized art form shines through. Lastly, we would like to acknowledge and thank the many artist-fabricators in whose work and creativity this book, and the exhibition from which it extends, is grounded.

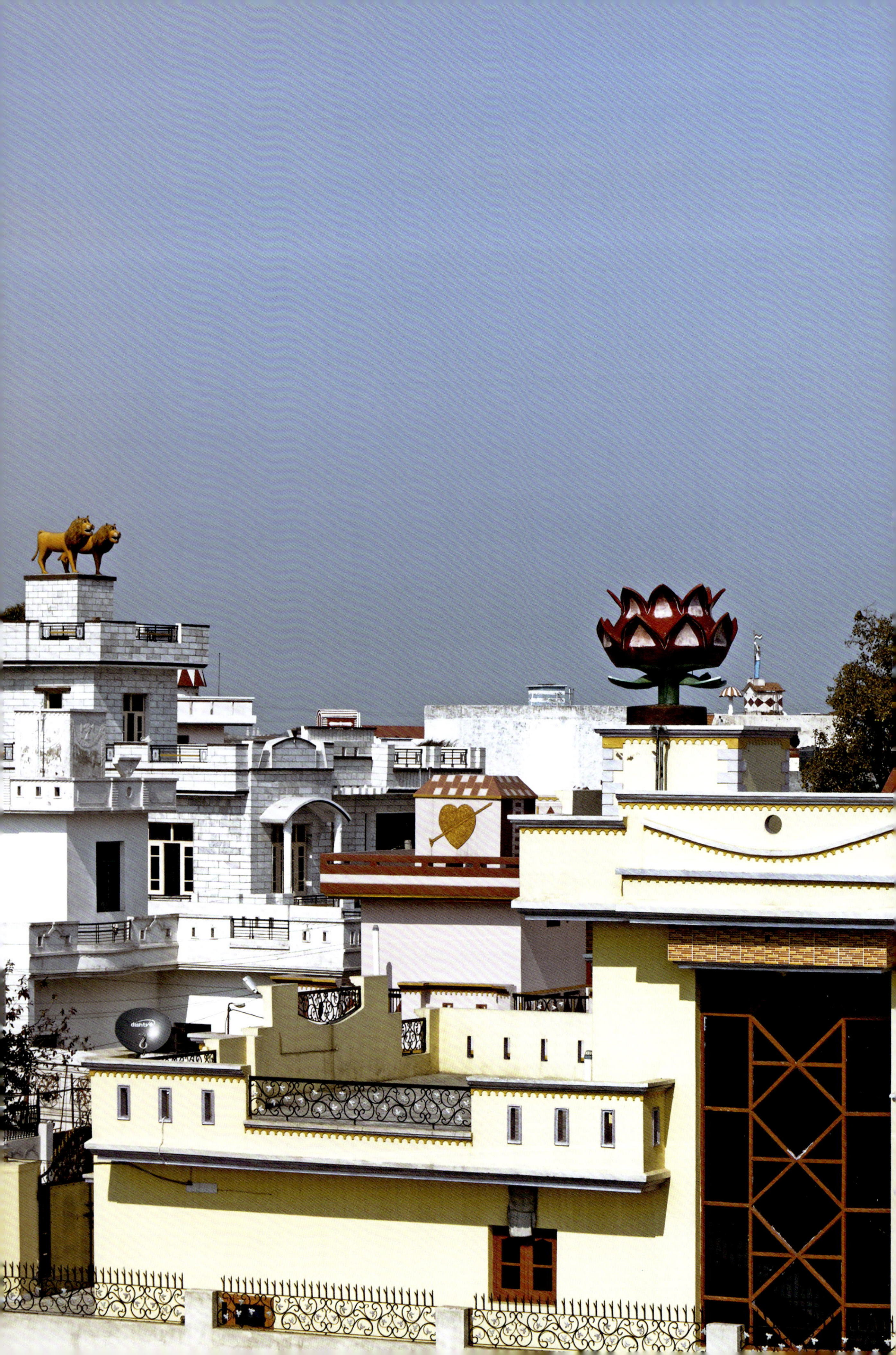

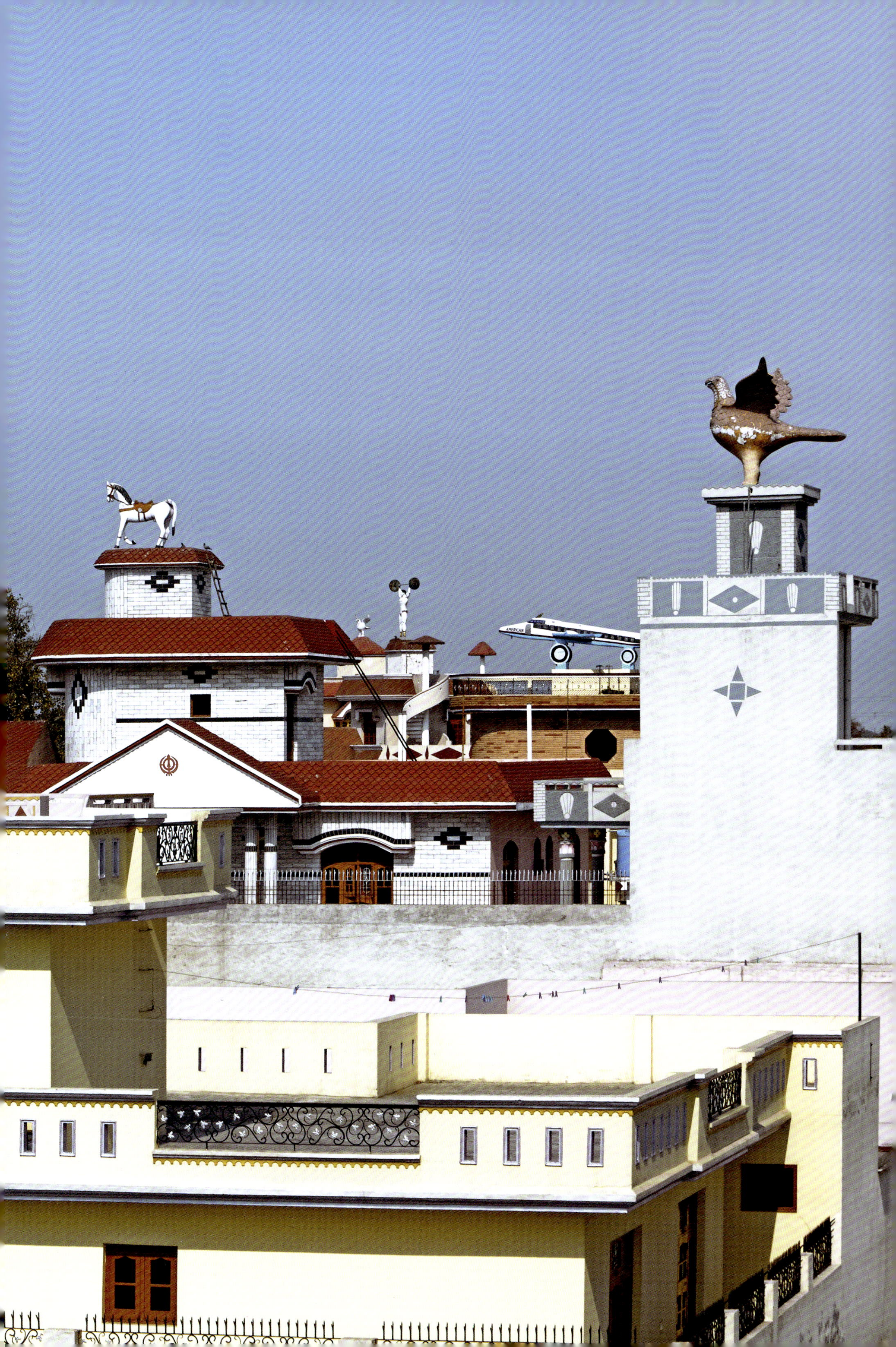
AMERICAN

# REIMAGINING THE HOME IN A TIME OF FLUX

RAHUL MEHROTRA

ARCHITECTURE, AND perhaps its most essential unit, the home, has historically been a codifier of a society's beliefs, achievements, and aspirations. It has also long symbolized stability: a haven to return to each night; a repository of memories contained in the images, artworks, and heirlooms that cohabit the space. And it is often more than that—the home is also a signifier of societal status through symbols of economic mobility, or sometimes their absence, representing beliefs both religious and cultural.

In India today, these basic assumptions stand challenged for a large portion of the population on account of three major factors. First is the massive scale of the informal settlements, wherein space and dwellings, whether in rural or urban contexts, are constructed and configured outside the formal purview of the state—a phenomenon that has become widespread in and beyond India in the last four decades. Second, massive demographic shifts are occurring around the world. Large groups of people are moving within and across regional as well as national boundaries because of economic aspirations and political instability. This will only increase as the depletion of natural resources and accelerating climate change cause more frequent natural disasters, which will further heighten general inequity and brutally dislocate communities around the globe. And last, digital influences are dissipating the once central role of architecture as a codifier of cultural symbols, imagery related to memory, and societal achievements and aspirations. All this results in an exponential increase in the population who are unhoused and often disfranchises the role of architecture in society, especially at the scale of the home.

It is in this context that Rajesh Vora's photographic project *Everyday Monuments* is pioneering as it unearths for us a unique situation where the binaries of stability and displacement, memories and their erasure, remote status and its codification in locality all become blurred in the artifact of the home in rural Punjab. More importantly, Vora frames the reading of the house at a visual decibel level exerting at times a disproportionate presence. He does this by displacing the house from the street and reframing it as a landmark—one that through its crowning rooftop sculptures modulates the skyline and becomes monumental. Here the aspirations of dwelling in a "modern" house confront a deep cultural impulse to adorn. Seemingly incongruous architectural elements coalesce to make the desires and achievements of the owners—albeit often in absentia—tangible and material not only in the specific imagery but in the sheer visual intensity of these homes. They can be read as venues at which an anticipated return can be celebrated, and as re-situating the status of the owner in a grounded relationship with their homeland.

This contextual crossover and hybridization of references through images signifying mobility has been used by diasporic populations in other places in India, such as the state of Kerala, and perhaps other parts of the world where conditions enable diasporic capital flows to transform the architecture of the home in visible ways. One might allude to this as "kitsch modernism" or a "new emergent vernacular." The homes in Punjab and the sculptures on top of them are moulded largely in reinforced cement concrete, which, with its ubiquitous presence, is clearly the vernacular building practice. Therefore, what makes the site of this work by Rajesh Vora particularly critical is that he extracts these images from the landscape of Punjab—where modernism was thought to have been firmly rooted in all its purity after its early establishment in the state capital of Chandigarh as the most vibrant site of the "modern project." It was the patronage of Nehru, the first prime minister of independent India, that made Chandigarh, designed by Le Corbusier in the 1950s, the symbol of modern India.

However, Chandigarh was somewhat of a *tabula rasa* situation, where modernism did not confront the many layers of tradition or the cultural milieu of Punjab and was not forced to confront any substantial existing built context. Furthermore, India's independence, although supposedly closing the debate on architecture and identity, did not produce the society for which the nation had hoped and yearned; instead, all efforts were directed toward dealing with the splintered society that the nation inherited. A society fractured by caste, class, economic disparities, rural–urban divides, and a multitude of beliefs and religious affiliations was welded together as a nation state.[1] Through this process, issues of uneven social and economic mobility threw up disparate aspirations, with the representation of each becoming increasingly challenging. It became overwhelmingly evident during these years that aesthetic modernity seemed to have arrived before social modernity through the small community of charismatic architects.[2] These were architects who introduced new ideas about spatial organization, building technologies, and, most critically, an aesthetic that jettisoned ornamentation.[3] Similarly, architecture in India continued to be largely handmade and dependent on craft. Reconciling these modes of production with the modernist tenets of predeterminacy and predictability was difficult for practitioners trained in Western sensibilities of architectural production when employed by the state or elites to design buildings. This resulted in the crafts staying below the register of the formal production of architecture while ensuring their continuity through engagement in the creation of the larger part of the built environment of India, which architects were not involved in moulding.

Here again, Rajesh Vora's work captures, perhaps unselfconsciously, these vernacular responses to modernisms in its formulation as kitsch. These responses are largely manifested in the everyday landscapes of settlements that are auto-constructed by inhabitants self-employing human resources and skills in the absence of a formal or state-provided housing supply. The internalization and assimilation of reinforced concrete and its sculptural possibilities as a common mode of construction in the post-independence landscape, which was skillfully demonstrated by Le Corbusier in Chandigarh, is now seamlessly employed or sculpted in the everyday landscape of Punjab. Vora's work also surfaces the broader ecology of production that involves local craftspeople, artists, and contractors, all supported by an economy buoyed by a robust diasporic network. In fact, the seeming ease with which these buildings sit in their local landscape while churning up associations within the larger circulation of capital and aspiration globally make them interesting sites for examining localized and internalized responses to modernism.

In a broader contextual reading of Rajesh Vora's visually stunning as well as provocative images, a compelling question arises from their location in the rural landscape of the small Indian village, where most of these homes are situated. This is clearly an indicator of the transitioning nature of the agriculture sector in Punjab and its deep historic ties with diasporic flows to and from the UK, Canada, United States, Australia, and many other parts of the world. But, more critically, these have become landscapes of transition, places where investments from "urban" albeit diasporic livelihoods are emerging within "rural" morphologies. The question is, what will these settlements look like as they evolve? Will these appear and operate like villages or cities or become small transitioning towns with their own urban form, logic, and relationship to the rural hinterland? This is where Rajesh Vora's work is extremely valuable, both as an archive and as a tool for speculating about these emerging landscapes. Seen through the lens of an insightful photographer, these homes and their rooftop sculptures ultimately ask us a critical question: How can we reimagine the home in a time of flux?

## NOTES

1 This post-independence scenario is succinctly described by Sundaram Tagore: "Independence unleashed waves of violence that seemed to be the wrath of supernatural powers. Indeed, in a metaphorical sense, the violence embodied the Indian philosophical tenets of creative and destructive forces—the cycle of chaos leading to order to only return to turmoil. Although modernity claims to decry chaos, its determination to oppose tradition breeds confusion." A phenomenon that continuously resurfaces in the coming decades and plays itself out in far more potent manifestations as the nation evolves. Sundaram Tagore, "The Legacy of Anti-Tradition," *The Art News Magazine of India* 2, no. 1 (1997).

2 Sibel Bozdogan, *Modernism and Nation Building* (Seattle: University of Washington Press, 2001).

3 These architects included Habib Rahman, the first Indian architect to be trained at MIT; Achyut Kanvinde, who was trained at Harvard; Gautam and Gira Sarabhai; Durga Bajpai; Piloo Mody and Lavina Colgan; Mansingh Rana; and, later, Charles Correa and B.V. Doshi.

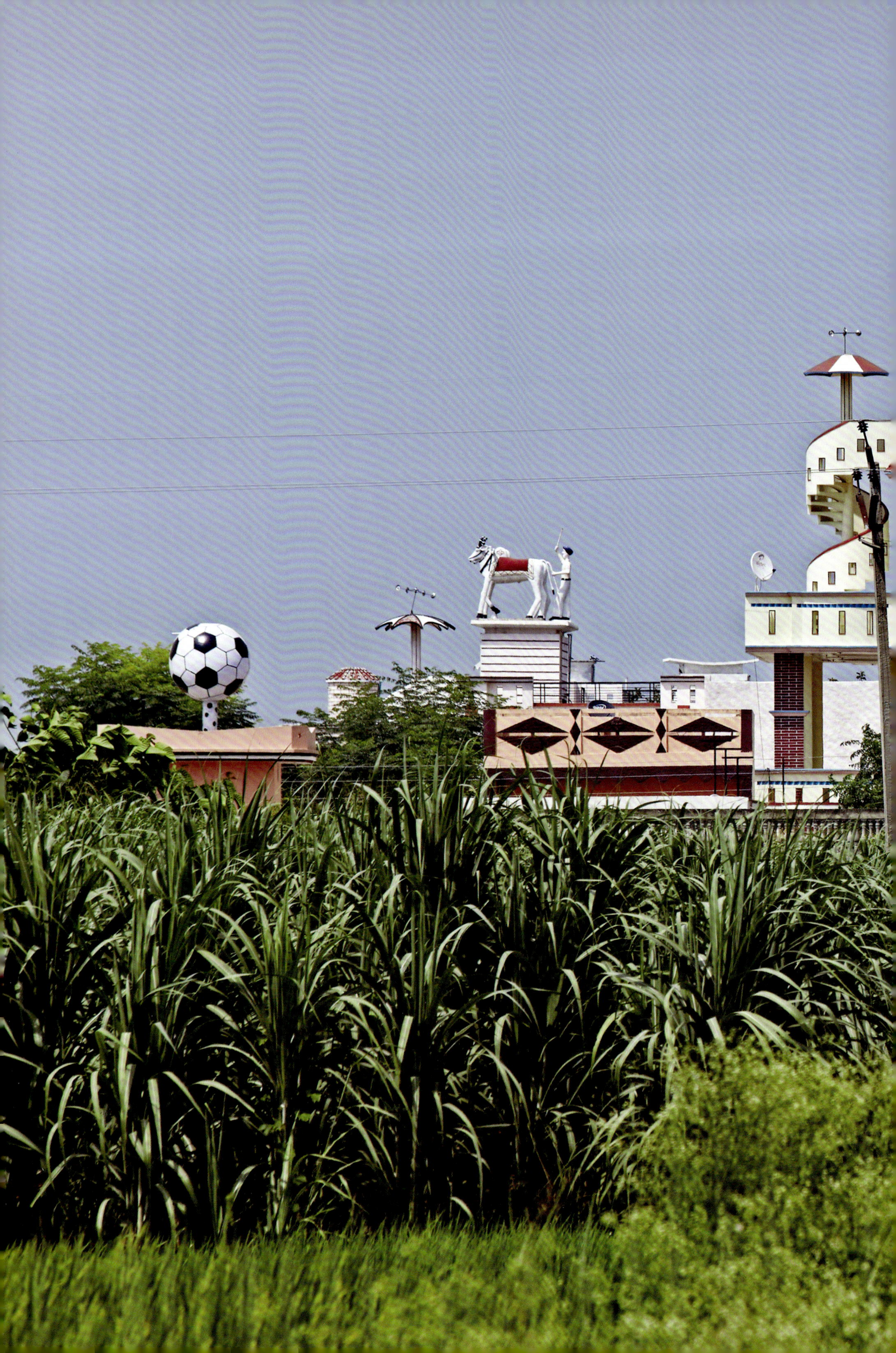

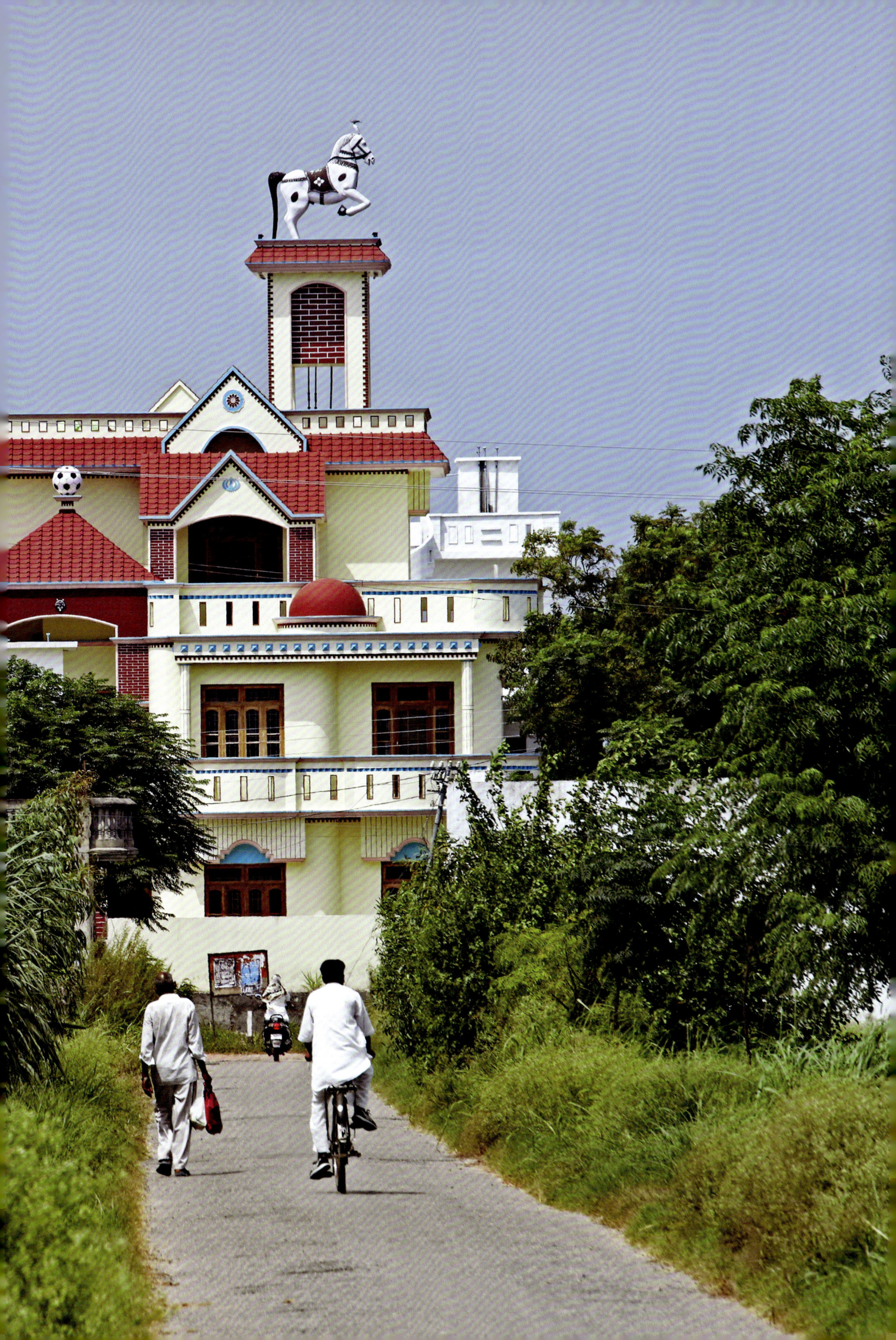

RAJESH VORA

# EVERYDAY MONUMENTS

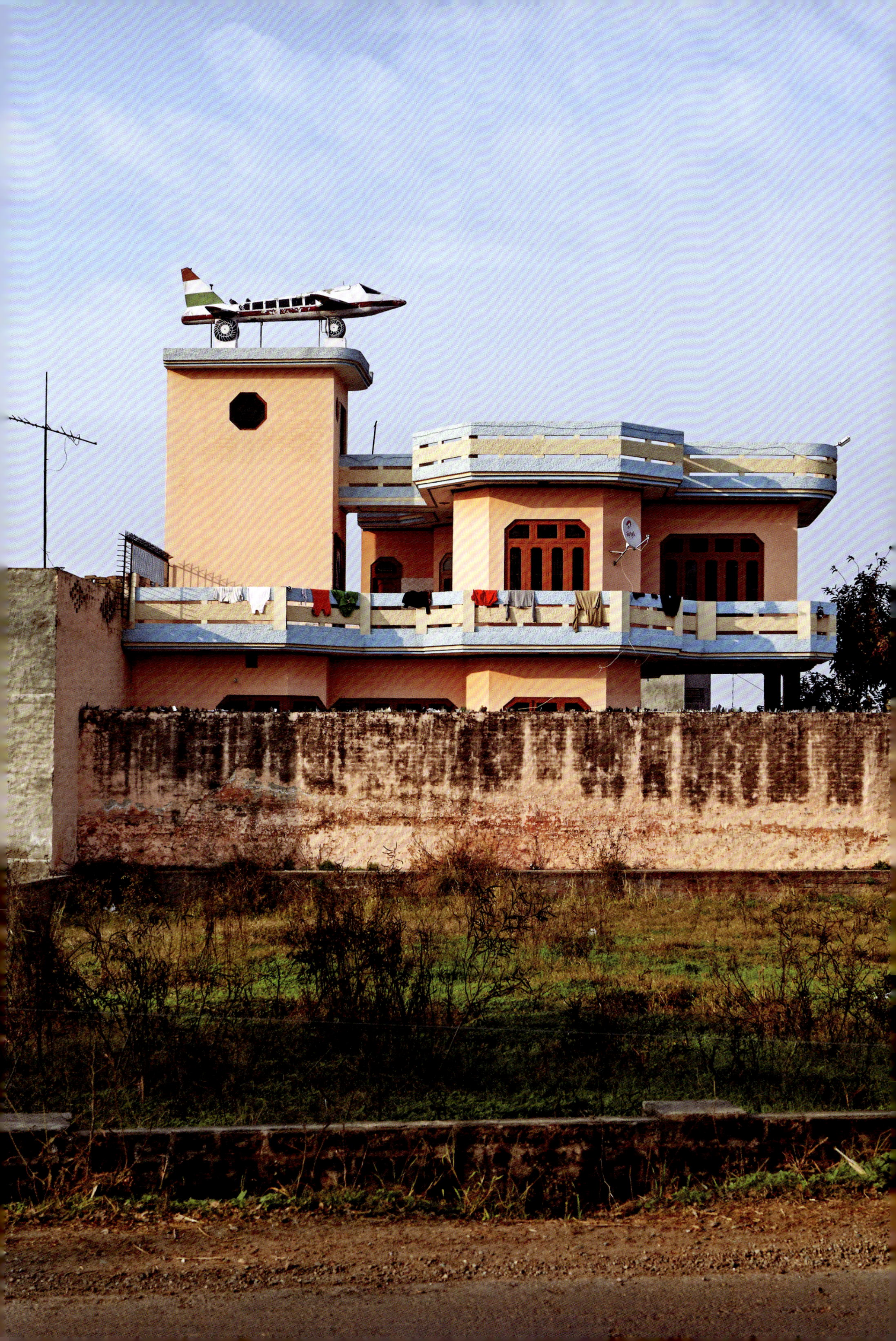

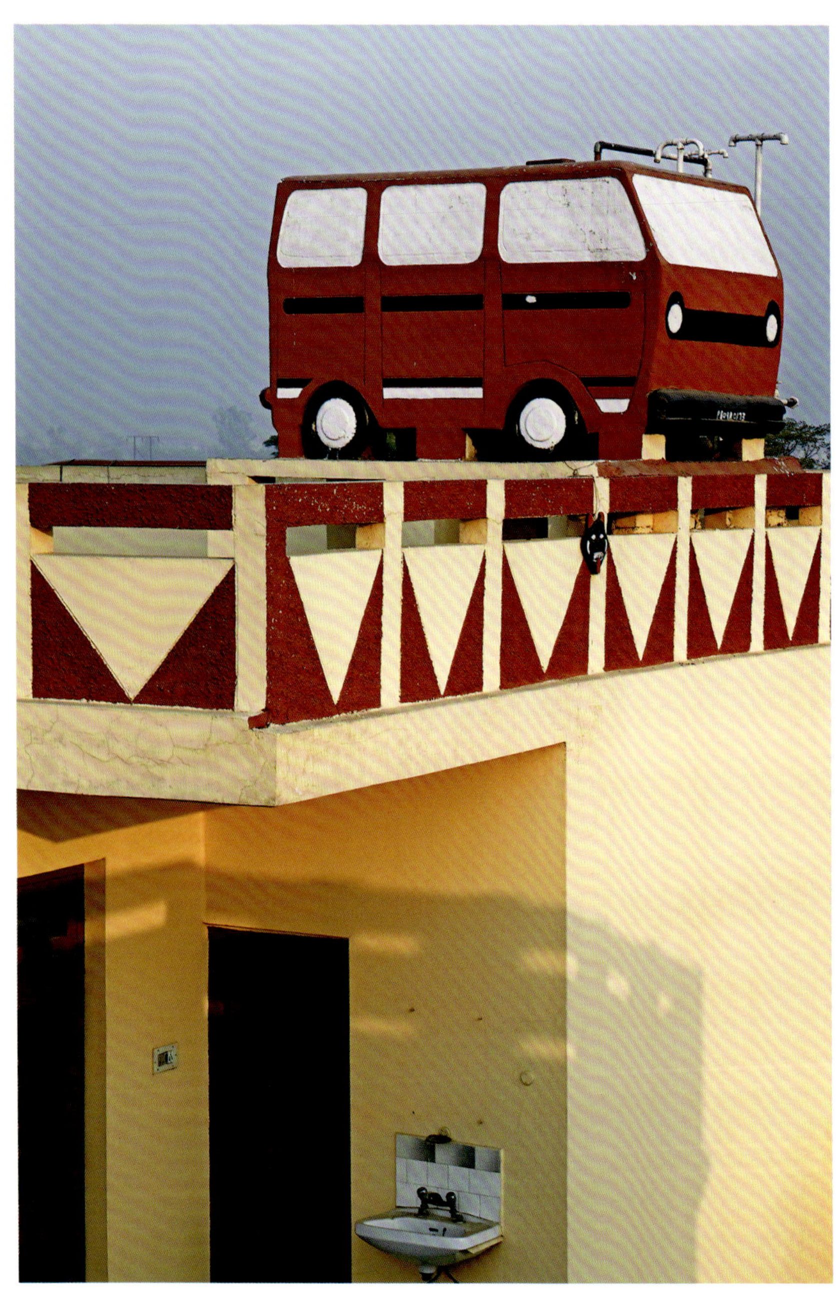

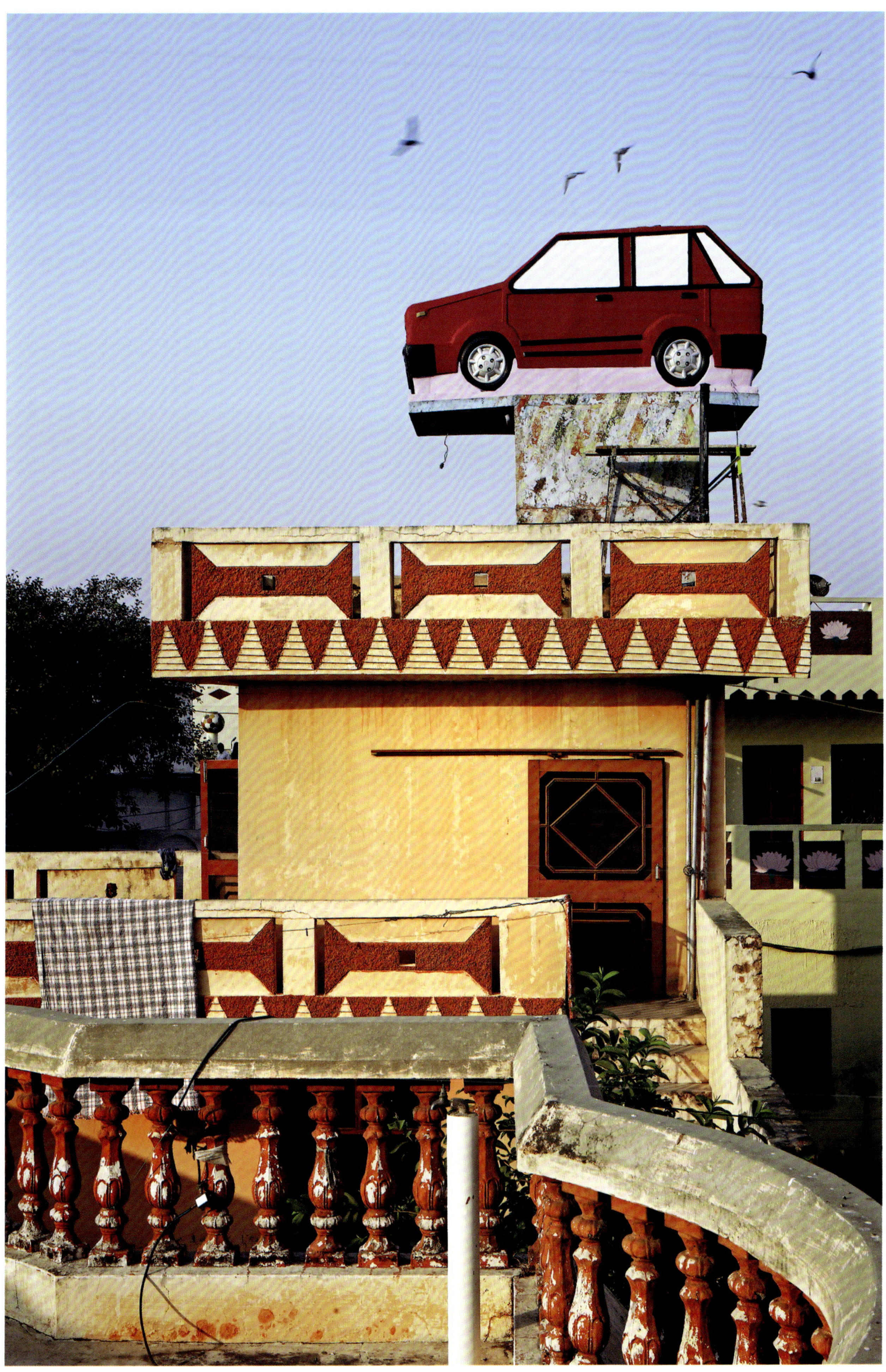

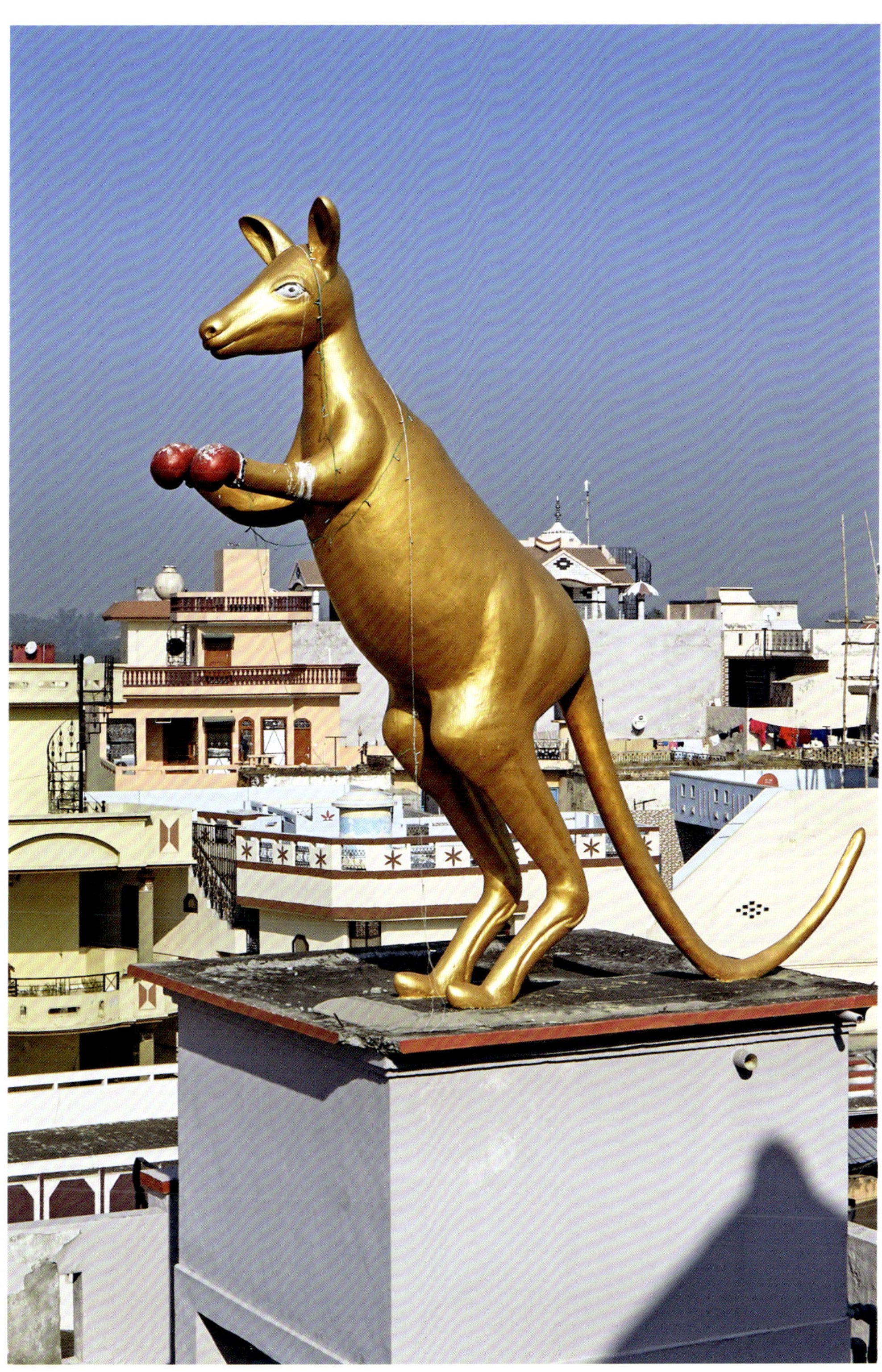

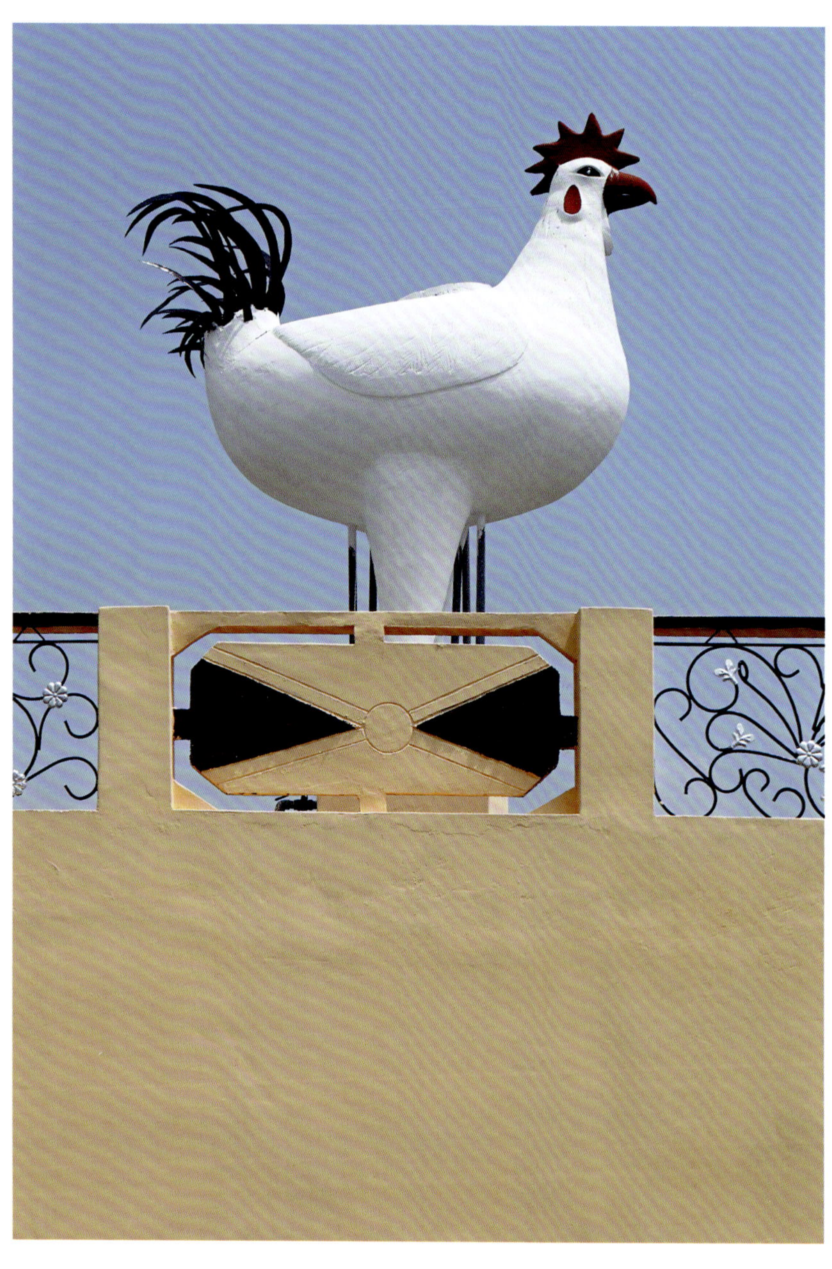

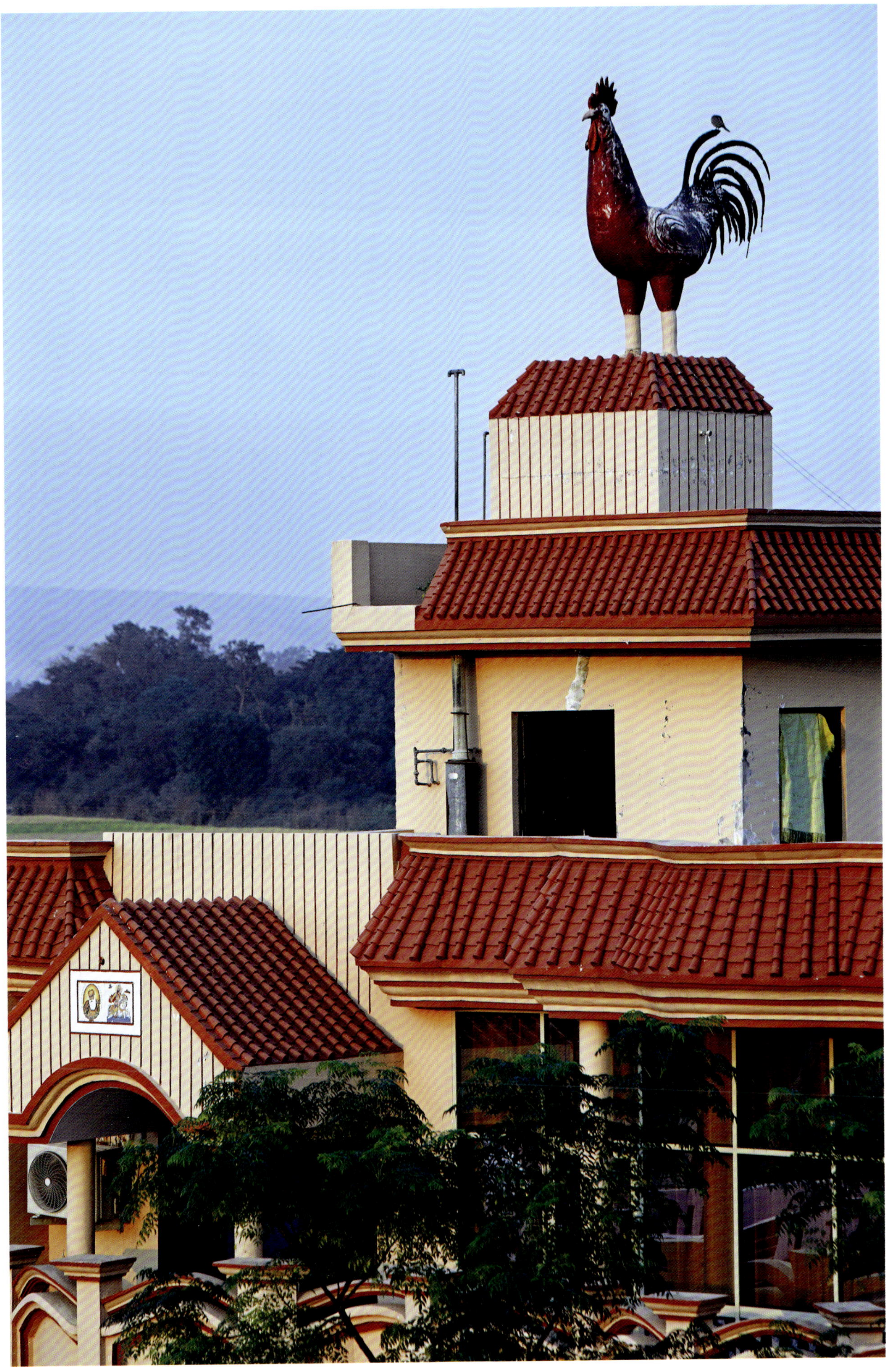

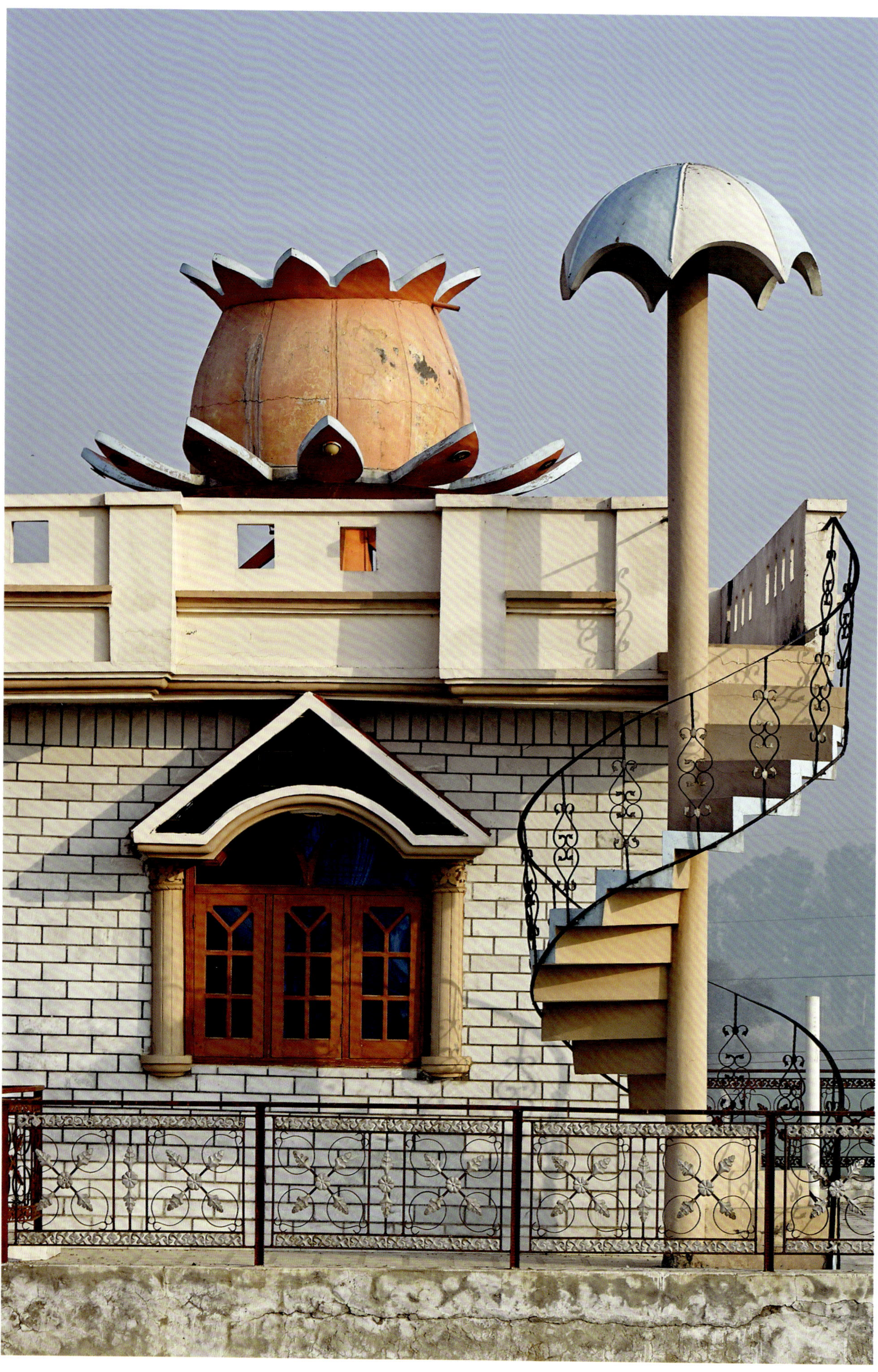

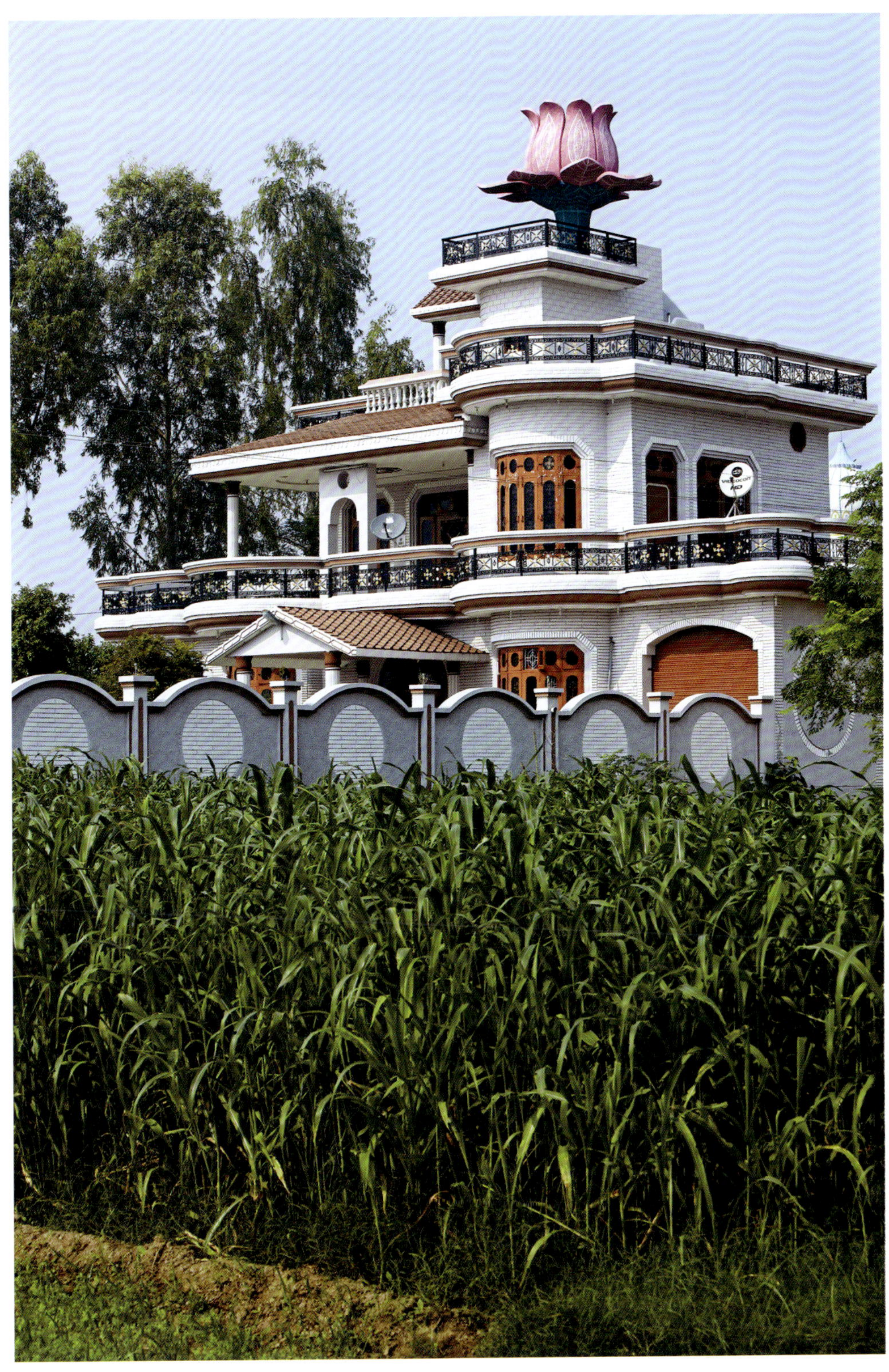

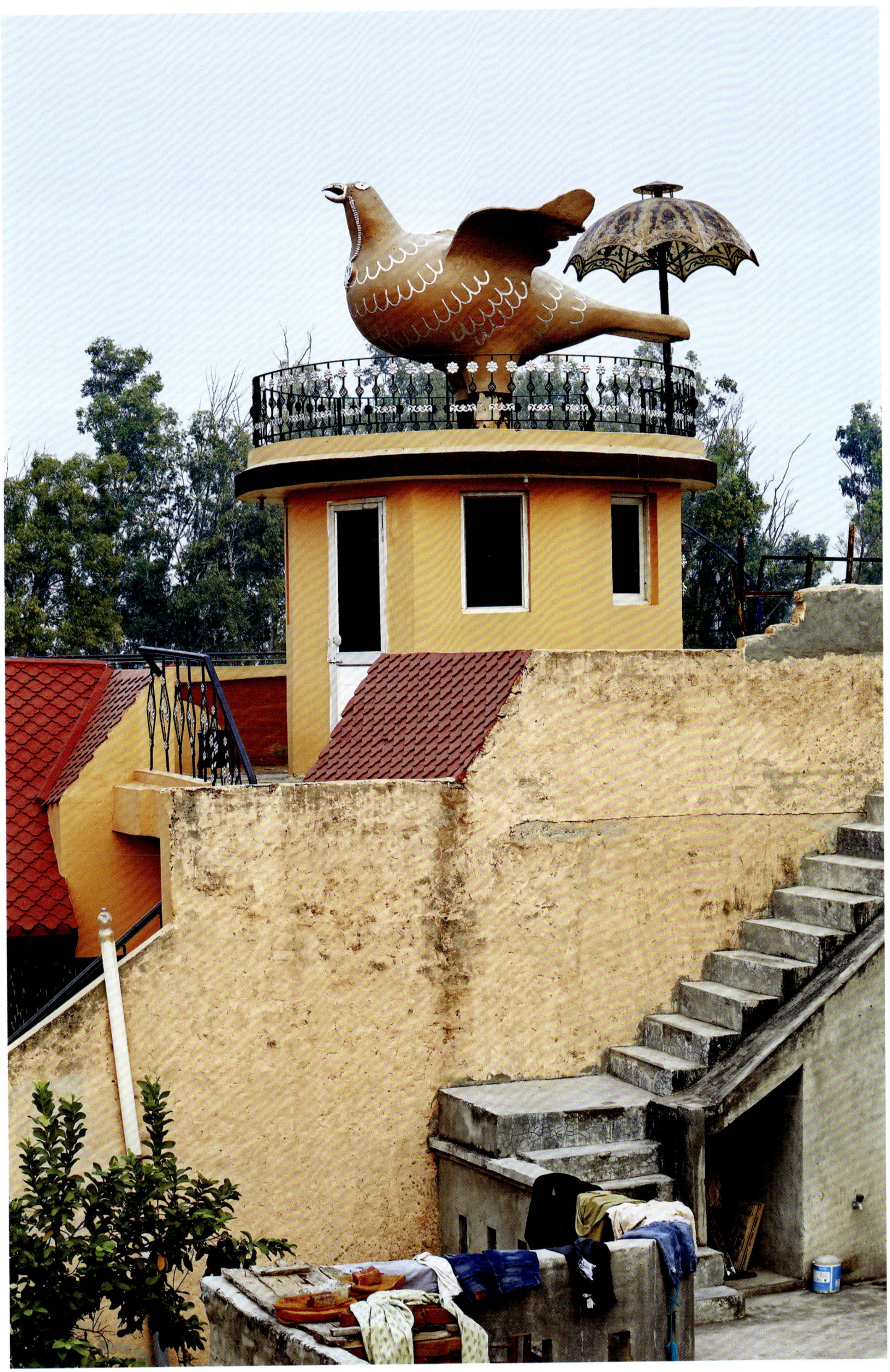

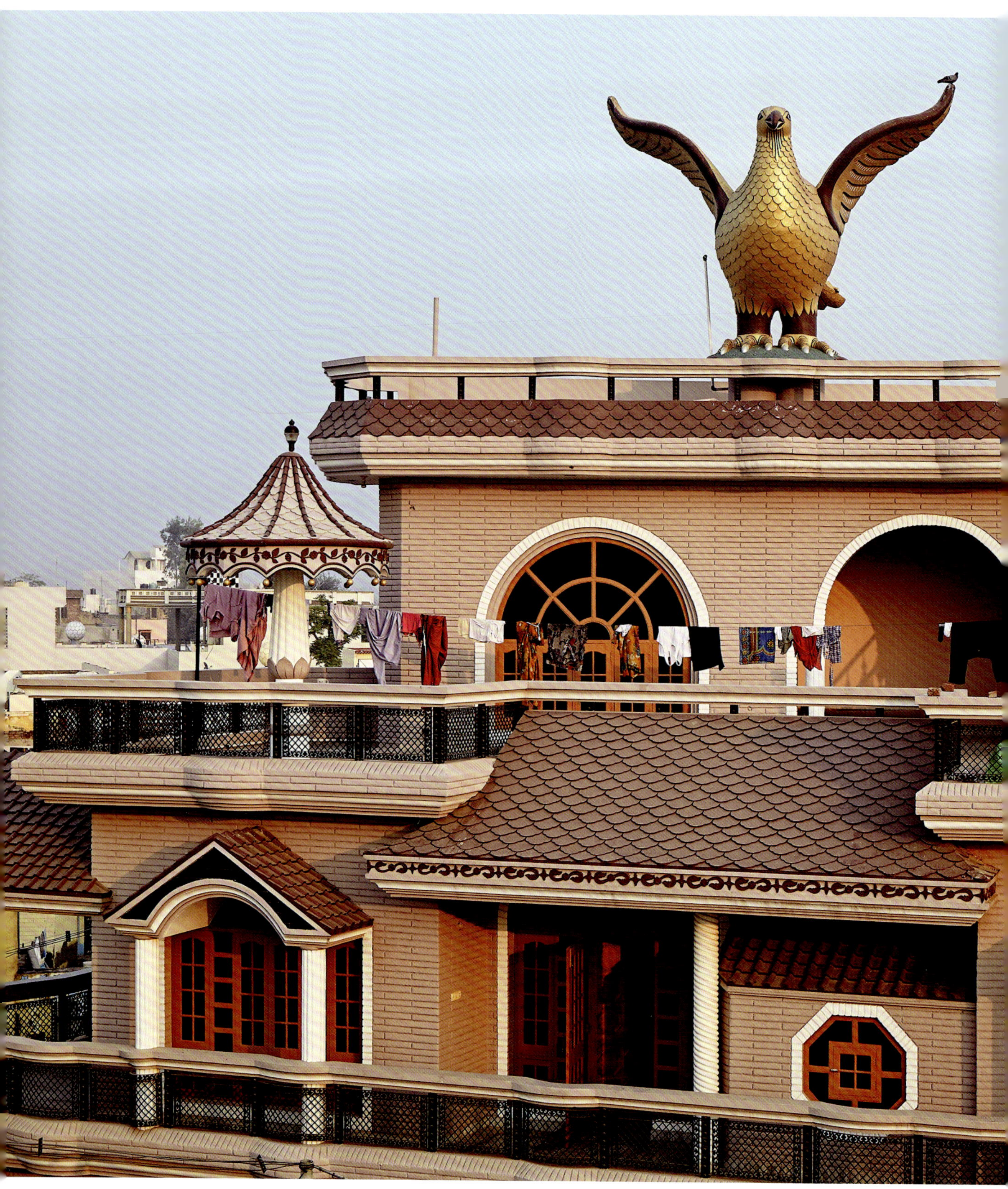

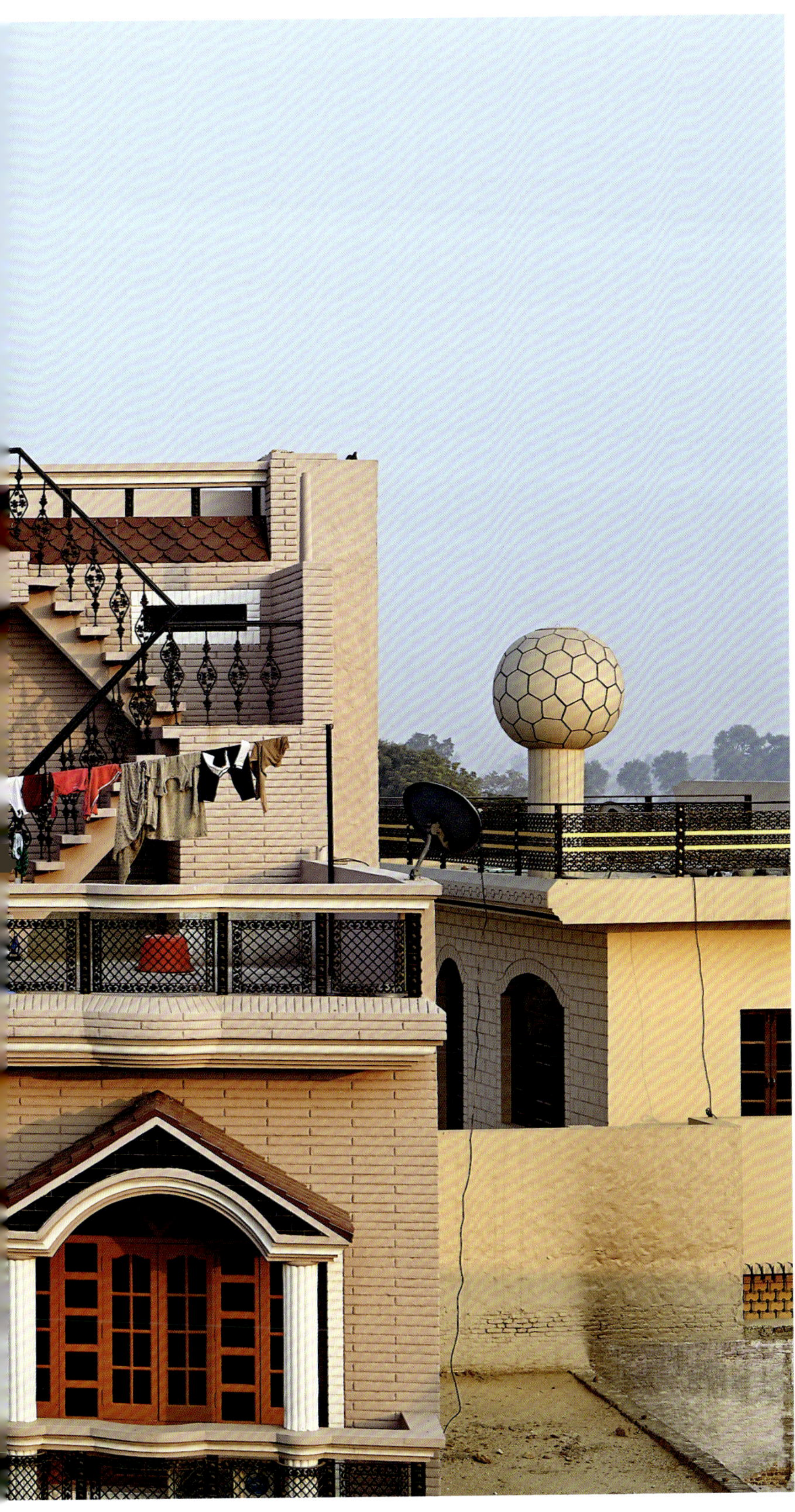

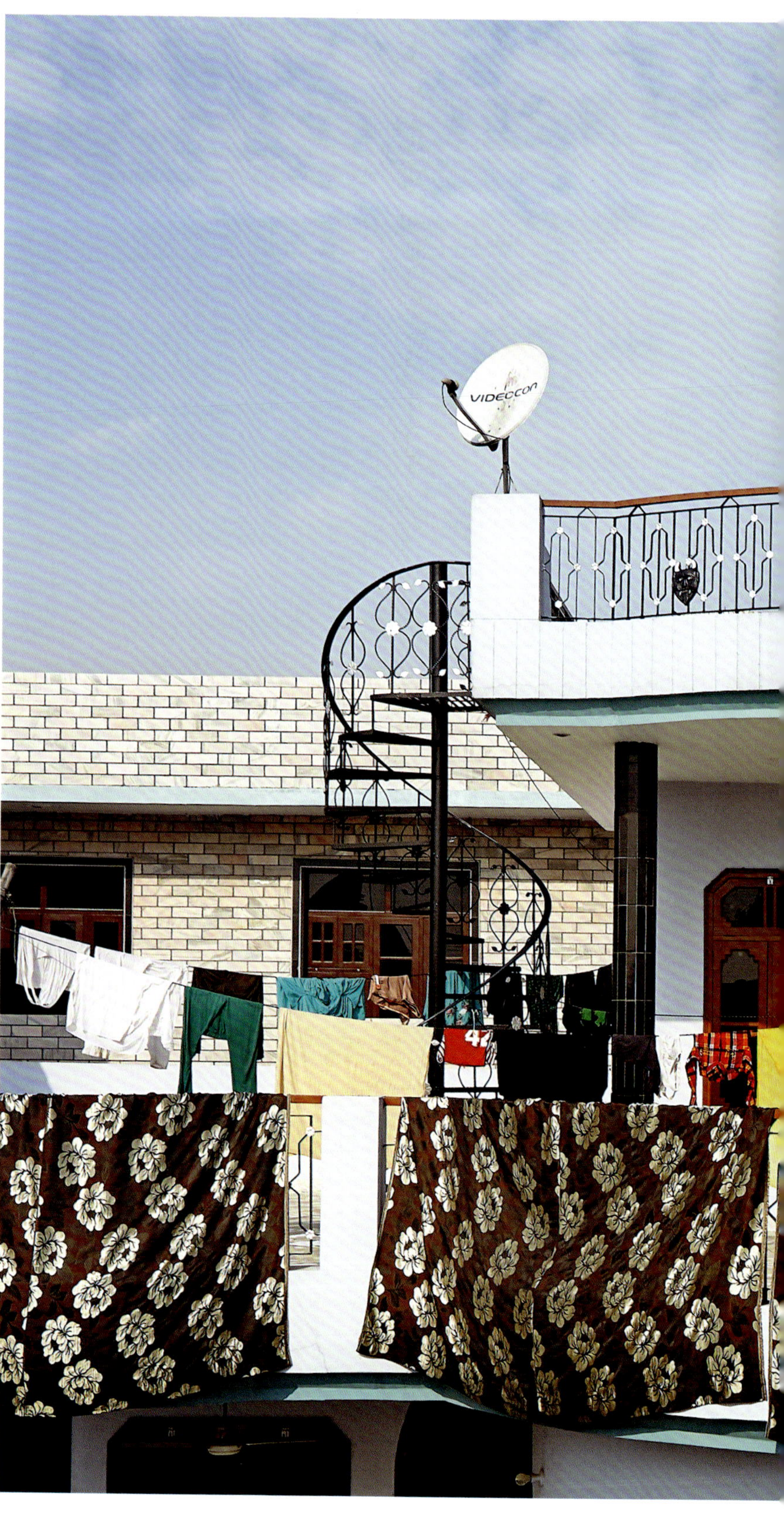
VIDEOCON

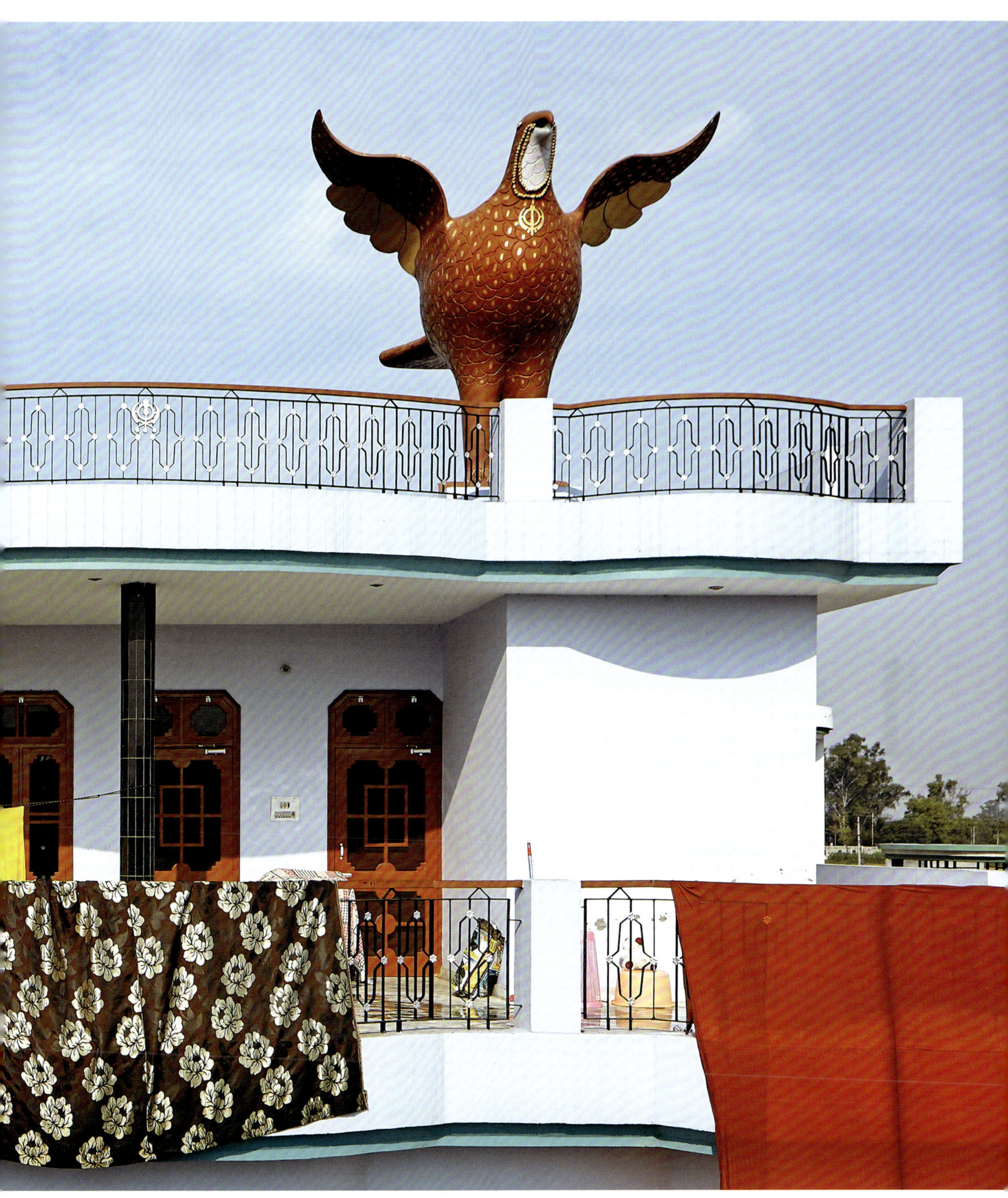

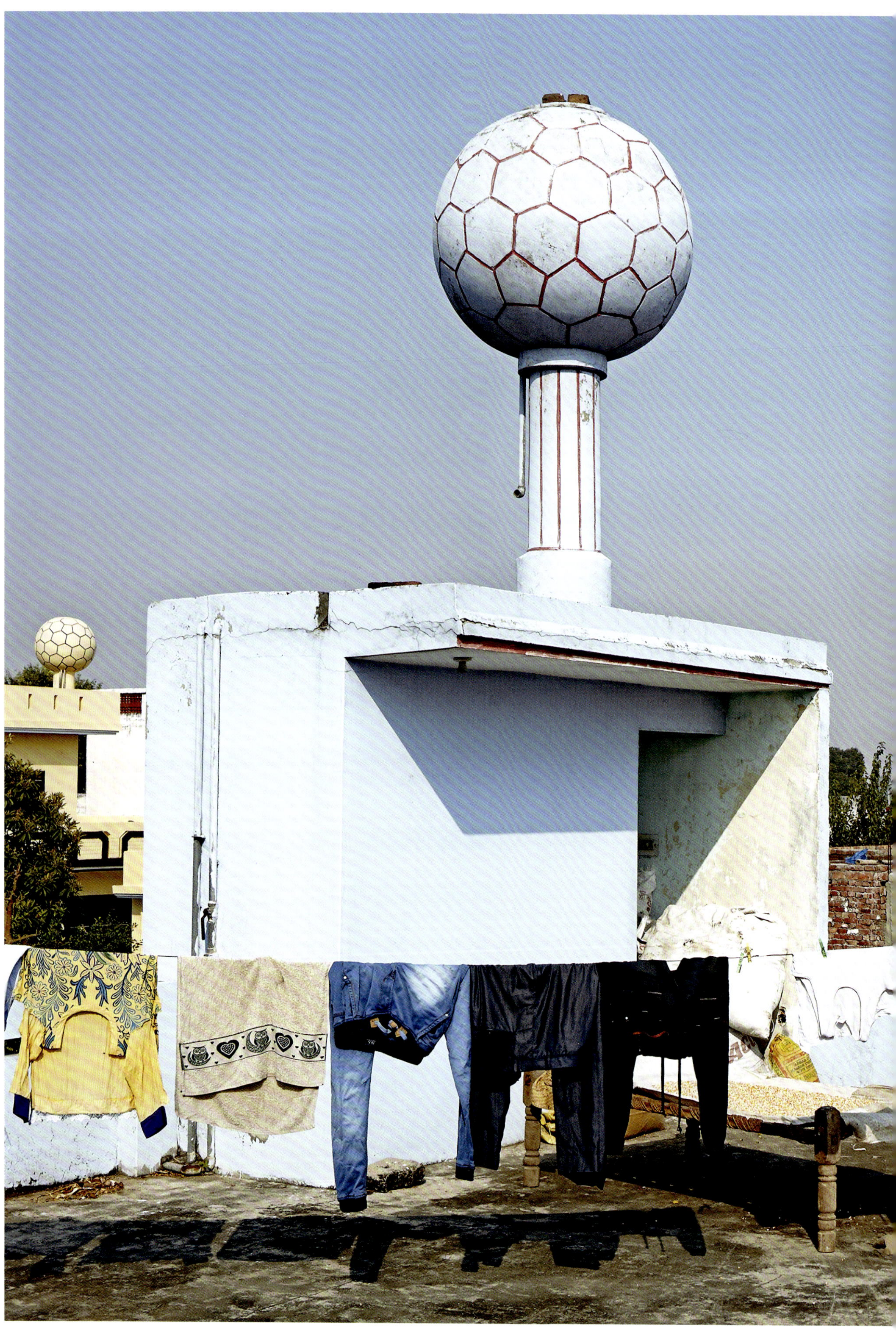

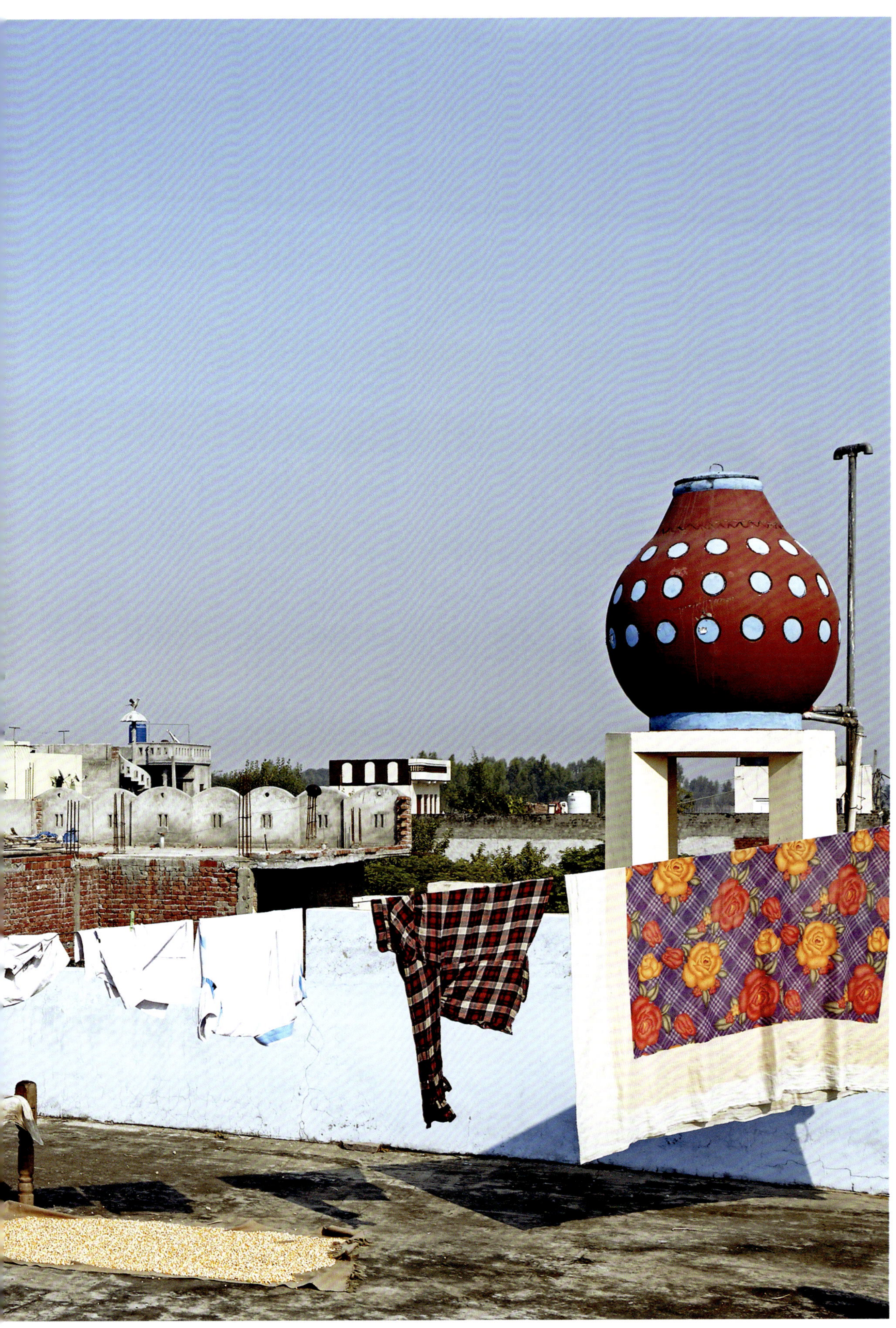

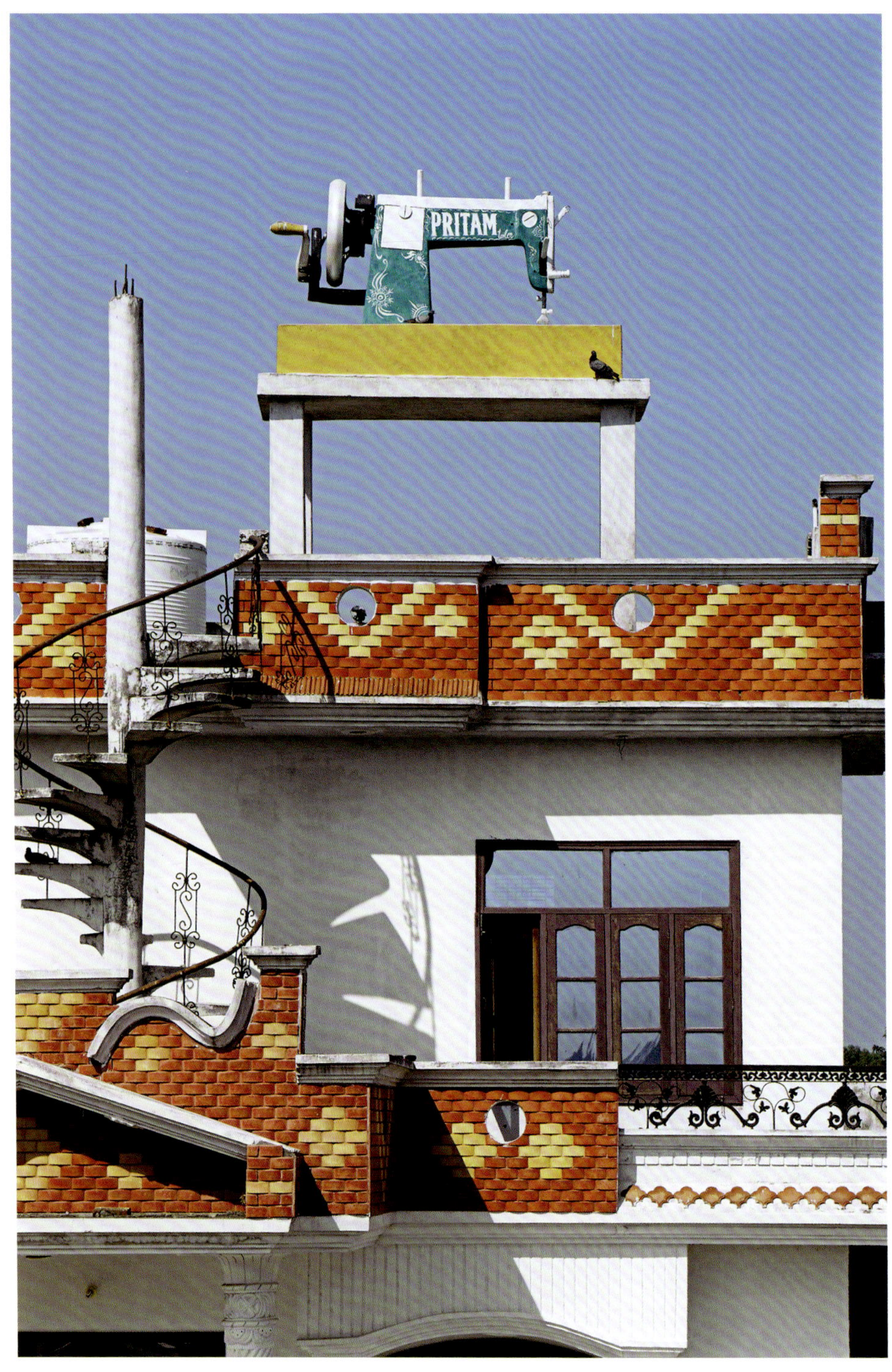
PRITAM

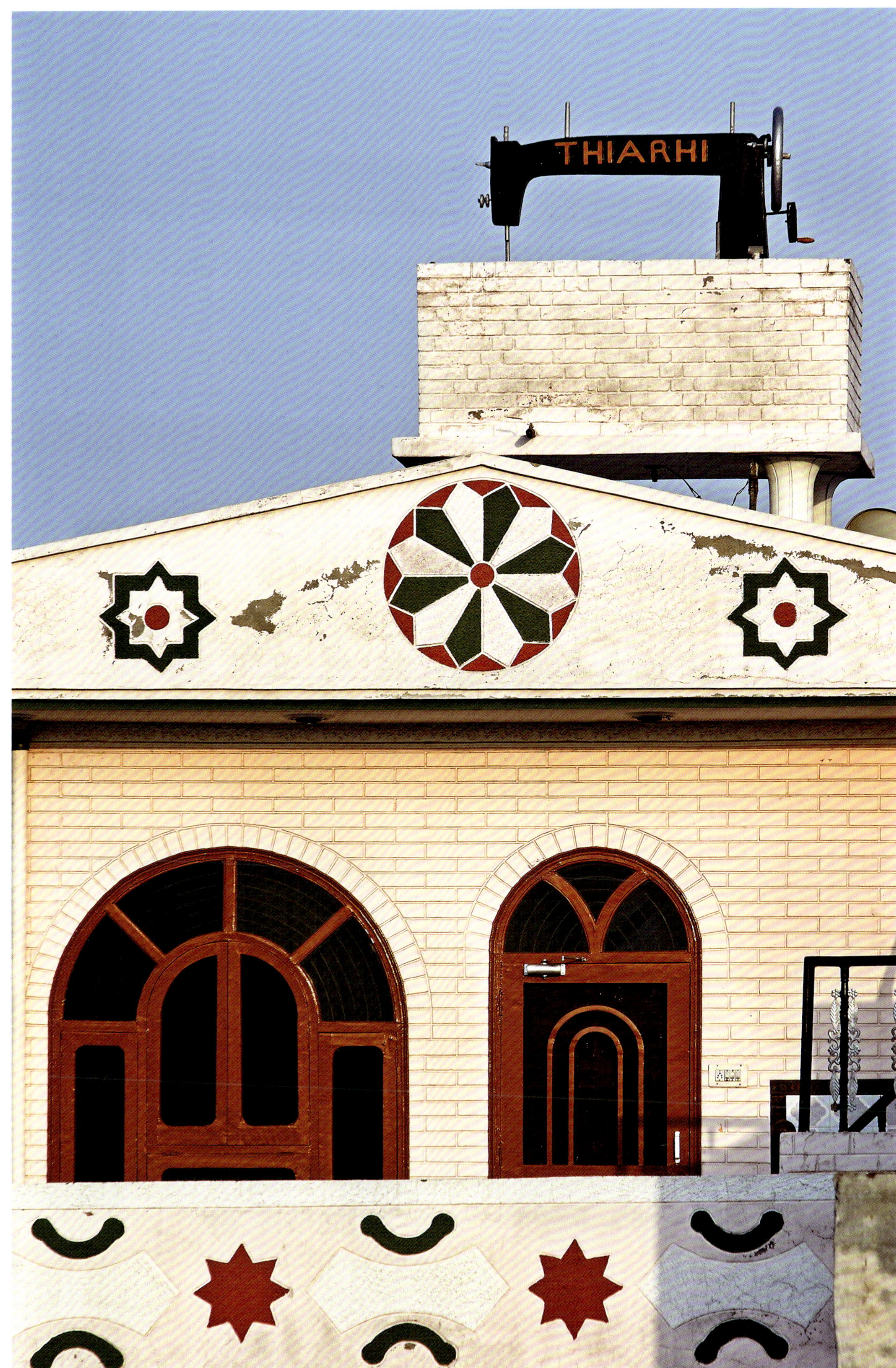
THIARHI

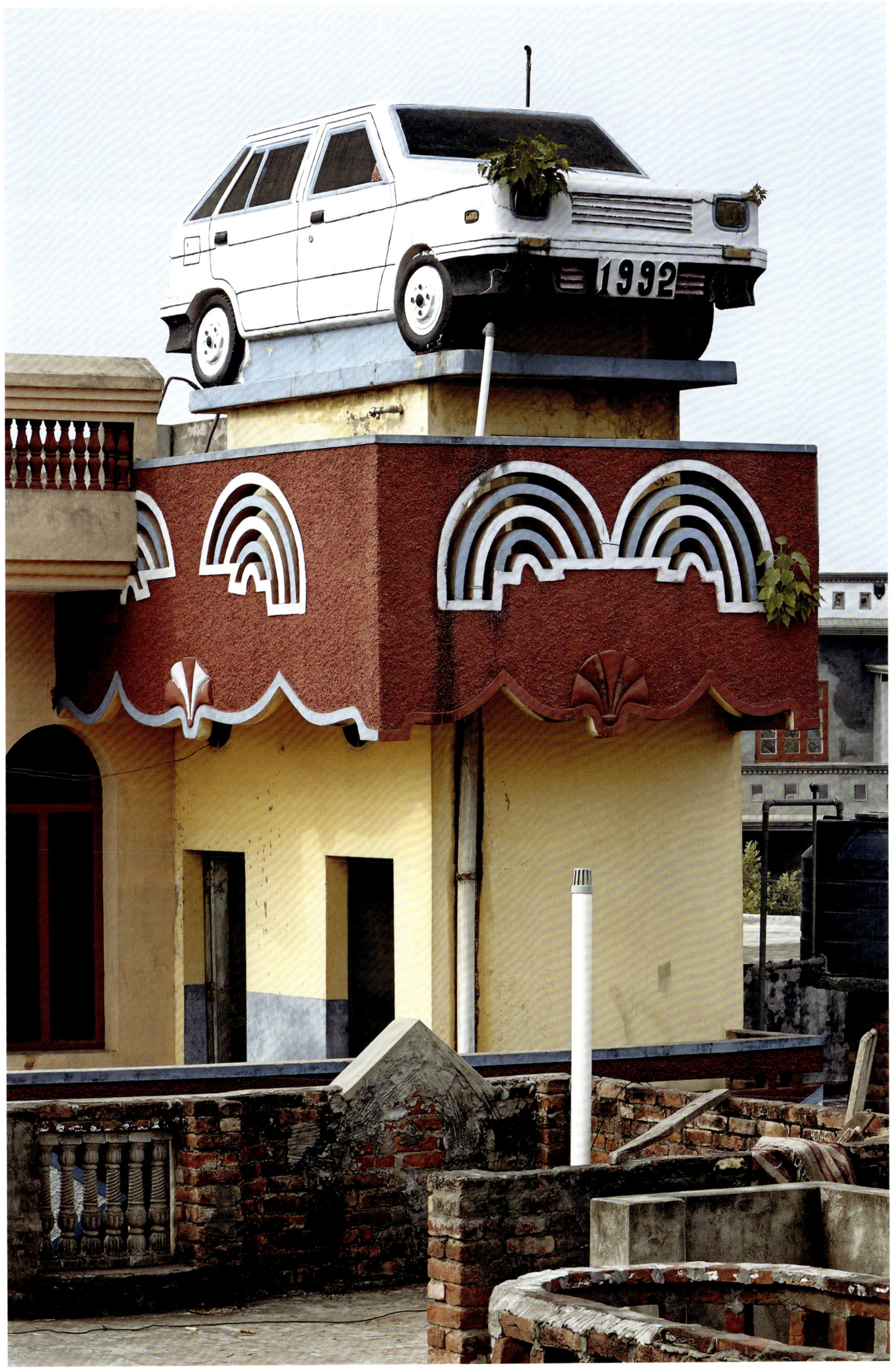
1992

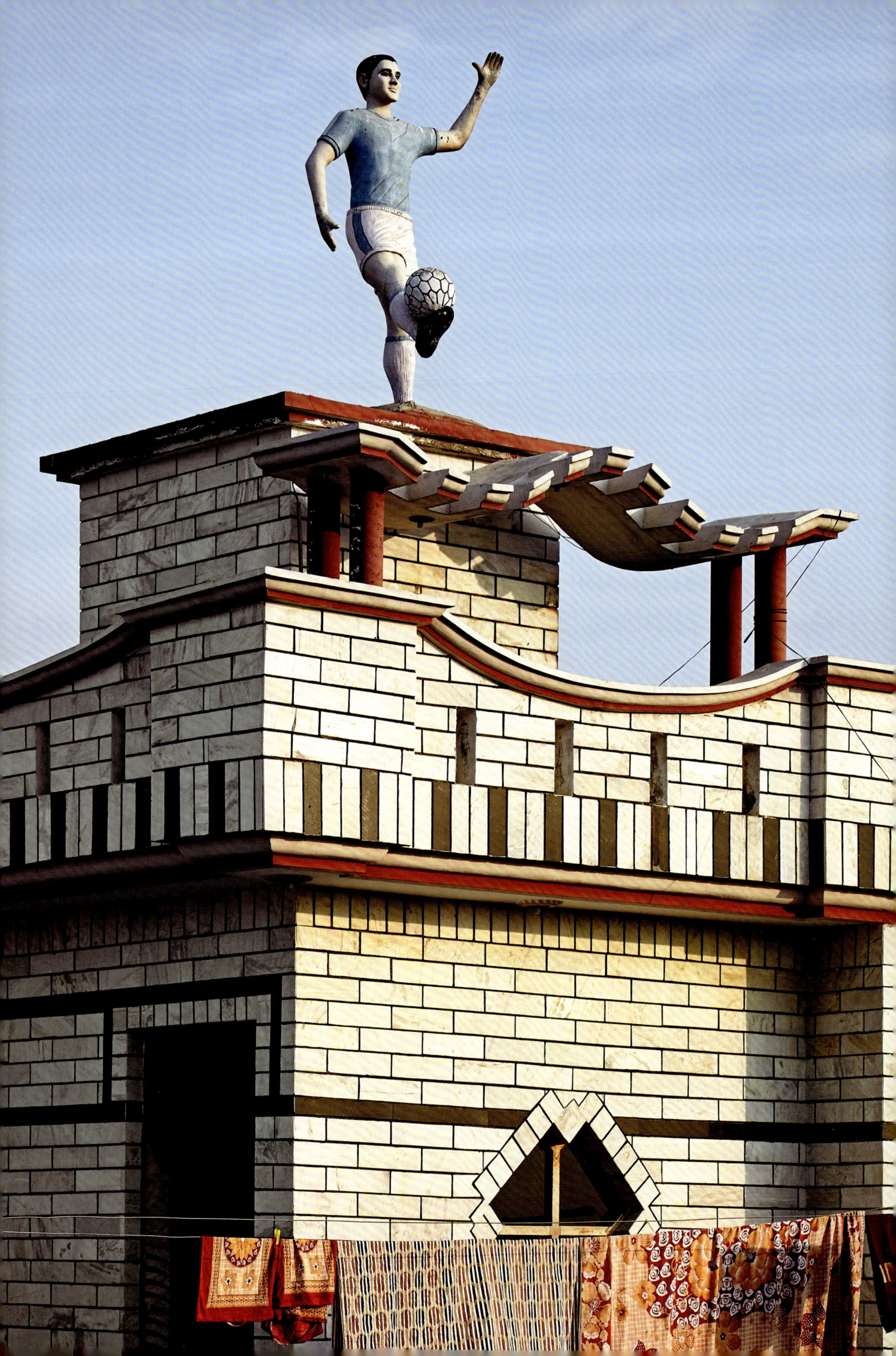

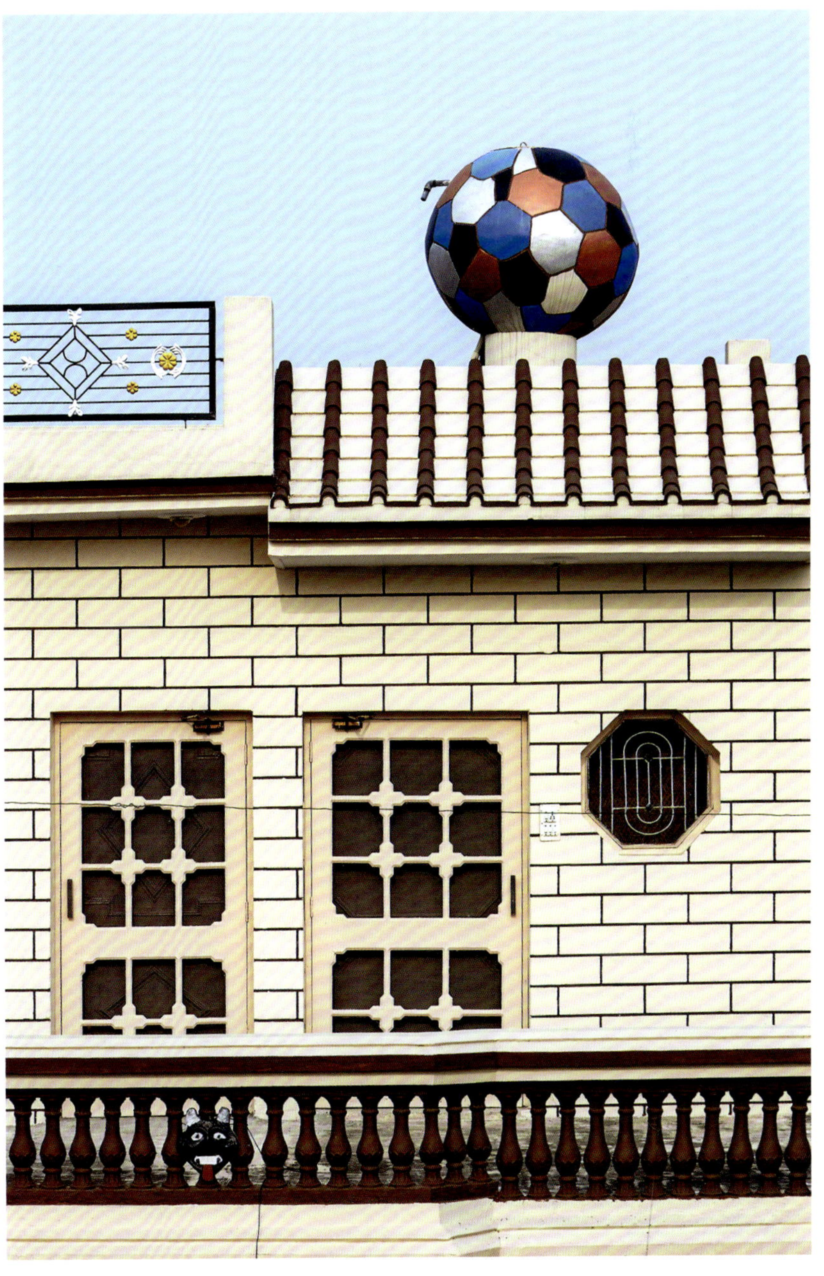

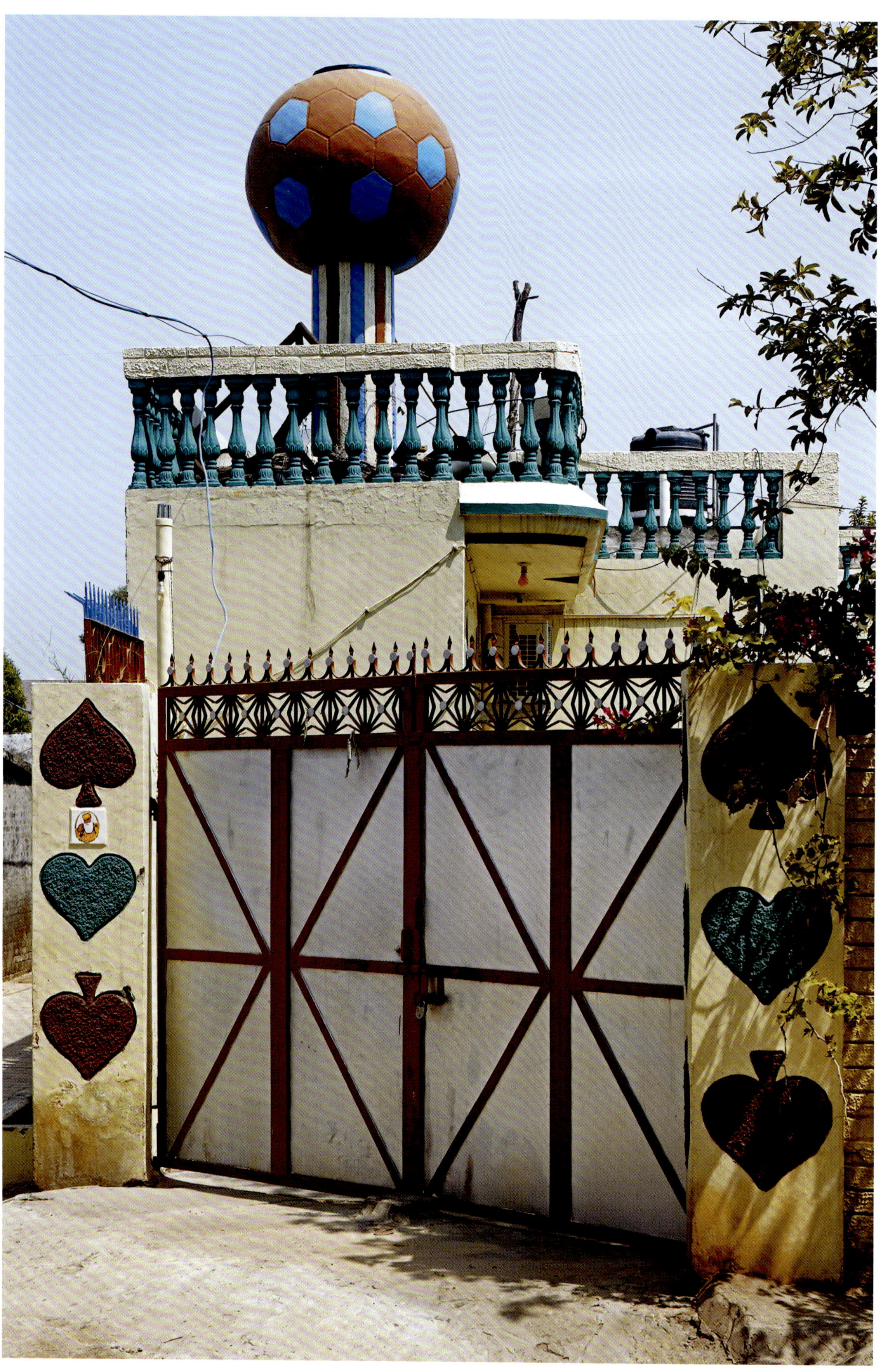

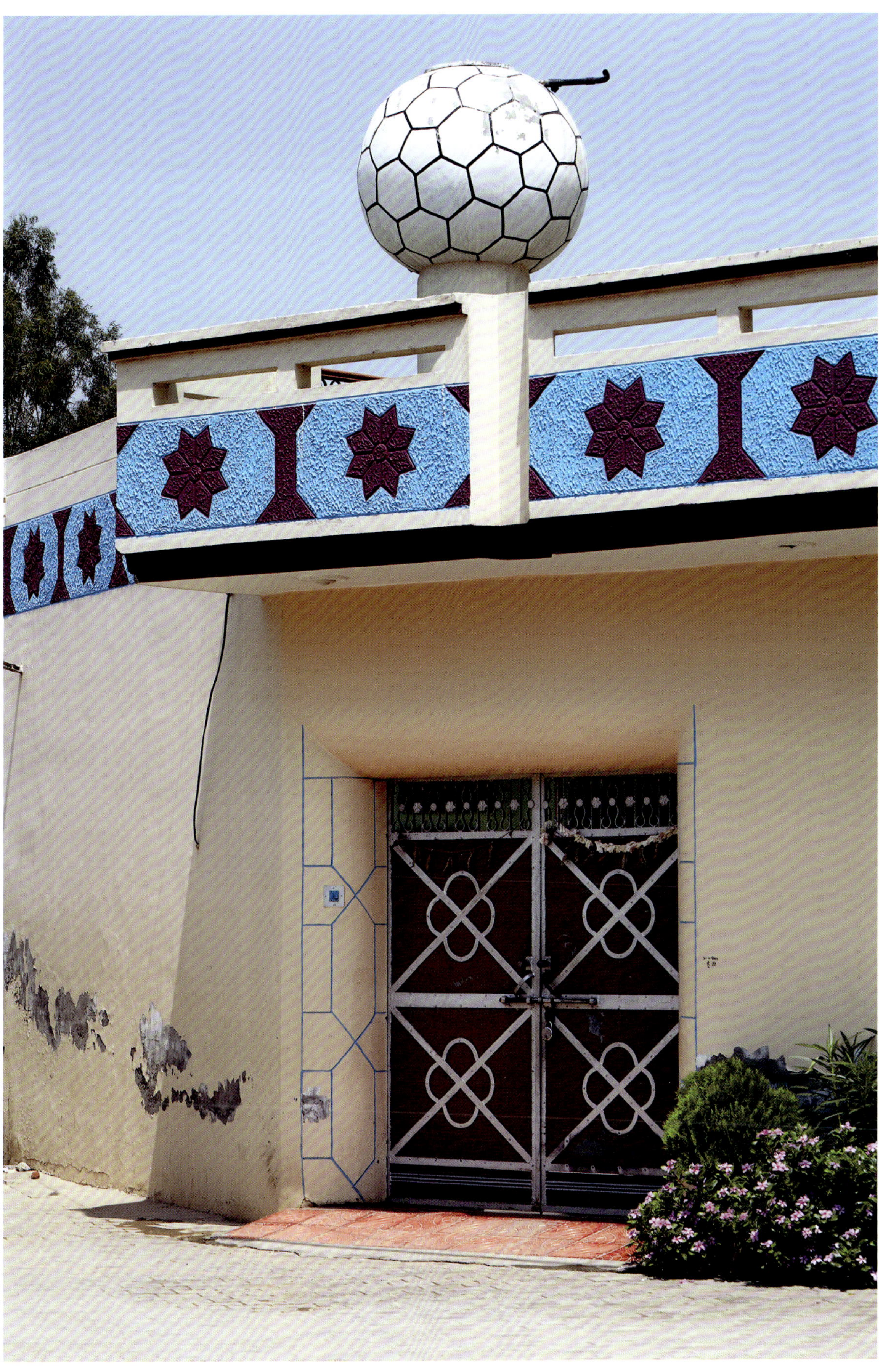

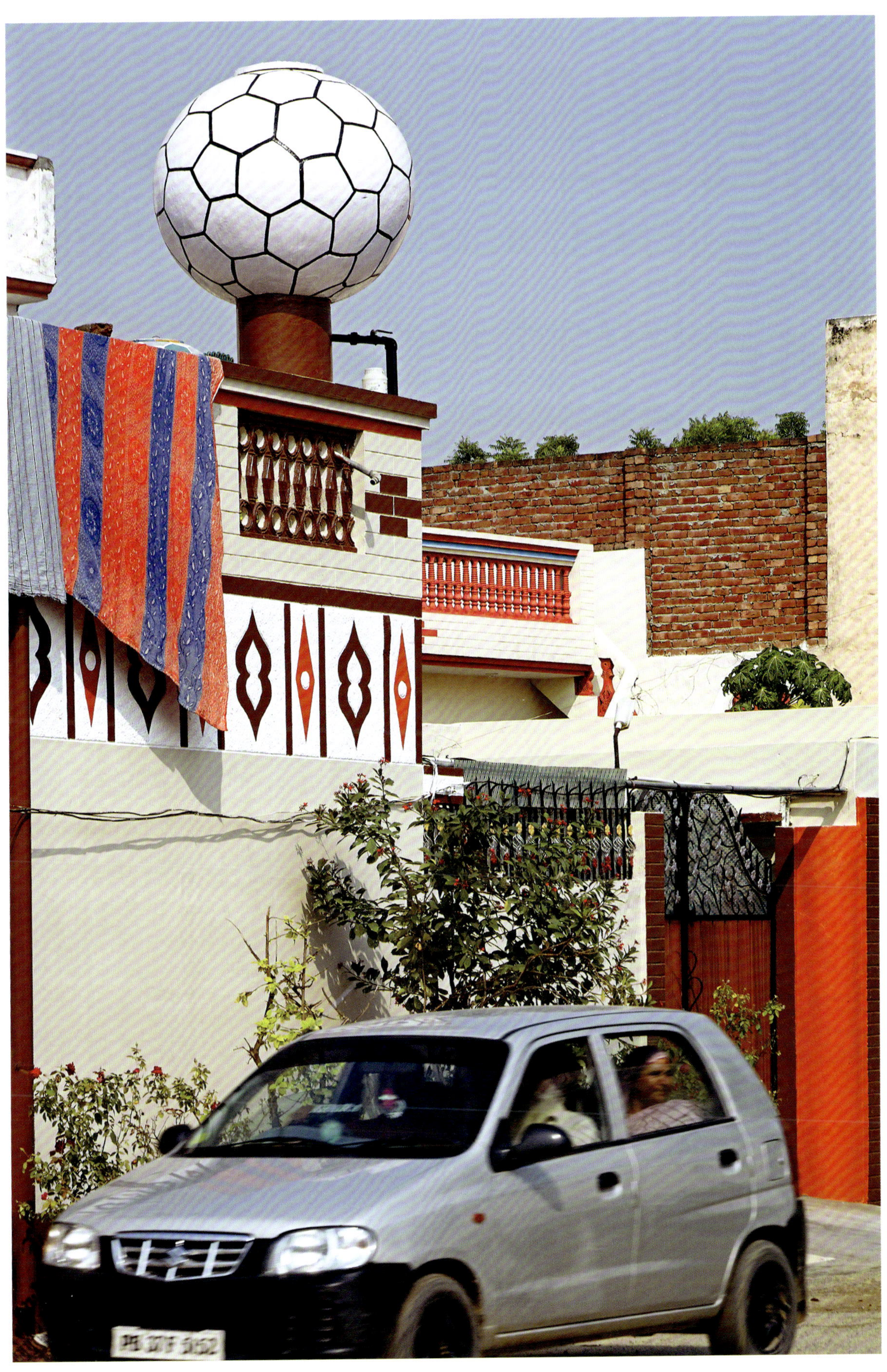

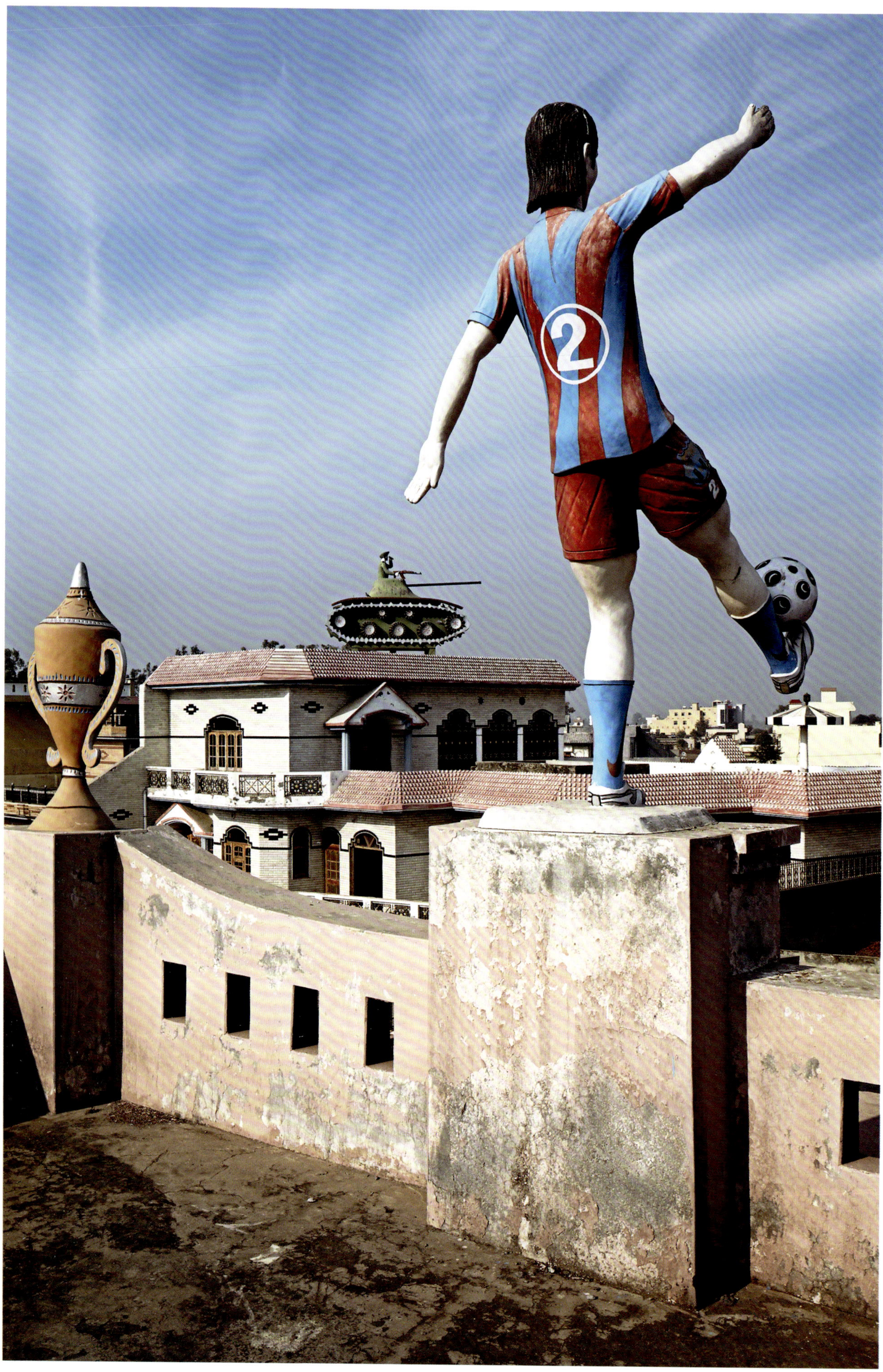
2

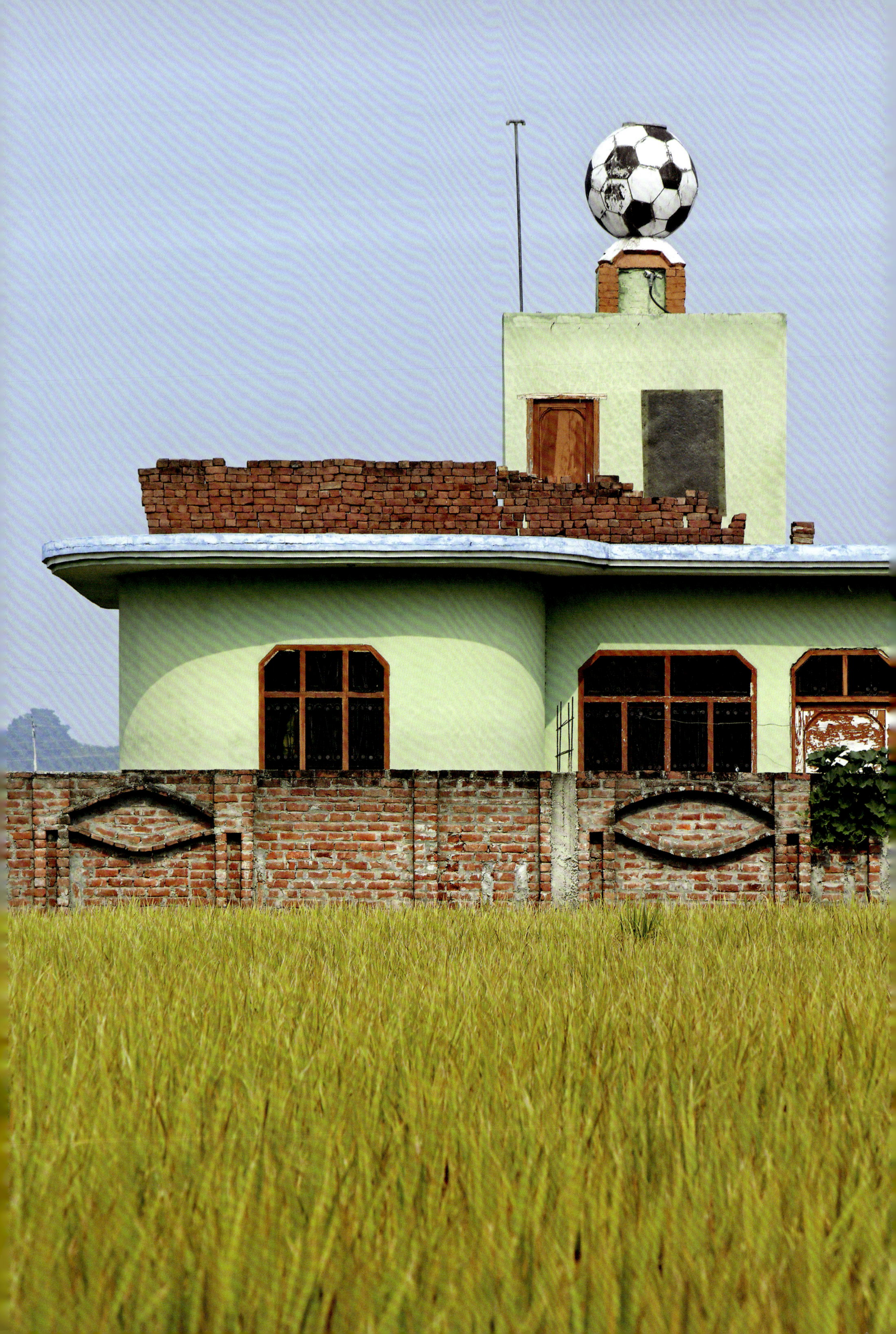

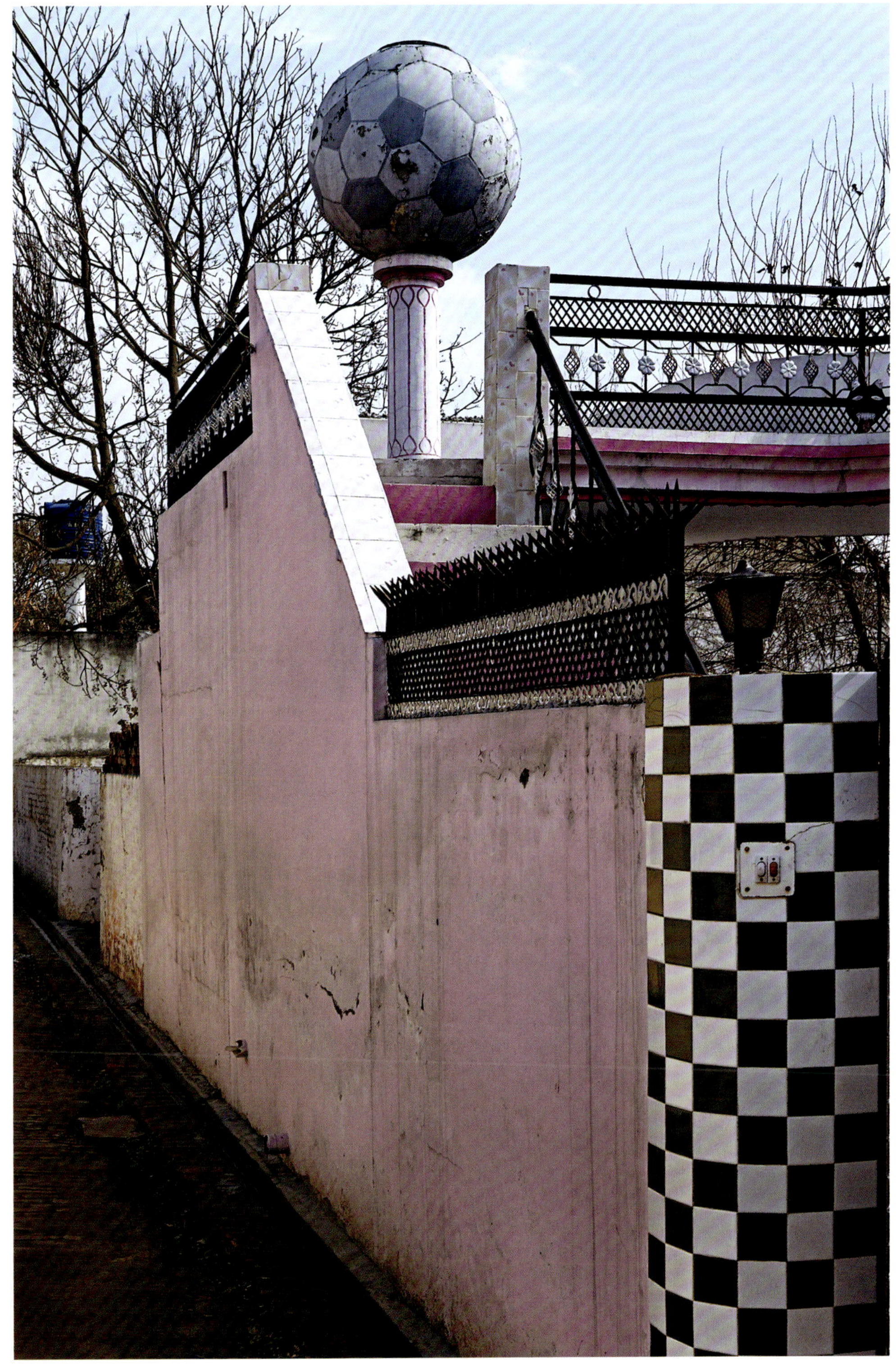

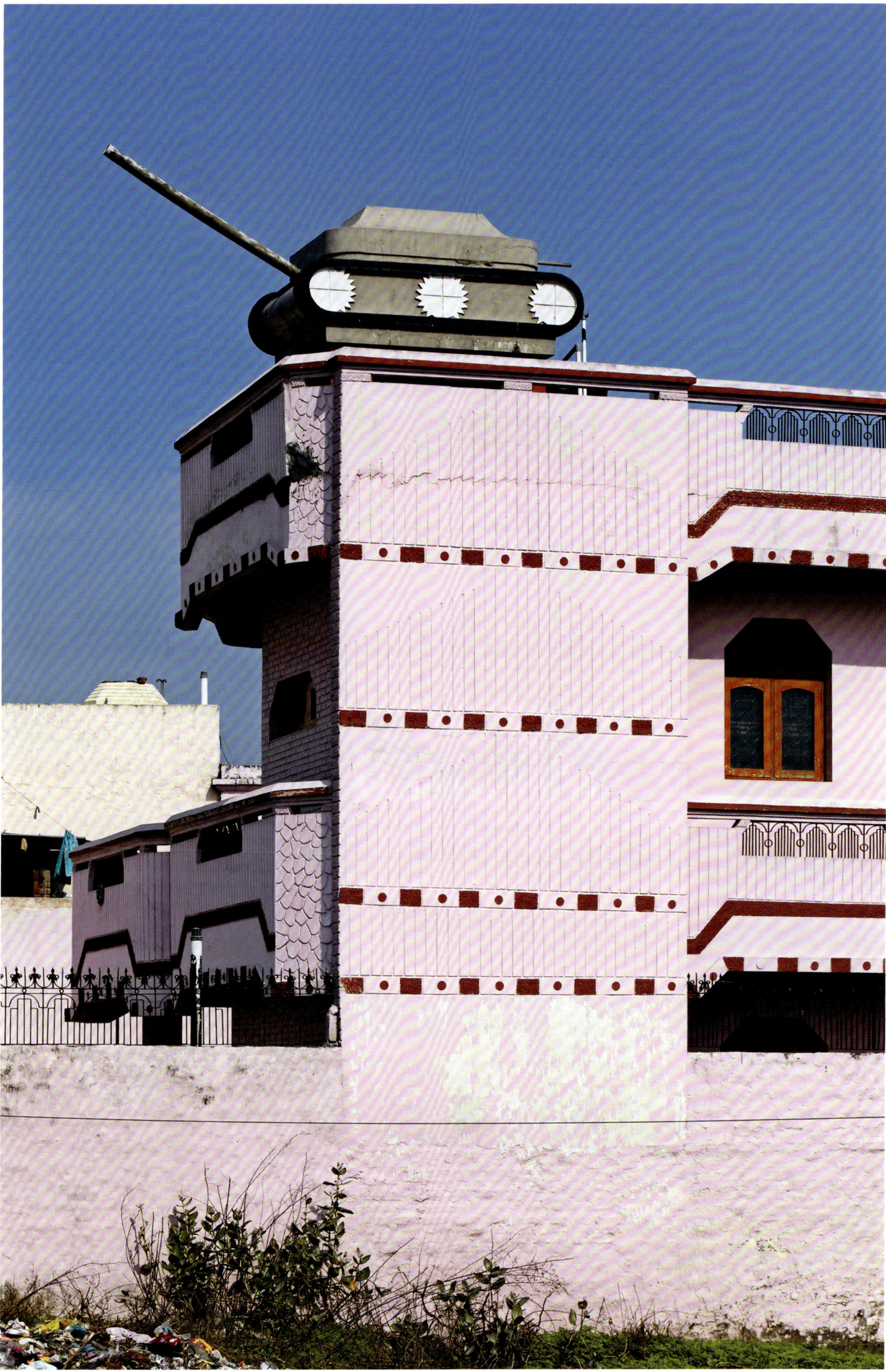

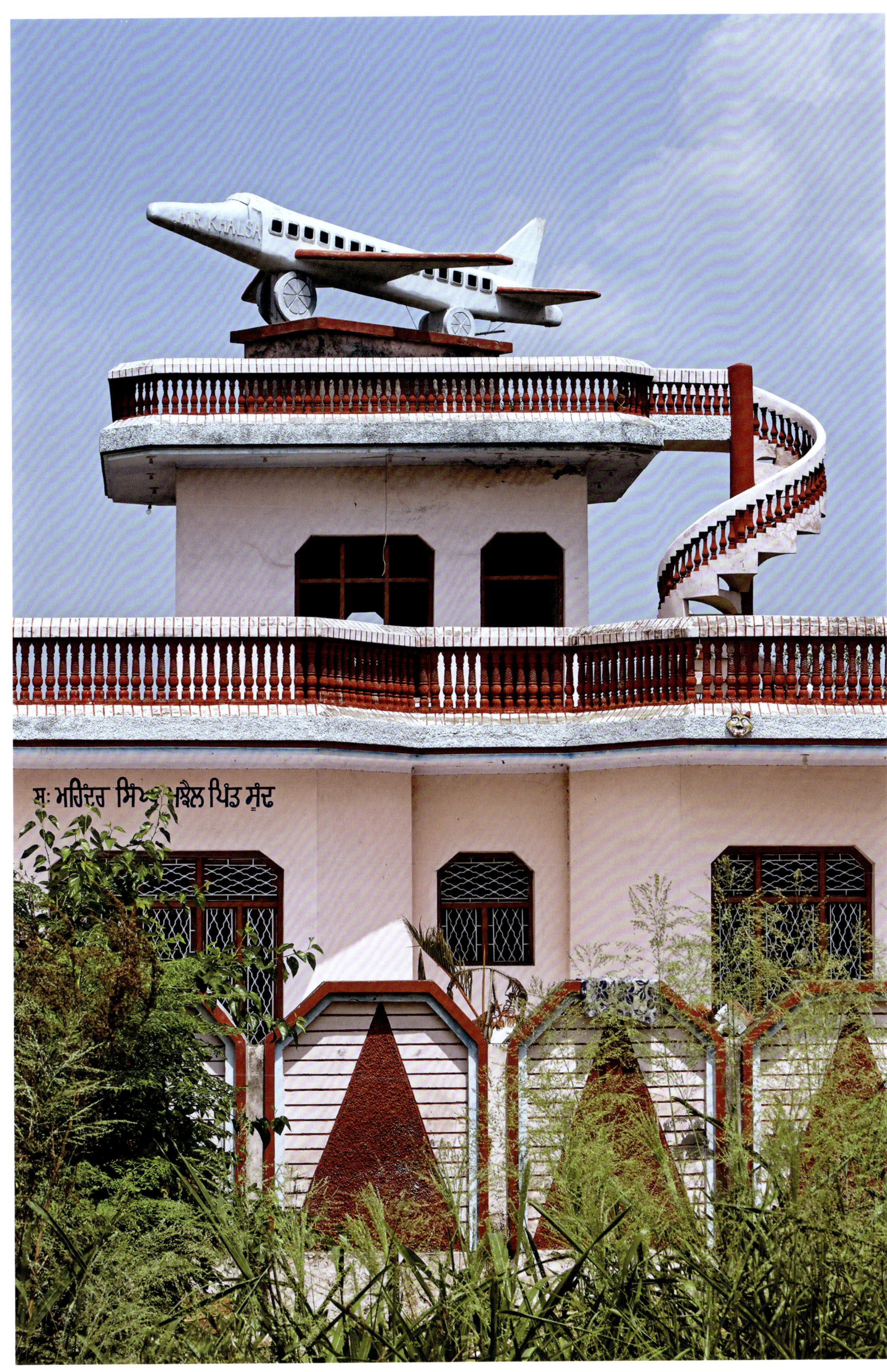
AIR KHALSA
ਸ: ਮਹਿੰਦਰ
ਪਿੰਡ ਸੂੰਢ

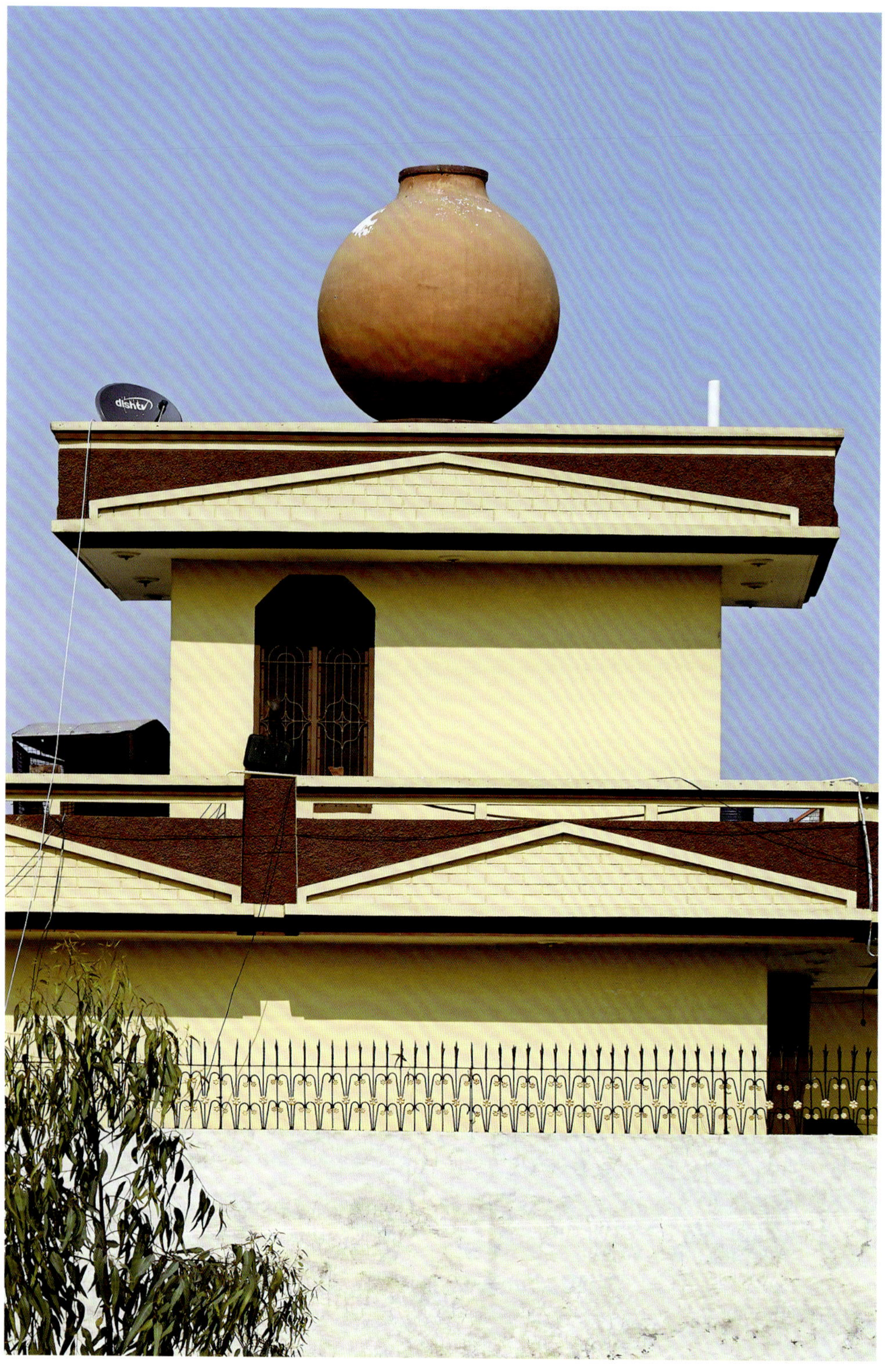
dishtv

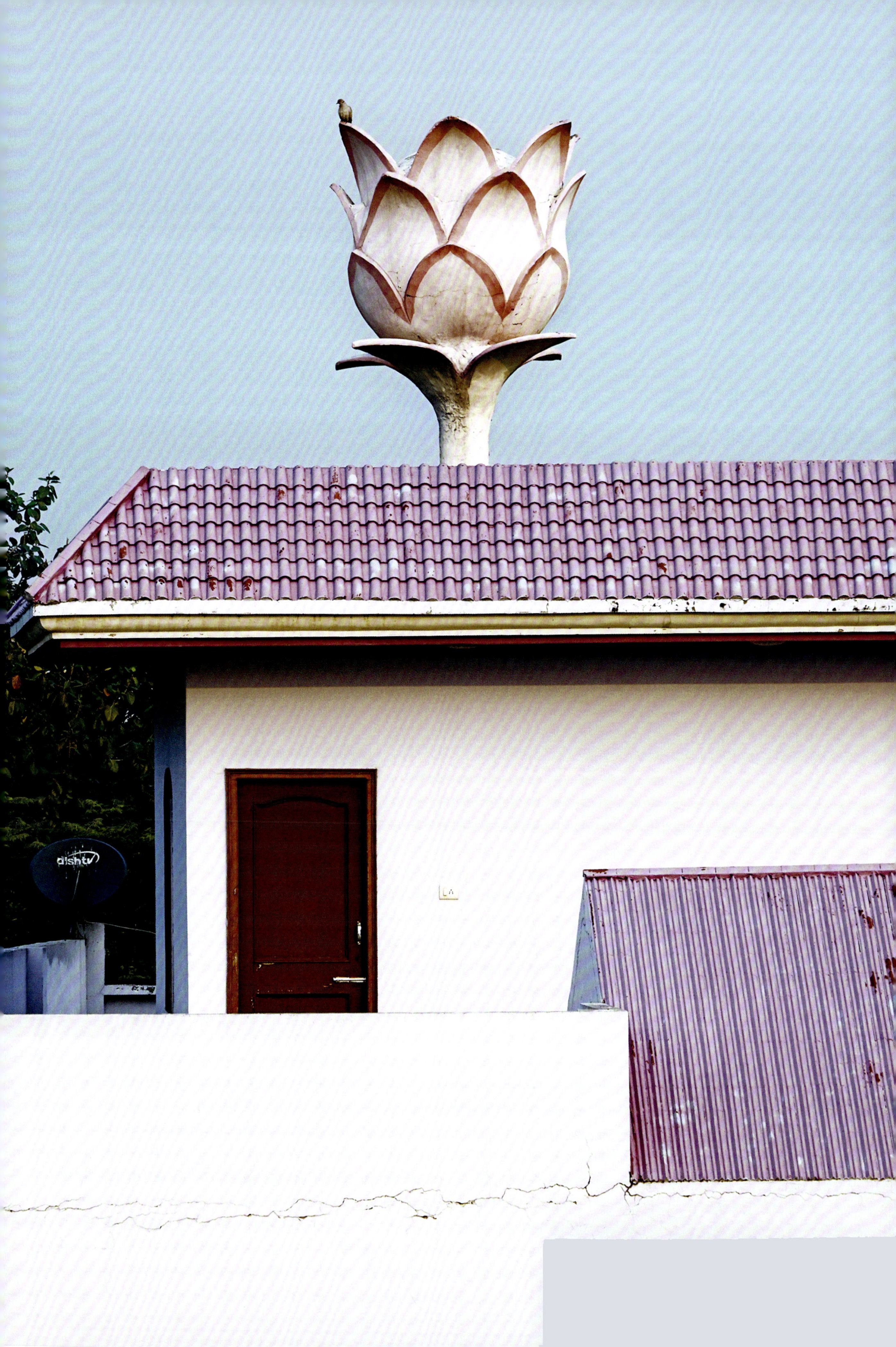
dishtv

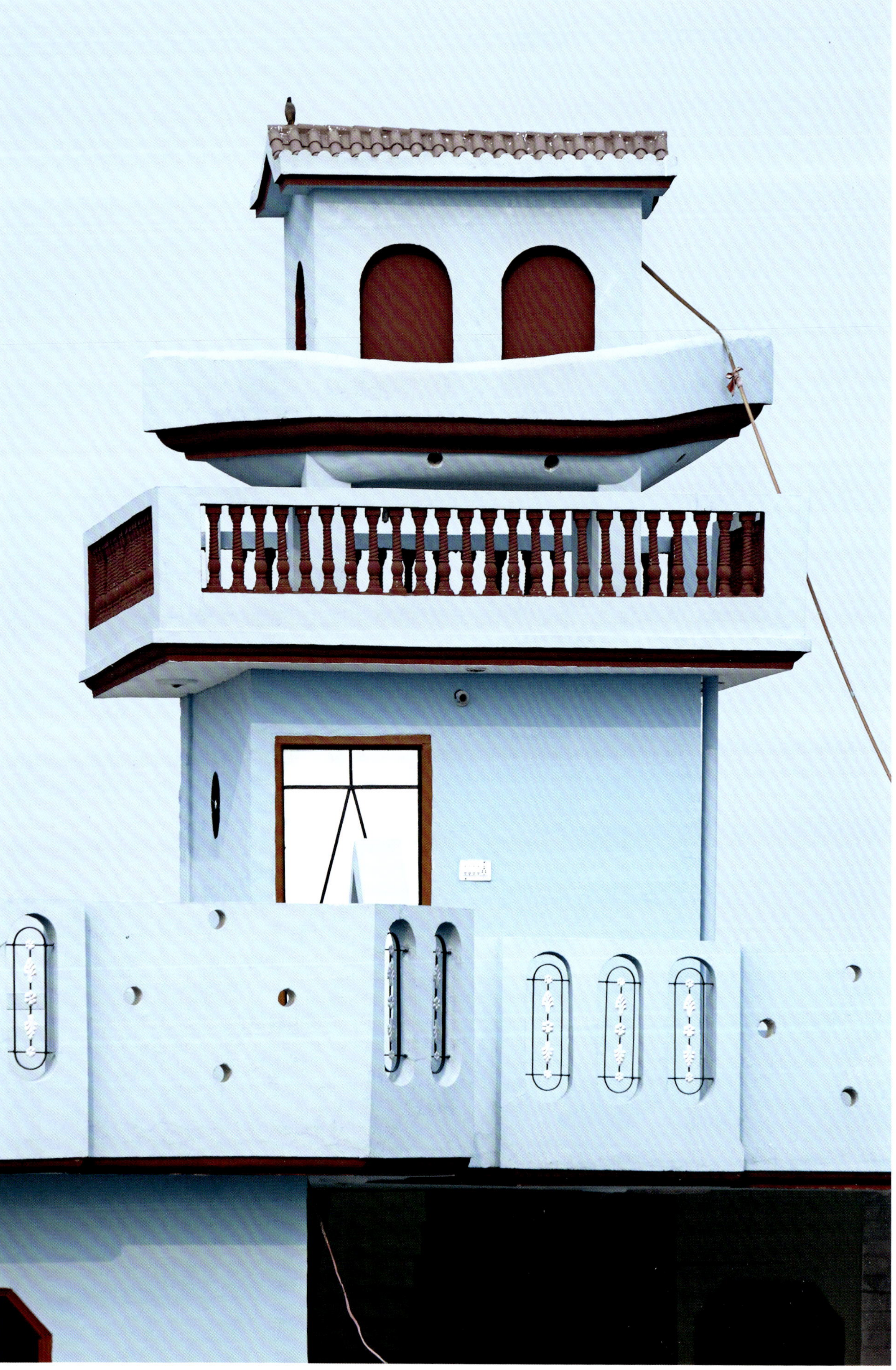

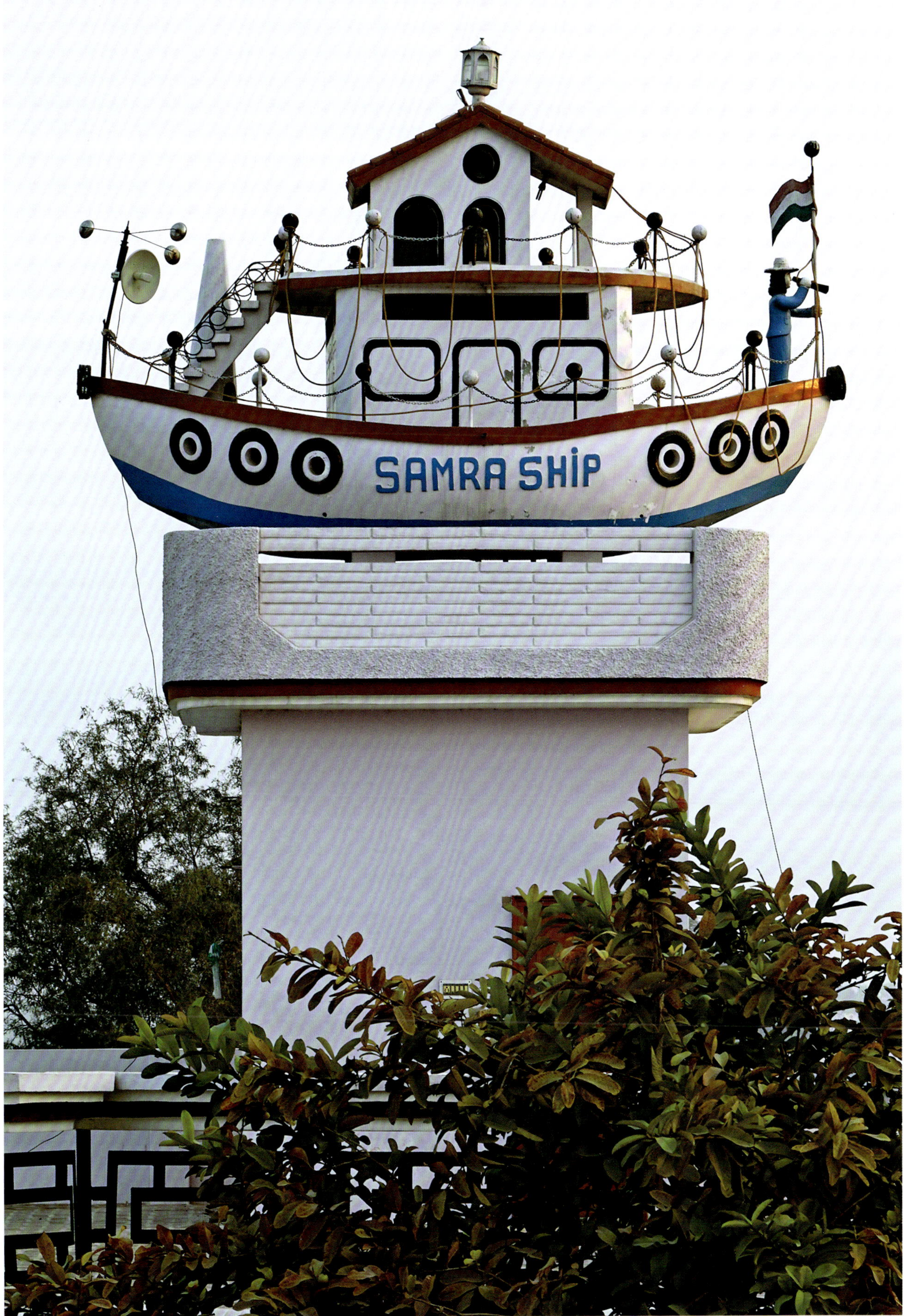
SAMRA SHIP

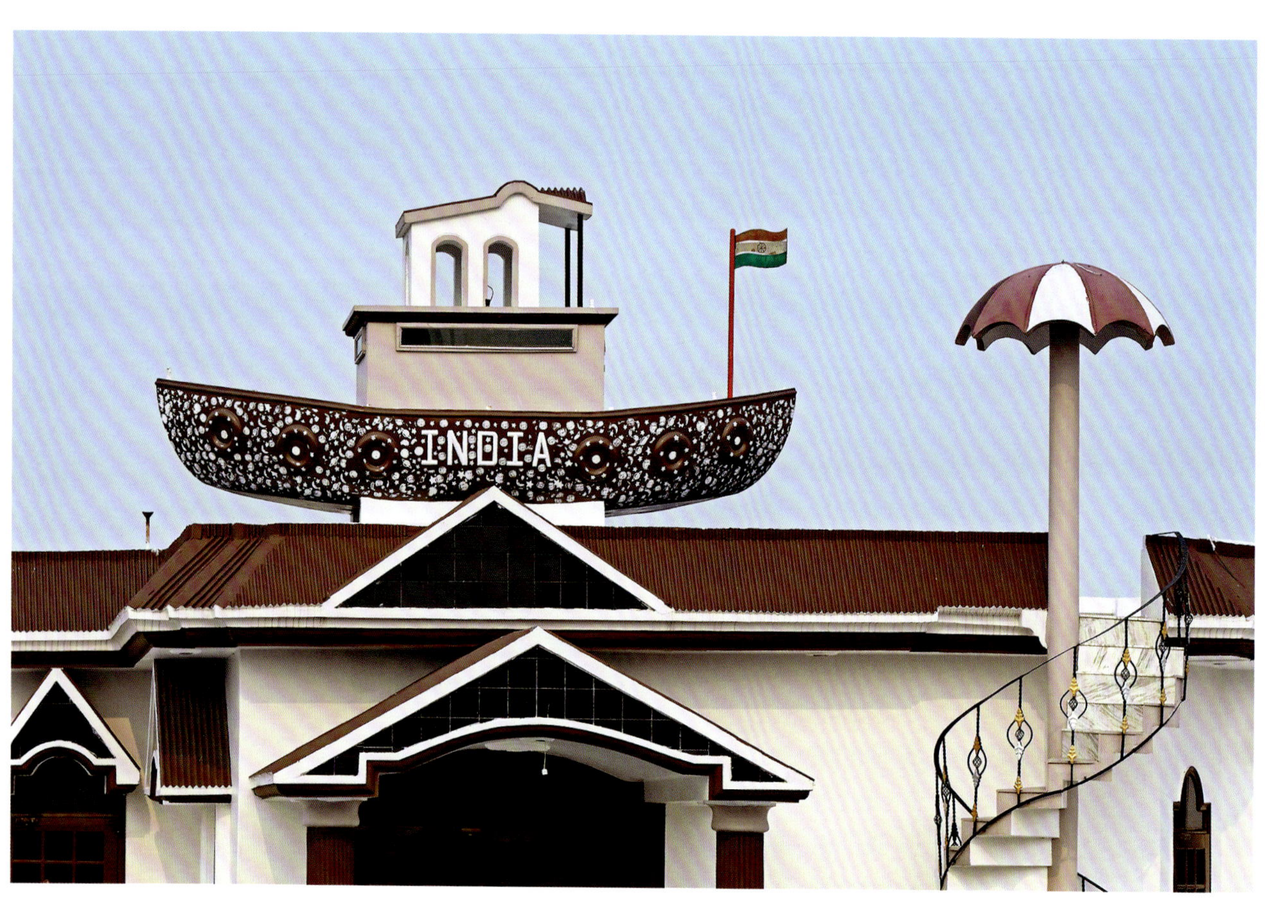
INDIA

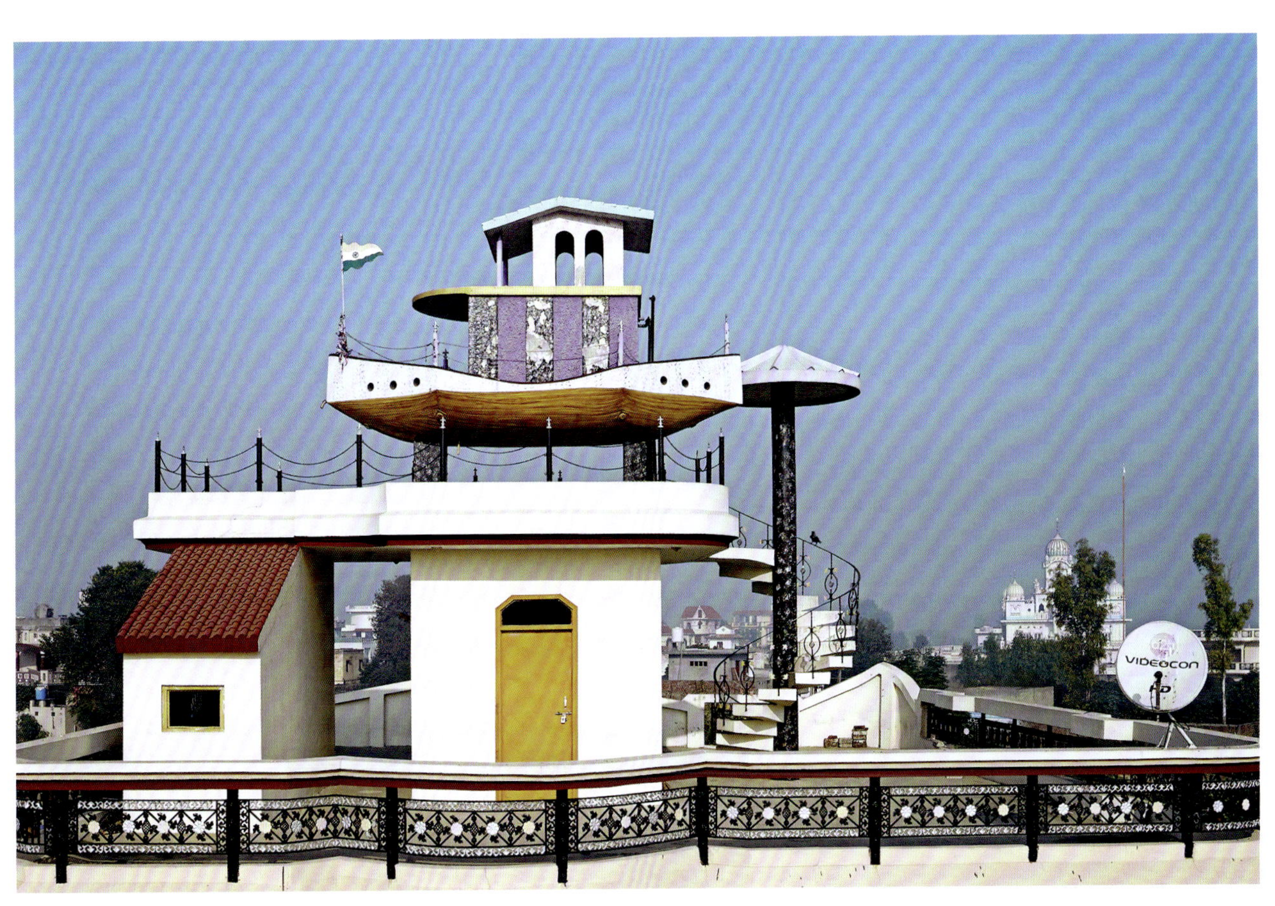
VIDEOCON

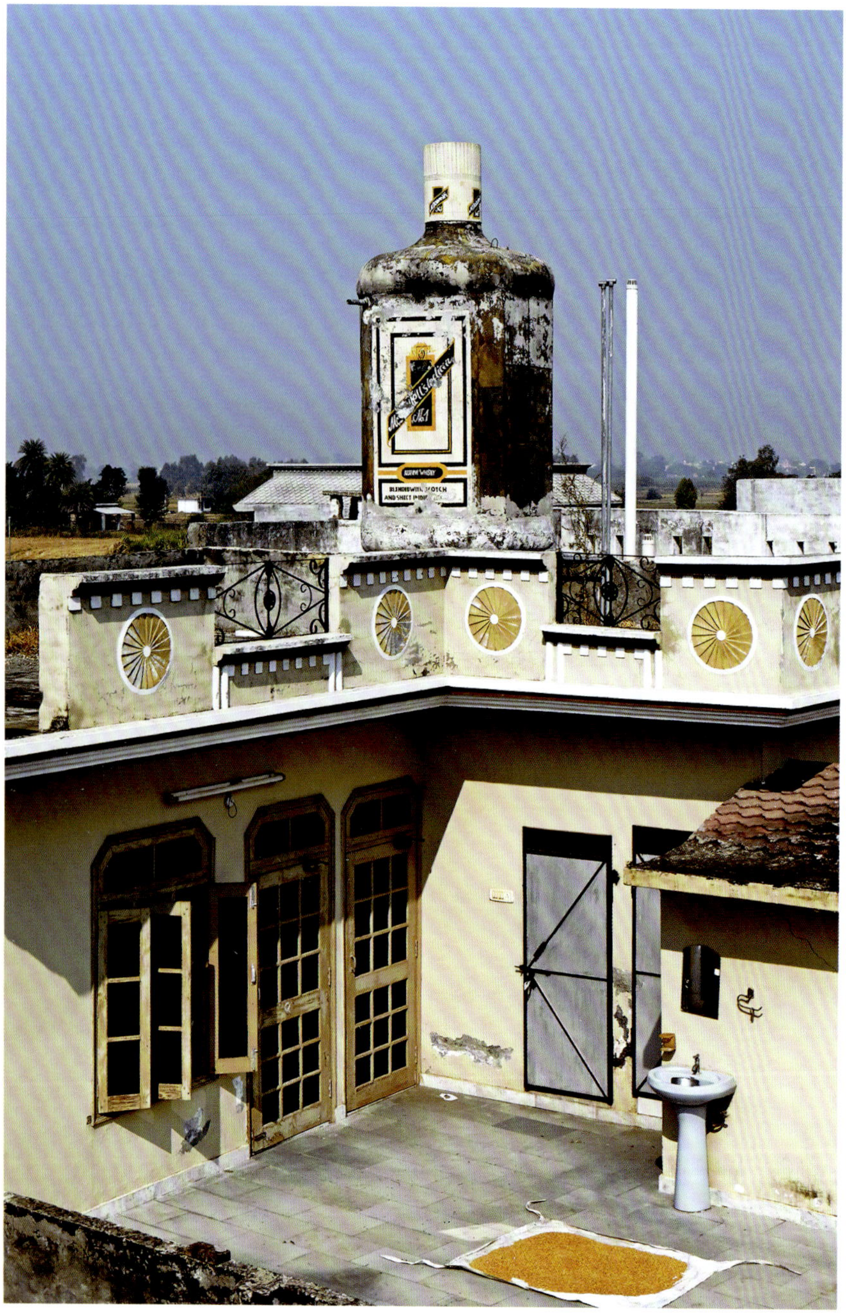

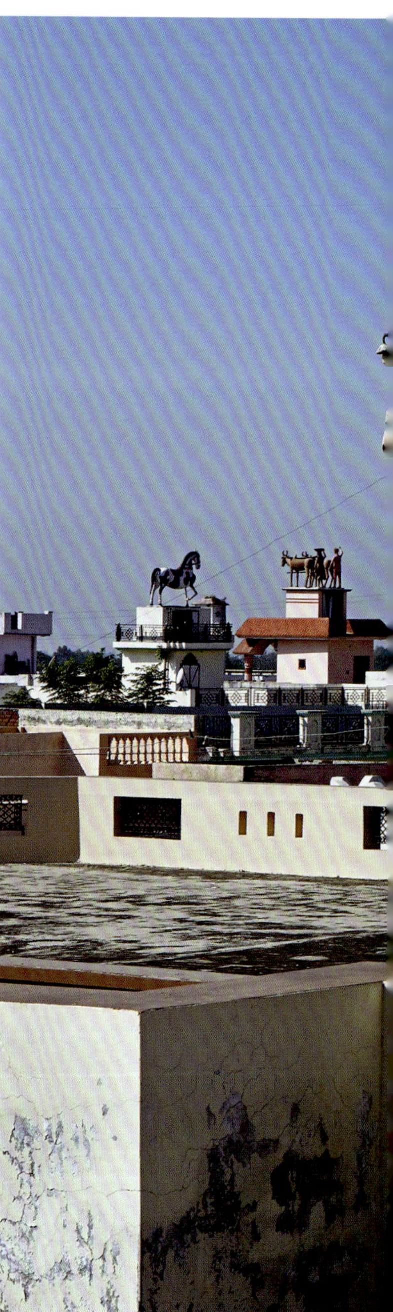

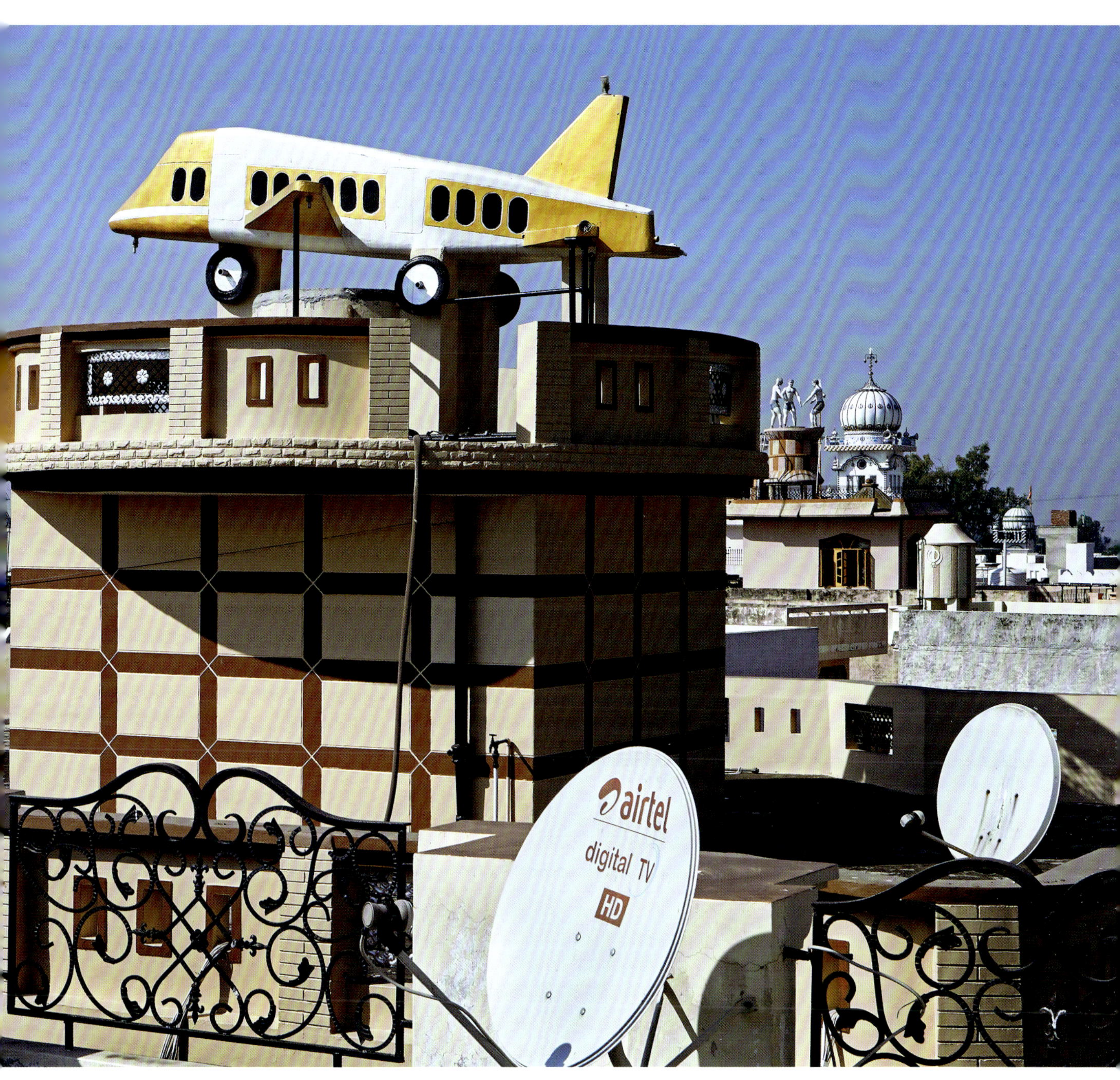
airtel
digital TV
HD

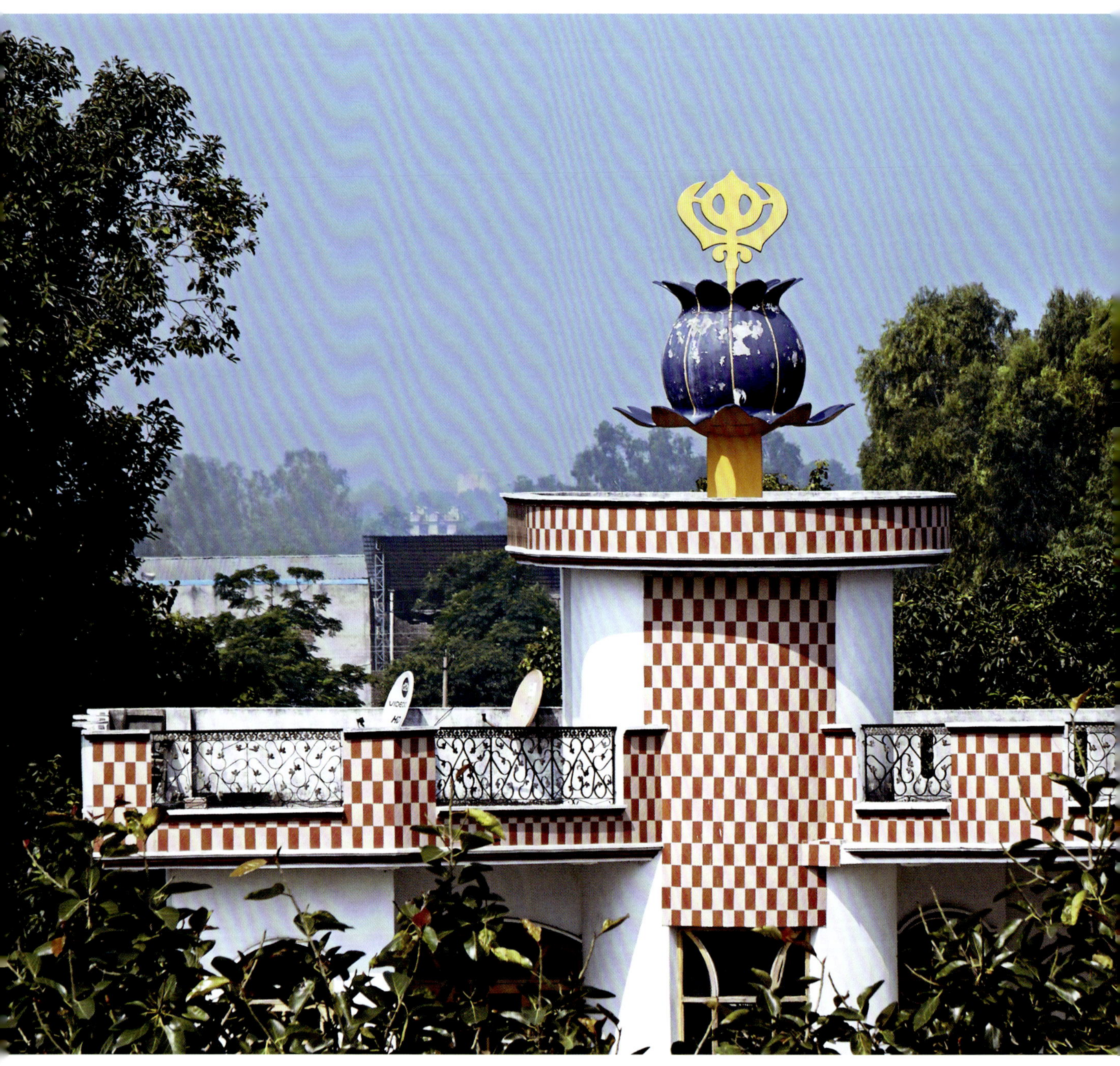

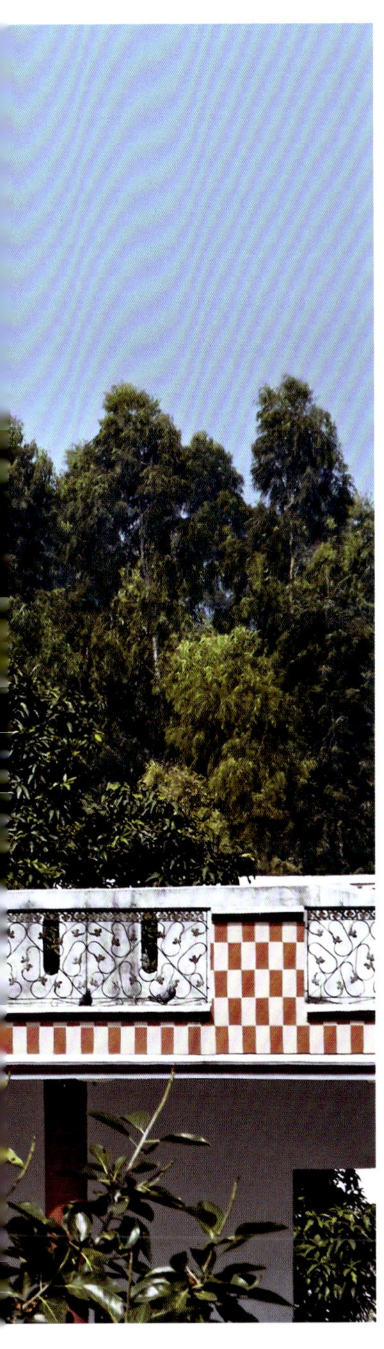

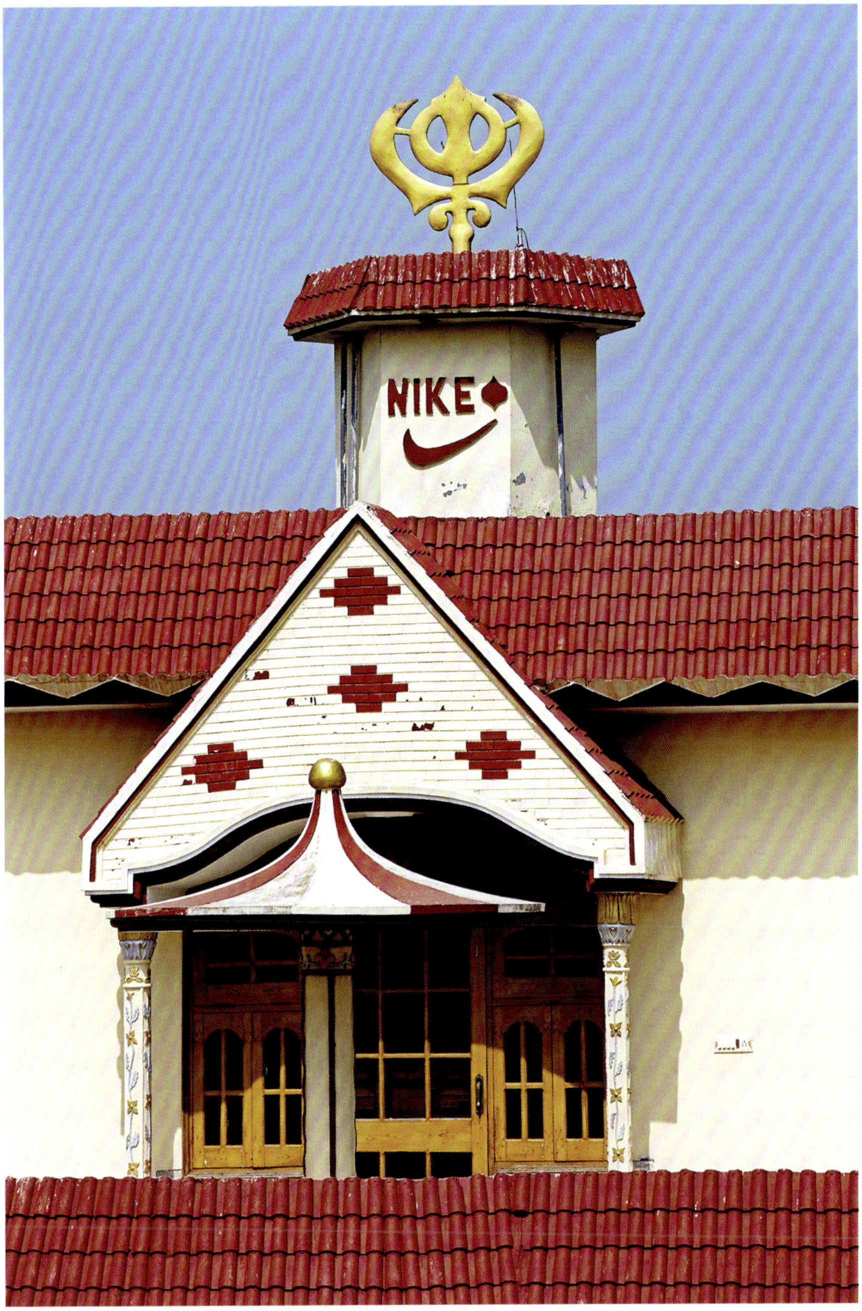

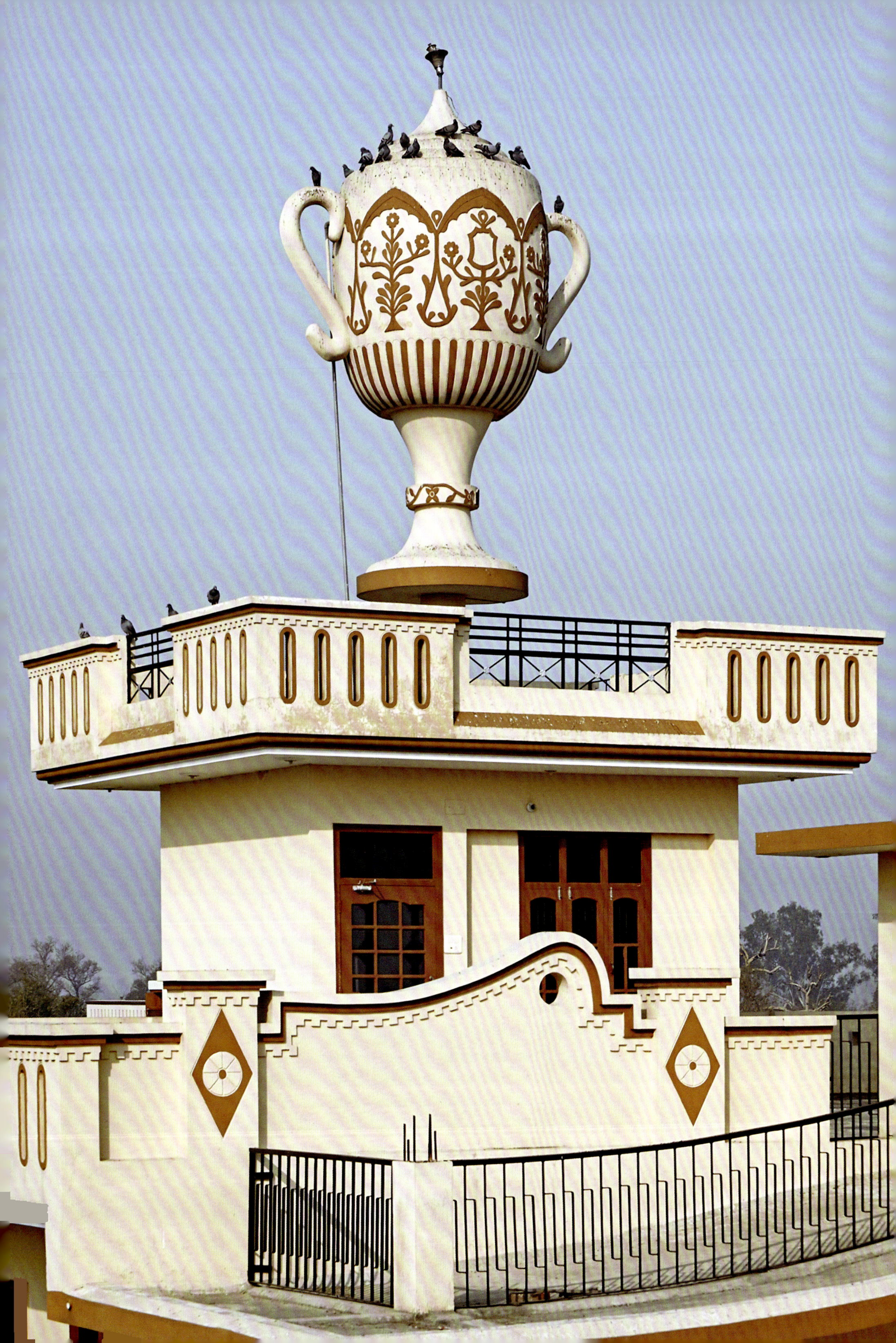

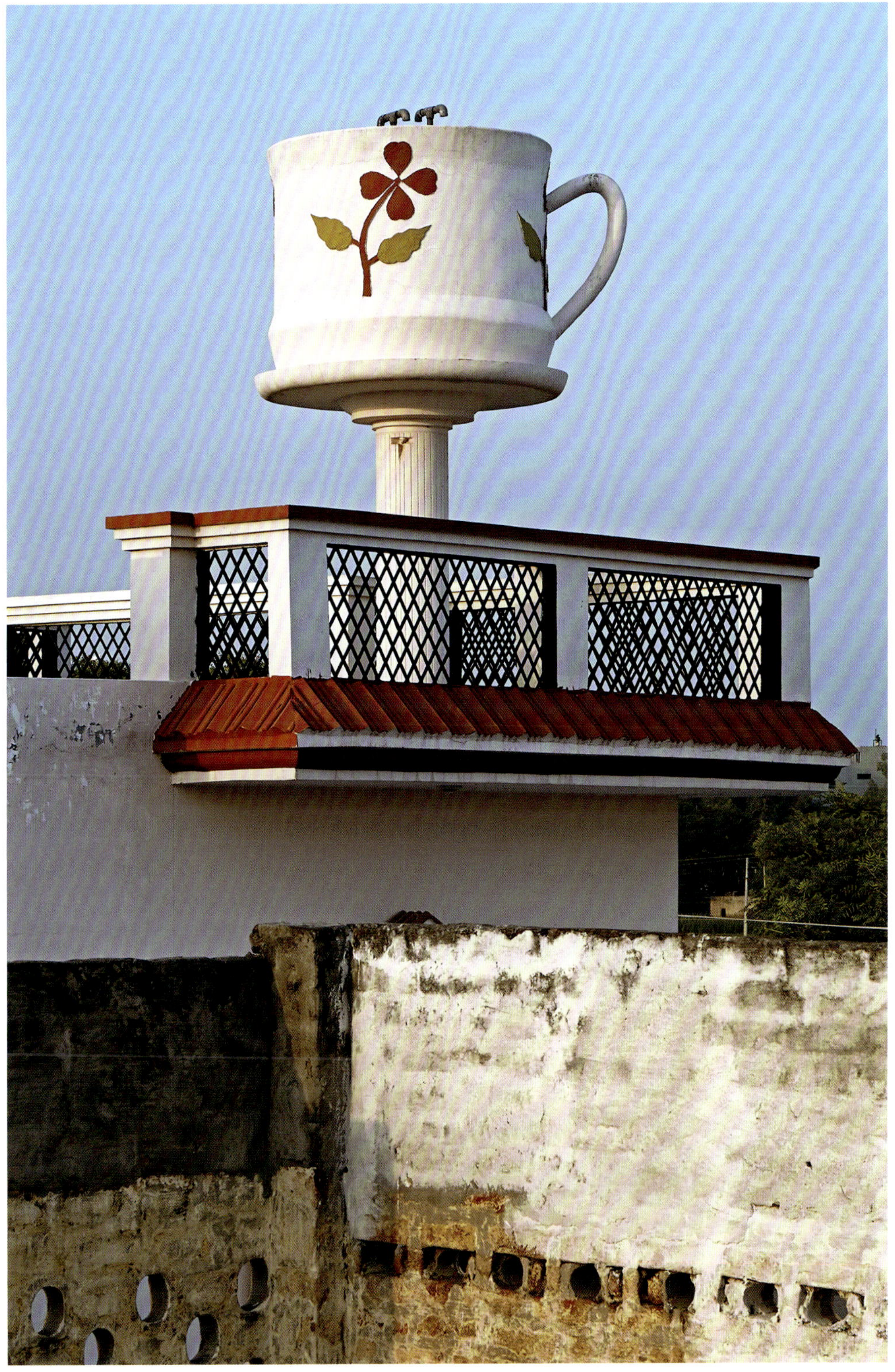

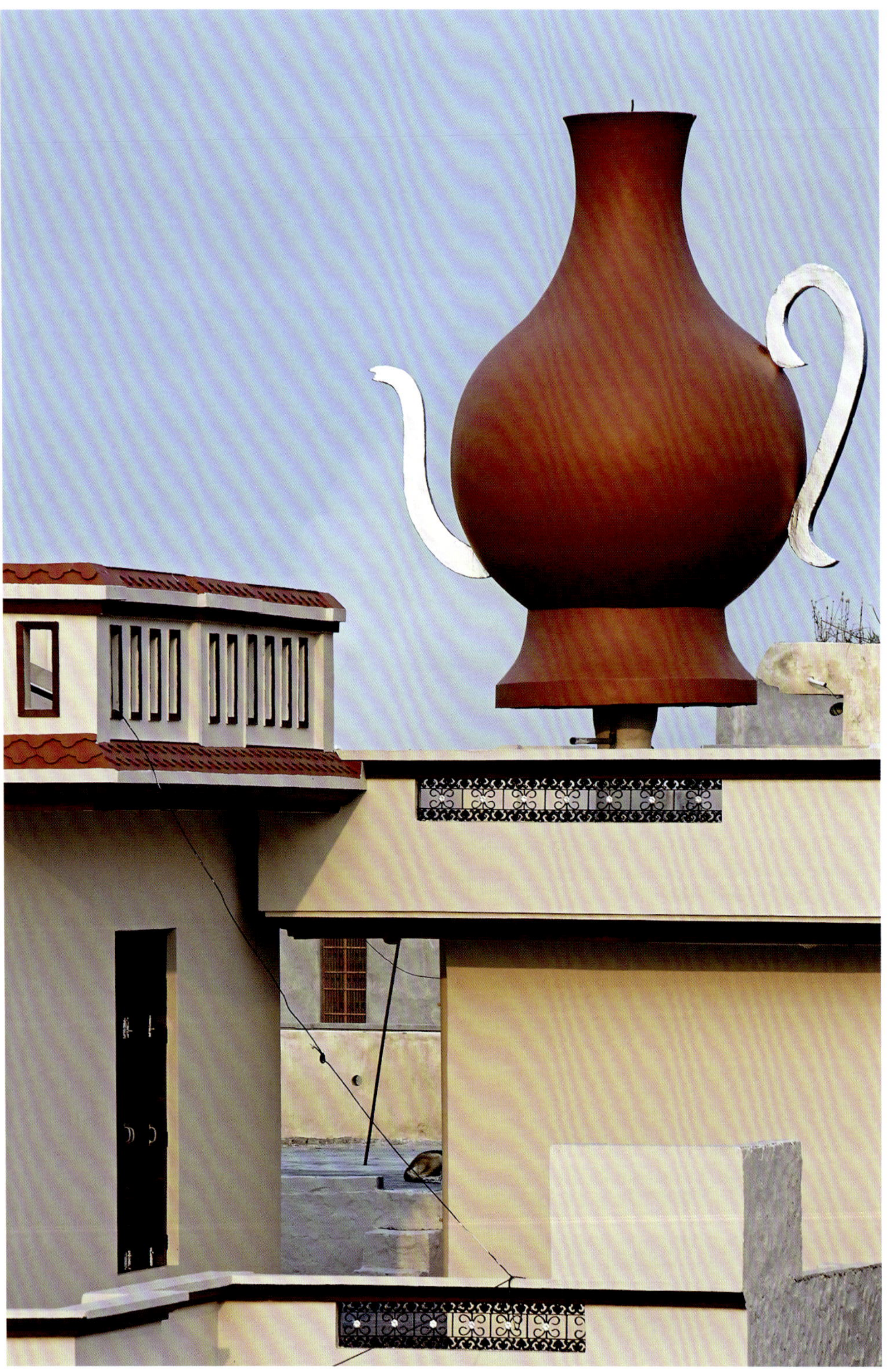

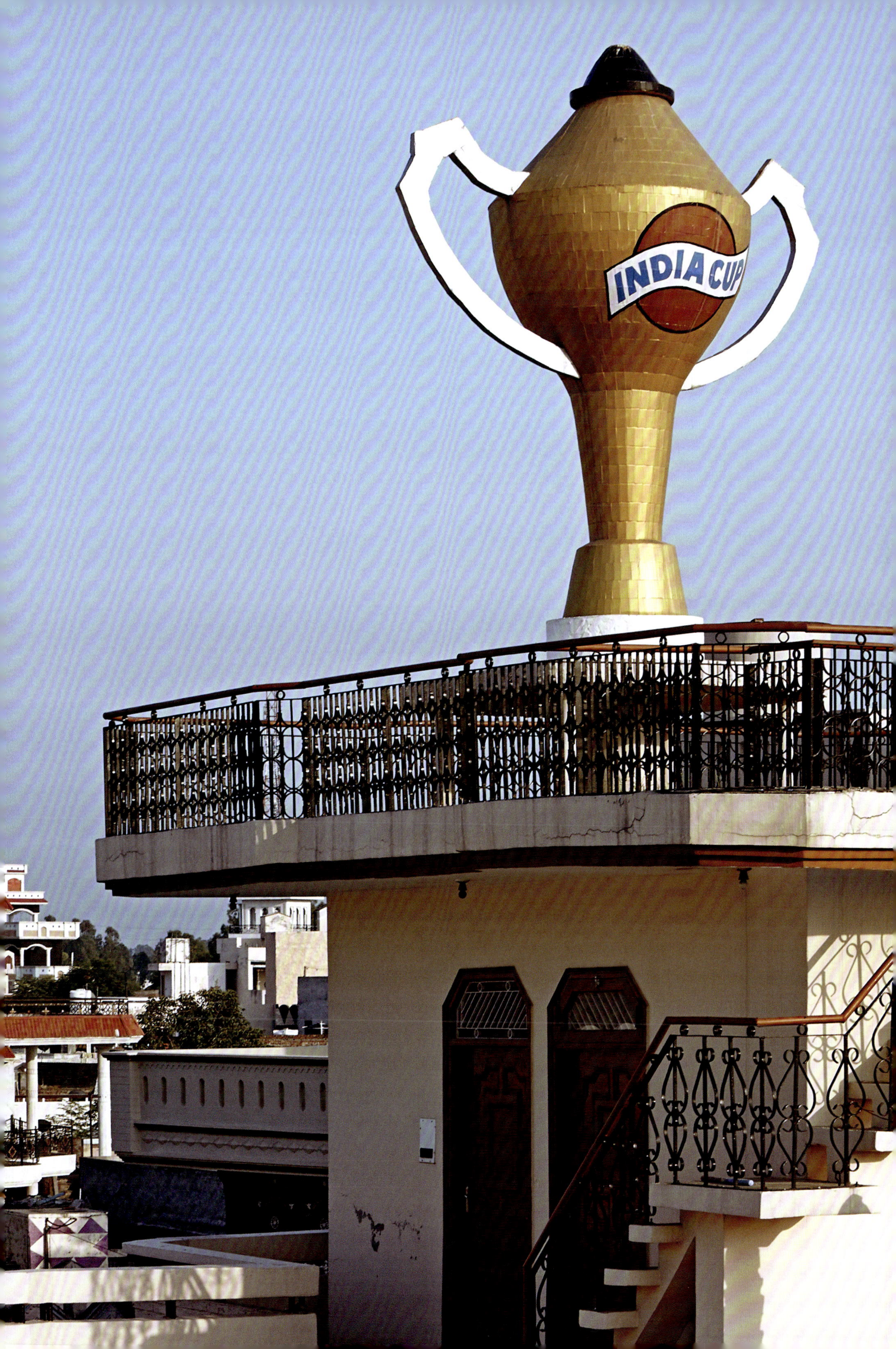
INDIA CUP

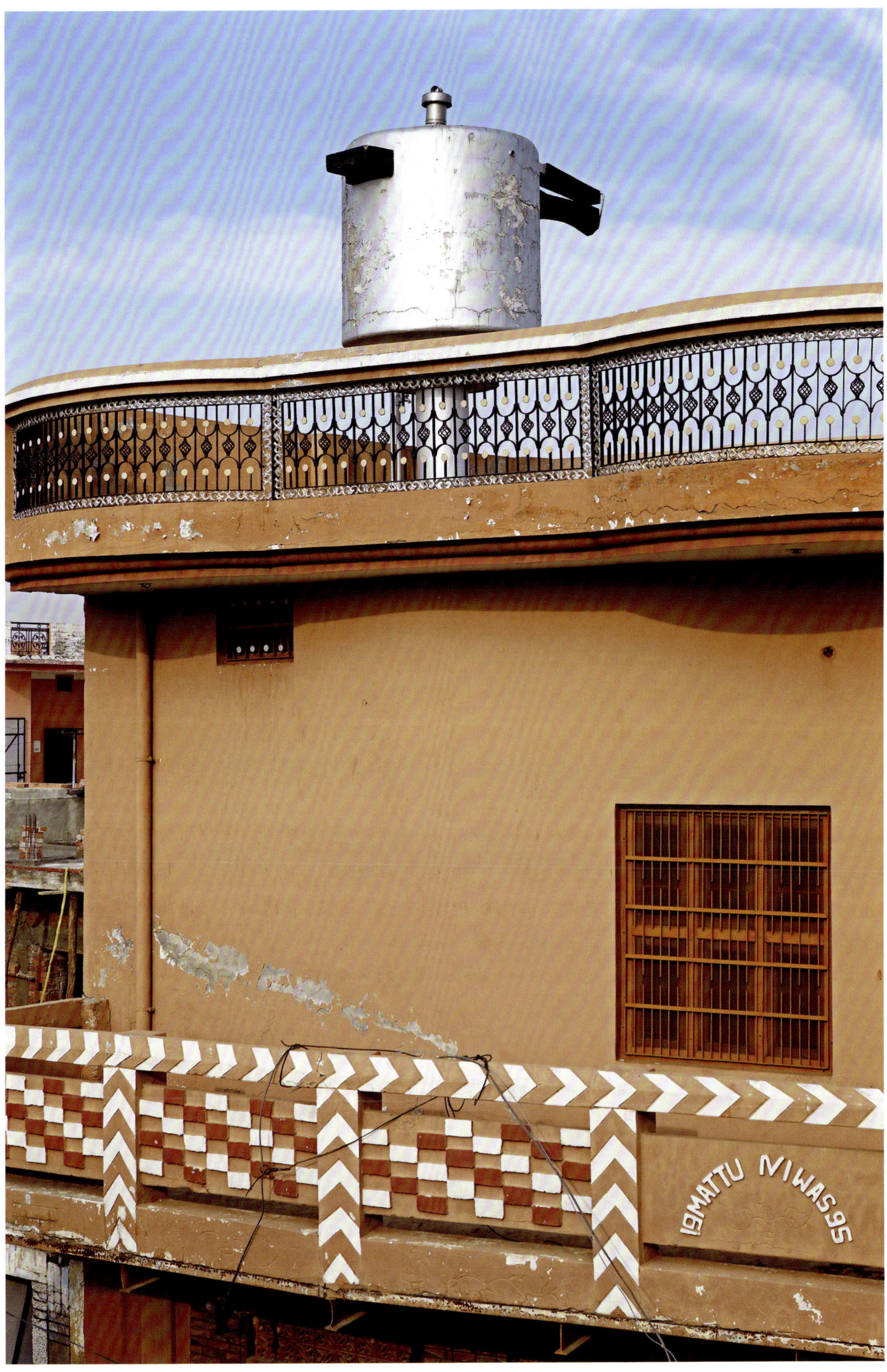
19MATTU NIWAS95

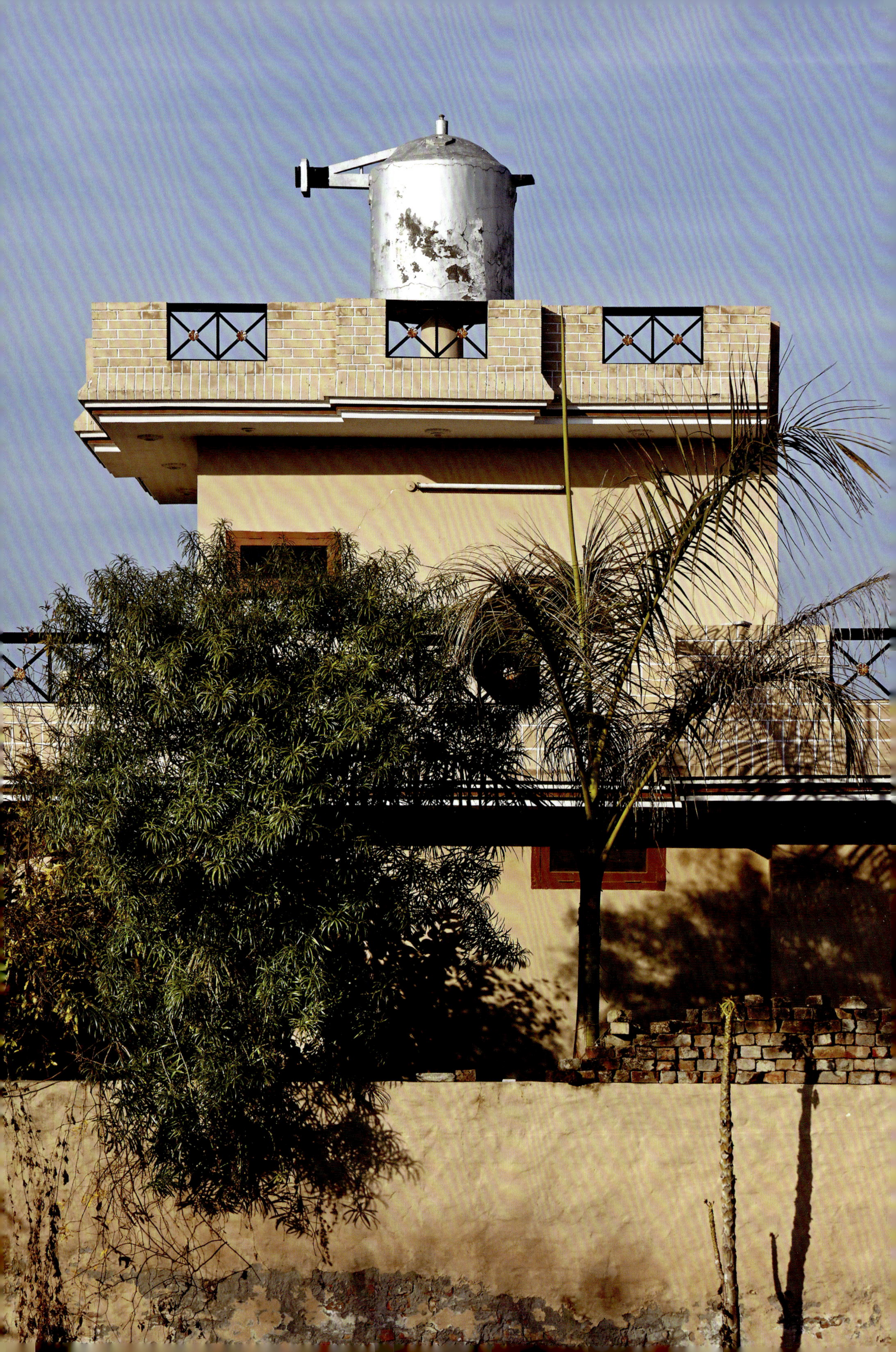

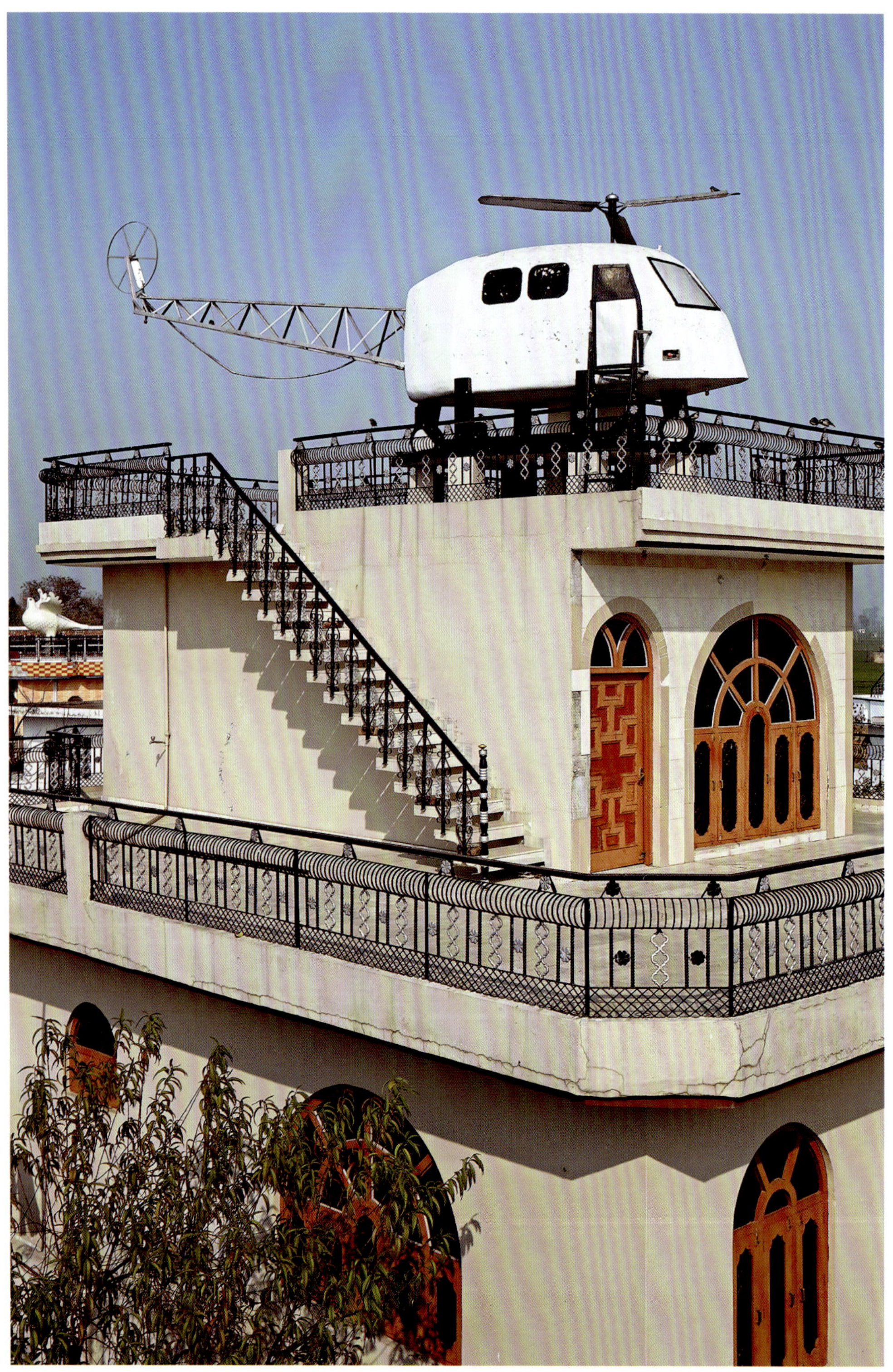

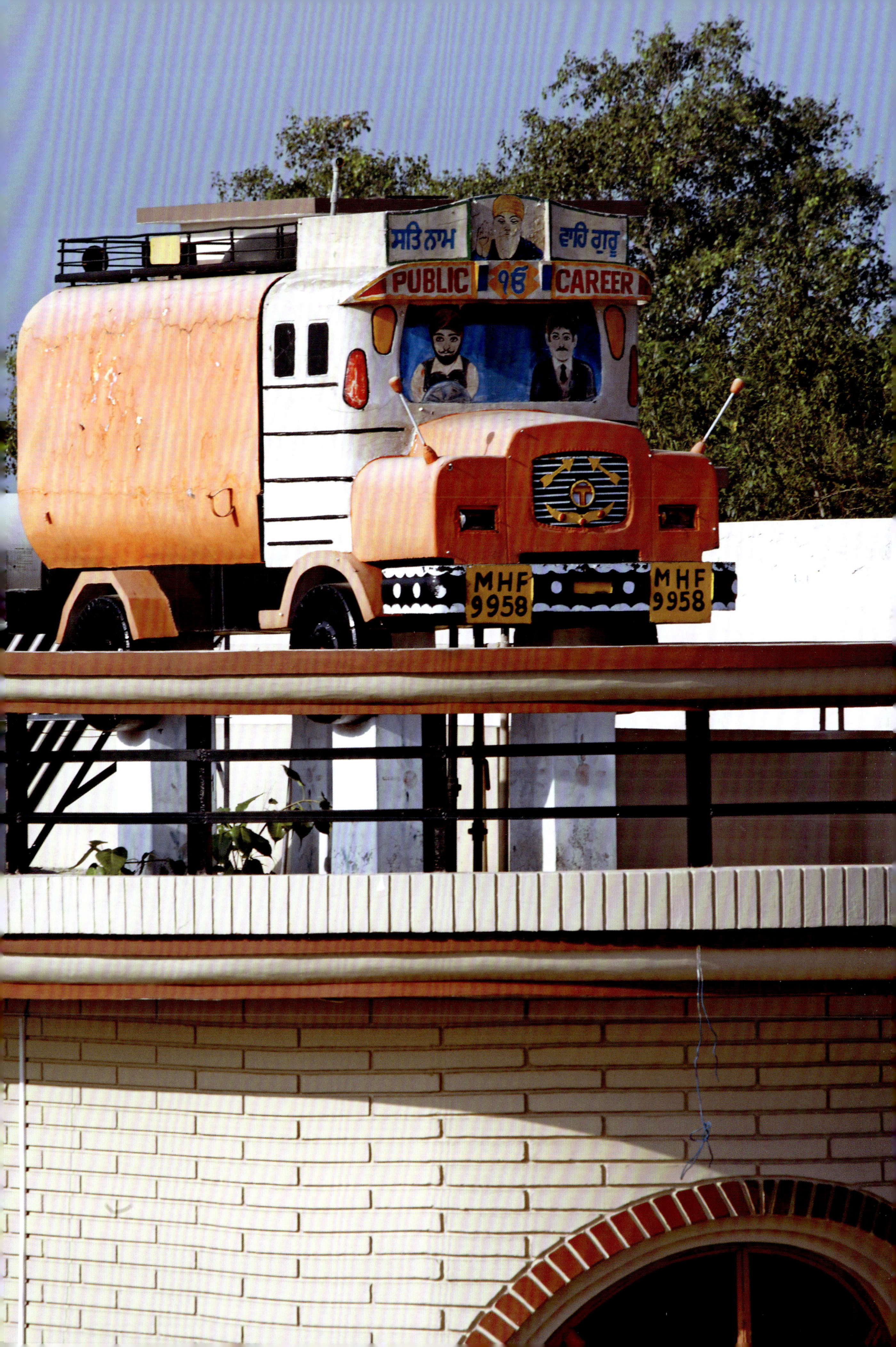
ਸਤਿ ਨਾਮ
ਵਾਹਿ ਗੁਰੂ
PUBLIC
ੴ
CAREER
MHF 9958
MHF 9958

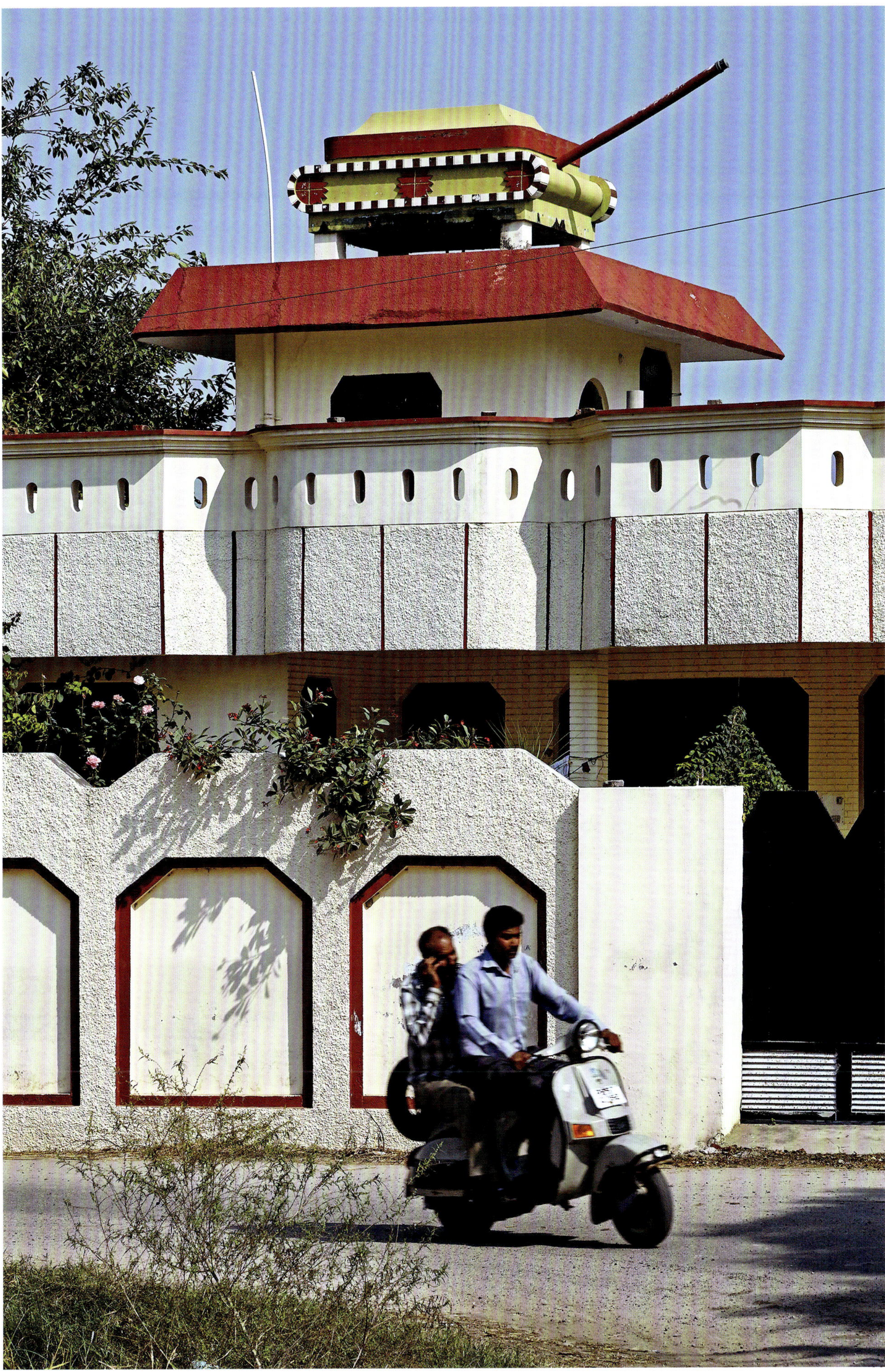

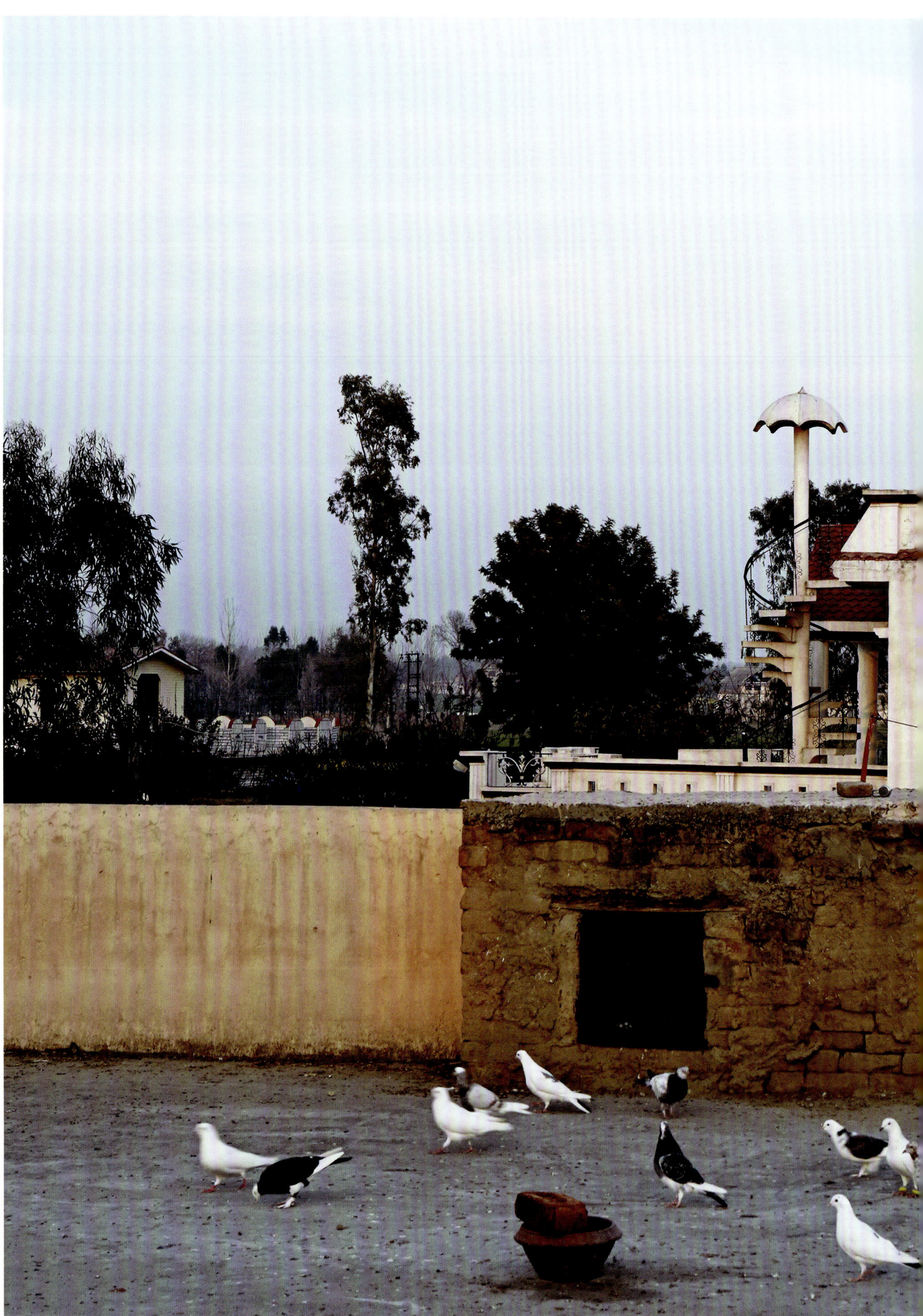

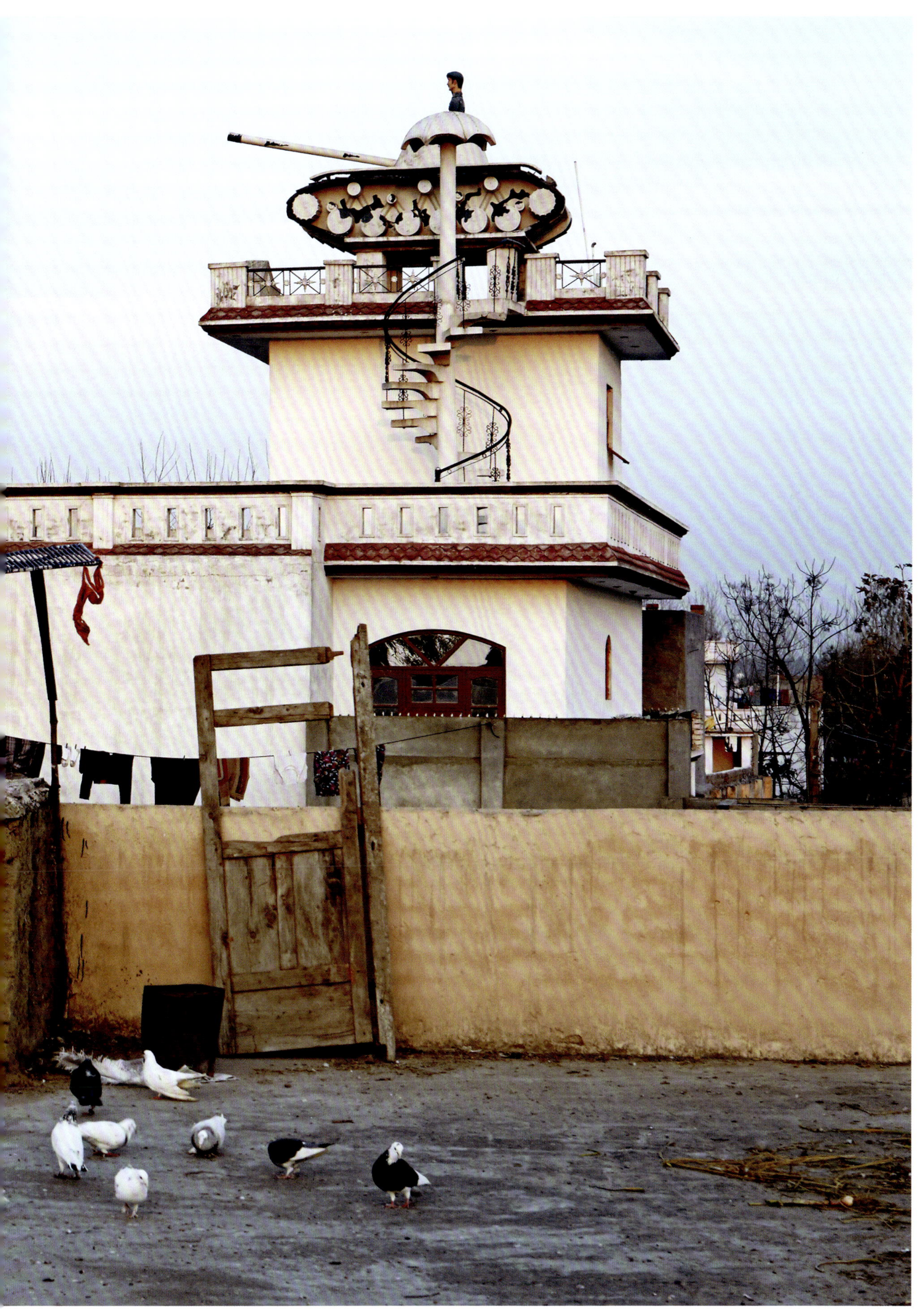

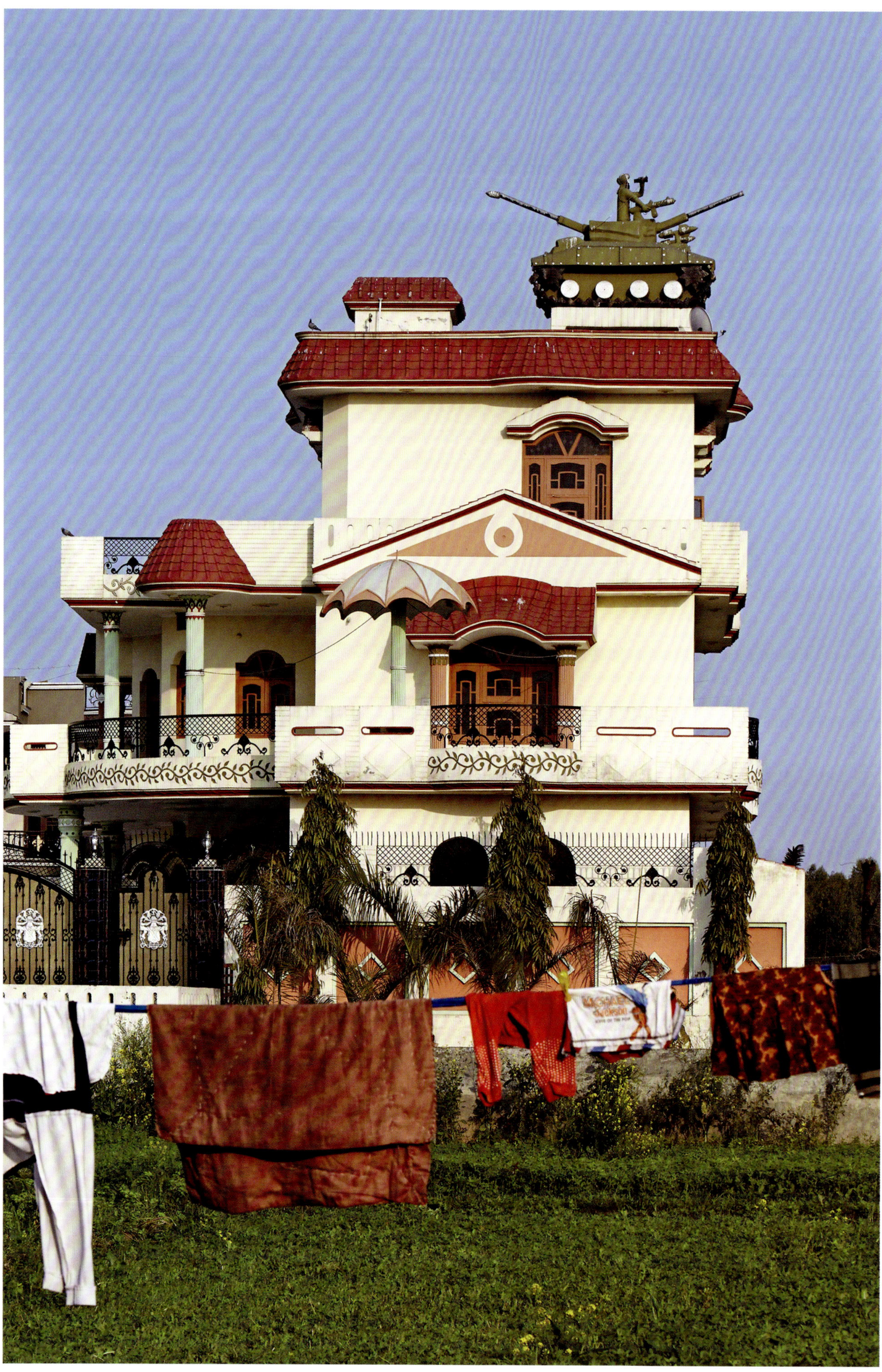

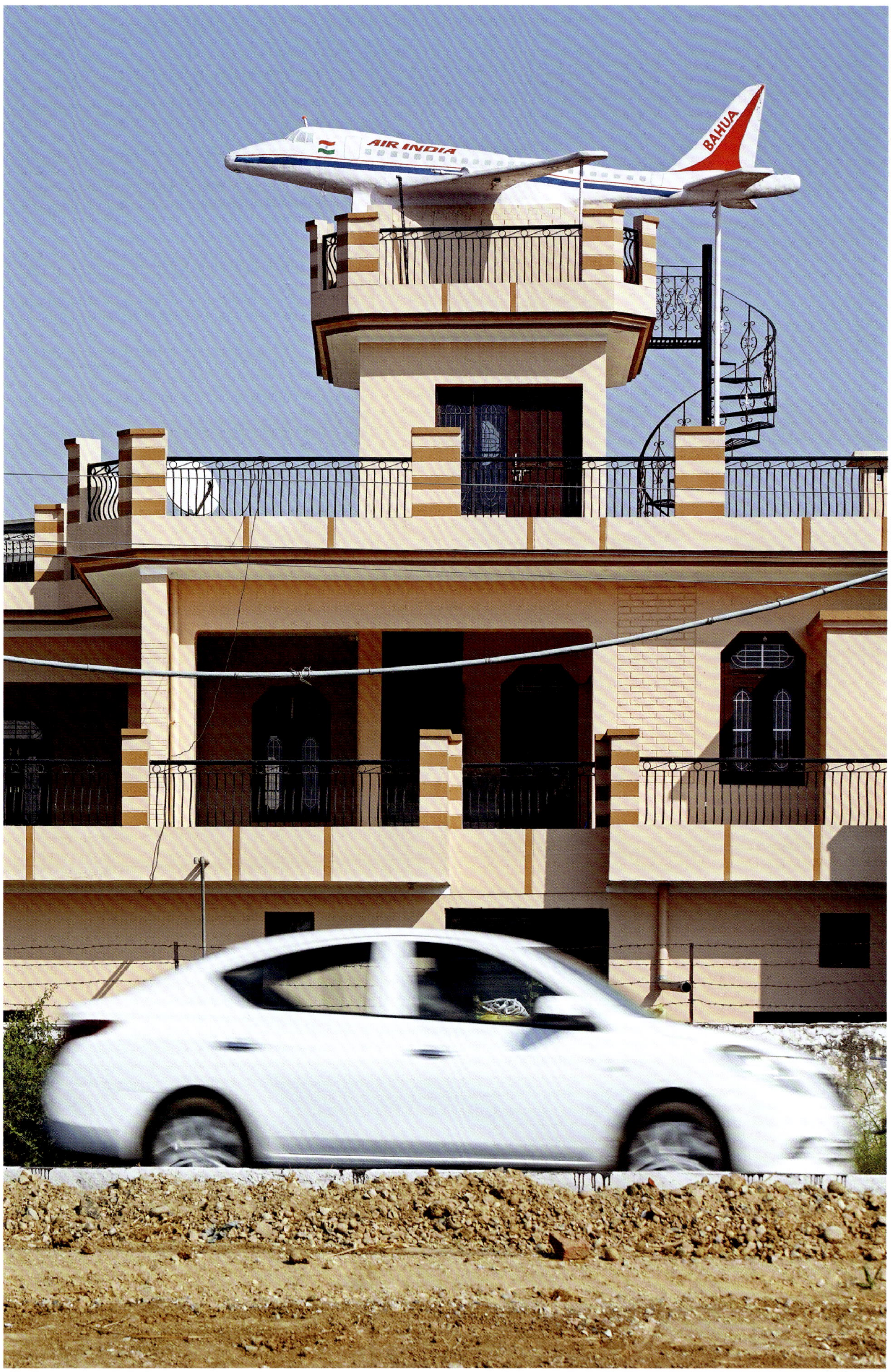
AIR INDIA
BAHUA

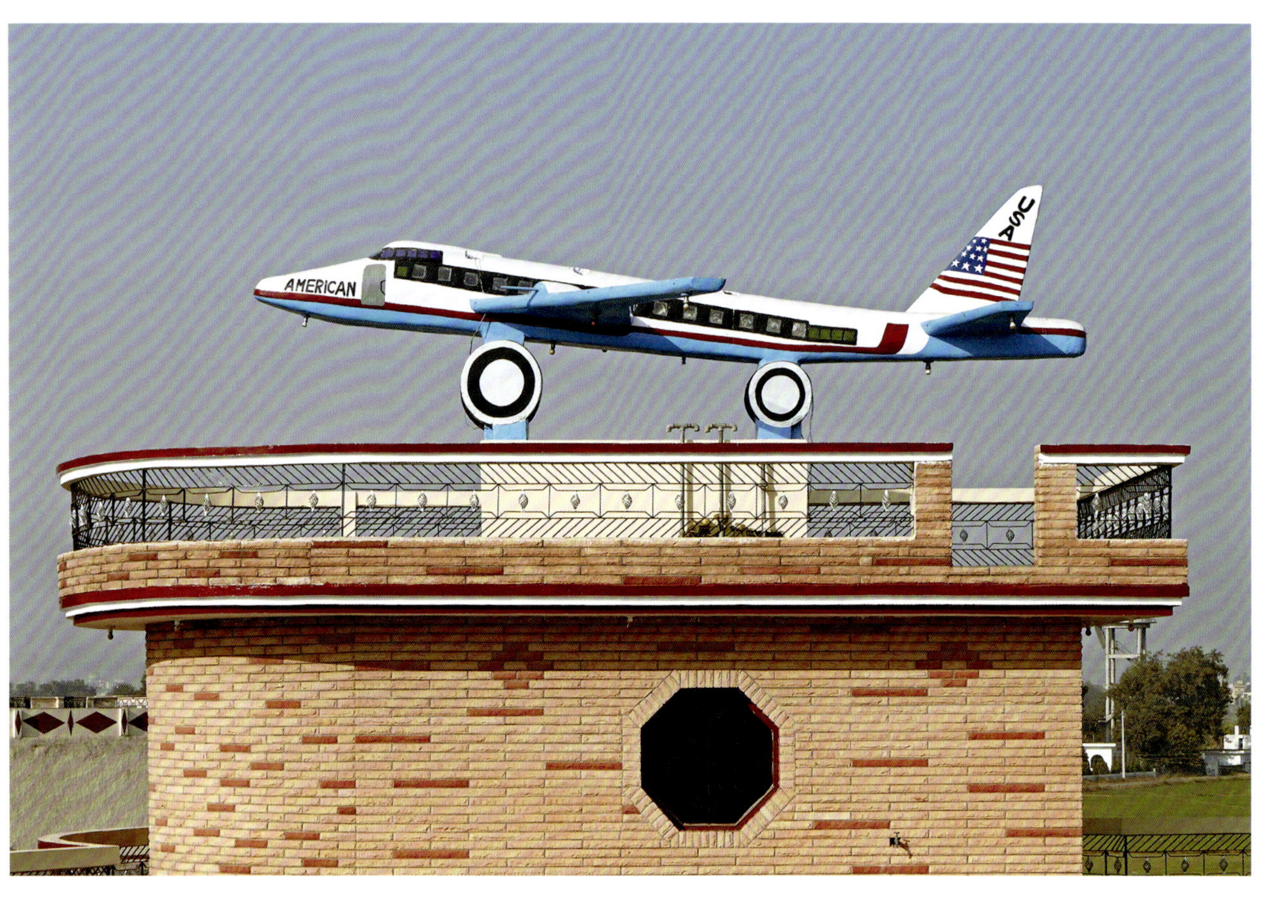
AMERICAN
USA

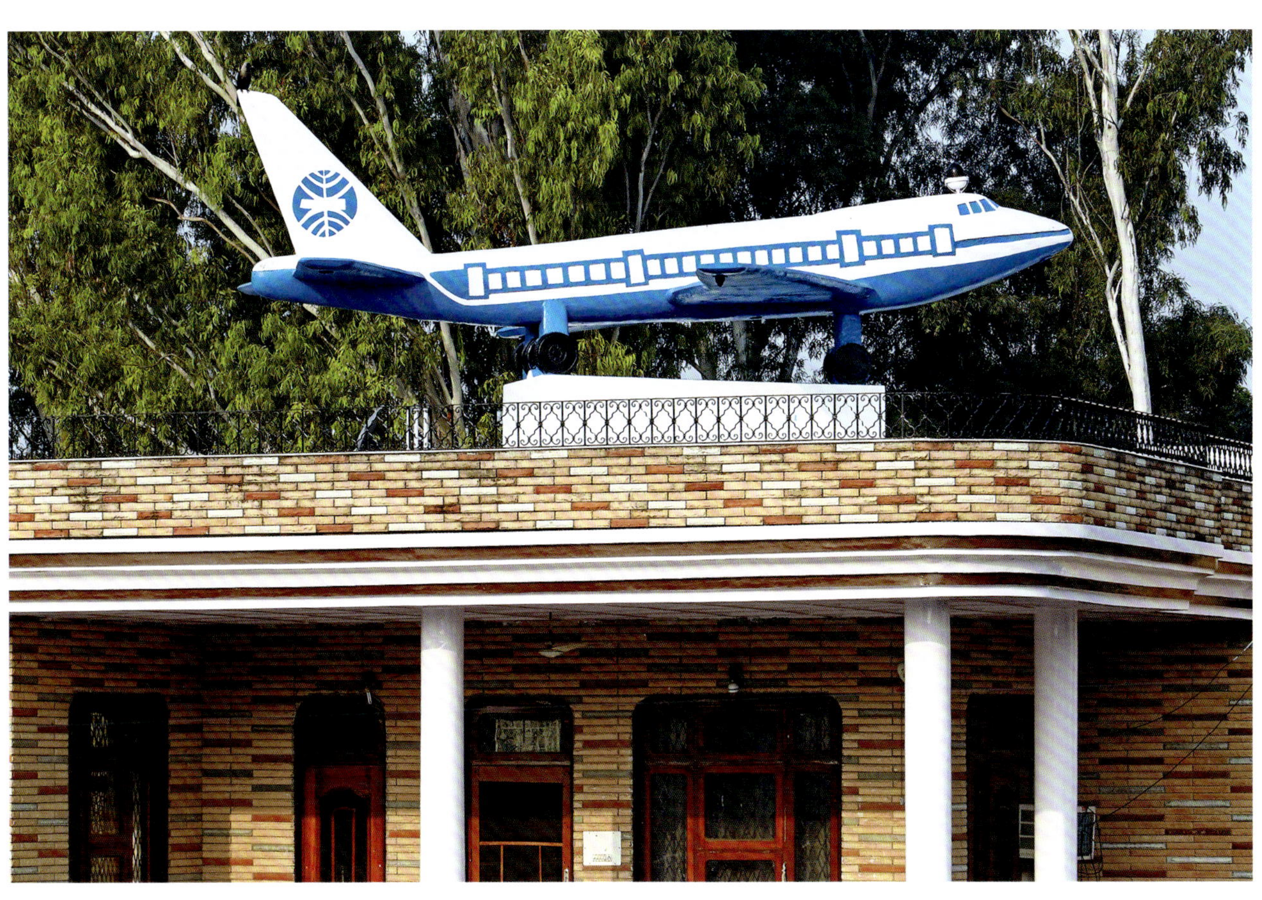

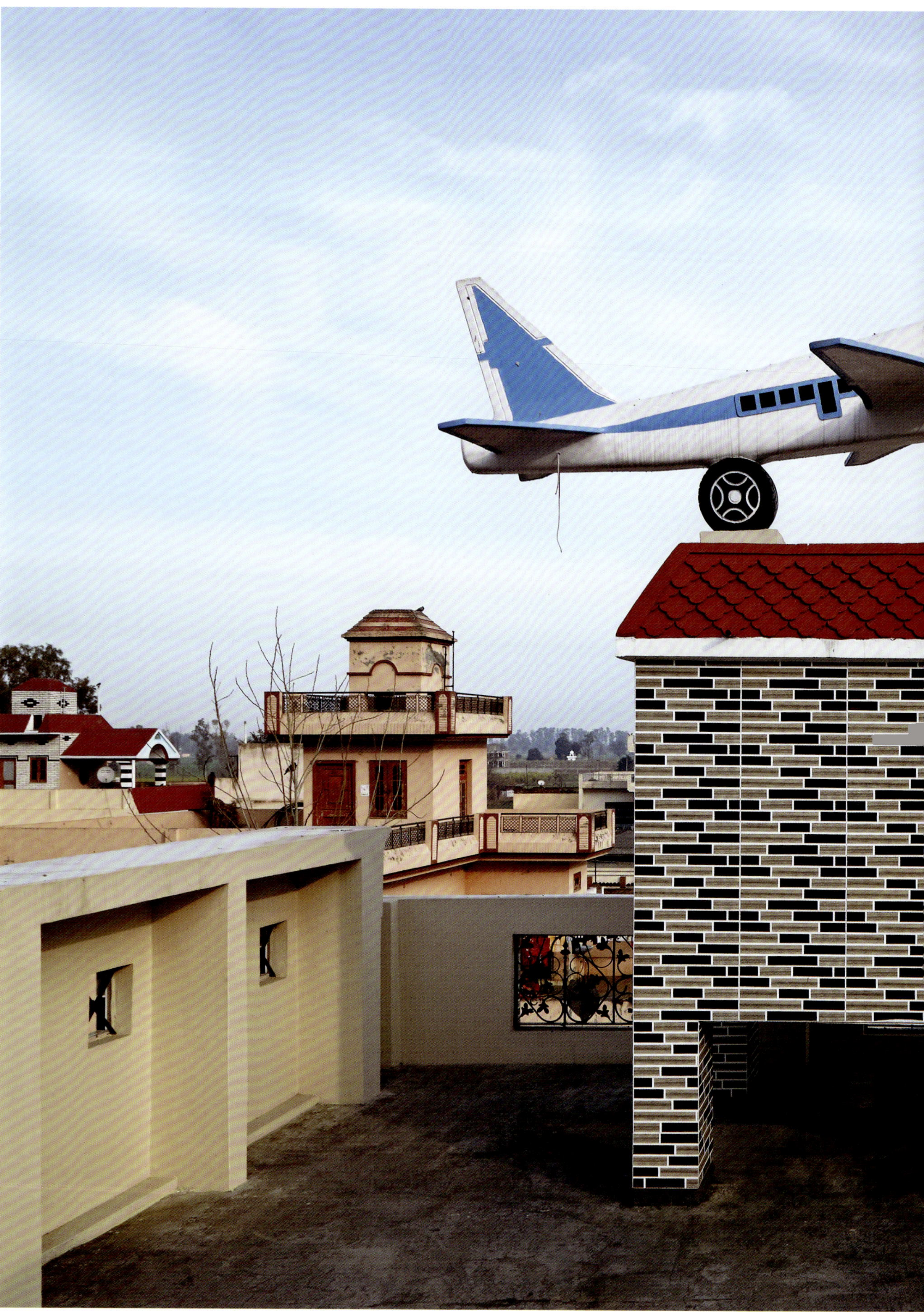

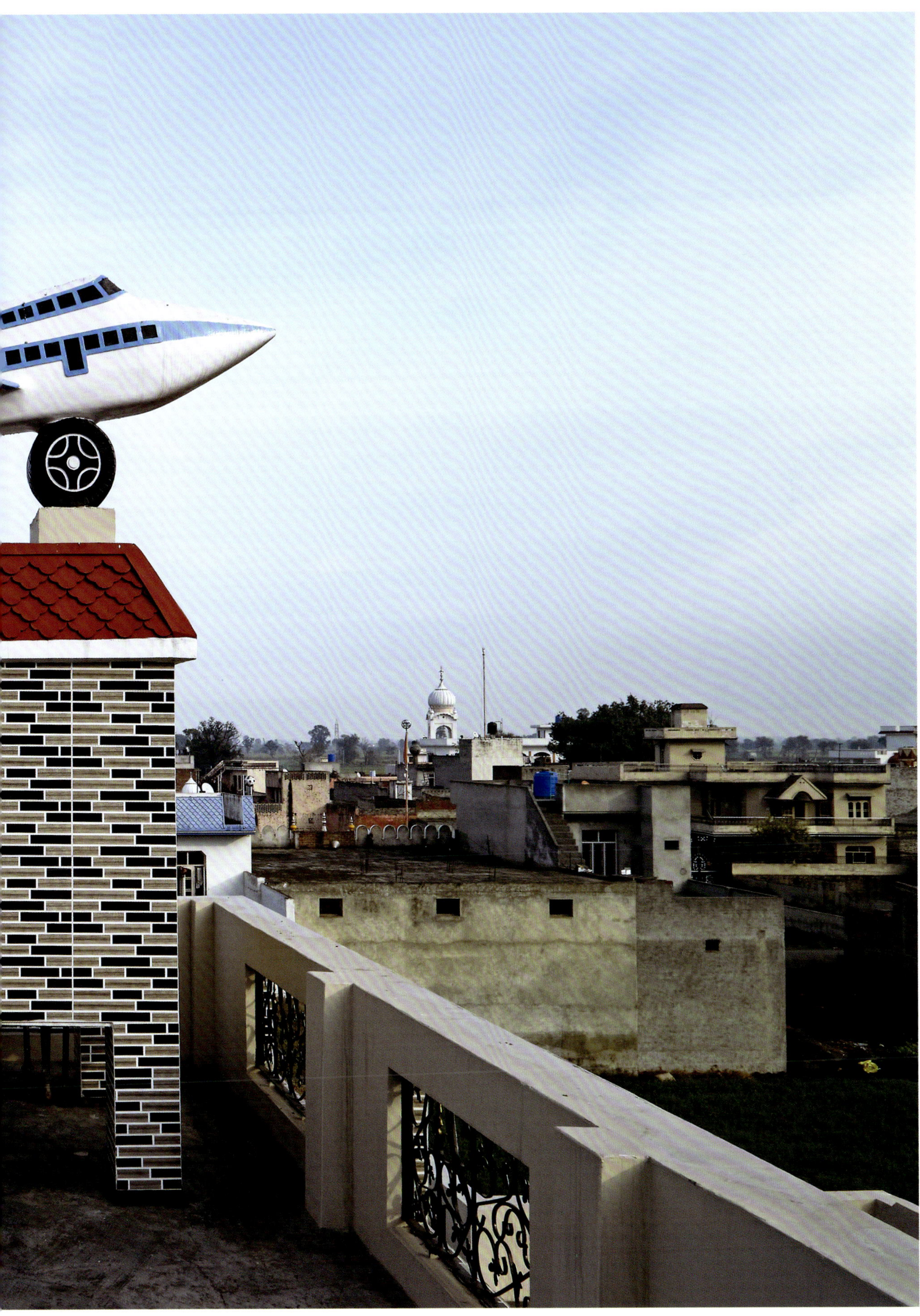

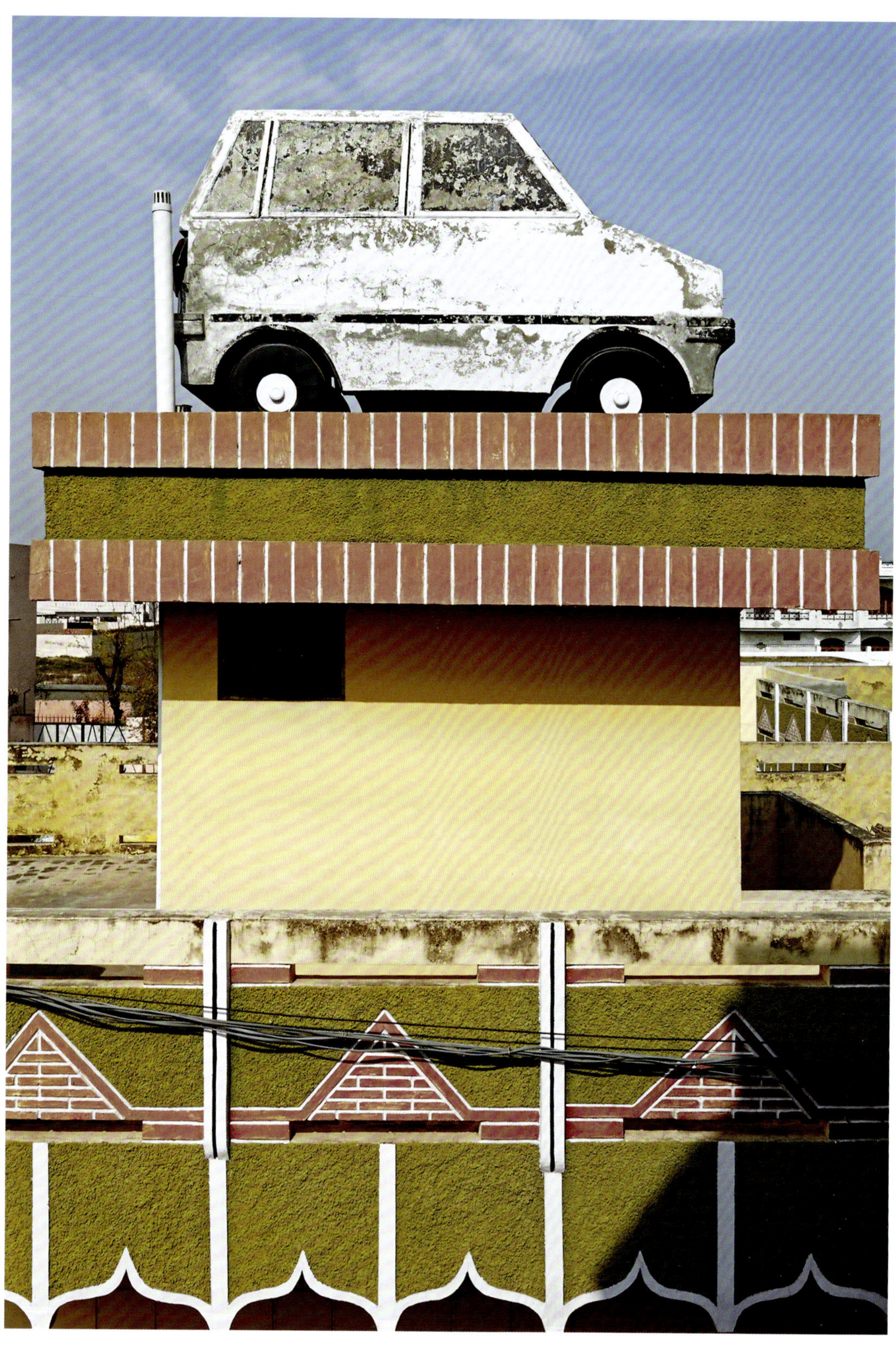

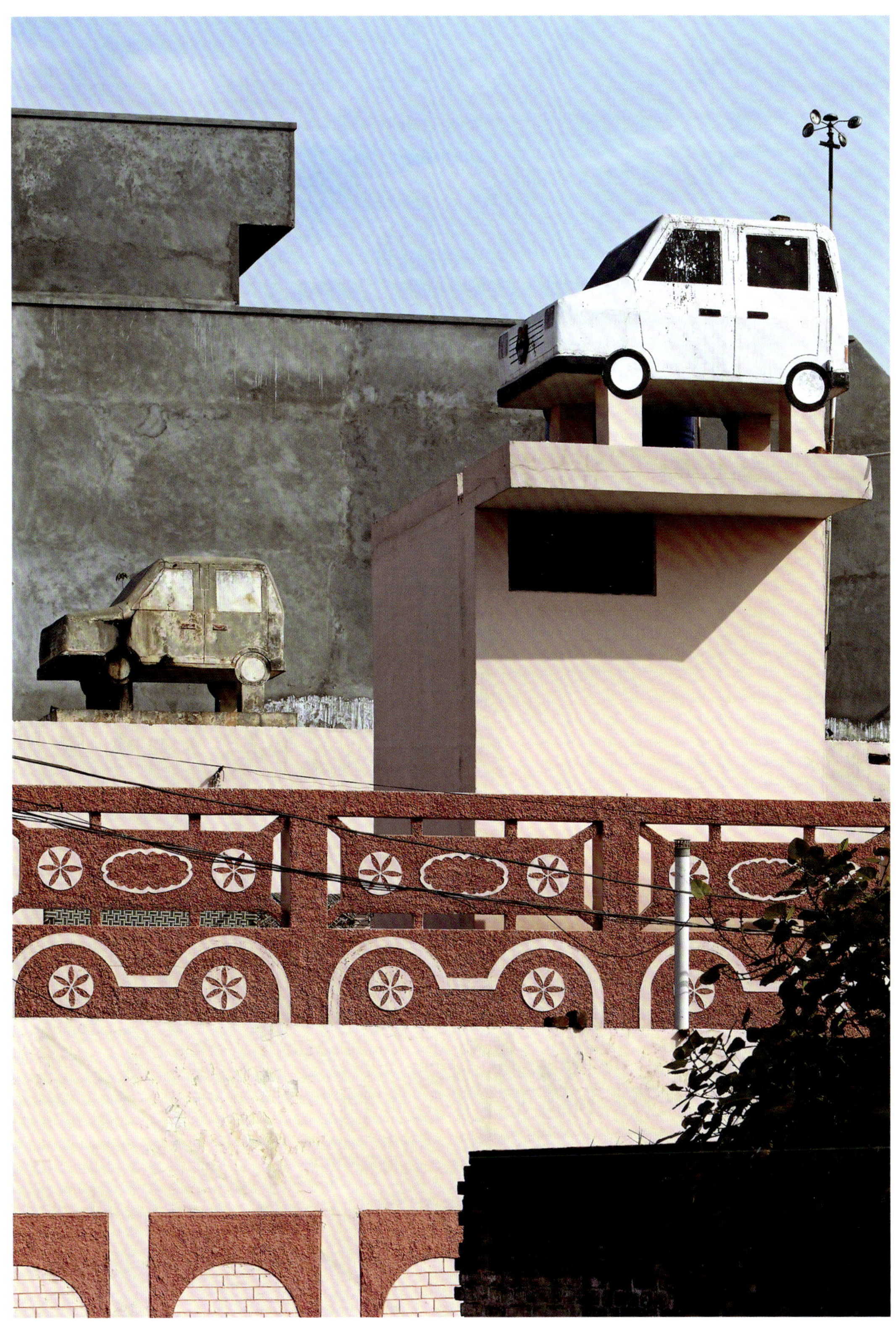

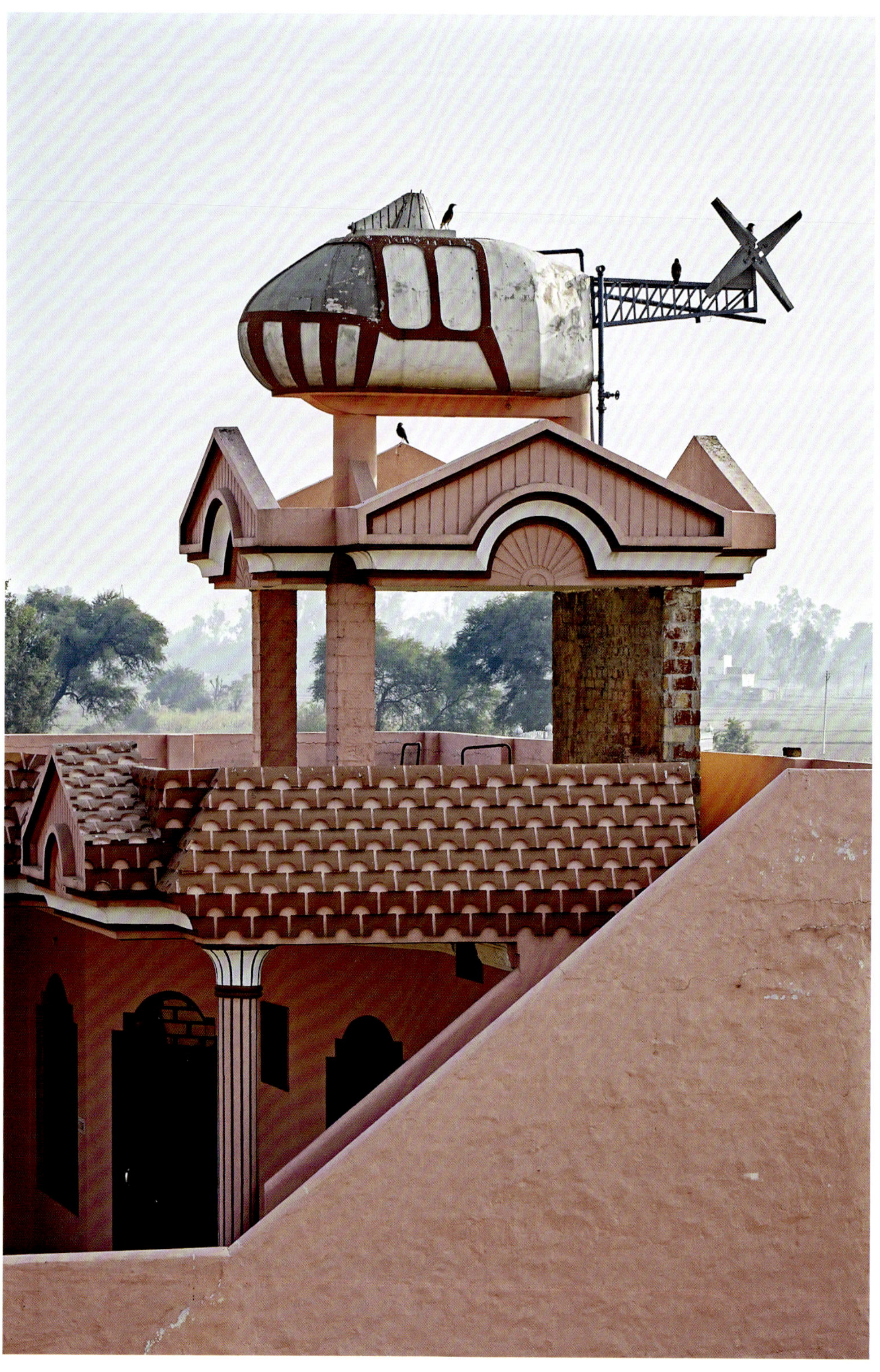

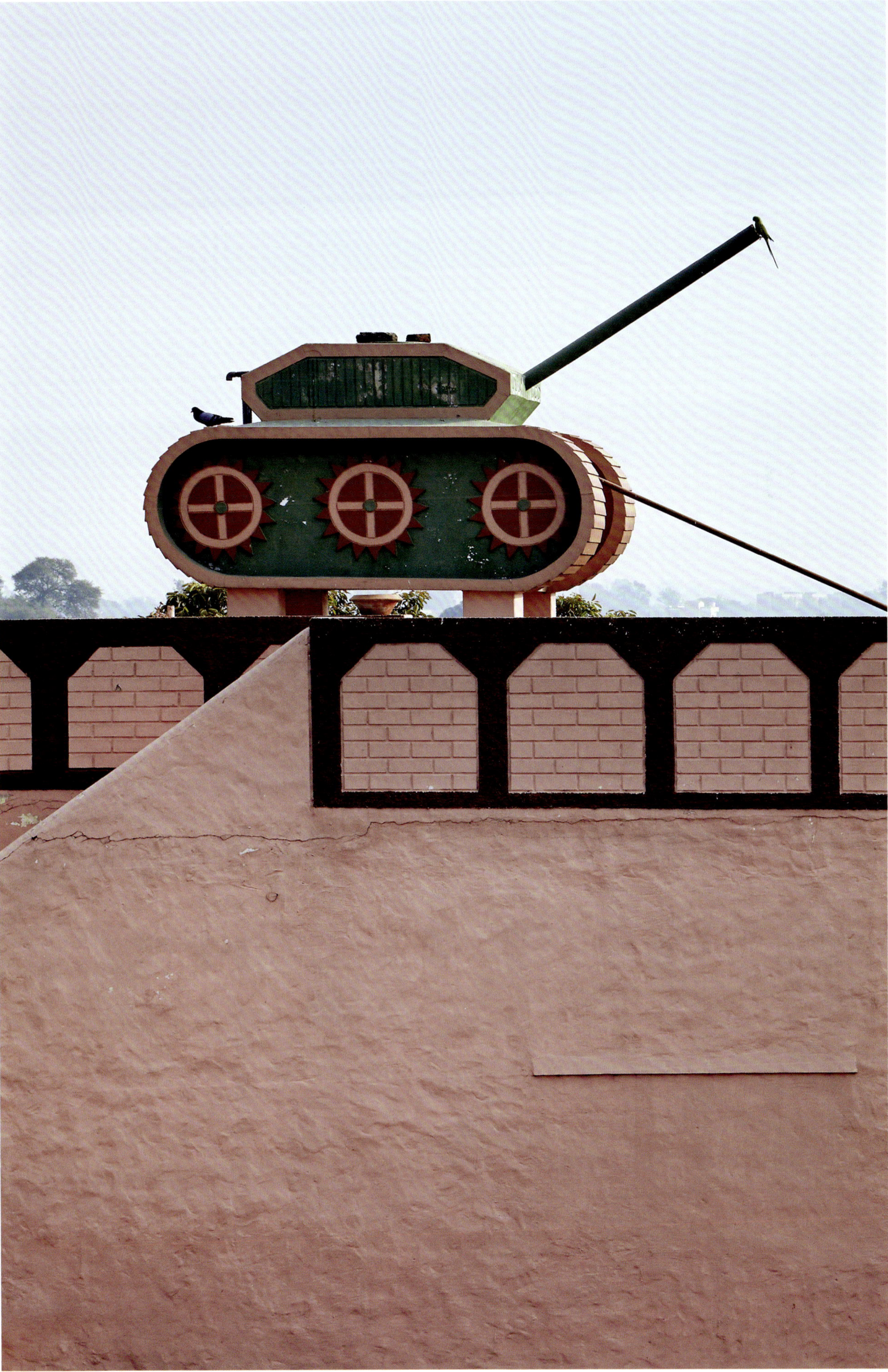

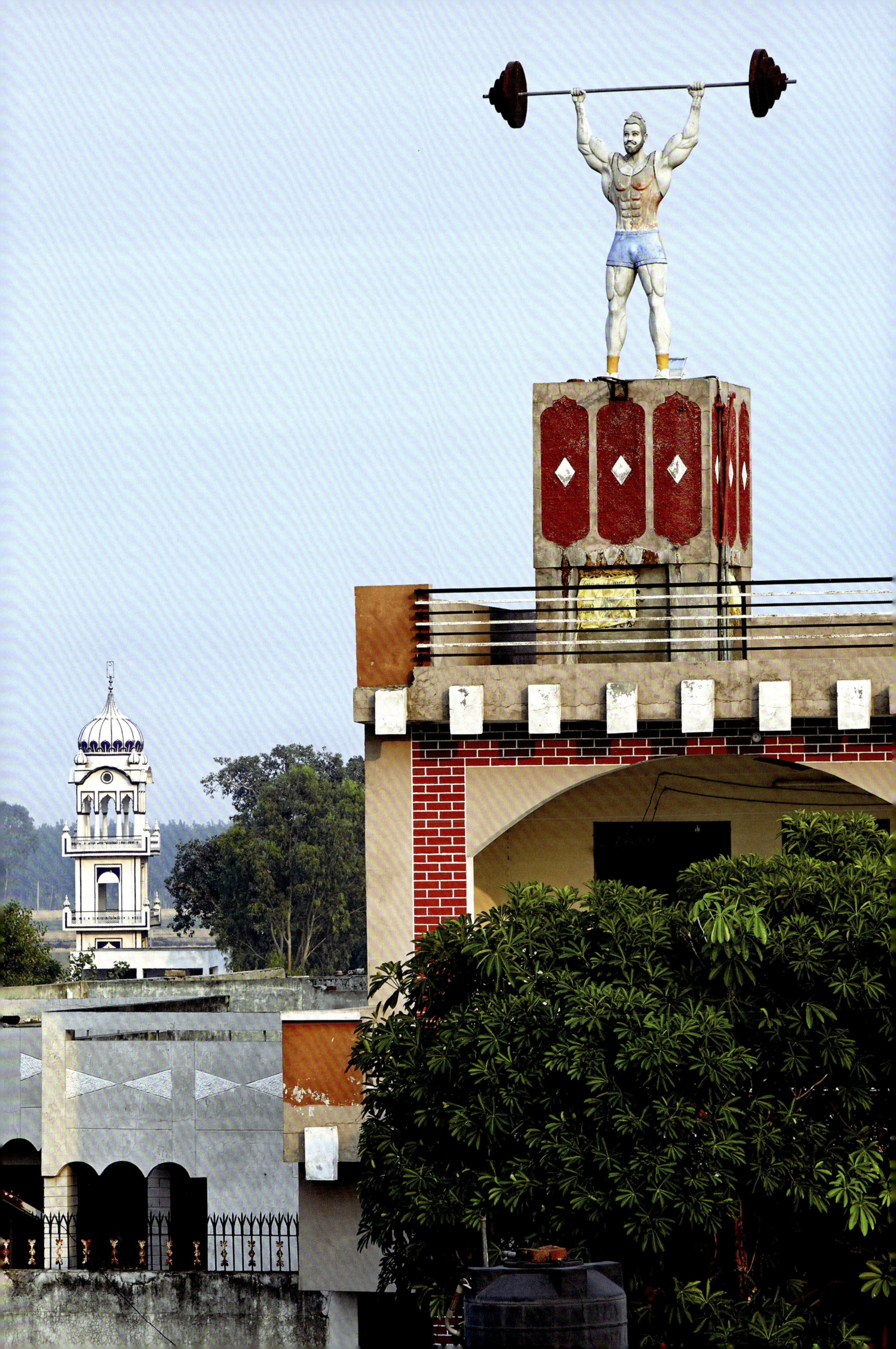

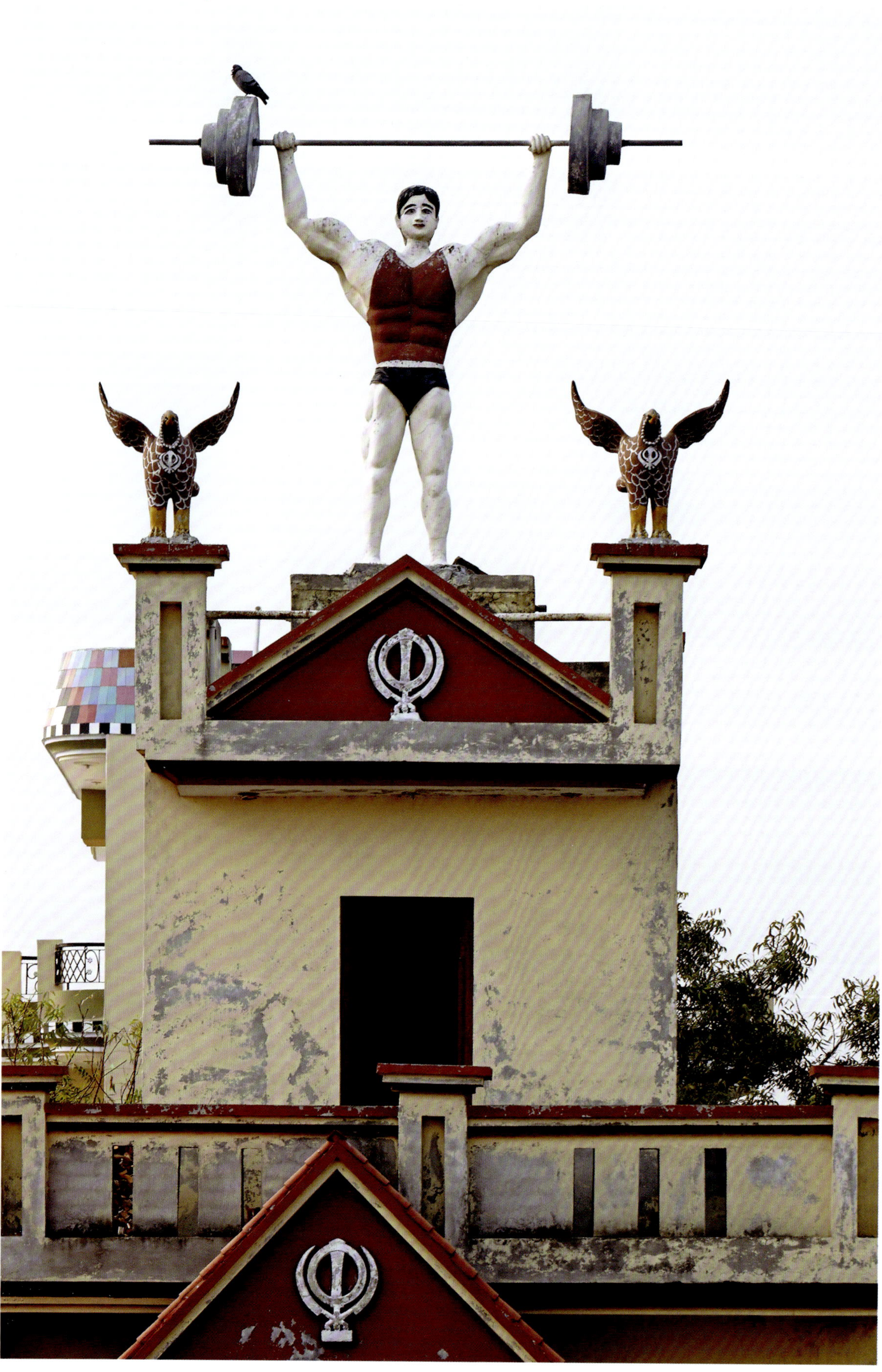

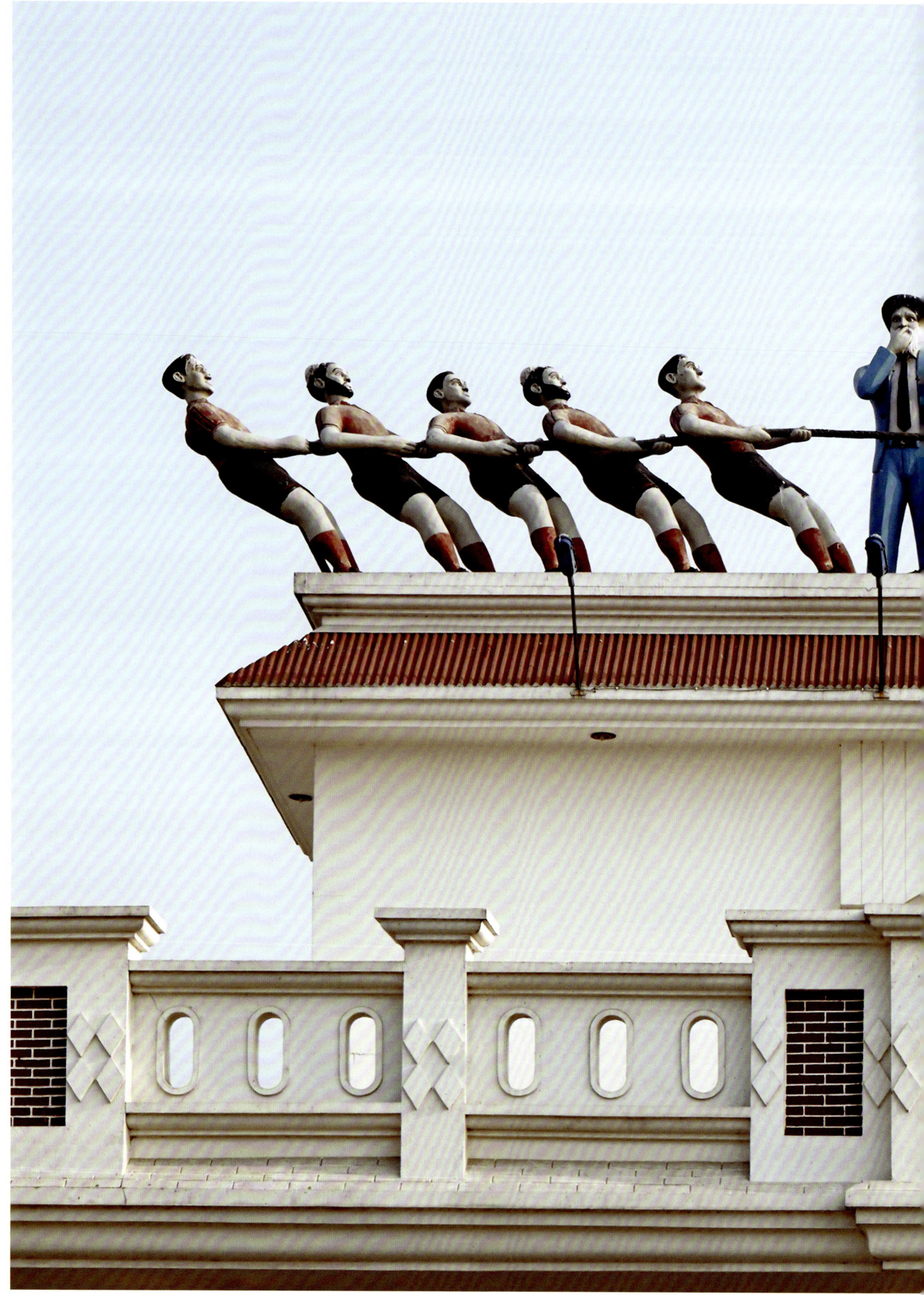

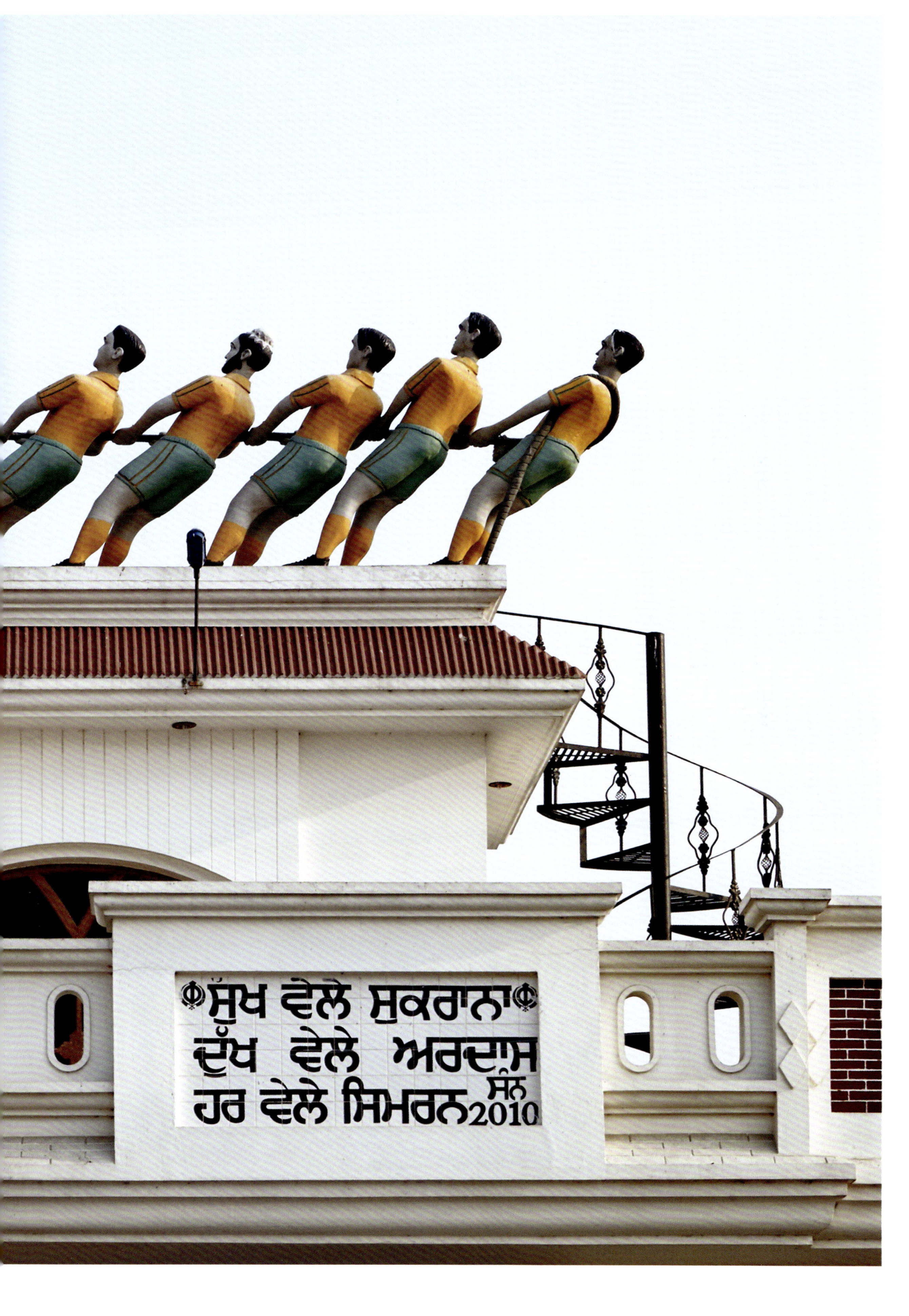
ਸੁੱਖ ਵੇਲੇ ਸੁਕਰਾਨਾ
ਦੁੱਖ ਵੇਲੇ ਅਰਦਾਸ
ਹਰ ਵੇਲੇ ਸਿਮਰਨ
ਸੰਨ 2010

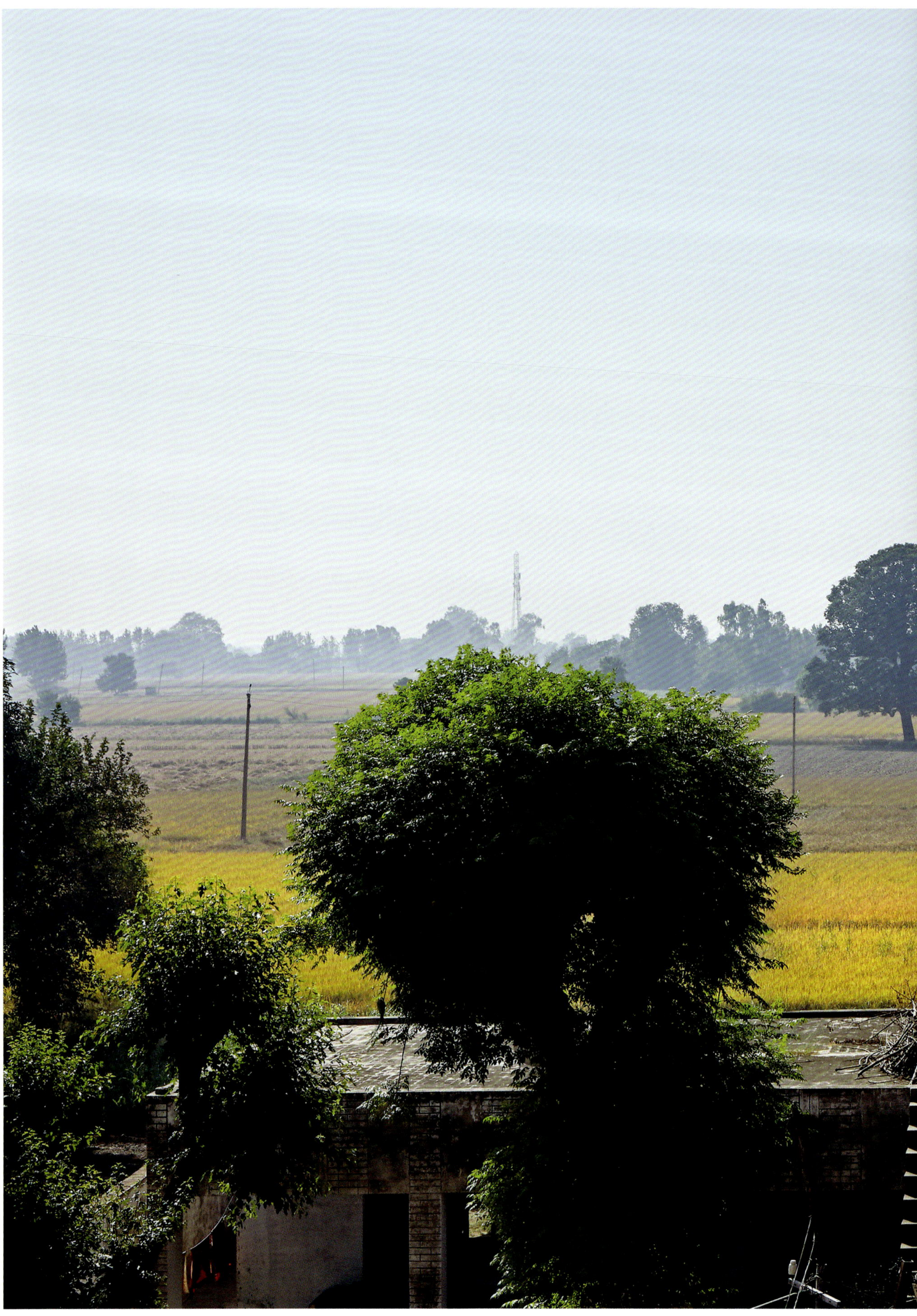

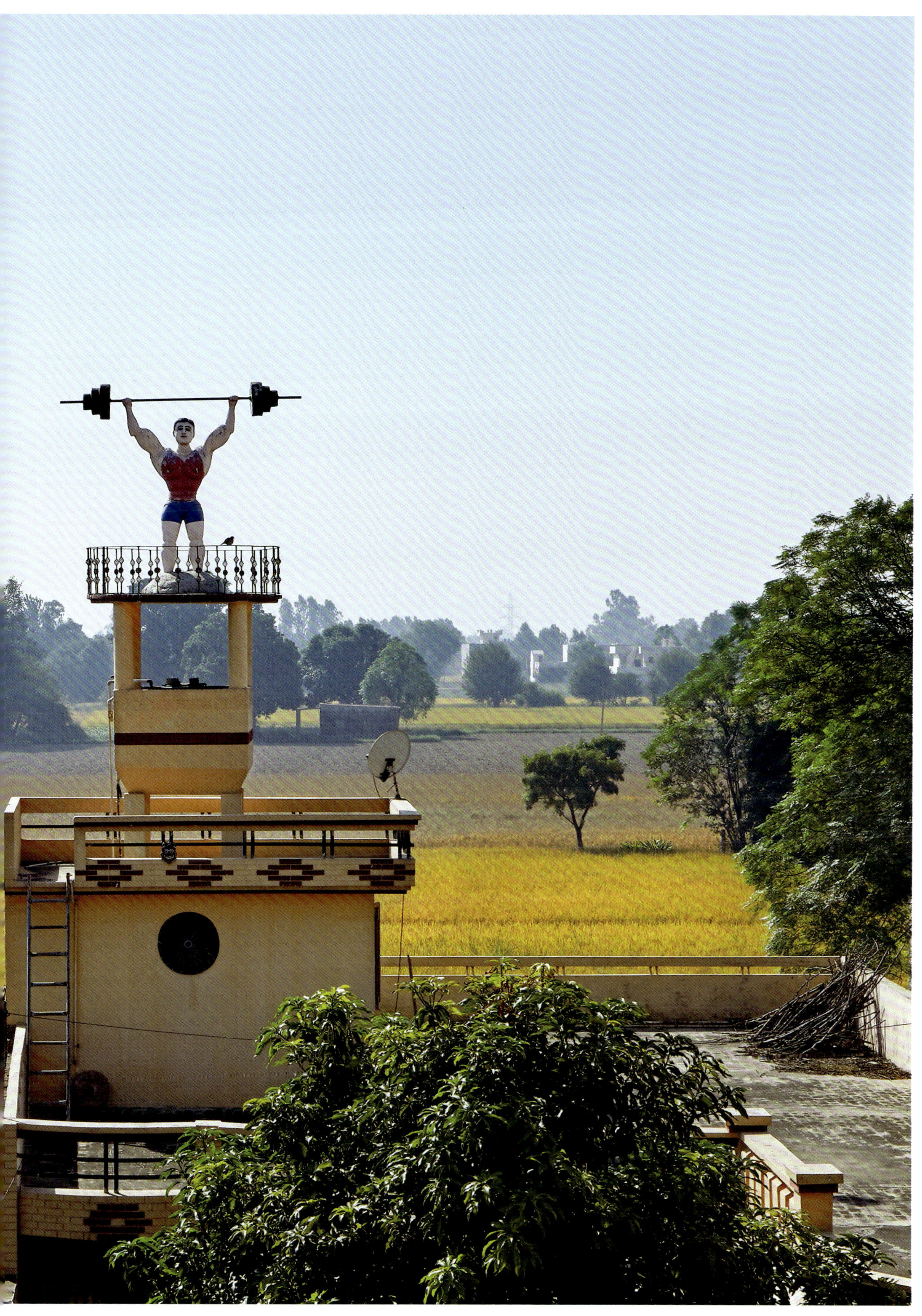

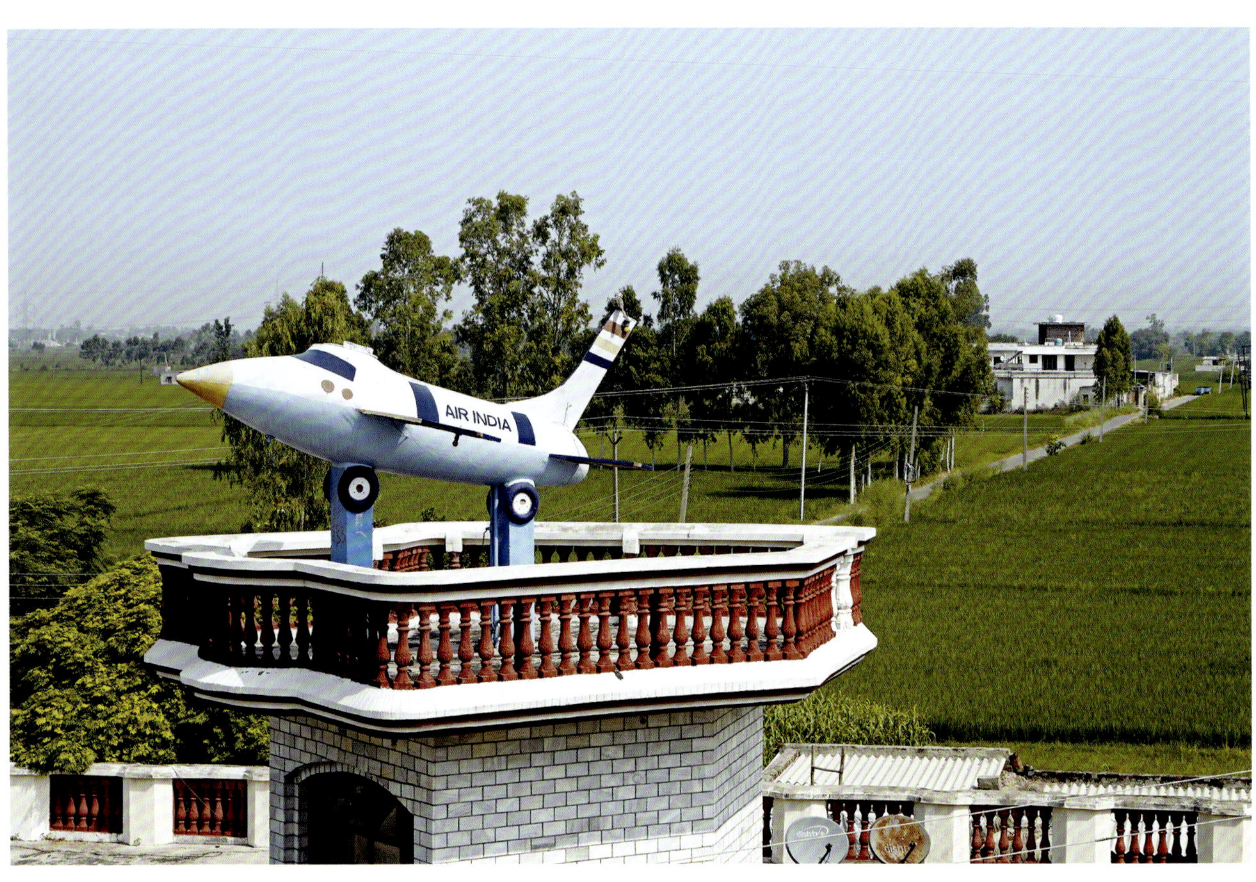
AIR INDIA

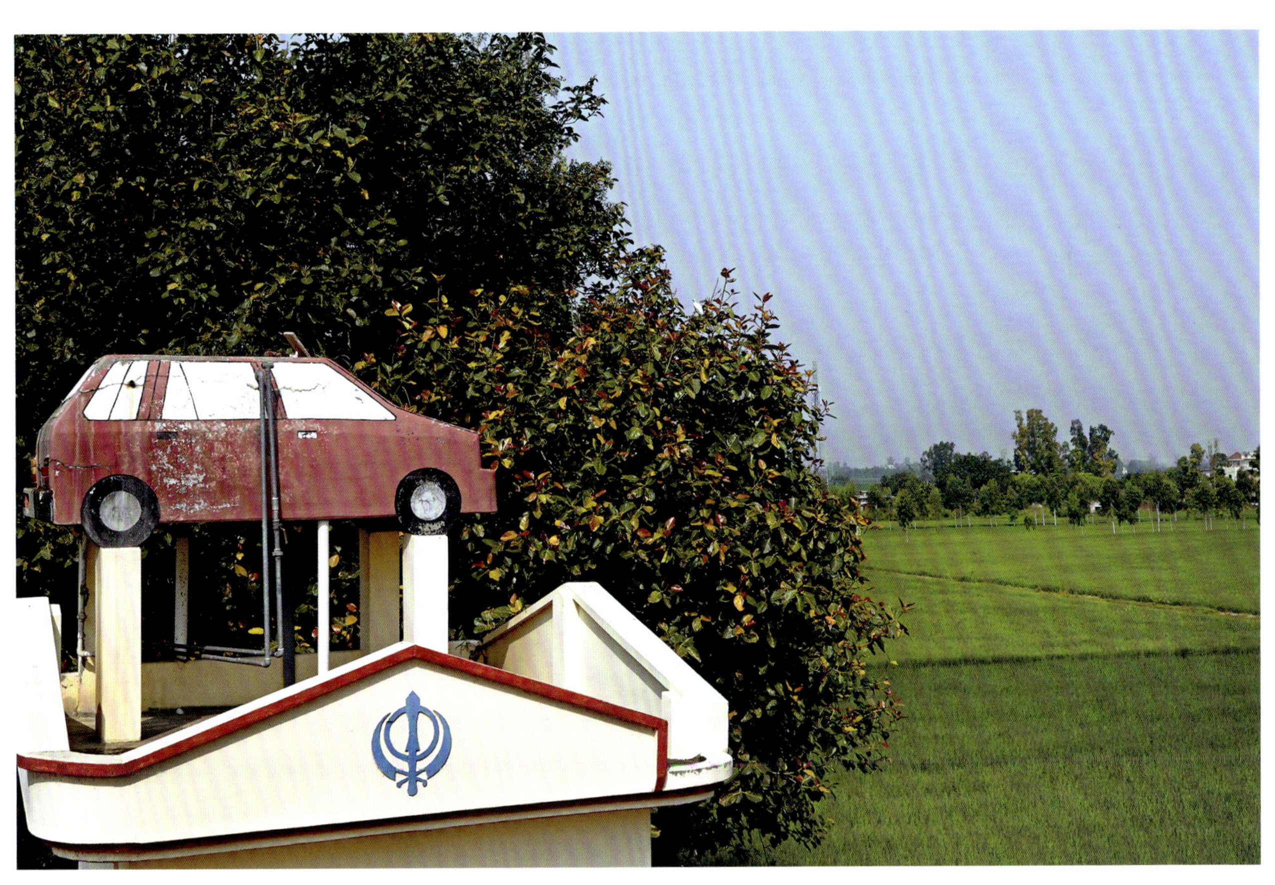

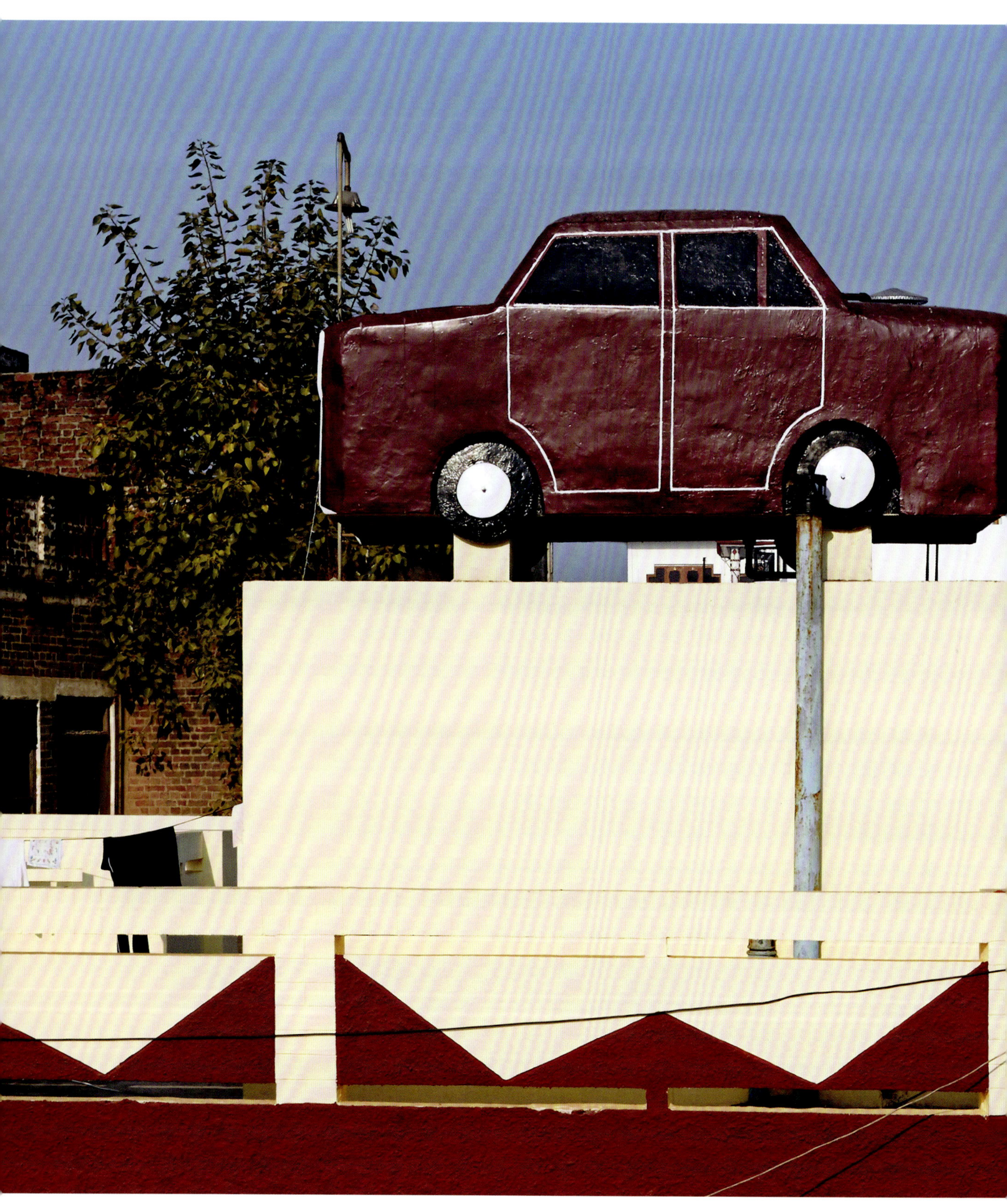

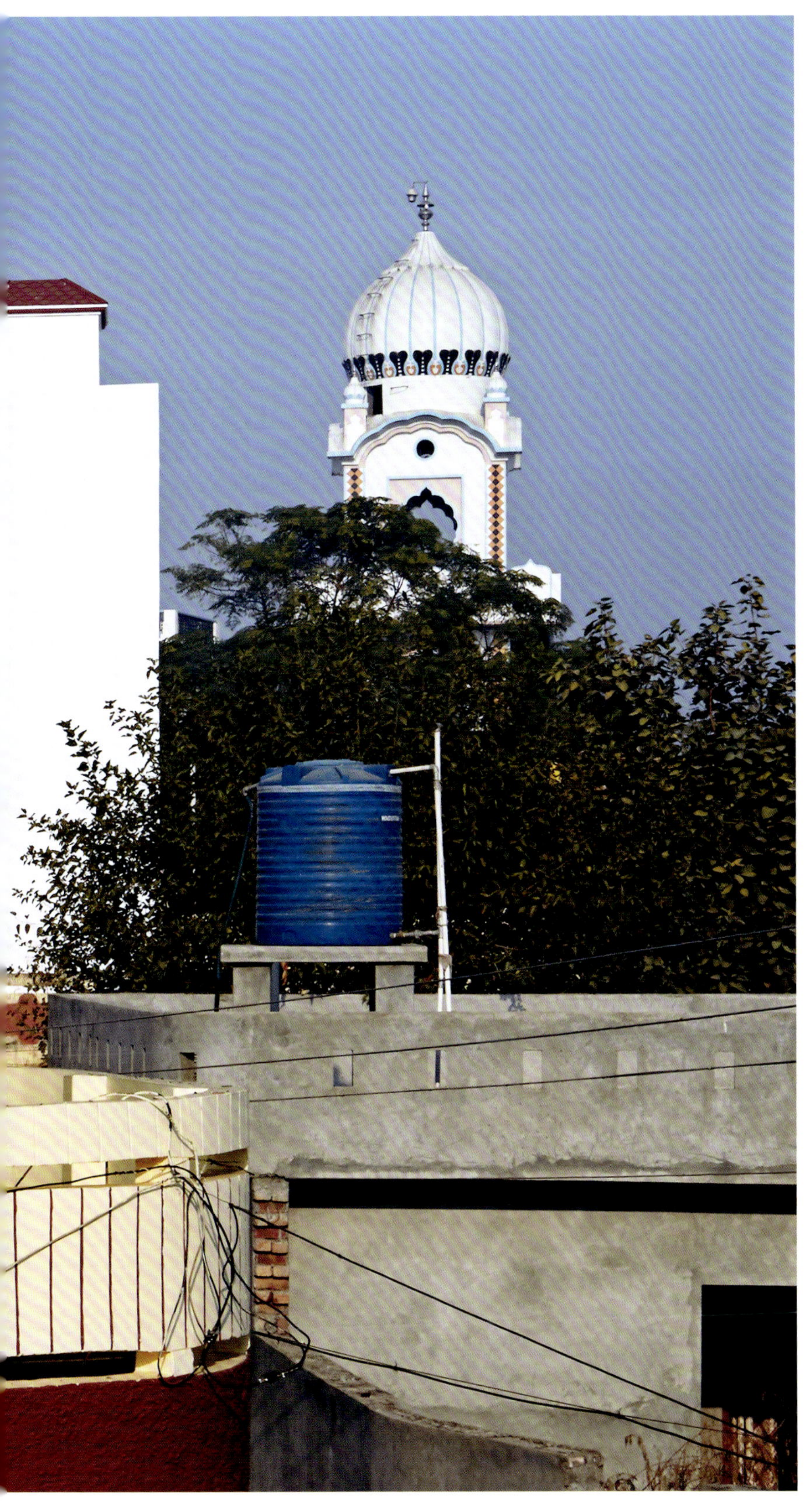

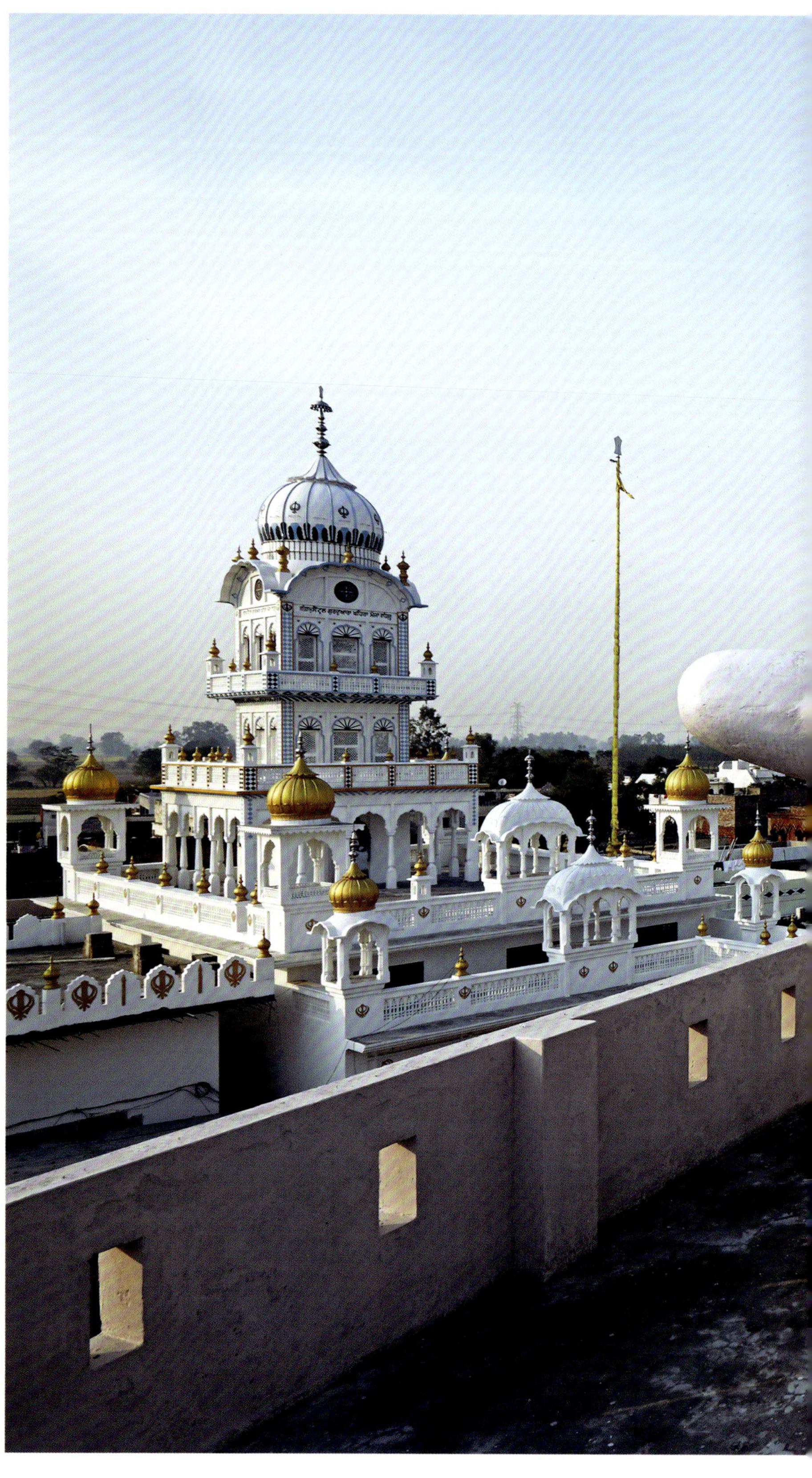

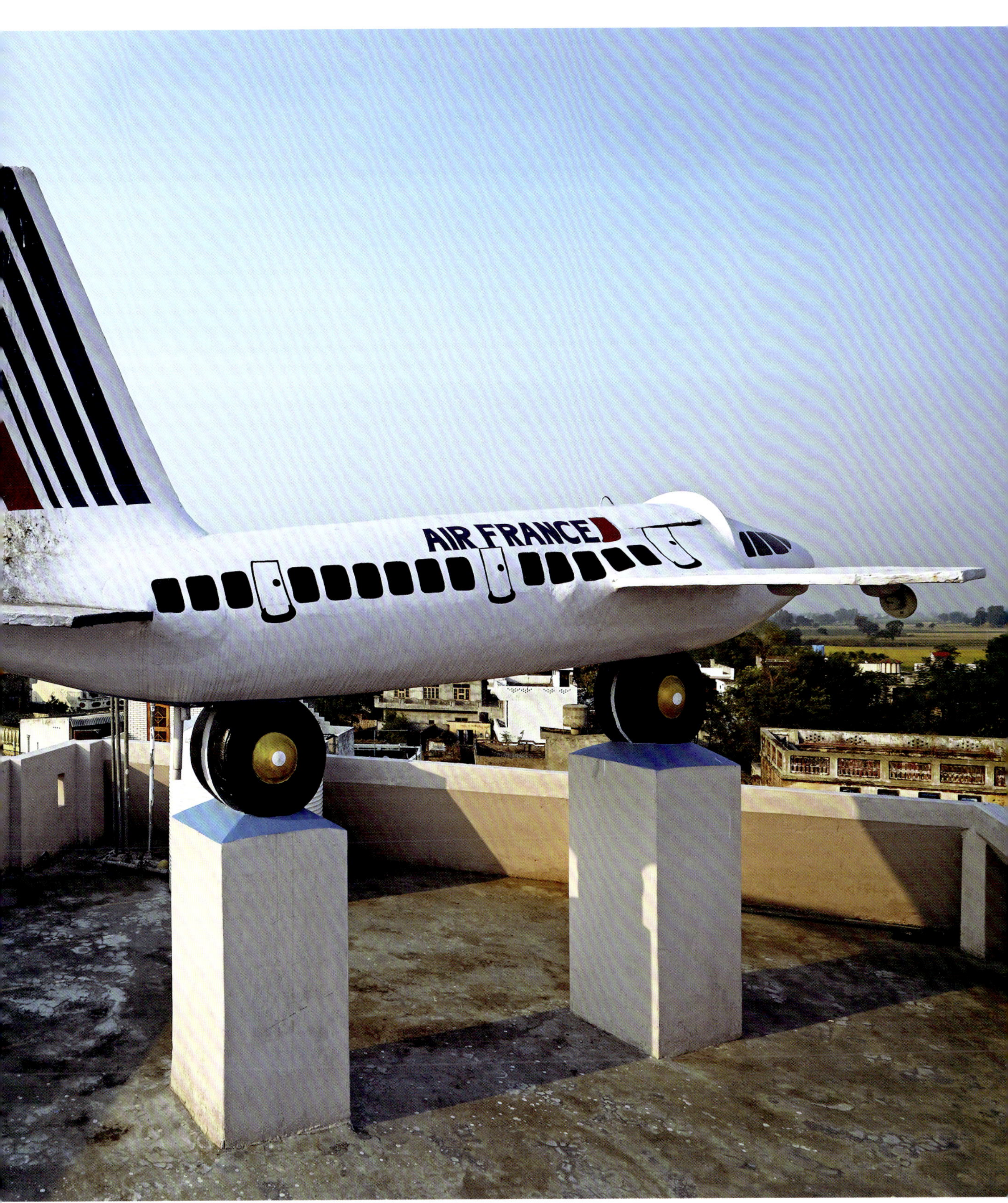
AIR FRANCE

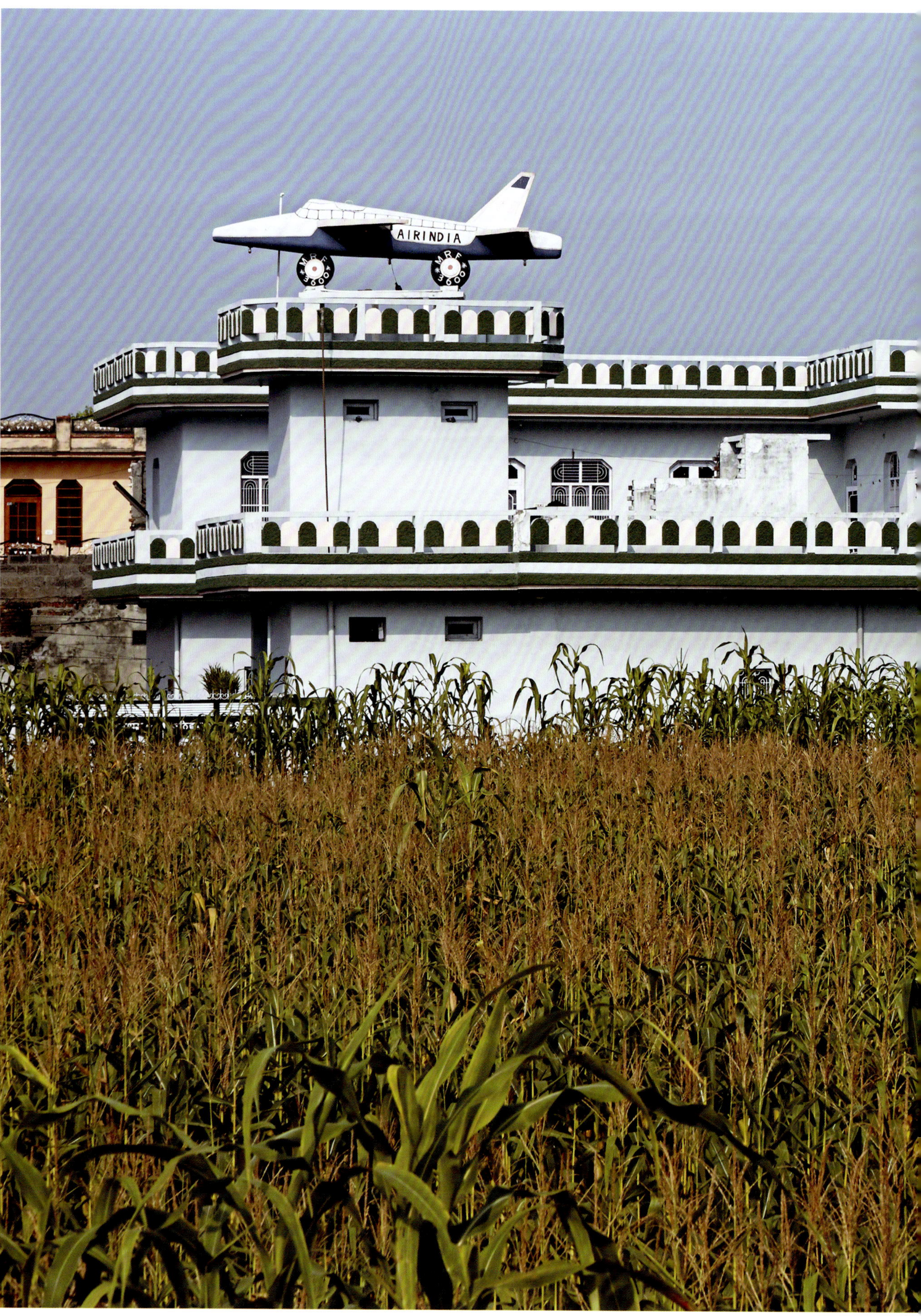
AIRINDIA
MRF 3600
MRF 3600

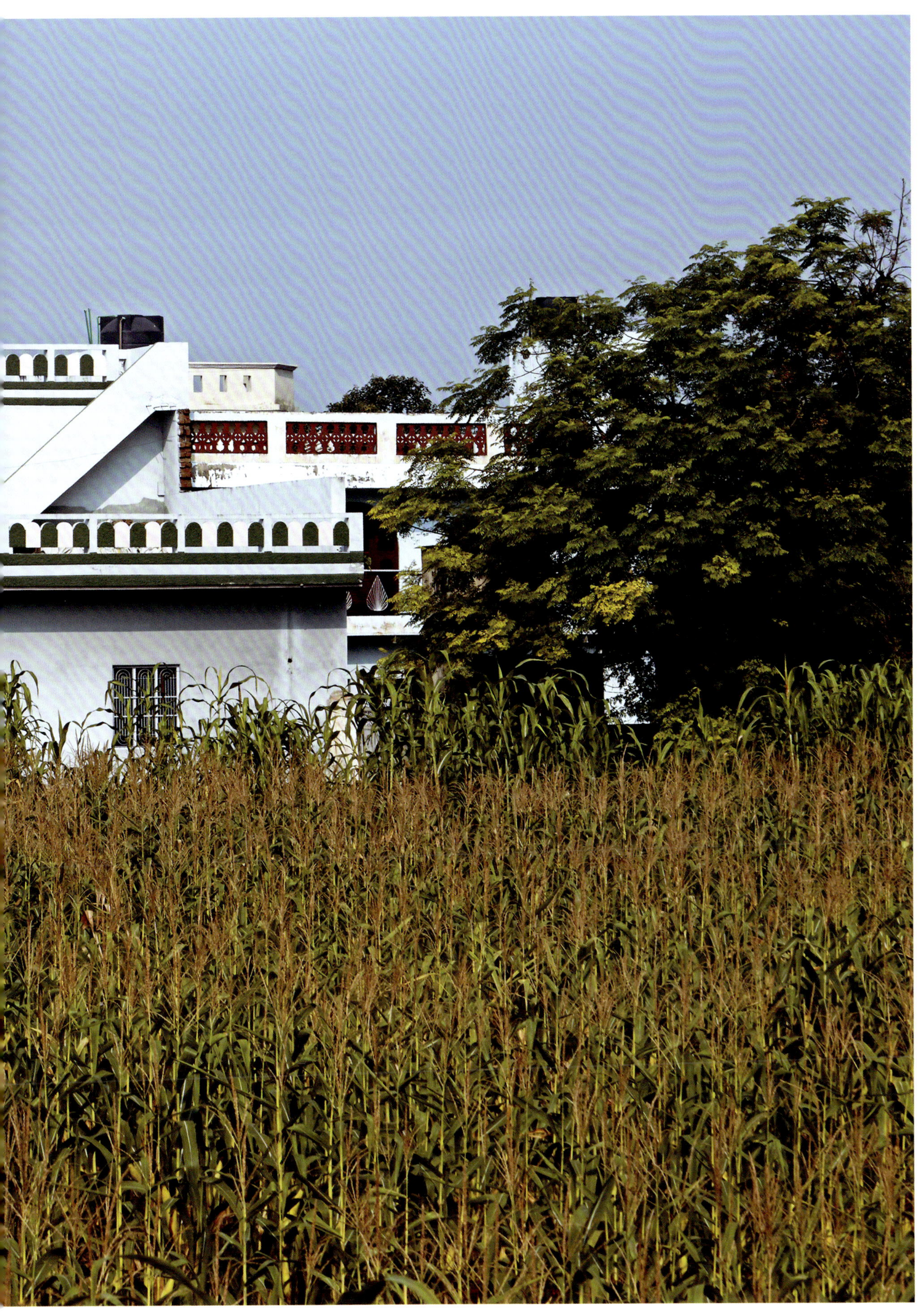

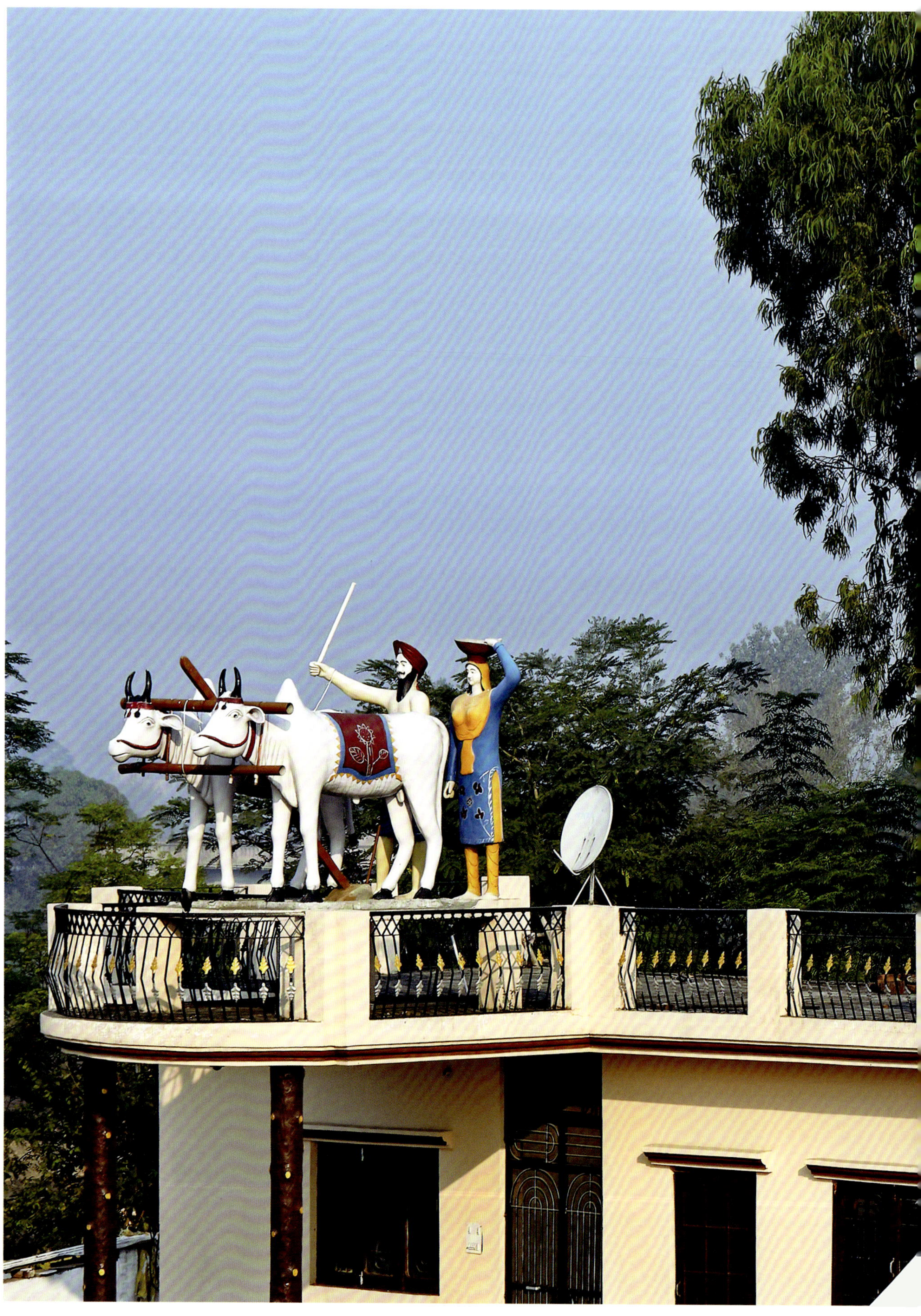

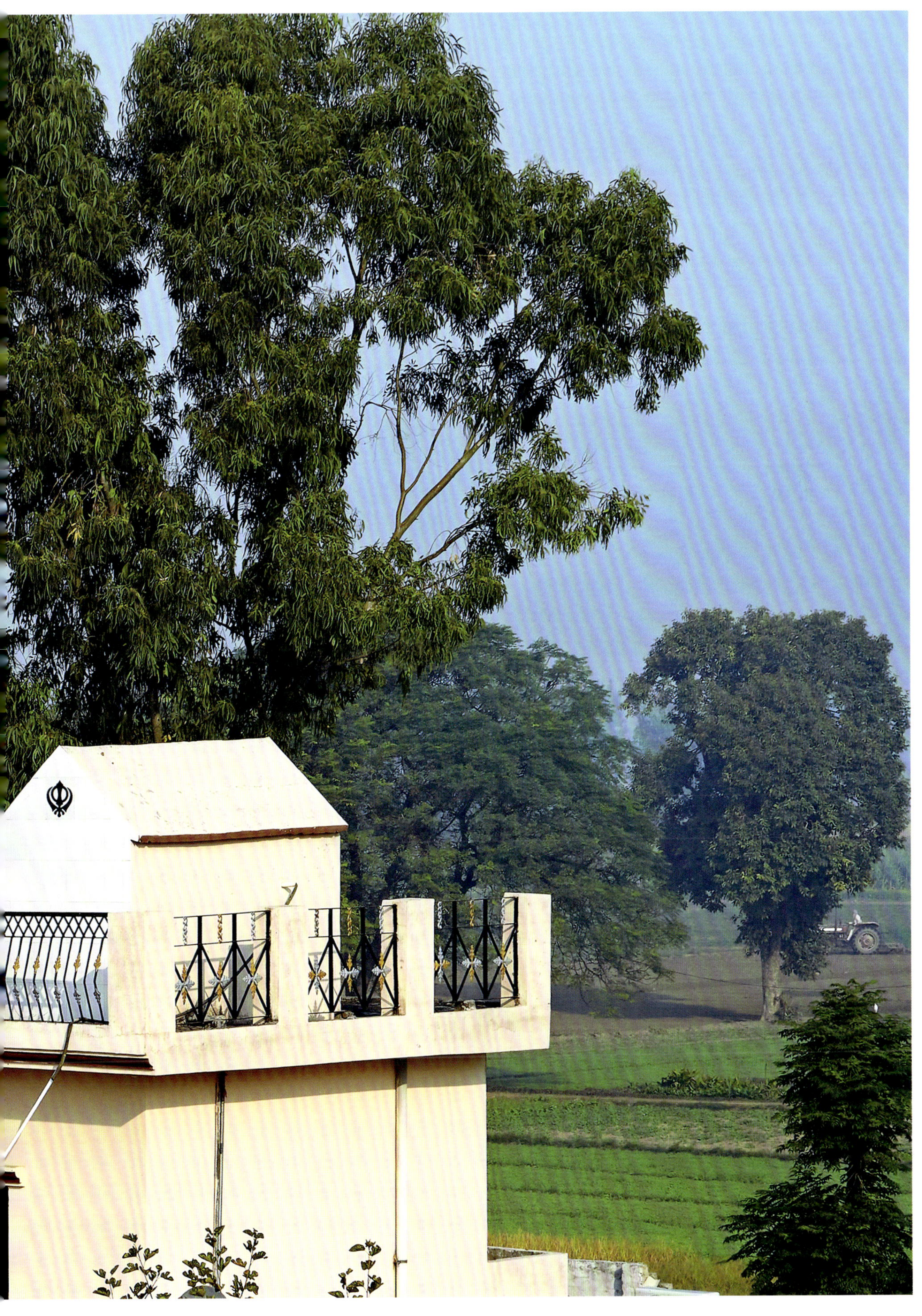

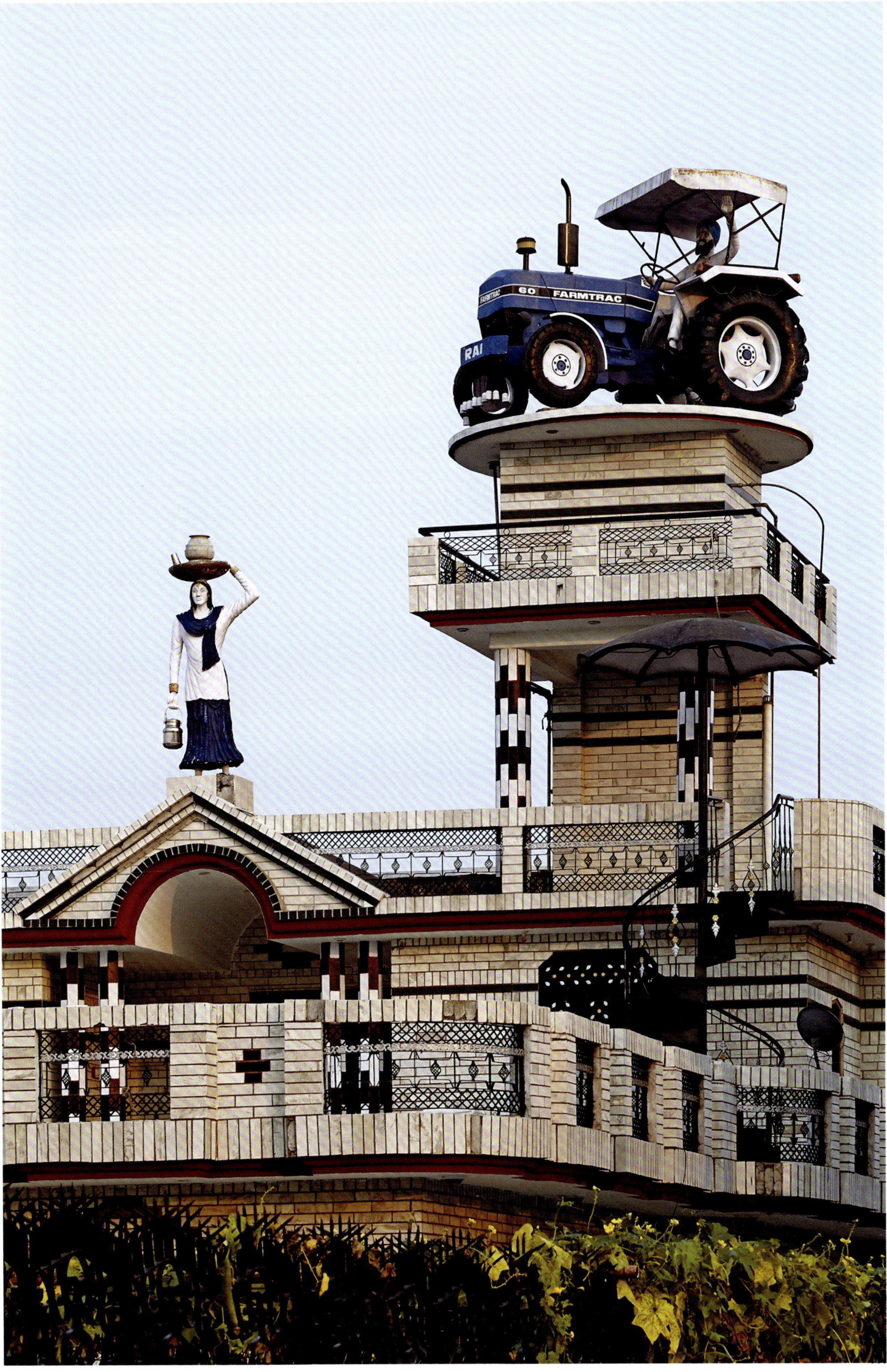
60
FARMTRAC

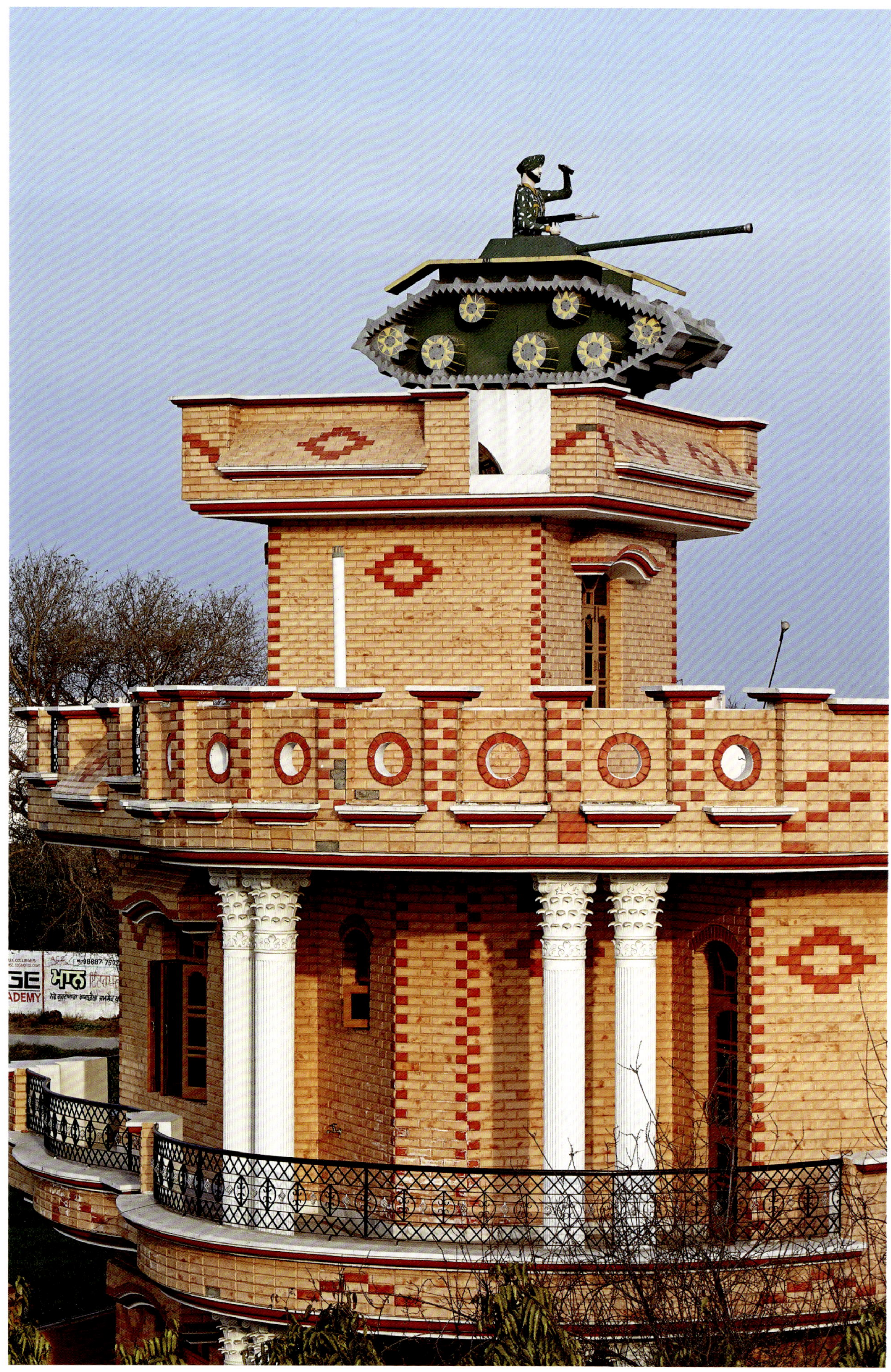

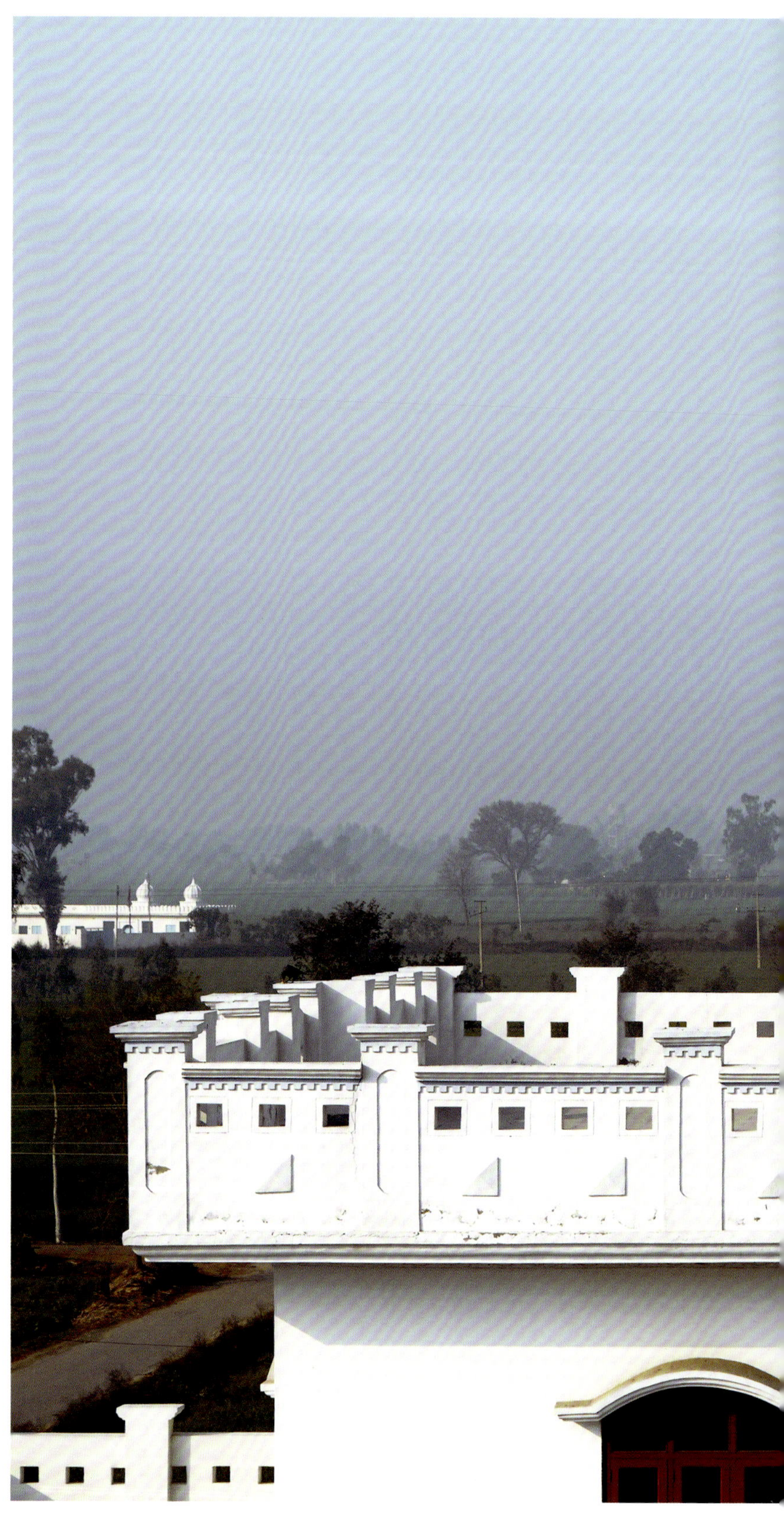

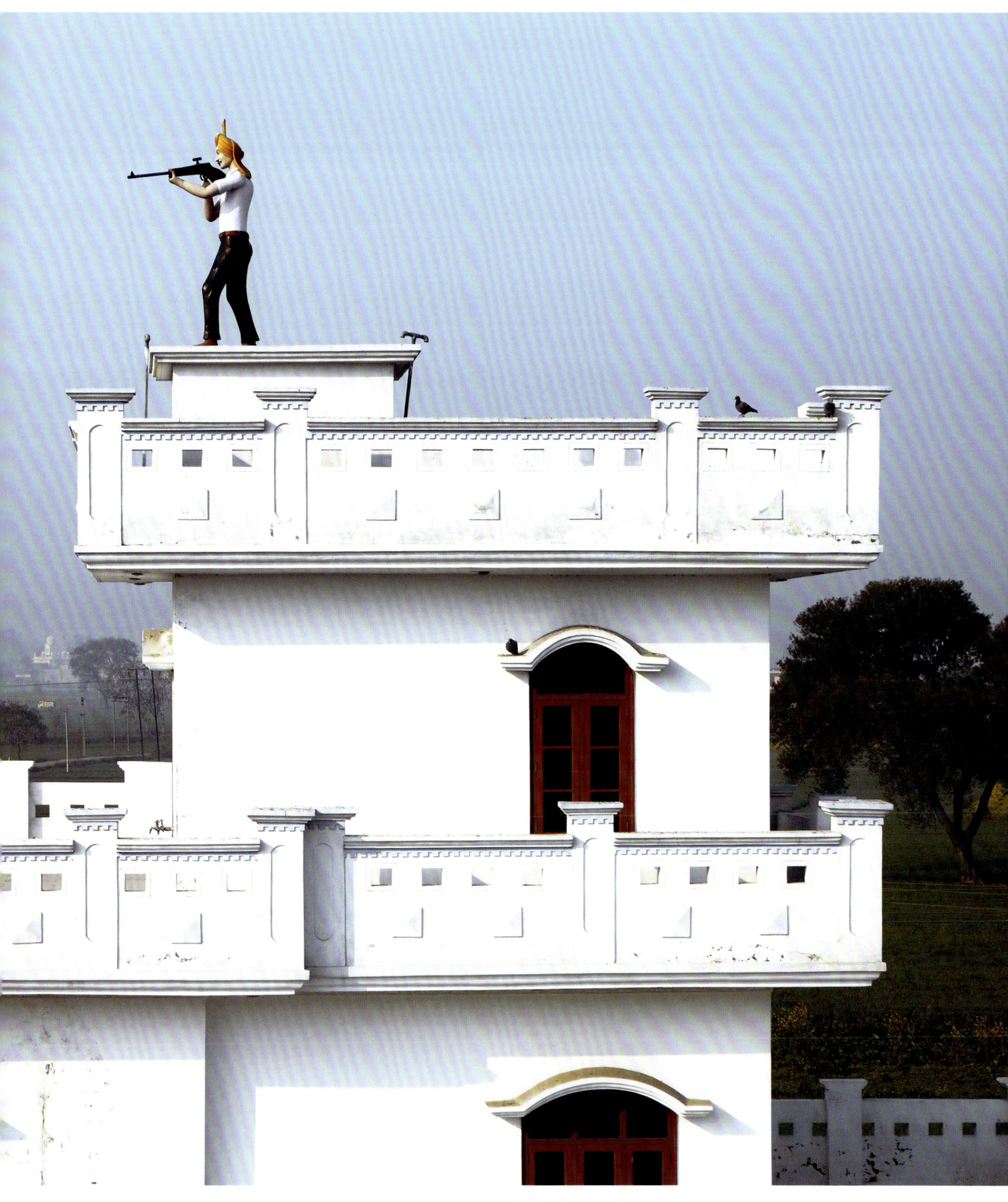

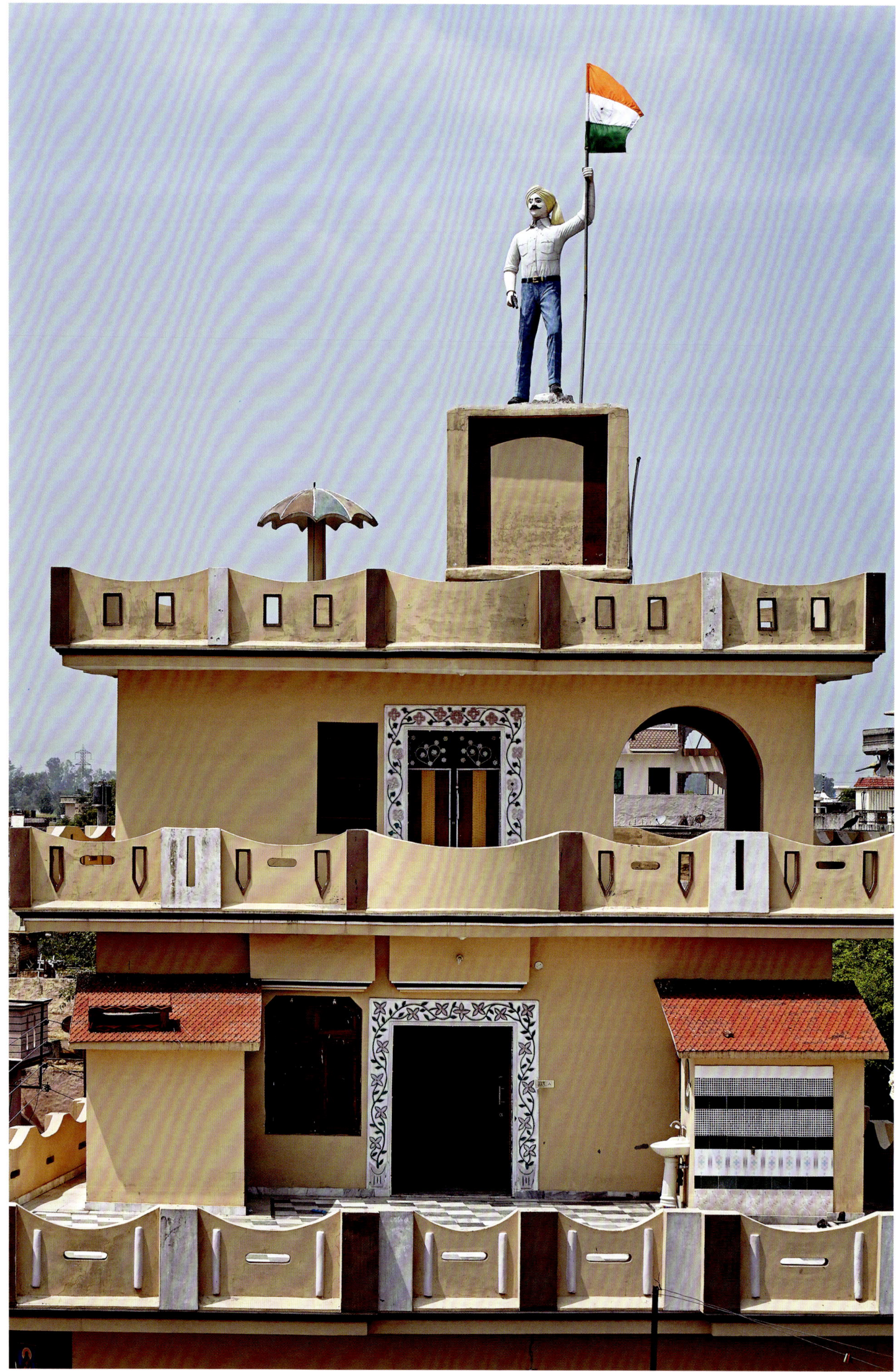

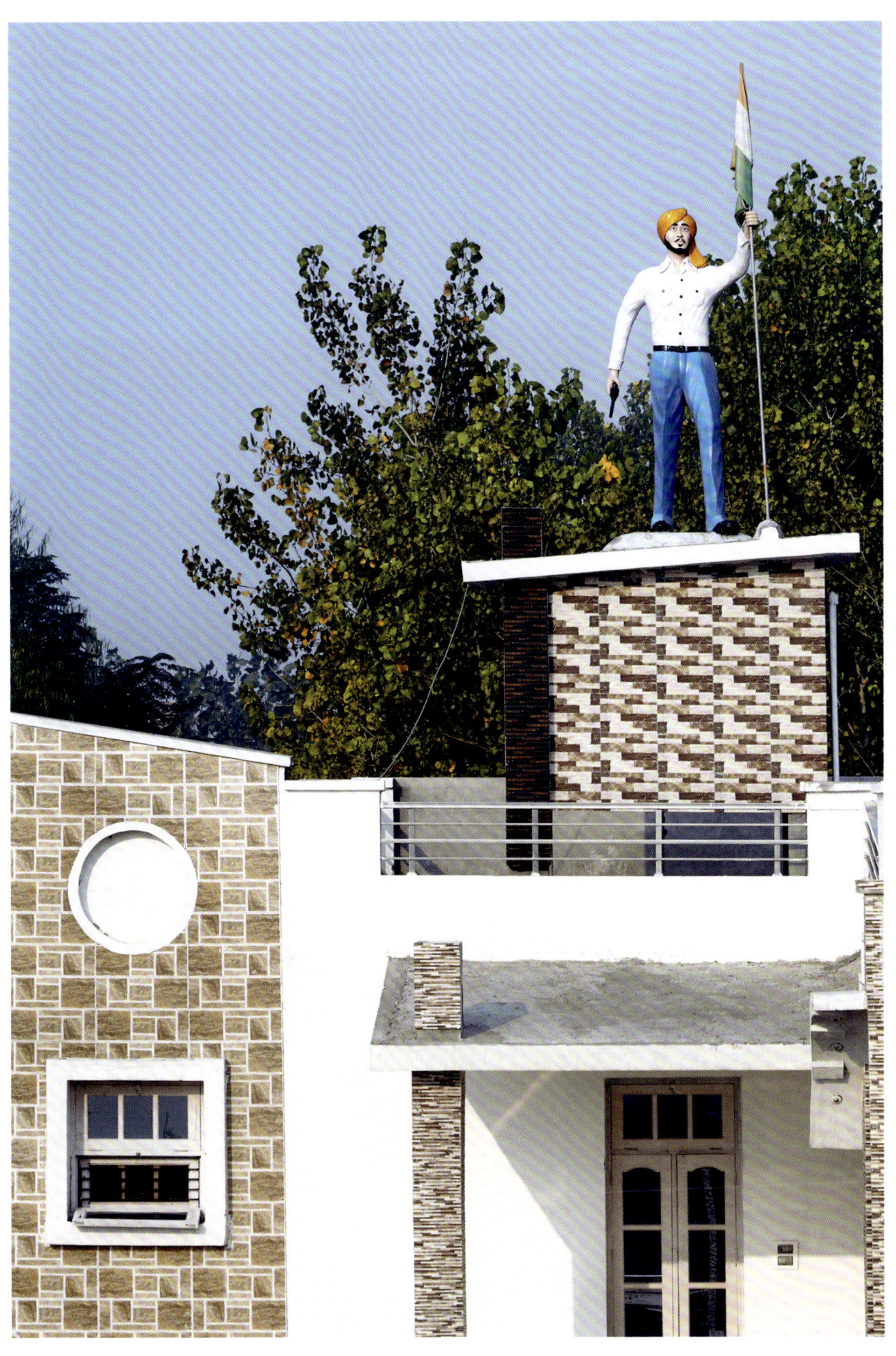

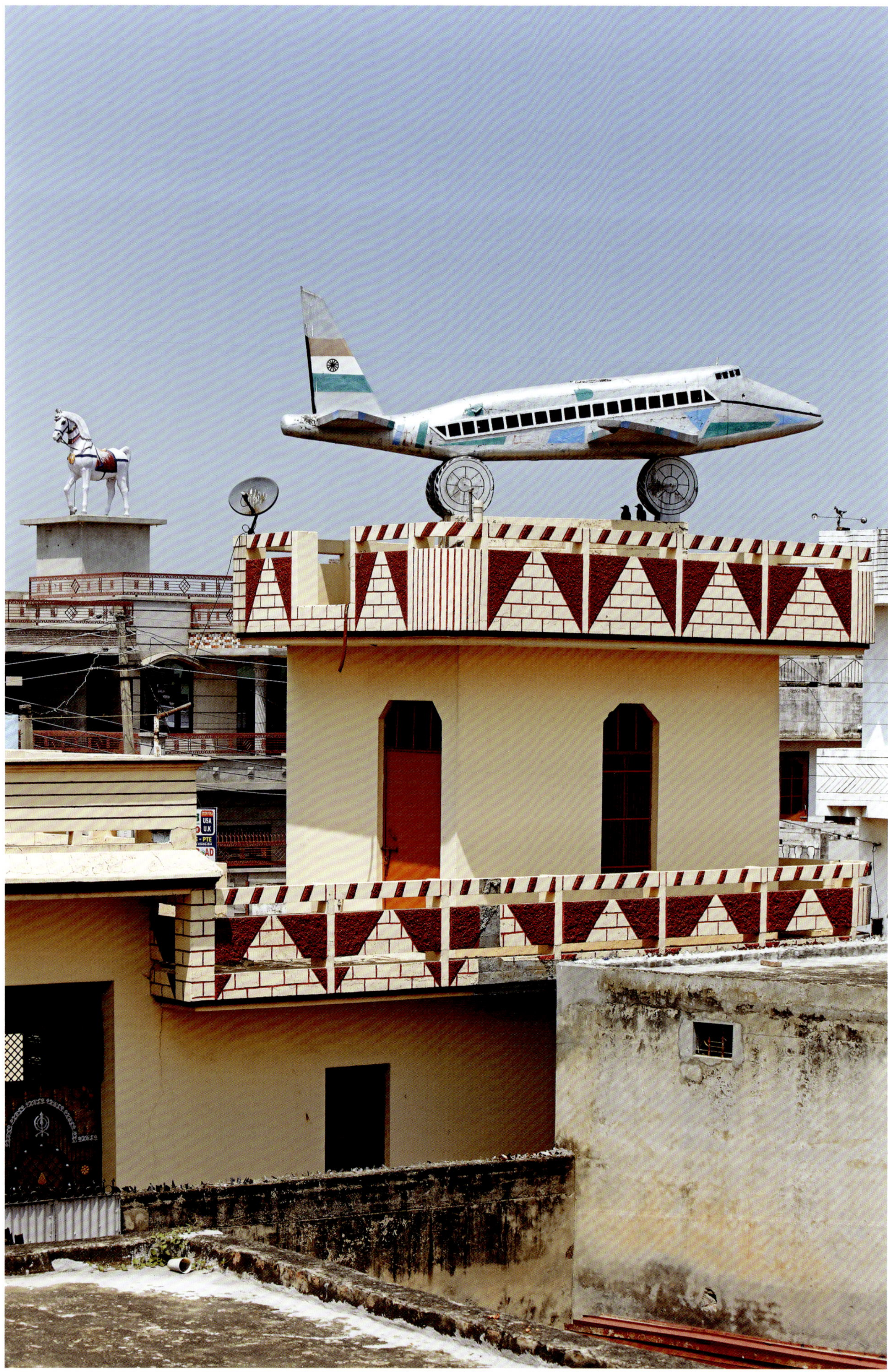
USA
U.K
PTE
AD

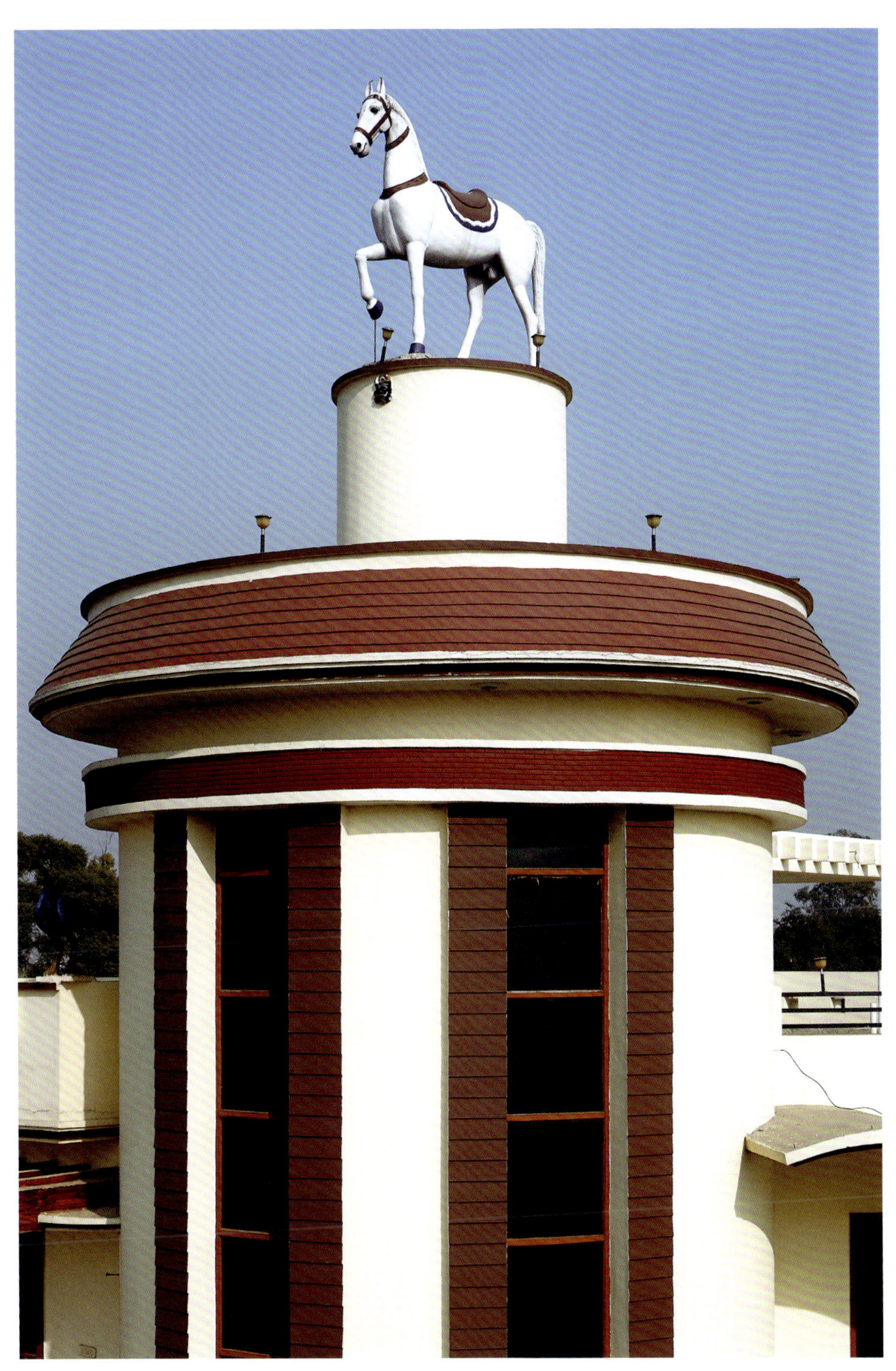

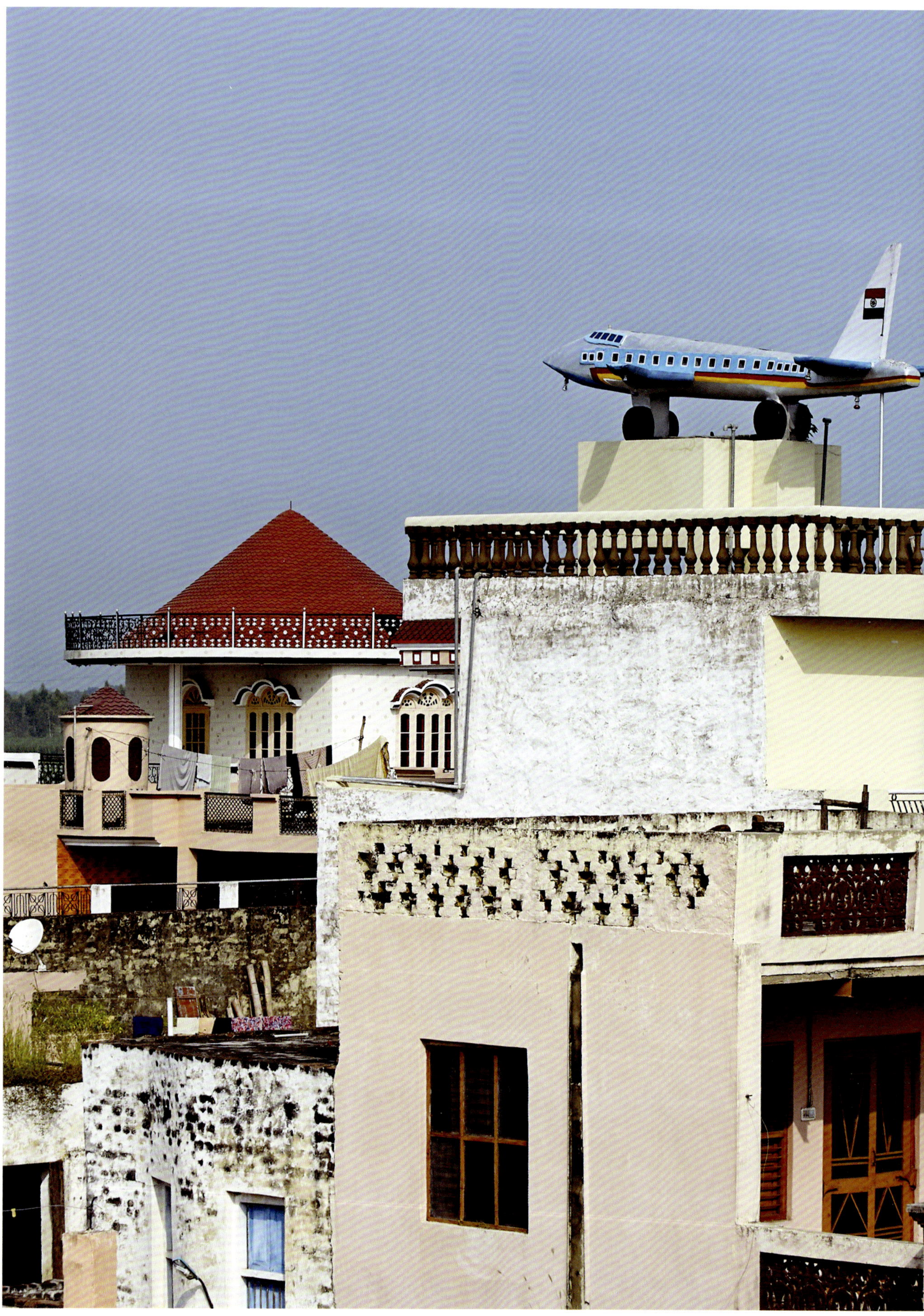

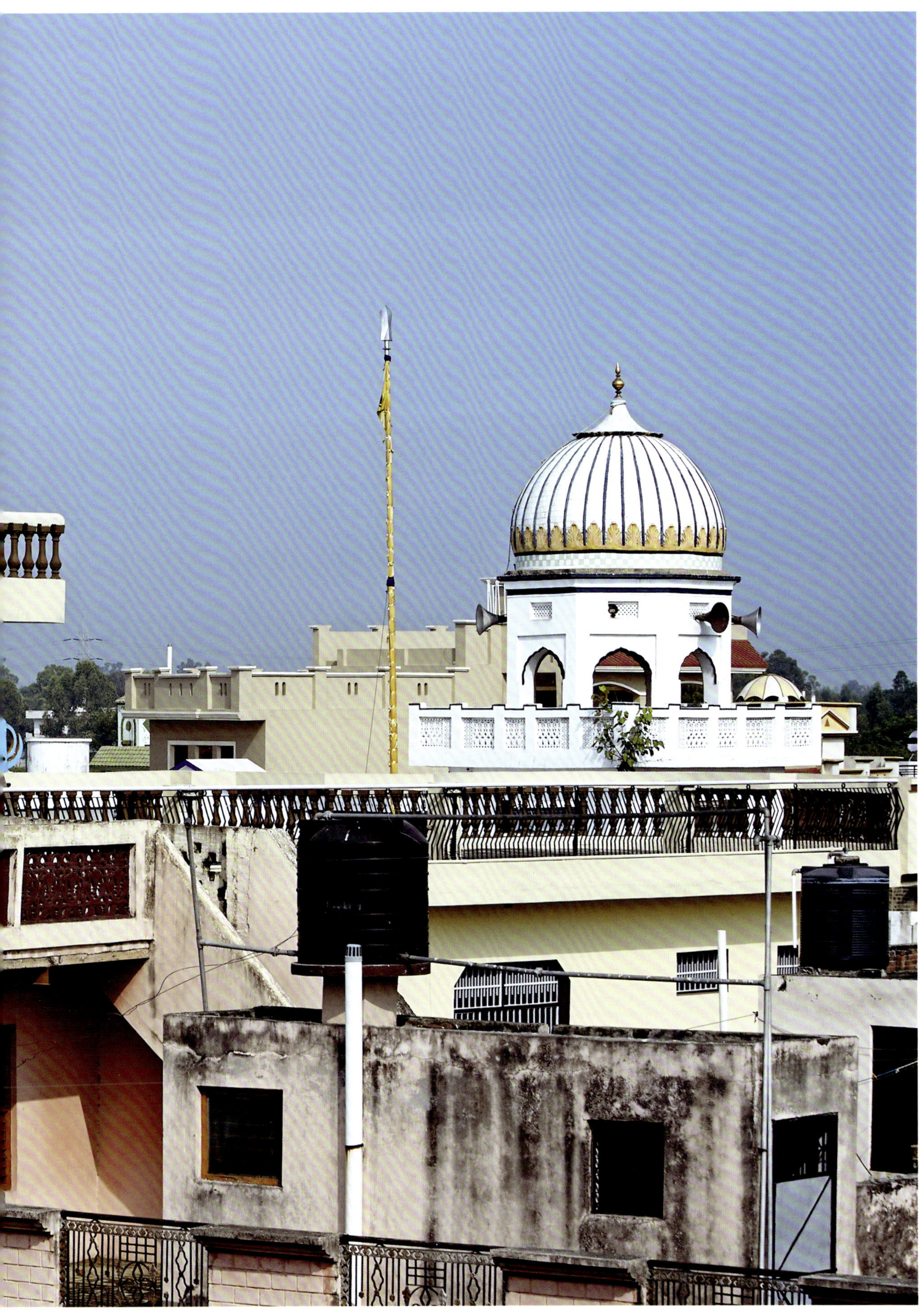

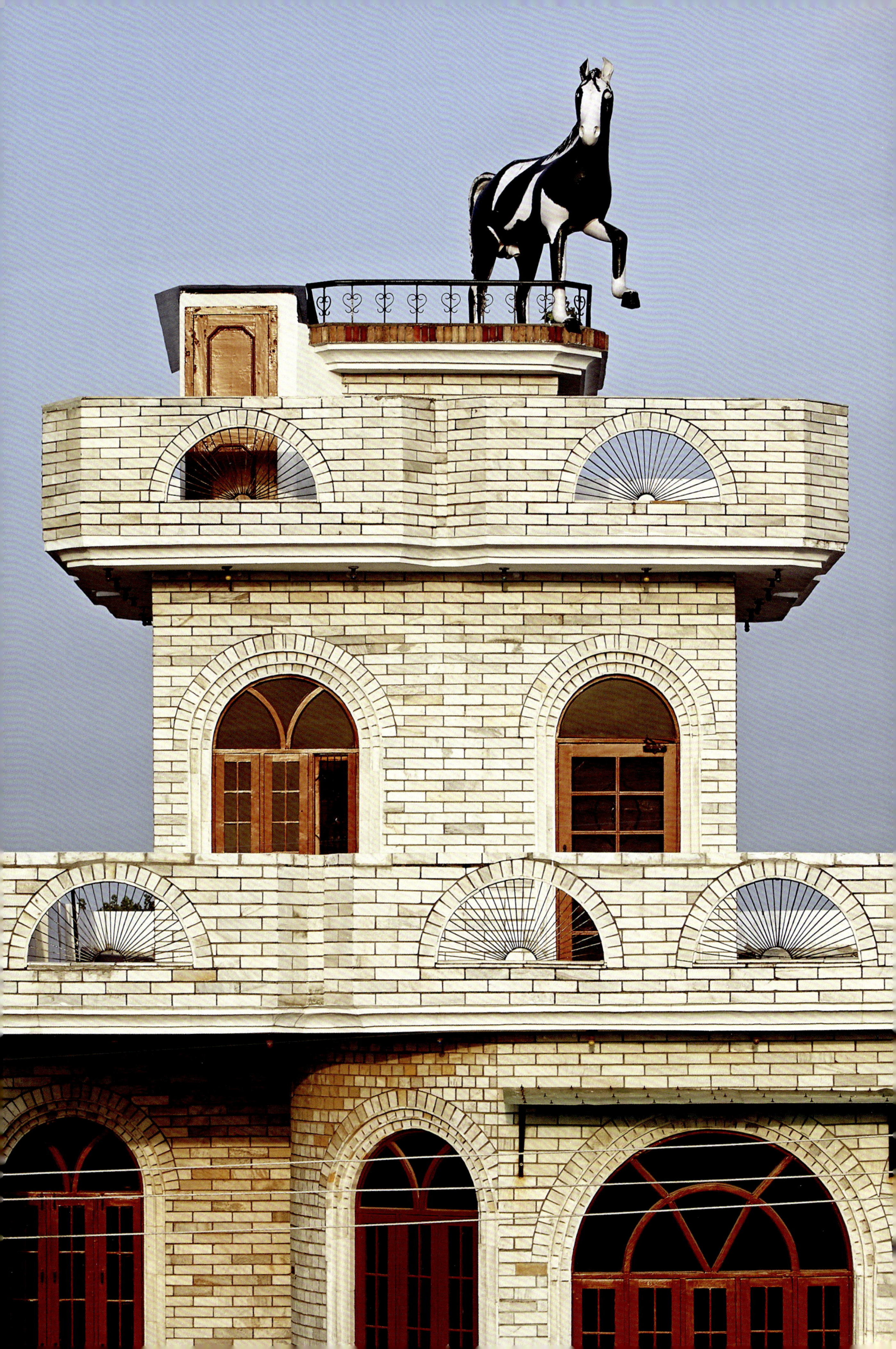

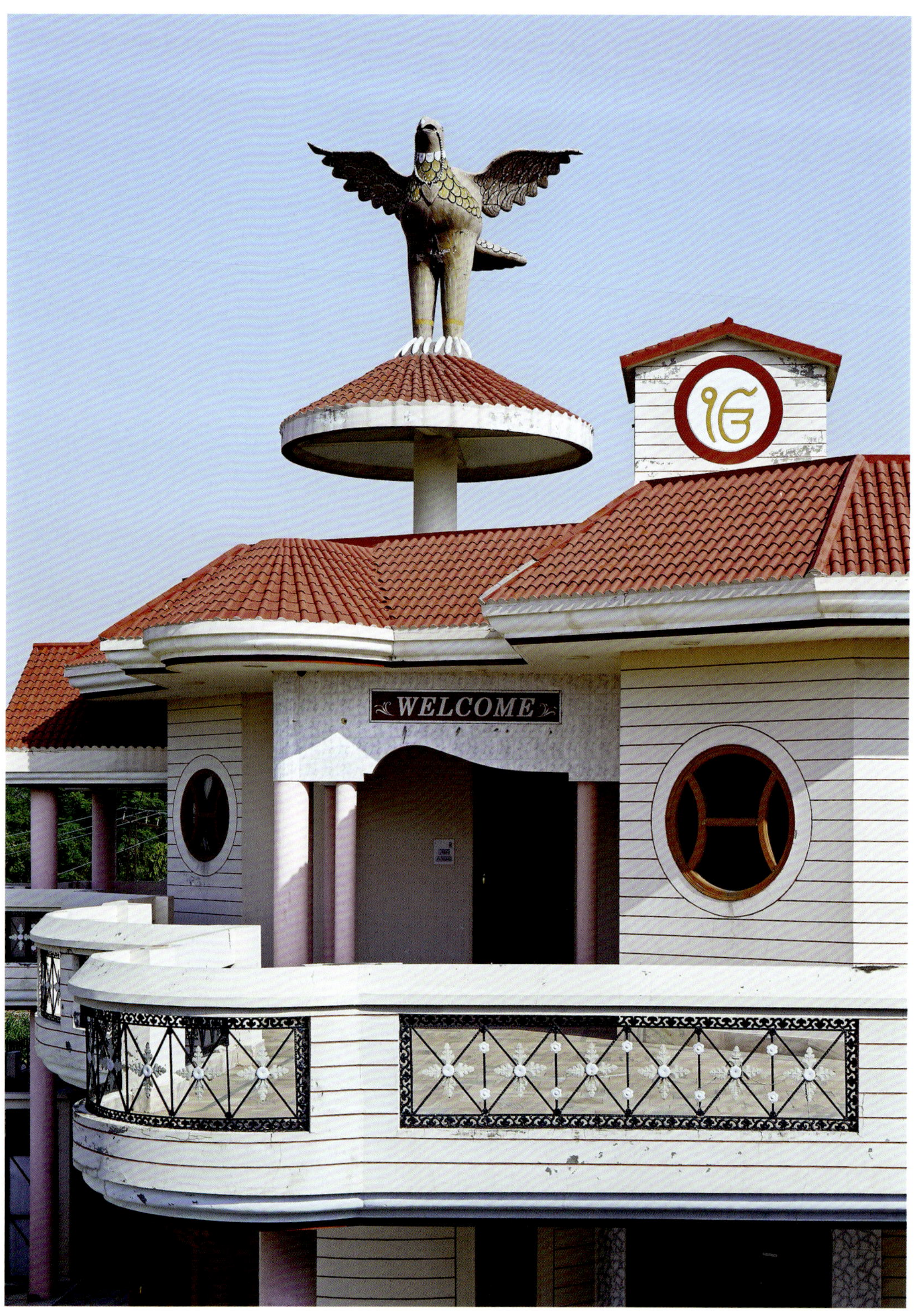
WELCOME

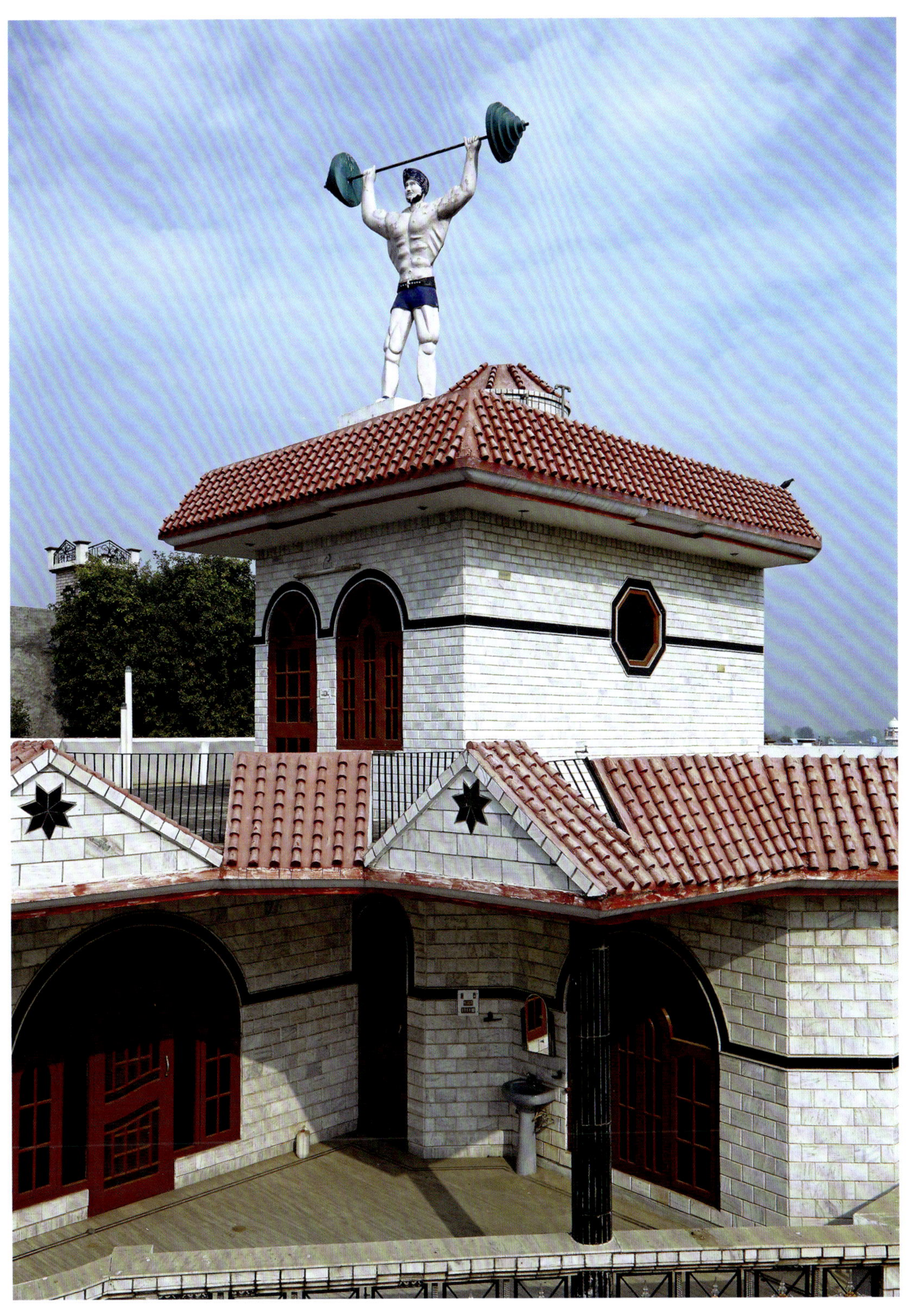

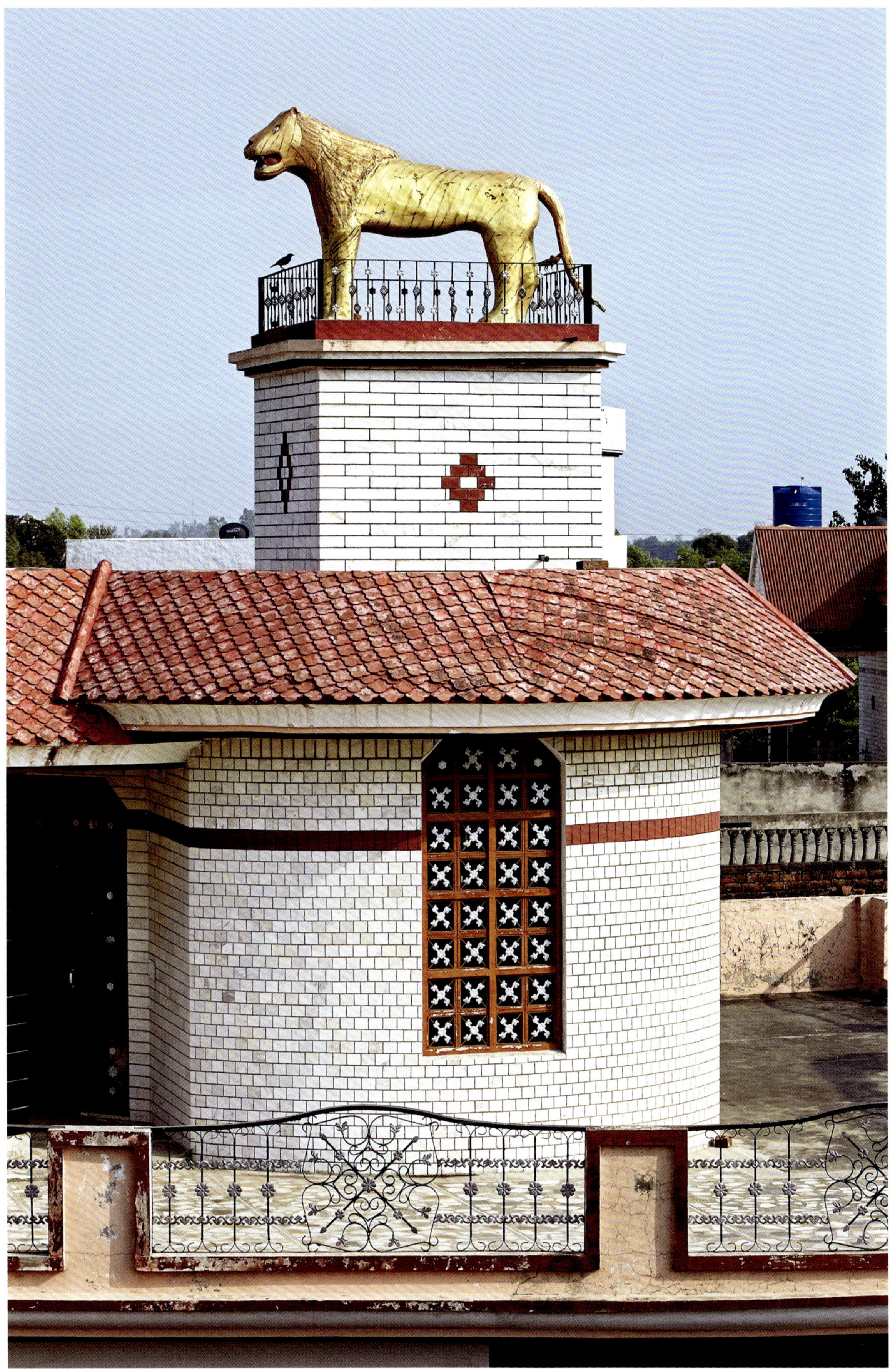

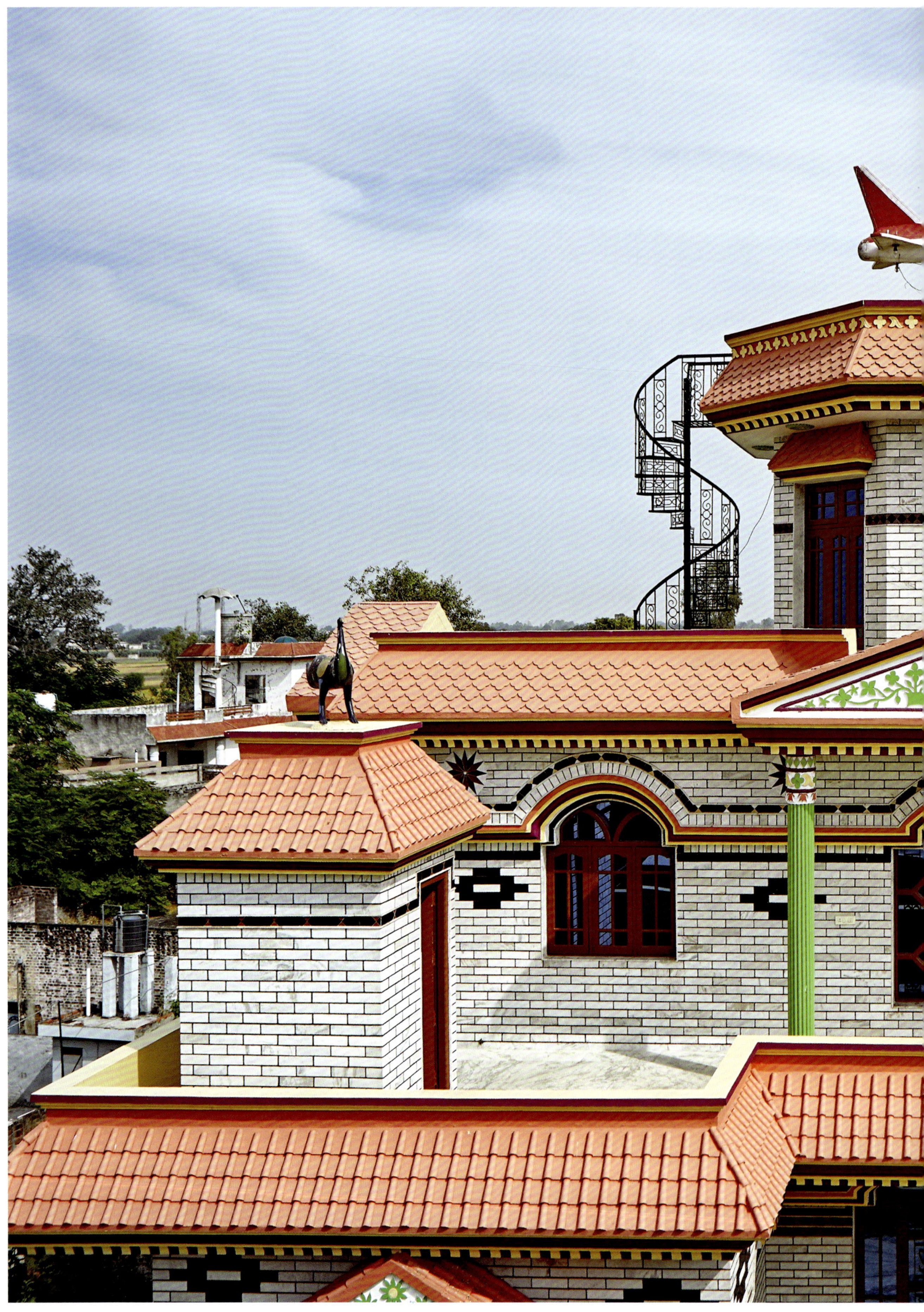

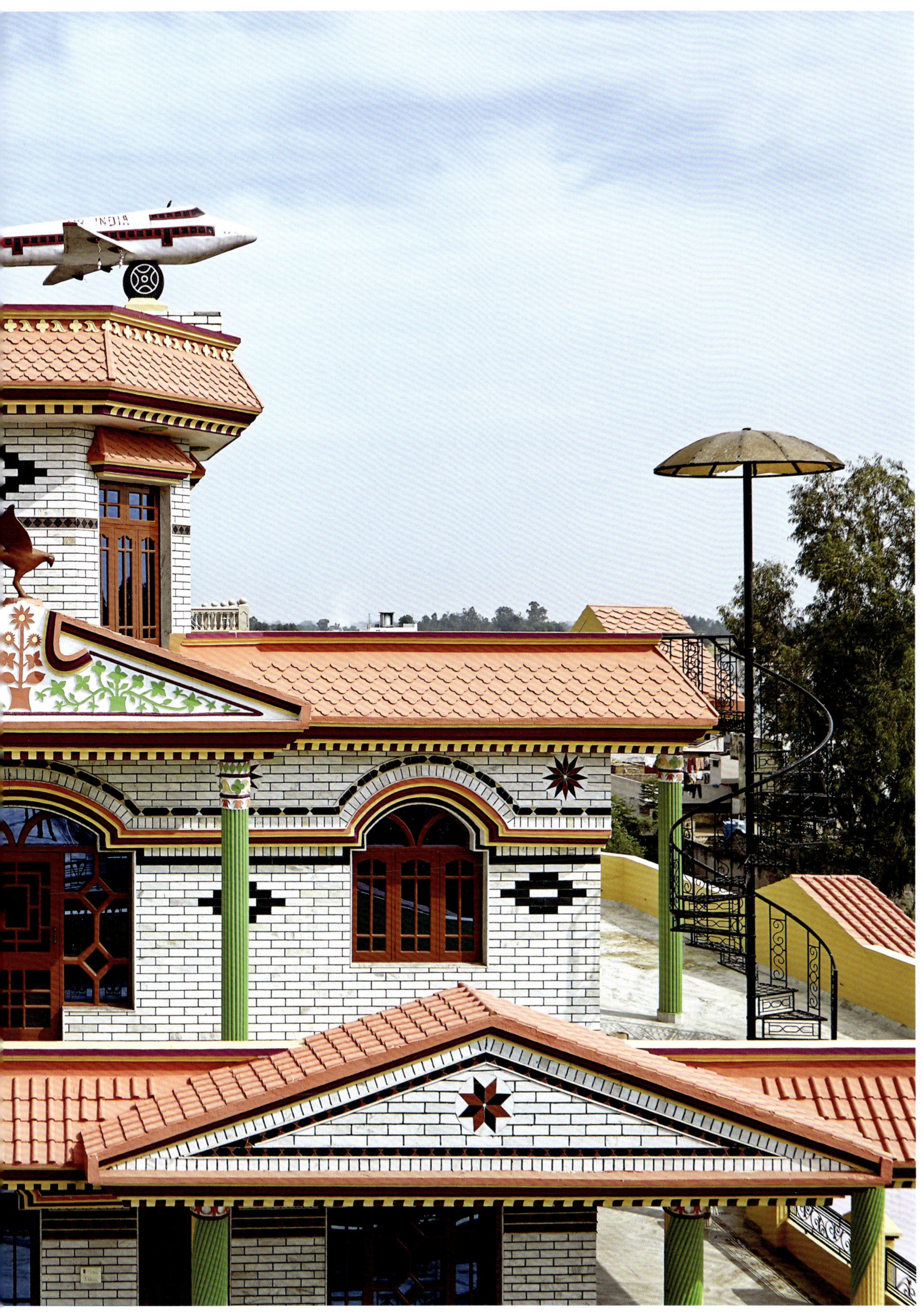
INDIA

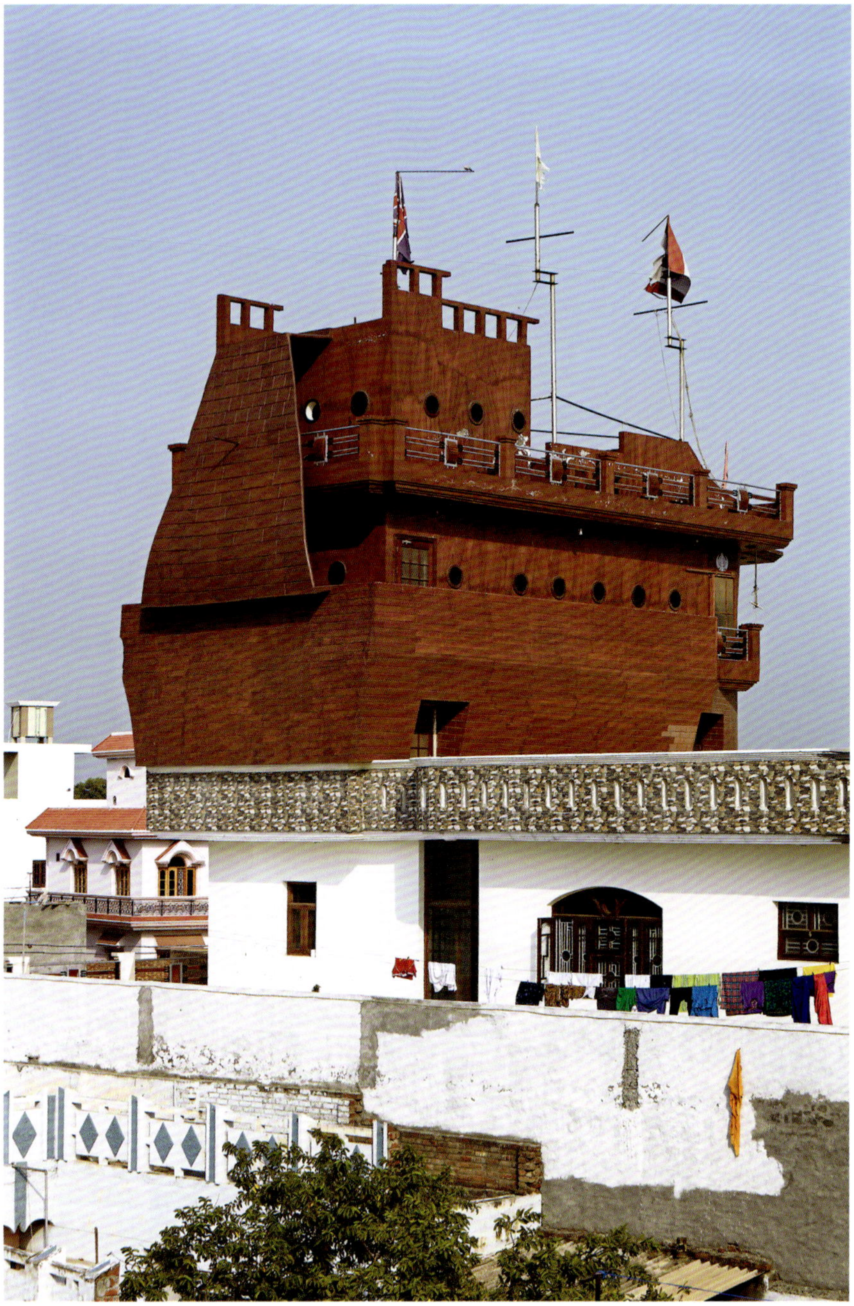

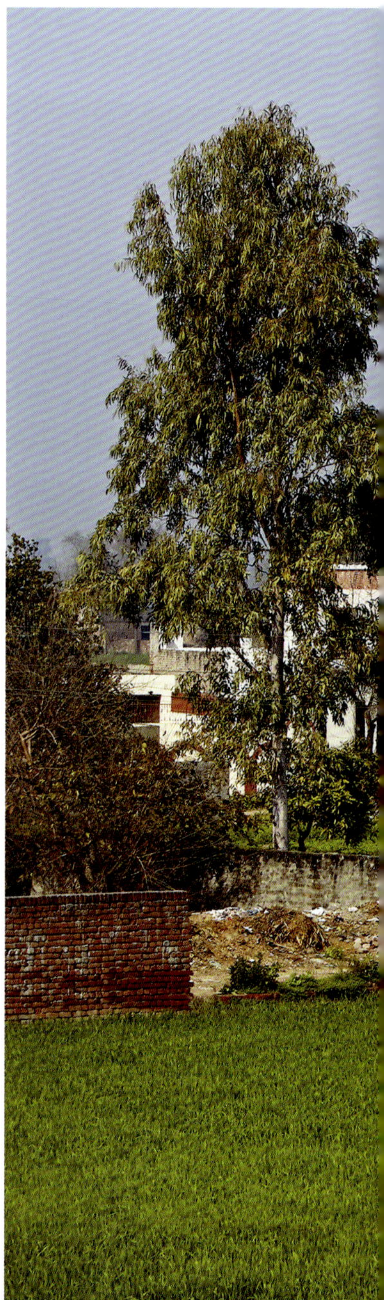

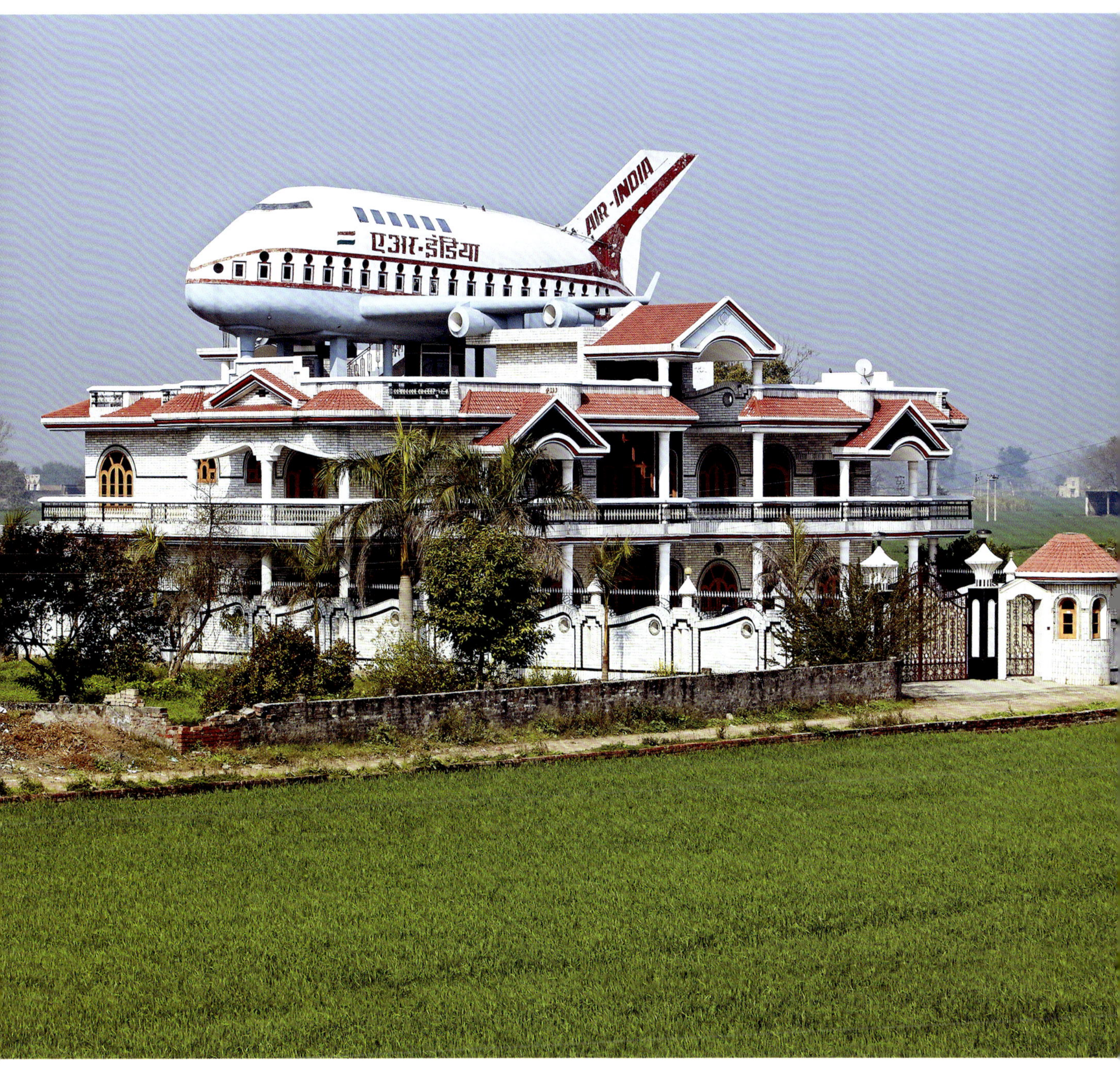
AIR-INDIA
एअर-इंडिया

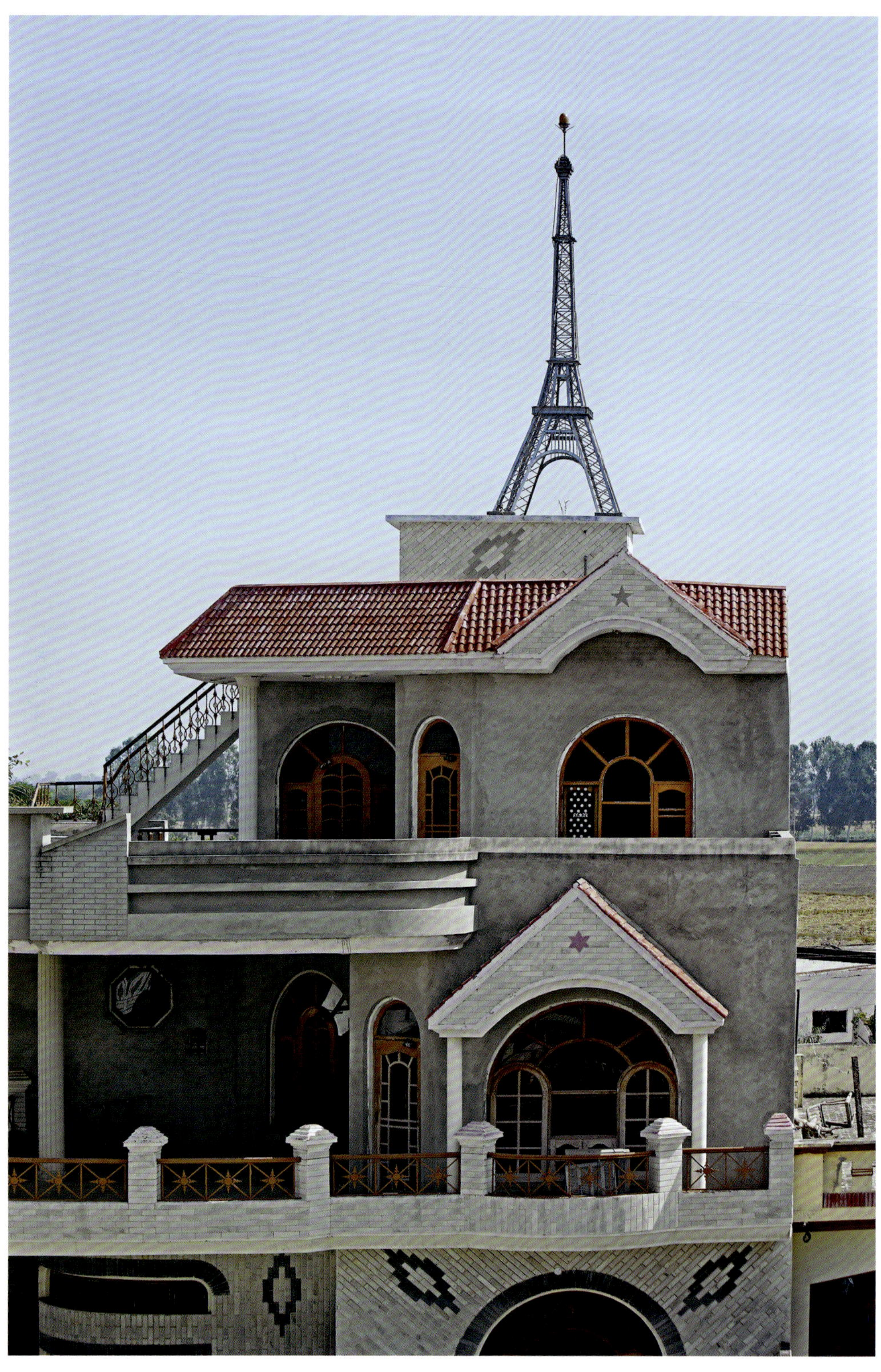

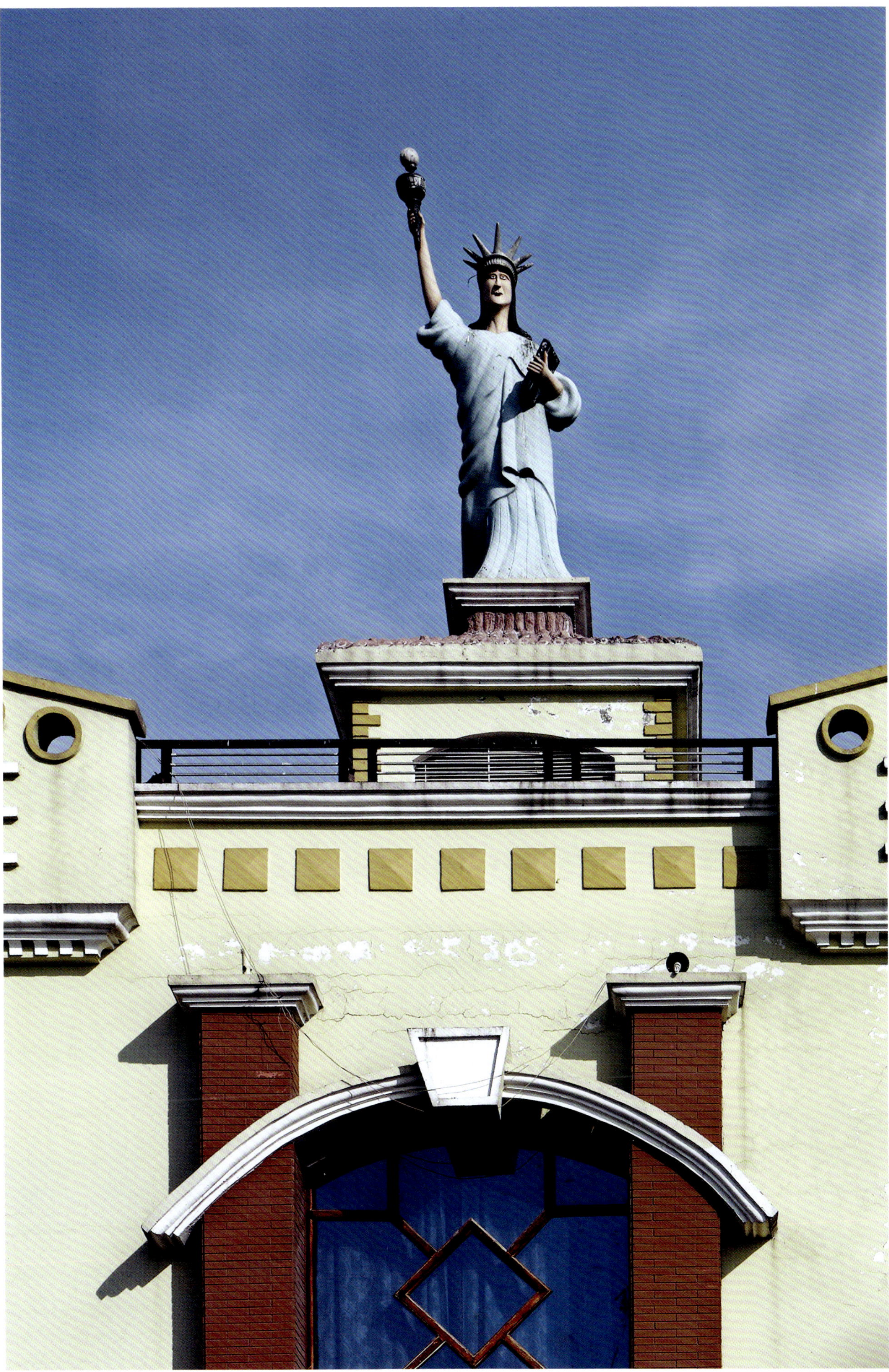

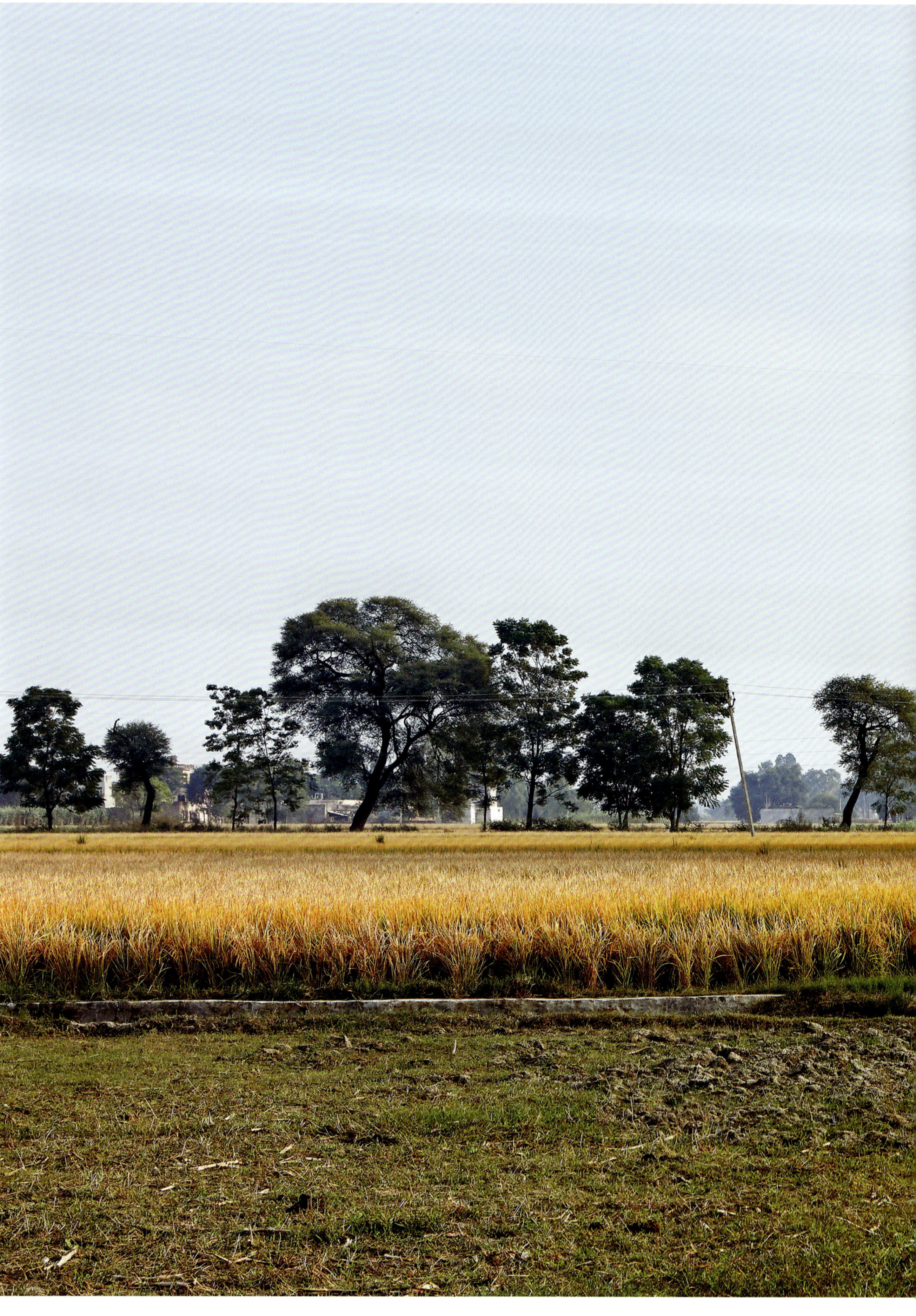

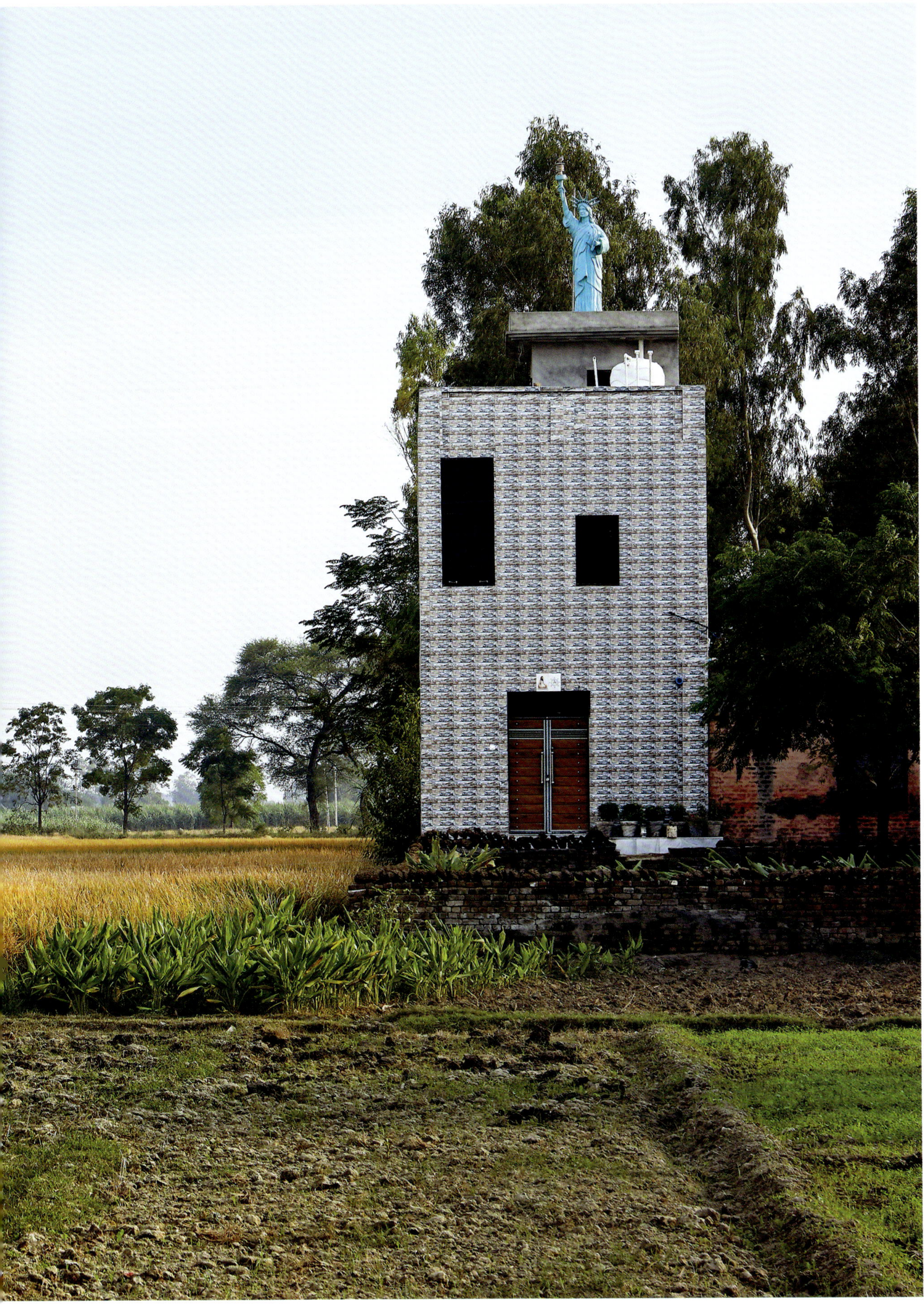

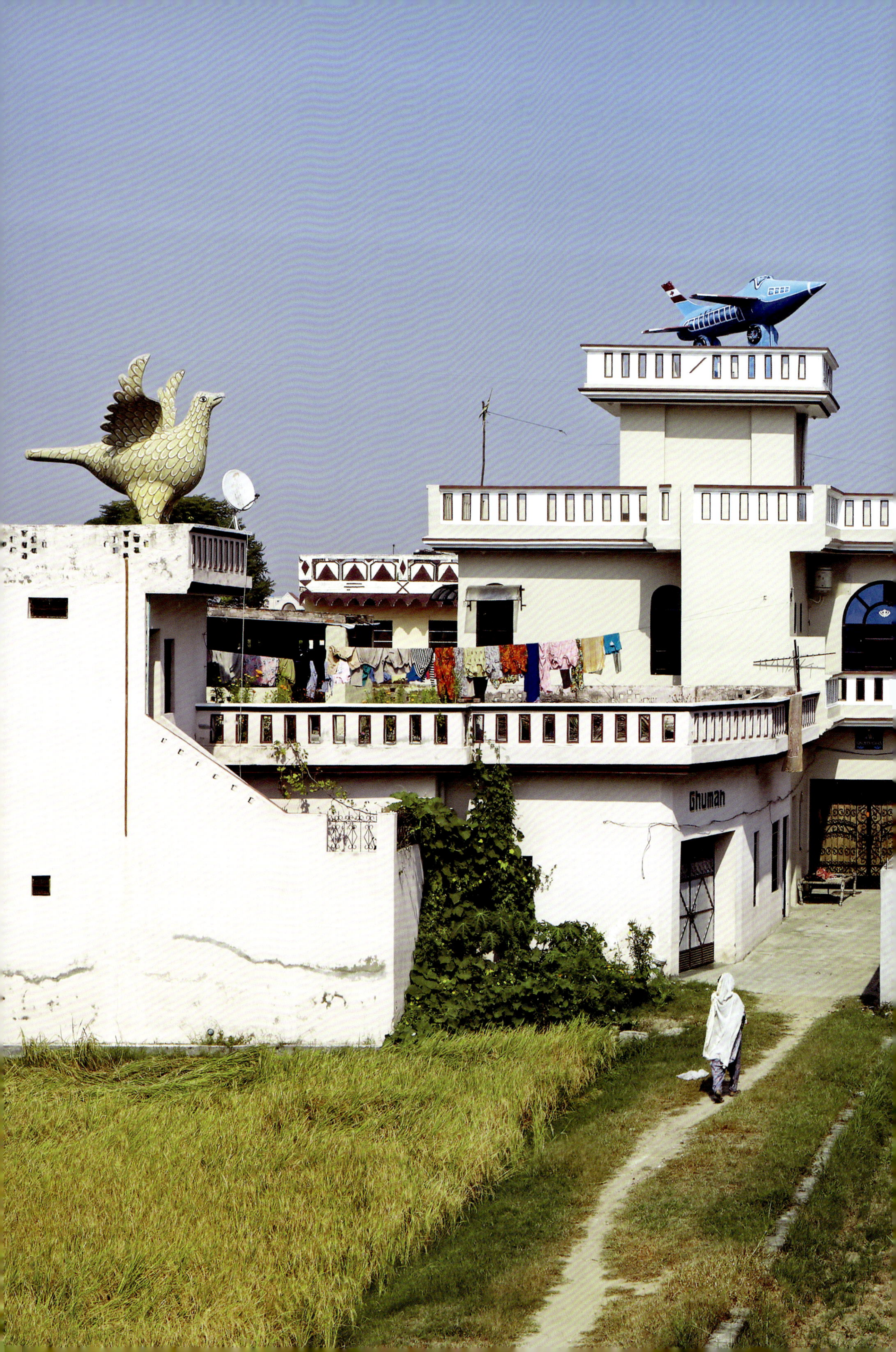
Ghuman

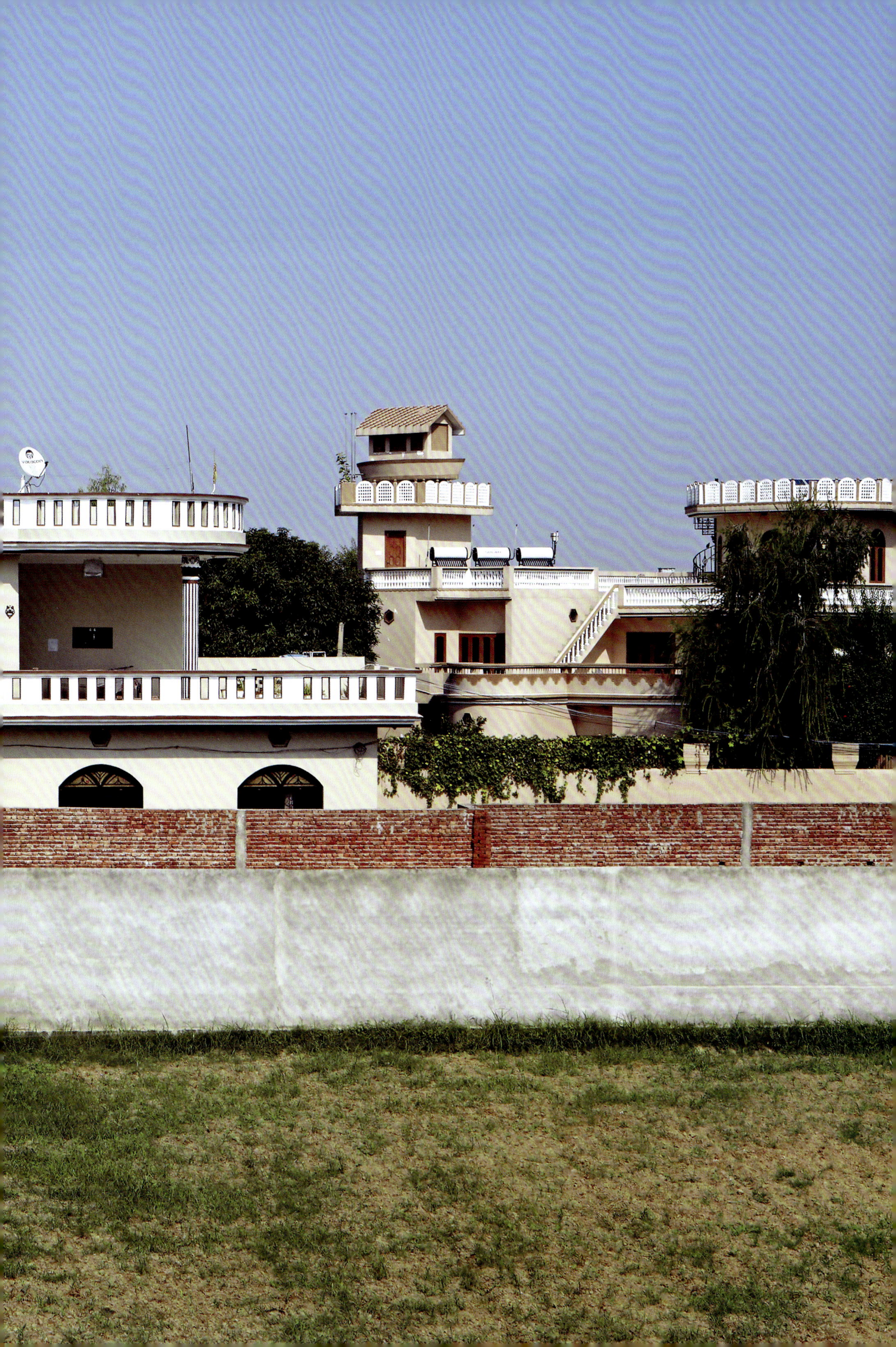

# THE ROOFTOP SCULPTURES OF PUNJAB

RAJESH VORA AND KEITH WALLACE

After independently encountering the rooftop sculptures in Punjab villages, in 2019 Rajesh Vora and Keith Wallace met and travelled together to research this distinct cultural expression. What the following discussion brings to light is little known outside of India but deeply rooted in the story of international Indian migration.

KEITH WALLACE Rajesh, you have been professionally photographing for over three decades, much of it architectural photography. Can you tell us something about your approach to photography and the difference between commissions for publications and your own personal work?

RAJESH VORA I would say that during my career as a professional photographer, besides the regular assignments, I was fortunate to work on commissions with select architects and organizations on a long-term basis. These didn't remain one-time assignments but developed into bodies of work mutually benefiting us and, in some cases, even leading us to ongoing collaborative projects. The experiences also helped to nurture my interest in personal photography projects and my interest in not adhering purely to the medium of photography but exploring other possibilities. For example, with my exposure to issues of urban planning, I assumed the role of activist and photographer to document and protect the ecosensitive mangroves along Mumbai's coastline. Working with filmmaker friends, we recorded a portrait of the metropolis as a pressure cooker that could boil over at any moment.

Over an extended period, to better understand the blurred lines of contemporary urbanism and the changing roles of people and spaces in urban society, I recently developed an extensive photo essay that appears in the book *The Kinetic City & Other Essays* by architect Rahul Mehrotra and explores its key themes of transaction, instability, spectacle, and habitation.[1] With this approach, there was not much difference between commissioned and personal work, and the overlap made it both an educational and an enjoyable experience.

When I created my personal photo stories at the beginning of my career, the subject of human faith within cultural and religious traditions attracted me. Also, in the 1990s, with the opening up and liberalization of the Indian economy to globalization, I did a photo project titled *Aspiring Models*, looking at a young generation's dream of walking in the footsteps of successful supermodels and Bollywood stars.

KEITH WALLACE When and how did you first encounter the water tanks and other rooftop sculptural embellishments in Punjabi villages that your *Everyday Monuments* project comprises? And what did you think of them? I remember when I first encountered them on a trip through Punjab in 2006, I was baffled; I had never seen anything like them anywhere else and did not understand the story behind them. It was only years later that my inquisitiveness was reignited through conversations with others, such as Delhi-based critic and curator Gayatri Sinha, who introduced me to your work and led me to making contact with you.

RAJESH VORA It was in 2014, on an assignment for the Italian-based *COLORS* magazine issue called "Moving House," about global migration. I visited a gurdwara [Sikh temple] in the village of Talhan, in the Doaba region of Punjab—it is popularly known as the Airplane Gurdwara. It was hard to believe that devotees who wished to migrate would offer a toy airplane bought at one of the many stalls located directly around the gurdwara in the hope of being granted a visa to enter another country. As I witnessed and documented this emotional ritual, I heard rumours of successful immigrants returning to their village and placing an airplane sculpture on their newly built home, which was equally fascinating to me. Not surprisingly, it drew me into a search for these sculptures in the Doaba region—popularly recognized as Punjab's NRI (Non-Resident Indian) hub—where Talhan is located, and from where many migrated to the UK, Canada, United States, Australia, and other parts of the world.

I had imagined a large-scale airplane model on top of the houses, but when I saw an airplane in the shape of a water tank, I couldn't help but marvel at its ingenuity, giving a twist to architect Louis Sullivan's famous axiom, "Form follows function." Besides its functionality, I noticed that the water tank was aesthetically placed in relation to the vernacular architectural style of the building. The initial builders of these houses, known as *mistris* [local construction artisans], were unschooled in formal architectural design, and their work reflects the rich diversity of India's climate, locally available building materials, and the intricate variations in local social customs and craftsmanship.

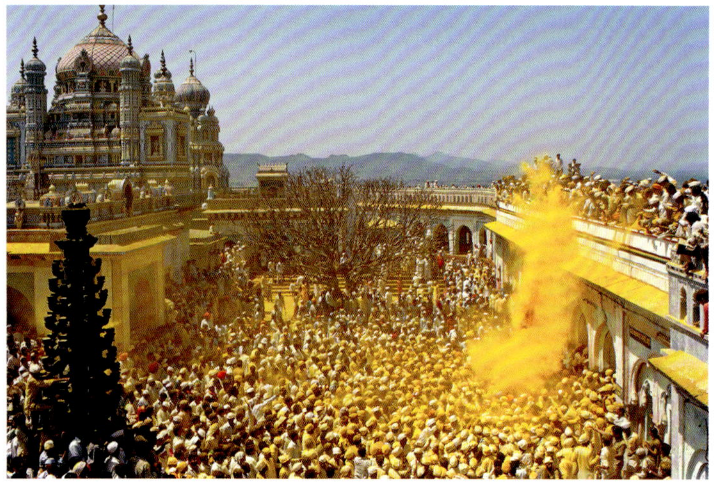

↙ Somvati Amavasya celebration at Khandoba temple in Jejuri. From the photographic project *Painting the Town Yellow*, 1993.

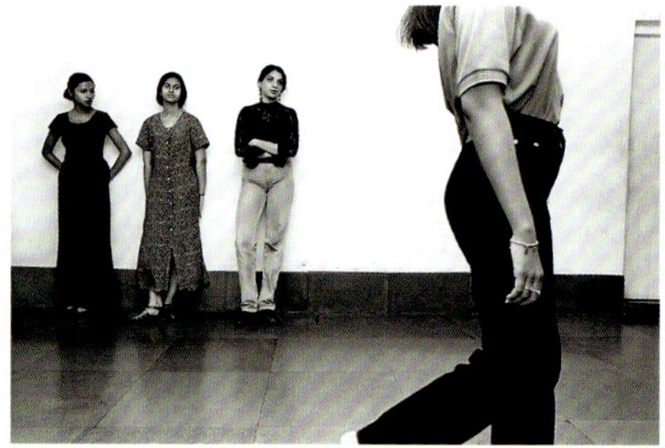

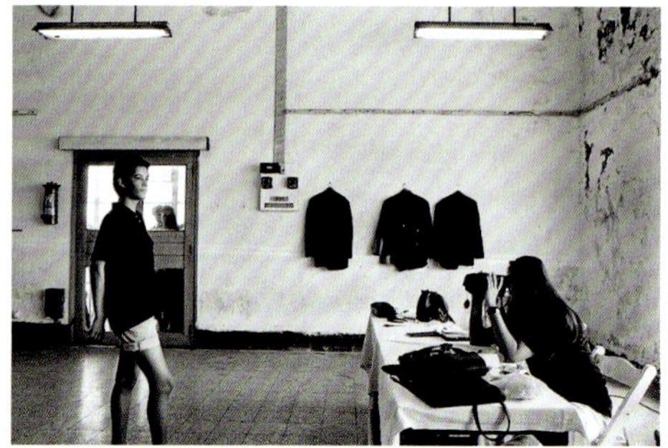

↓ From the photographic project *Aspiring Models*, 1997–98.

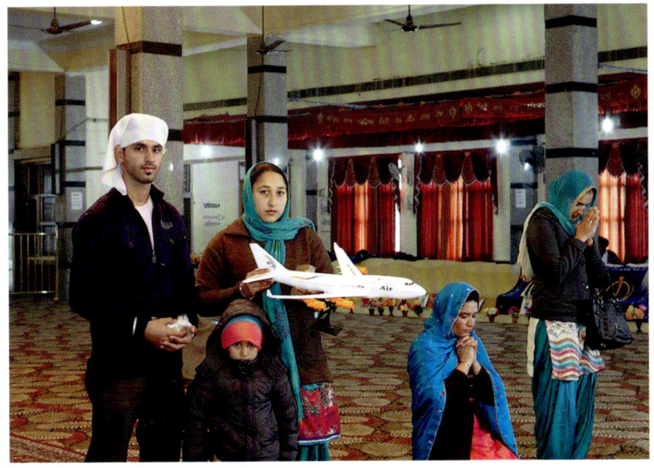

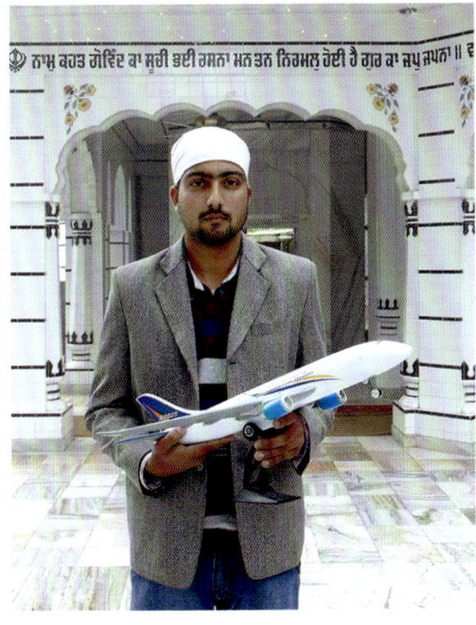

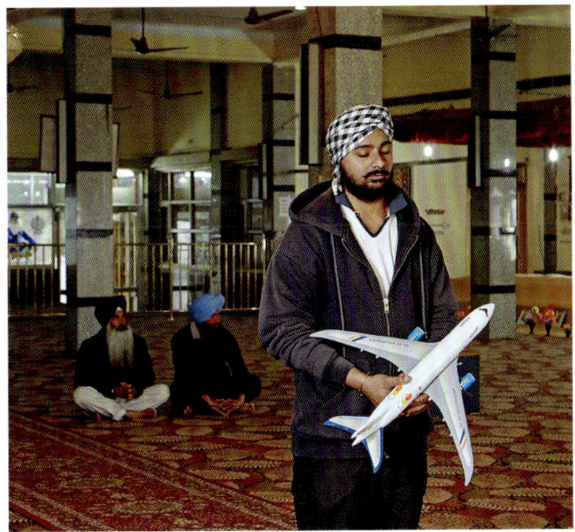

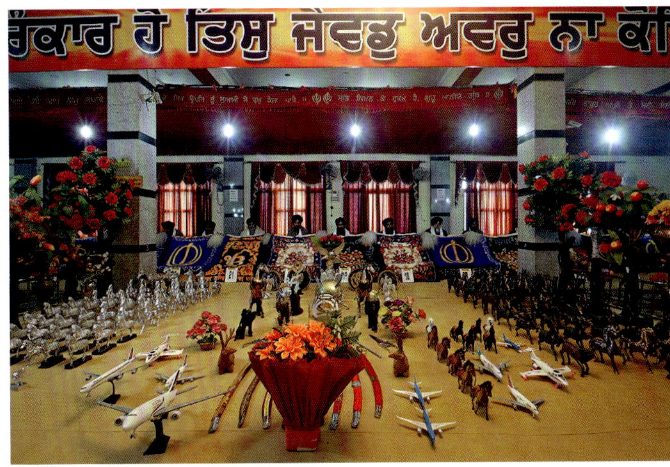

Devotees make offerings at the Airplane Gurdwara, village of Talhan, in hopes of receiving a visa to leave Punjab. Originally published in *COLORS* magazine, January 2014.

But as I travelled away from the main roads and farther into the villages, I saw water tanks that weren't airplanes but were instead in the shape of army tanks, falcons and animals, footballs, vehicles, and even figurative sculptures of weightlifters and football players, some of which I learned did not necessarily function as water tanks but were placed on top of the water tank.

Before I understood their purpose, these sculptures first brought to mind the different turbans that people in India would have adorned themselves with since the eleventh century and that indicate the wearer's social class, caste, and region of origin, and the occasion. On top of these houses, I had found these fantastic metaphorical headdresses and was now curious to know more about the owners and those who gave shape to them. I couldn't help but ask myself, who would put these sculptures on top of their houses, and why?

KEITH WALLACE There are three main regions in Punjab: Majha (bordering on Pakistan), Doaba (between the Beas and Satluj rivers), and Malwa (the southern part of the state). As you note, the Doaba region experienced significant international emigration, which especially increased in the 1970s as many countries implemented policies encouraging immigration from Asia; the largest percentage of Punjabi NRIs are in fact from Doaba, and more recently Malwa. Where I live, on the west coast of Canada, there is one of the largest Punjabi populations outside of India—migration here extends back well over a century—but I had no awareness of these sculptures before actually going to Punjab. And I had to ask myself, why? How did you locate the houses and their sculptures? Did you find owners? Make contact with the fabricators?

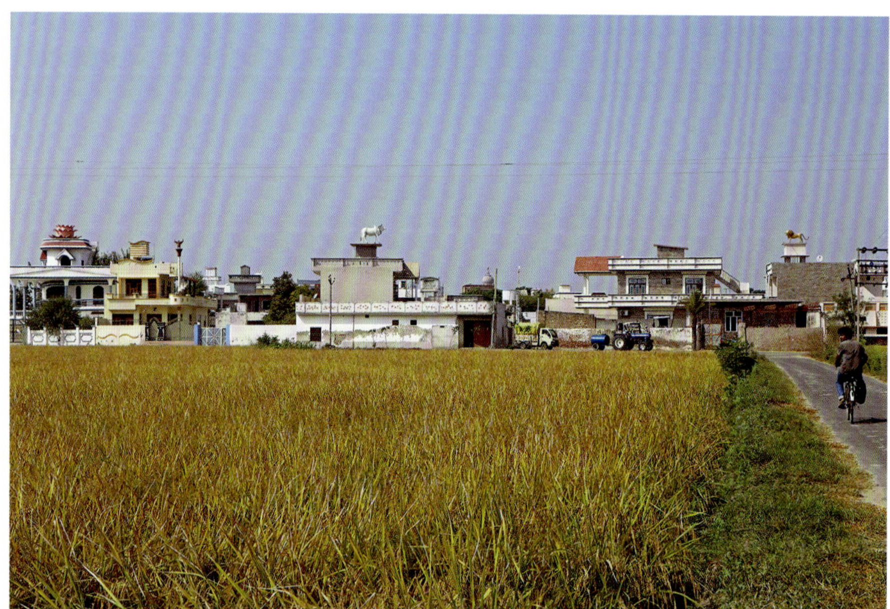

Houses with rooftop sculptures, village of Littran, 2019.

RAJESH VORA It wasn't always easy to find these houses. I had neither map, GPS, guide, address, nor any available research, and even though Ram Pratap, my taxi driver from Jalandhar—the largest city in Doaba—offered to assist me in my search, I still had doubts about successfully locating them. He could neither read nor write, but he could speak Punjabi, and, more importantly, he had travelled frequently in the Doaba region ferrying NRIs from Amritsar Airport to their respective villages.

Keeping Jalandhar as our base, every morning we would head in the direction of one of the four districts of Doaba—Kapurthala, Jalandhar, Hoshiarpur, and Shaheed Bhagat Singh Nagar (known prior to 1995 as Nawanshahr). Driving along the National Highway, we would take detours and visit villages on both sides of the highway. We were often unlucky as some villages would have no houses with the rooftop sculptures. Undeterred, we would ask villagers about whether any such houses existed in nearby villages. With their often imprecise replies, we had to choose whether to follow their lead or return to the highway and continue our search. Throughout six different expeditions over a five-year period, we criss-crossed these four districts to 150 villages and travelled 7,500 kilometres; some days we would find fifteen to twenty houses with sculpted water tanks, and other days we would spot only a few.

Typically, we would reach a village and stop at the *sath*, a raised platform under a large tree where men would gather to rest from work, share news, and discuss village affairs. Ram Pratap would introduce me and enquire in Punjabi with the elders if there were any houses in the village that might have sculpted water tanks. Fingers would point in different directions and a few names be dropped as to who the owners of the homes were, and we were on a mission. Following their instructions, we would circumnavigate the village ring road—called *bahari sadak*—sometimes more than once in hope of spotting the sculptures. If we did spot one, the next task was to find a vantage point from an opposite house in order to photograph it. Sometimes we were lucky, and from nowhere, we would end up in front of a house with a sculpted water tank fully visible as if waiting to be photographed.

In most cases we were not fortunate enough to meet the owners as these houses often lodged either elderly members of the family or caretakers who would occupy a corner room on the ground floor. A few houses remained locked because they were occupied only during seasonal visits by the NRI owners. Thus, I had to be satisfied with what little information Ram Pratap could gather from the neighbours, family members, or caretakers about the owners of these houses and the names of those who fabricated the sculptures.

But one thing we were assured of were cups of Punjabi *chai*, and an invitation for *roti* or a freshly cooked meal as we moved from village to village.

I was curious to meet and learn more about the sculptors of the water tanks and their history, but finding them was also a challenge. The sculptors have their workshops in small towns spread throughout these districts, and they travel quite some distance to install and assemble the water tanks or the nonfunctional sculptures—the latter of which at least two of the sculptors referred to as "showpieces." When I finally contacted a few of them, I understood their work better, but they were unable to shed much light on the origin and evolution of these sculpted water tanks.

KEITH WALLACE Yes, these sculptures are not always easy to find. One sees them every so often from one of the National Highways or railway lines that interconnect Punjab. In 2018, while visiting Chandigarh, the capital city of both Punjab and Haryana states, I hired a driver to help me look for them. When I told him I was looking for domestic water tanks, I am sure he thought I was a bit *pāgala* [crazy]. Why would anyone be interested in that? Driving down the highway, I didn't see any, which got me questioning if I even would, but just before reaching the town of Nawanshahr, I noticed a village far in the distance, where I detected sculptures jutting into the sky. I directed the driver to the village and got out to take some photographs. We were soon surrounded by villagers who wanted to know what we were doing. I expect being a *gora* [a fair-skinned Westerner], likely a not-so-common sight in their village, piqued interest. And Rajesh, you've told me that with your beard, head covered with a cap, a fancy camera hanging from the neck, and a backpack, village elders initially thought you might be an NRI Sikh on holiday. After explaining what I was looking for, they offered in Punjabi all kinds of suggestions that they passed on to the driver, who now understood my quest and who became excited by the search for water tanks. In one afternoon we encountered a considerable number.

Something I found so interesting is that these sculptures—and as I later found out there are hundreds of them throughout Punjab—are located primarily in the villages, most of which are not intersected by the major highways, and rarely ever in the larger towns, certainly not in cities such as Jalandhar or Chandigarh. I came to realize just how much this cultural phenomenon is embedded in village culture. Punjab is primarily an agricultural state and not really on the tourist radar, aside from the Golden Temple in Amritsar, and even local visits to the villages are not a common activity except by other villagers and NRIs. And there are more than 3,500 villages in Doaba alone.

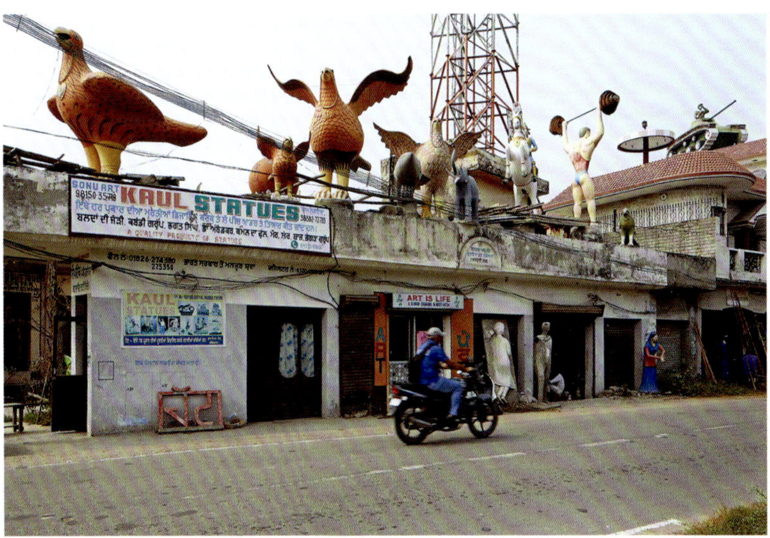


Workshop of Kaul Statues, village of Jandiala Manjki, 2019.

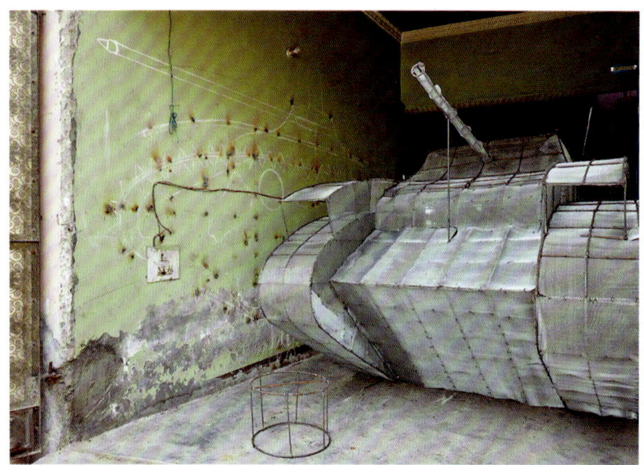

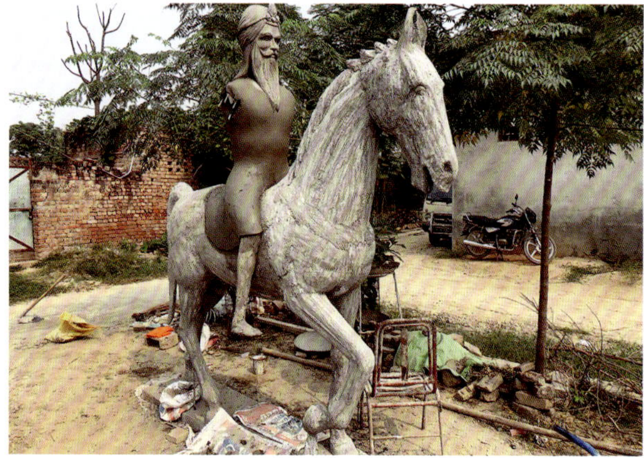

Army tank sculpture in progress at Kaul Statues workshop, village of Jandiala Manjki, 2019.

A sculpture in progress at Davinder Kumar's workshop, village of Banga, 2019.
Photo: Keith Wallace

During the visit you and I made together to Punjab in 2019, it was instructive to meet with those who actually make these sculptures and gain some understanding of the process of how they work with clients and physically create the sculptures. These sculptors are for the most part not trained in art schools. They learn their skills through mentorships and even through elder family members, a process that is likely related more to folk art and craft traditions in rural India—traditions that result in artworks that are more utilitarian. Punjab is known for its basketmaking, pottery, Phulkari embroidery, carpet weaving, leatherwork, etc. So the question arises of what to call the sculptors—fabricators, artisans, artists? While it is an entrepreneurial enterprise, they do see their work as a creative process and mentioned that others do refer to them as artists.

Tarsem Lal, a building contractor in the village of Khalwara, near Phagwara, surmised that there are about twenty-five to thirty artists in the Doaba region with commissions generally secured by word of mouth rather than advertising. Also, Saba, a sculptor based in the village of Attowal, said each artist has a general area within their district that they serve, perhaps a 60-kilometre radius, and that they are aware of and able to identify each other's work.

The owner, the owner's family, or the building contractor may come to the artist with an idea, often through a photo, about what they are interested in and then they leave the final product up to the artist, with some communication between the two, until the sculpture is completed. Of course, not all negotiations will be the same with each artist; there are no standard rules for the process. And depending upon the workload, the artist may oversee the fabrication, hiring of assistants, and then take over on the finishing details.

The sculptures themselves are made of rebar, wire mesh, cement concrete, and paint. The process might start with a to-scale drawing on the wall of the studio, as in the case of Sonu Lobhiya; a small model; or even an image downloaded from Google. Depending on the scale of the sculpture, it can be completed in the studio or, if heavy, the steel structure is at times lifted onto the roof by ropes and pulleys, or even a crane, then finished with the cement concrete and paint. Because of the scale of some of the sculptures, there are artists whose studios are located outdoors on their home properties.

But it appears that client needs are shifting. According to the artists we met, there are now fewer functional water tanks being made and more of what you mentioned earlier: showpieces—sculptures that are more elaborate and stand alone as embellishments that can be placed anywhere on the roof. Most often they are placed at the highest point of the house—on top of the water tank—so in that respect they are still part of the water tank, with the tank becoming a kind of exhibition plinth. Also, what was primarily identified with NRIs is increasingly being taken up by locals for their own houses, and in some cases by businesses. As well, gurdwaras are commissioning pieces for their buildings and gardens.

Rajesh, did you notice a shift from earlier sculptures to the more recent ones, either in terms of functionality or those who are commissioning them? What is your understanding about how these sculptures originated and how they have changed? And what can one call them? As with the artists, I find they are difficult to neatly situate within the realm of contemporary art.

RAJESH VORA Before I move on to the origin of the water tank, there is one thing I want to add to your observation about the artists working within a radius of about 60 kilometres. I, too, noticed that the architectural style of the houses, building materials, ornamentation, colour schemes, and even the design of the water tanks would change as one moved from *tehsil* to *tehsil*—the subdivisions within a district. This localized approach is practical and has other plus points. It helps with the logistics and economics of the construction. Due to the familiarity and trust between the client, contractor, and service providers, there is a certain harmony reflected in the house, giving a personalized touch, adding variety to the ornamentation on the façades of these vernacular houses. Still, it could also resonate with the popular aphorism that depicts India's linguistic diversity: *Kos par badle paani, chaar kos par baani* ("The language spoken in India changes every few kilometres, just like the taste of the water"). With the ever-increasing presence of sculpted water tanks in different villages, one could apply the above aphorism to Punjab.

But during my last trip in 2019, with the ever-enterprising spirit of Punjabi NRIs, I could see trends that gave rise to this aphorism have expanded to describe not just a few kilometres in rural Punjab but countries across the world. The early vernacular style of the houses—using local materials and expressions, varying from district to district—had adapted to global ideas translated by the NRIs' innovative understanding of what a home should look like. This even seems to have influenced some local artisans and contractors, giving birth to a style of architecture in rural Punjab that is yet to find its name—maybe *Videshi* architecture—or "foreign" architecture—or even NRI architecture?

The evolution of decorative water tanks seems to have started sometime around the late '70s in the Doaba region of rural Punjab, although no one I spoke with had an exact date. The upgrading of rural homes at this time with a washroom and toilet requiring running water

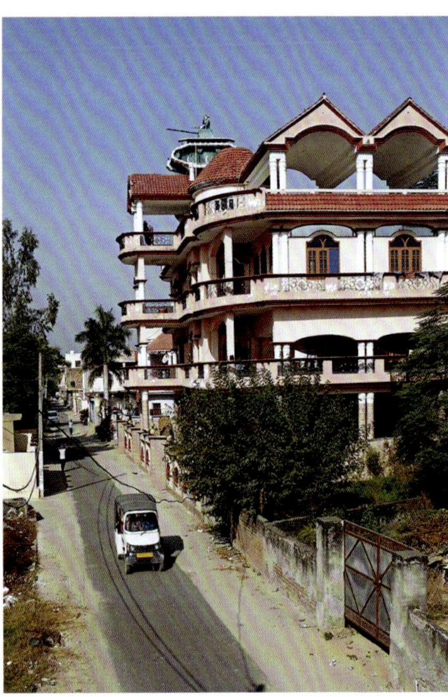

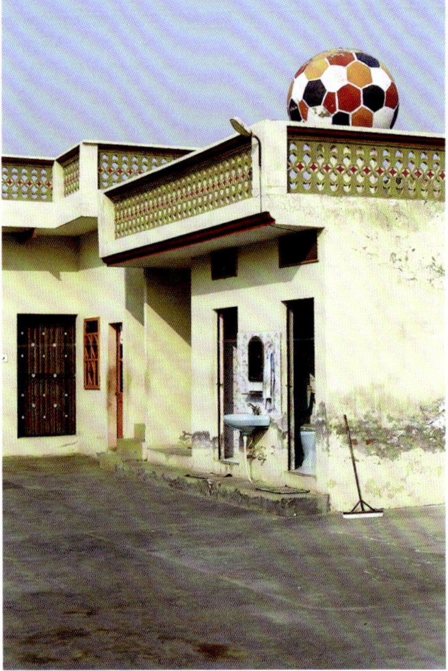

Army tank on top of four-storey house, village of Chaheru, 2015.

Football on top of attached washroom, village of Mohem, 2014.

could be one of the reasons as people were starting to install submersible electrical water pumps on their properties that reached down to the water table rather than relying upon community sources such as mechanical hand pumps. With the introduction, also in the '70s, of concrete cement as a building material in rural Punjab, some of the earliest examples of the water tanks were conceived in the shape of a football with a diameter of 100 to 150 centimetres and could be easily fabricated by joining two cement concrete moulded spheres with an opening on top. This functional water tank, resembling a *matka*—the Indian clay water pot—was placed on top of these utility areas, typically located at the side of the house near the entrance gate. Jalandhar's famous football-manufacturing industry may well have inspired these early football-shaped water tanks, which are still seen throughout rural Punjab because they can be mass produced. The introduction of modern plastic tanks in black and blue colours is no match for these more personalized brilliantly painted football-shaped water tanks of various designs.

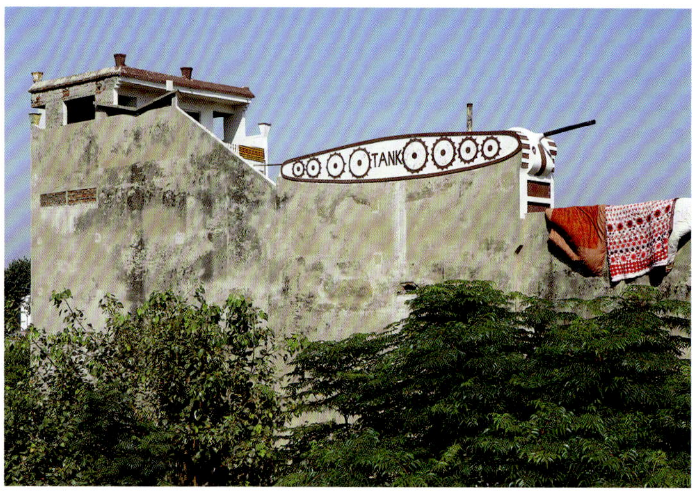


↑ An early water tank sculpture built by Gyani Mahendra Singh Makh in 1970, village of Chachoki, 2019.

It seems Gyani Mahendra Singh Makh, of Chachoki village near Jalandhar, who was a government building contractor, could be considered one of the fathers of the modern-day sculpted water tanks of rural Punjab. In 1970 he built a reinforced concrete cement water tank that not only visually announces a sculpture of an army tank, but also has TANK spelled out across its side, prominently positioned on top of his four-storey house, apparently the first multi-storey house in the village. He cleverly installed a smaller water tank that was concealed inside the outer shell of the sculpted army tank in order to keep the water cool—a technique in common use today.

While Gyani Mahendra Singh Makh was not an NRI, remittances started pouring into the Doaba region from the migrant members of local families, many who had left Punjab in the 1960s and early '70s and whose prosperity is manifested in these renovated or newly

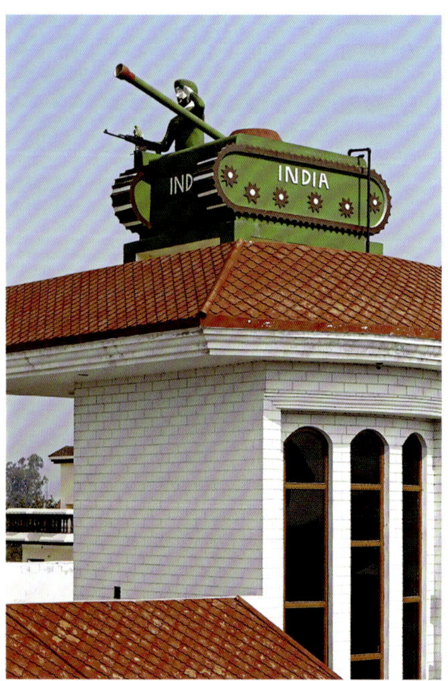


← The simplicity of this army tank water tank suggests that it is an early example of the form; village of Khela, 2015.

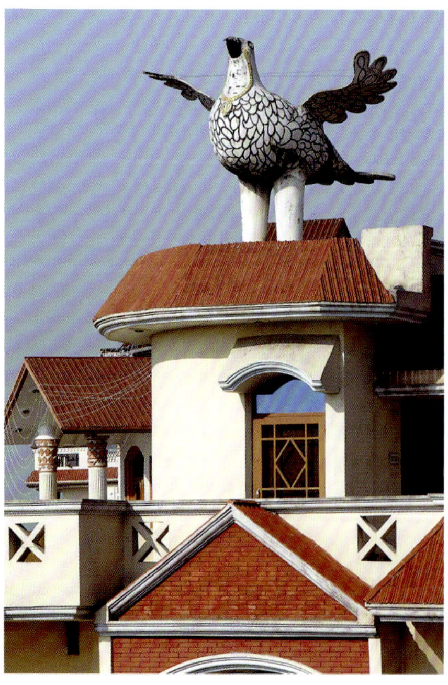

Early falcon (*baaz*) water tank, village of Hapowal, 2019.

constructed rural homes. Either an extra level or two was added or new houses were built from the ground up, with the water tank finding a conspicuous spot within the building's overall composition—increasingly at the top, where the water pressure would be more effective. The early football-shaped water tanks were gradually joined by airplane-shaped water tanks, also cast in concrete cement. Realistically painted, these airplanes often proudly carried the name of the country's national carrier, and even the family's surname—a humble tribute to the aircraft that took them to their future lives.

By the late 1980s, the skyline of rural Punjab was witnessing a significant change. With the rising NRI financial contributions, these houses grew larger, the airplane-shaped water tank became increasingly emphasized, and other avatars, individually commissioned rather than mass produced, took birth. With the long association of Punjabis in the armed forces, and paying homage to their family members who served in the Indian army, air force fighter planes and army tanks were another early theme. Villagers told me stories of the bravery and courage of family members, and some, with a cunning smile, would draw my attention to the tank's gun muzzle pointing toward Pakistan. Since Independence in 1947, India and Pakistan have been in four wars, including one undeclared war, and many border skirmishes and military stand-offs. In addition, Guru Gobind Singh's *baaz*, the majestic falcon one sees in the portraits of the tenth Sikh guru, also took the shape of a water tank on the homes of many devout Sikhs. *Baaz* is a symbol of strength and tenacity, as well as good luck if one lands on your house. During the 1990s, with an increase in the variety of sculptures, the water tanks became landmarks in the village. Serving a functional need while simultaneously adding aesthetics to the house, they soon became a symbol of success resulting from a migrant's hard work overseas.

As you said earlier, there also was a shift to having the sculptures, especially those too complicated to function as a water tank, installed atop the actual tanks, thus becoming more an architectural embellishment. Aside from the *baaz*, Sikhs began commissioning Guru Gobind Singh's horse or a lotus flower, representing enlightenment. And then many other forms began taking shape—a nationalist would proudly install a statue of freedom fighter Shaheed Bhagat Singh, who is revered as a hero of India's early independence movement in the 1920s; a farmer, his pair of bullocks or a tractor; a sports enthusiast, perhaps weightlifters or a representation of sporting events; and a migrant who now lives in

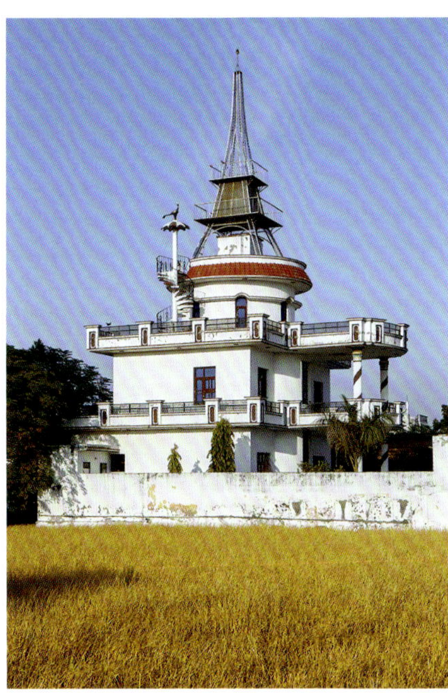

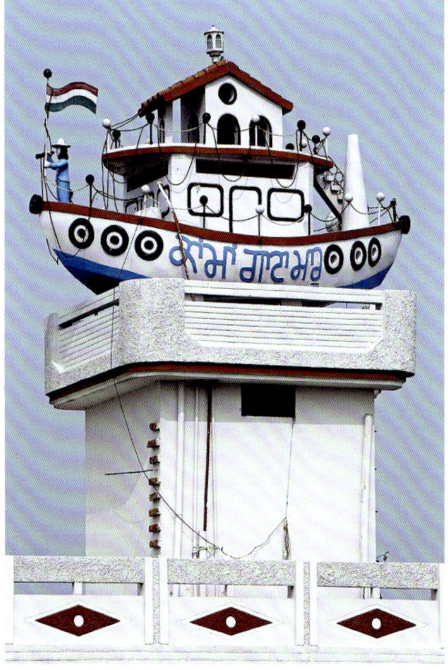

Eiffel Tower on top of water tank, village of Mohanwal, 2019.

This ship water tank references a pre–air travel era of migration; village of Mehatpur, 2015.

New York or Paris would display the Statue of Liberty or Eiffel Tower. Added to this growing list were Marutis, India's first domestically designed car; ships, some highly elaborate in their construction, which reference the pre-airplane era of migration and are incongruous in that there is no ocean in close proximity; as well as helicopters, trucks, pressure cookers, water pots, bottles of India's most popular whisky (McDowell's No. 1), etc.

You are right that it is difficult to situate these sculpted water tanks within the realm of contemporary art. One may call it the study of the intricate relationship between form and function, or "anonymous sculptures," as the German conceptual artists and photographers Hilla and Bernd Becher called the subjects of their photographs. Punjabi sculpted water tanks remind me of a comment by the Bechers, "We photographed water towers and furnaces because they are honest. They are functional, and they reflect what they do—that is what we liked. A person always is what s/he wants to be, never what s/he is. Even an animal usually plays a role in front of the camera."[2]

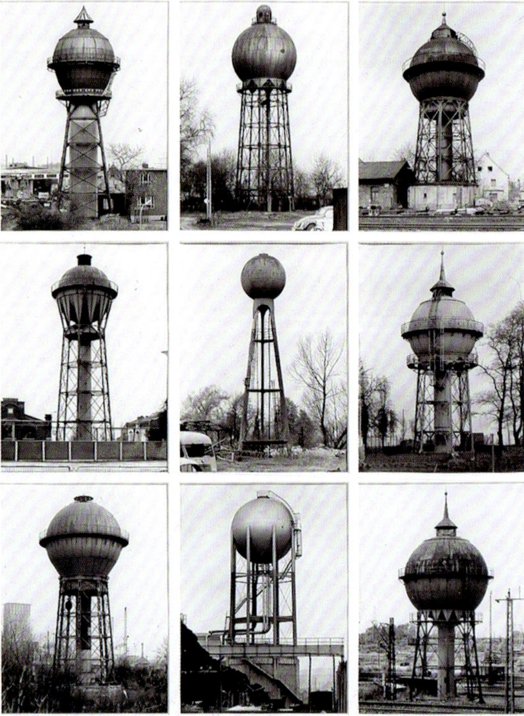

Bernd and Hilla Becher
*Water Towers*, 1972
nine black and white photographs
133.7 × 103.2 × 3.8 cm.
The Eli and Edythe L. Broad Collection. © Estate Bernd & Hilla Becher, represented by Max Becher.

KEITH WALLACE Oh yes, what to call them? I have struggled with this, and I think that struggle is one thing that contributed to my interest in these sculptures. Working outside the prescribed space of professional art, these artists actually challenge my assumptions about what art can be. They are in fact sculptures; it is just that their reference points are local and have functional, traditional, or familial symbolic purposes, rather than what might be considered fine art, which is connected to formal institutional training and where the work of art exists primarily to be appreciated as a sign of an individual's aesthetic or conceptual creative vision. However, it is important to note that many contemporary fine art Indian artists—and artists in other parts of the world, for that matter—reference folk art or craft traditions even though these works, unlike those in the villages, are rarely shown in the context from where the references were sourced. Thus, the rooftop sculptures are more than just aesthetic objects and, for the most part, do not possess the refinement, both materially and intellectually, expected of traditional fine art sculpture. For example, the rendering of muscles on the weightlifters—physical sports such as kabaddi, cricket, and football are a passion in Punjab—differs greatly from one sculpture to the next and is often audaciously exaggerated in a raw kind of way. Army tanks vary from simple minimalist representations to highly complex compositions complete with a figure, gun in hand, scanning the distant landscape with his binoculars. These sculptures are not cerebral propositions but more pragmatic in intent.

Aside from being sculpture, these works likewise can in fact be considered a form of public art: they are in your face; they are not made for a gallery or museum context; they are just there, very present, and embedded within a collective social experience. Again, many contemporary artists in other parts of the world are actively exploring ways of engaging with public space outside of the museum or gallery. In the case of Punjabi water tank sculptors, it is a process where art, architecture, and everyday life seamlessly meld together. So while the water tanks the Bechers photographed are of a very different aesthetic from that of Punjabi water tanks, as well as the showpieces, there is, I believe, a shared honesty in acknowledging a practical and social function in the objects themselves.

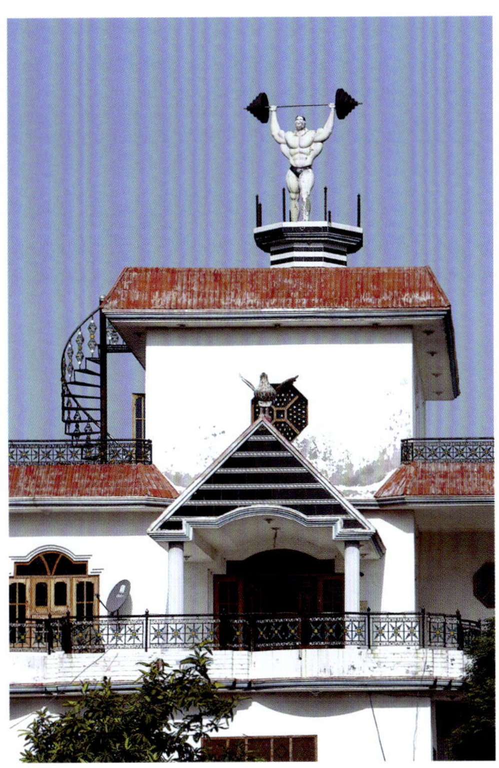

Weightlifter on top of water tank, with a *baaz* below, village of Pader, 2015.

RAJESH VORA You are raising a critical point, and—though this is a departure from the Bechers' water tank typologies—I had a different approach to my documentation. With the sheer variety of the sculpted water tanks, I decided to photograph them like an outdoor studio portrait, thus exercising a certain restraint and regard for each subject. It was also essential for me to be face to face with my subject; I could not achieve this by photographing them from street level, and accessing the rooftop terrace of a house located opposite was the best option. Negotiating this approach also had its charm. I would knock on the door of homes and, explaining my purpose, I would politely ask to go up to the balcony, take a peep from a higher-floor window opening, or best, to reach the rooftop terrace, a request that was never refused. Someone would accompany me or simply give instructions about the staircase to climb and even give me the door keys to meet my awaiting subject. In a way, with the rooftops serving a variety of functions such as drying laundry, siting a TV satellite dish, storing things, and offering nighttime respite from summer heat—and these components are visible in many of my photographs—I also encountered what they would see every day, but I was capturing the moment through my own specific aesthetic approach.

With some homes remaining locked, I missed photographing a few subjects, but I had no regret as it taught me to accept the situation and move forward, as I was sure there would be other surprises ahead.

KEITH WALLACE Building upon the idea of you seeing these sculptures as portraits, I want to return to what you suggested earlier—that they also tell stories, many a product of frugal diaspora lifestyles that within a decade or two led to prosperity—and for me this emerges as a central aspect in understanding them. Again, rather than considering these sculptures only through the lens of fine art, it is more constructive and meaningful to consider them from the perspective of material culture, that these objects are specific to their cultural contexts, which lends an anthropological proclivity to your project. In the case of Punjab, it is often a family reference making itself publicly present on the skyline.

This idea of a domestic identity marker is common in many cultures around the world. In Israel and Palestine it is less celebratory, with plastic domestic water tanks being colour-coded black to indicate the homes of Palestinians whose water resources are regulated by the Israeli government; in some neighbourhoods the abundance of these water tanks is referred to as the "black forest." On the west coast of Canada, First Nations longhouses traditionally have carved wood posts supporting the interior roof beams, but also outdoor carved house poles or planks at their entrance that announce to the community a memorial for an ancestor, an association with clan membership, or an accounting of a historical event. Ghana is well known for its "fantasy coffins," and although they do not serve as house markers, they are individually commissioned to honour a deceased family member and are now a commonly accepted instance where craft and art converge.[3] These examples evolved for a variety of reasons, and in Punjab we find an emphatic form of cultural expression that seems to have emerged in its own organic way. Who would ever think of representing a pressure cooker on one's roof? Someone who owns a successful restaurant abroad? And then there is the kangaroo with boxing gloves presumably commissioned by a family that migrated to Australia, or the full slate of tug-of-war participants complete with a referee

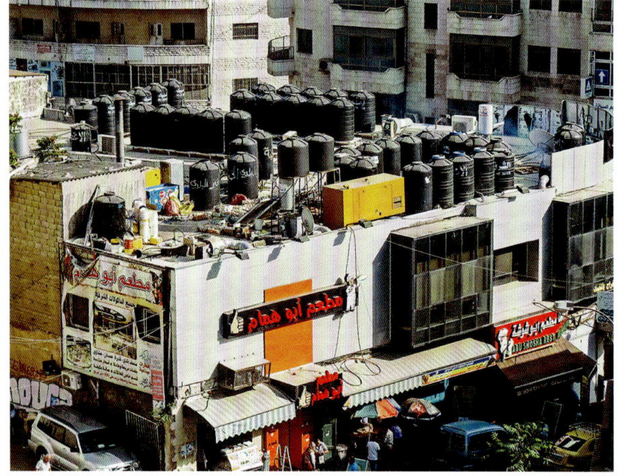

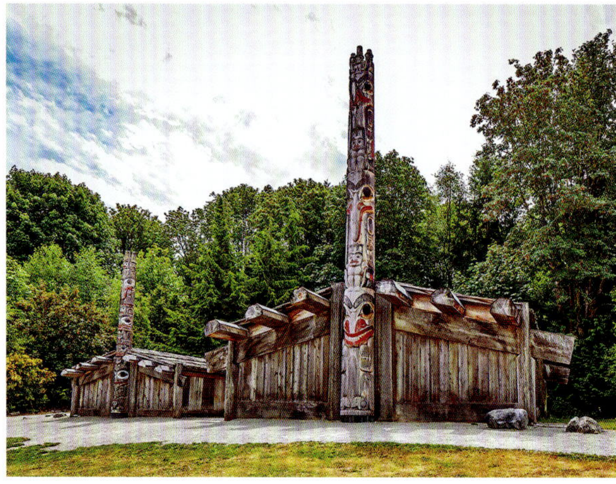

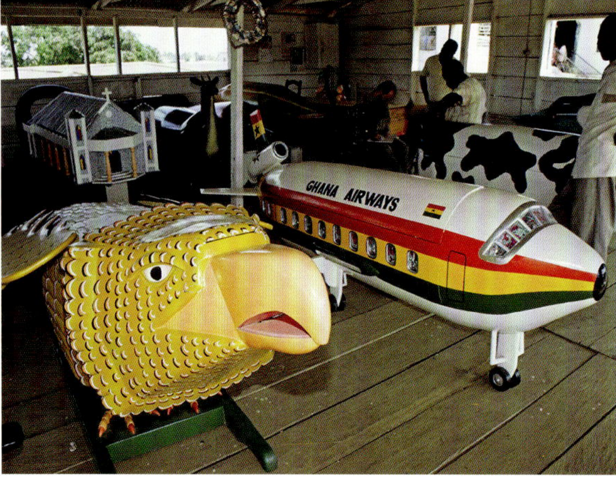


↖ Water tanks atop buildings in the Palestinian city of Ramallah, 10 kilometres north of Jerusalem.
Photo: Lu Yang

↑ These Haida housefront poles from the Northwest Coast of North America represent an enduring form of domestic identity marker. The one on the left was created between 1958 and 1962 by Bill Reid and Doug Cranmer, and the one on the right in the early 2000s by Jim Hart.
Museum of Anthropology at the University of British Columbia, Vancouver, Canada.
Photo: Peng Ge

← In Ghana, "fantasy coffins" such as these, shown in a funeral director's store in Accra, are commissioned from specialized carpenters to commemorate deceased family members. The coffin of this airplane was made for a high-ranking executive of Ghana Airways.
Photo: Nick Haslam

commissioned by a sports enthusiast in the UK—there is a playfulness embedded in these family markers that indicates where the owners have been or where they are coming back to, creating a sense of connection between one place and another.

The idea of "everyday monuments," the title you have given your project, is so fitting. These sculptures are indeed monuments in that for the most part they are commemorative of a family's journey or occupation or faith. But unlike the public monuments of politicians or war heroes plopped into a public square, these Punjabi monuments either serve an everyday function—storing water—or are incorporated as part of an everyday domestic space—a house.

RAJESH VORA At the same time, it is easy to see these sculptures and the houses they are placed on as simply showing off a migrant's success, which carries some truth to it, especially for those houses whose scale is literally over the top. These houses are for the most part so different from the earlier one-storey courtyard-style house surrounded by a wall and an entry gate, and conceivably could provoke resentment, and in some cases likely do, from villagers who have not gained the same opportunity to migrate. On the other hand, the construction and maintenance of these houses have created employment in many villages that otherwise offer few opportunities, even within the agricultural sector that Punjab is so recognized for. In addition, a new domestic form of artistic expression—the sculptures—has been launched.

But beyond the construction of these houses and the commissioning of the sculptures, it is important to acknowledge the financial contributions NRIs have made to other aspects of village life. Such projects include hospitals, schools, infrastructure, and even more modest offerings such as market stalls, bus shelters, and sponsorship of sports teams. Even though some family members have been living elsewhere in the world for decades, the connection to "home" is not lost. For example, there are families who migrated to Canada as early as 1906 who continue to maintain a close relationship with their family village.

Punjabi exuberance is often cited when referring to these everyday monuments. But why? Historically, monuments were built by kings and commoners and illustrated an idea or something commemorative. Punjabi houses with water tanks demonstrate this as well, but more democratically; it is becoming a common practice irrespective of socio-economic standards and differences. Earlier water tanks and sculptures were primarily commissioned by Jat landowners who were able to migrate, but now Punjabi Dalits, the farm labourers, are also migrating and building new houses and adorning them with sculptures.

*Shaukeen*, they are—the word often used to refer to one who is extremely fond of something and therefore practising it simply for the love of it. They proudly put sculpted water tanks of different sizes and shapes on top of their homes, fulfilling their dream of building their own Taj Mahal and creating a contagious art form with each subsequent home owner imitating and trying to better the other!

In reflecting upon my project *Everyday Monuments*, I was fortunate to document a particular period of a diasporic culture as an architectural artefact. As time goes by, the second generation, who, for the most part, are born outside of India and have adapted more completely to their respective cultures, may over time further shift the trend of sculpted water tanks started by the first-generation migrants. However, as the migration of families from other levels within Punjab society continues, we might see different manifestations of sculpted water tanks. Or we might see its natural demise.

## NOTES

1 Rahul Mehrotra, *The Kinetic City & Other Essays* (Berlin: ArchiTangle, 2021).

2 Tobias Haberl and Dominik Wichmann, "Klar waren wir Freaks," *Süddeutsche Zeitung Magazin*, May 15, 2008, https://sz-magazin.sueddeutsche.de/kunst/klar-waren-wir-freaks-75418.

3 "Fantasy coffins" were first presented in relation to fine art in the exhibition *Les Magiciens de la terre* at the Musée National d'Art Moderne in Paris in 1989. Since that landmark exhibition, many museums around the world have exhibited folk art and crafts as fine art, the meaning of which has subsequently become increasingly fluid.

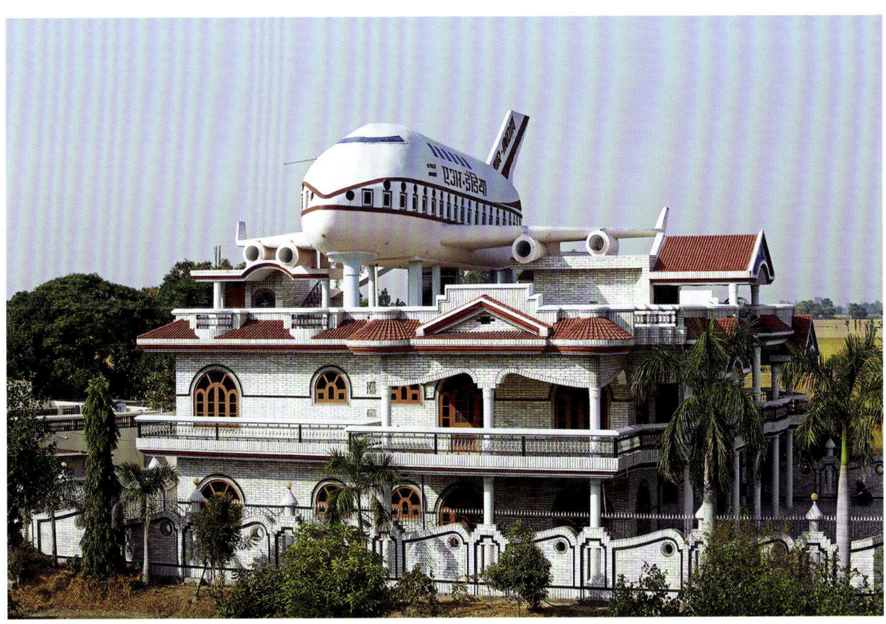


Airplane on top of house, village of Uppal Bhupa, 2019.

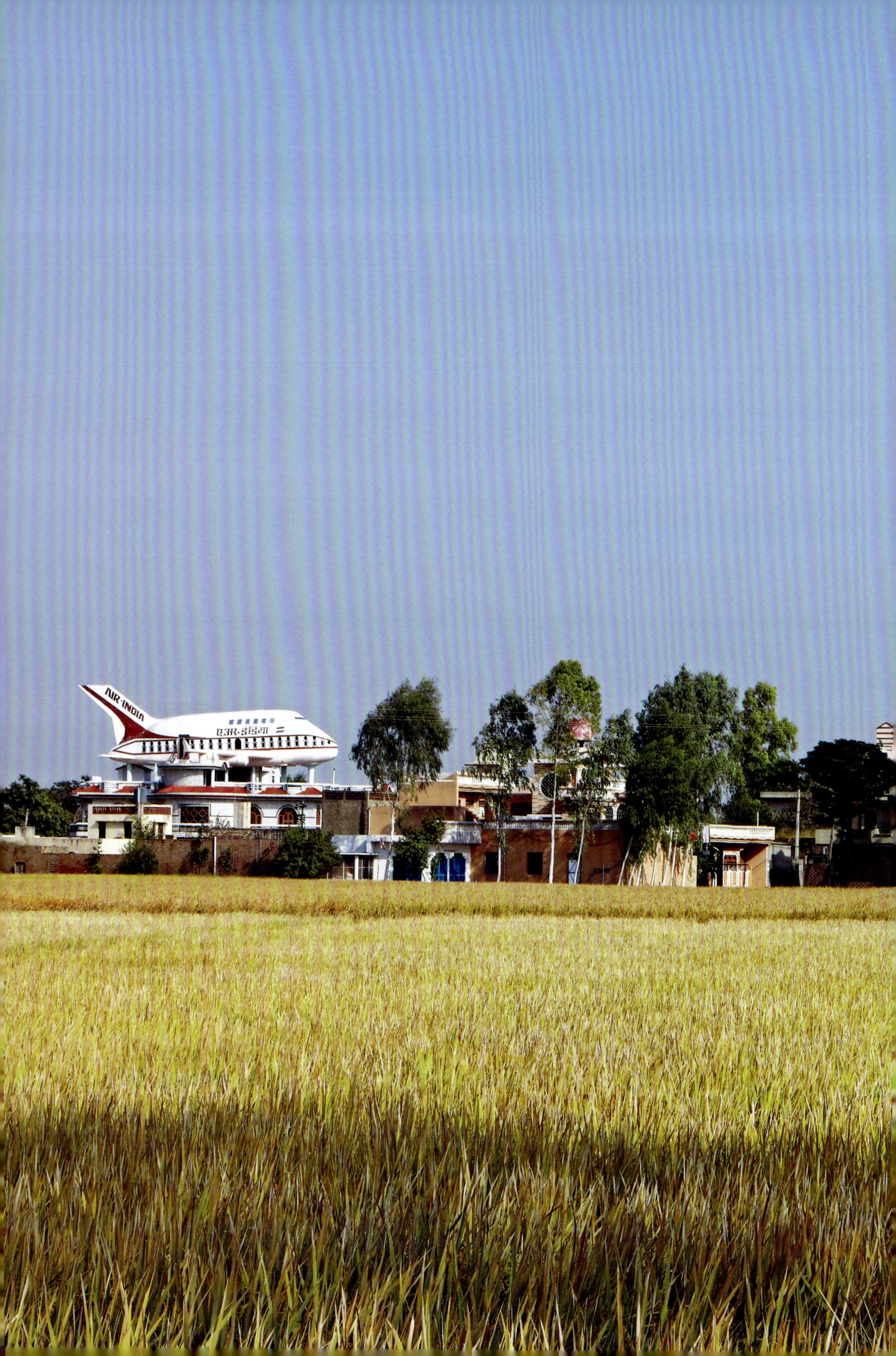
AIR-INDIA
एअर-इंडिया

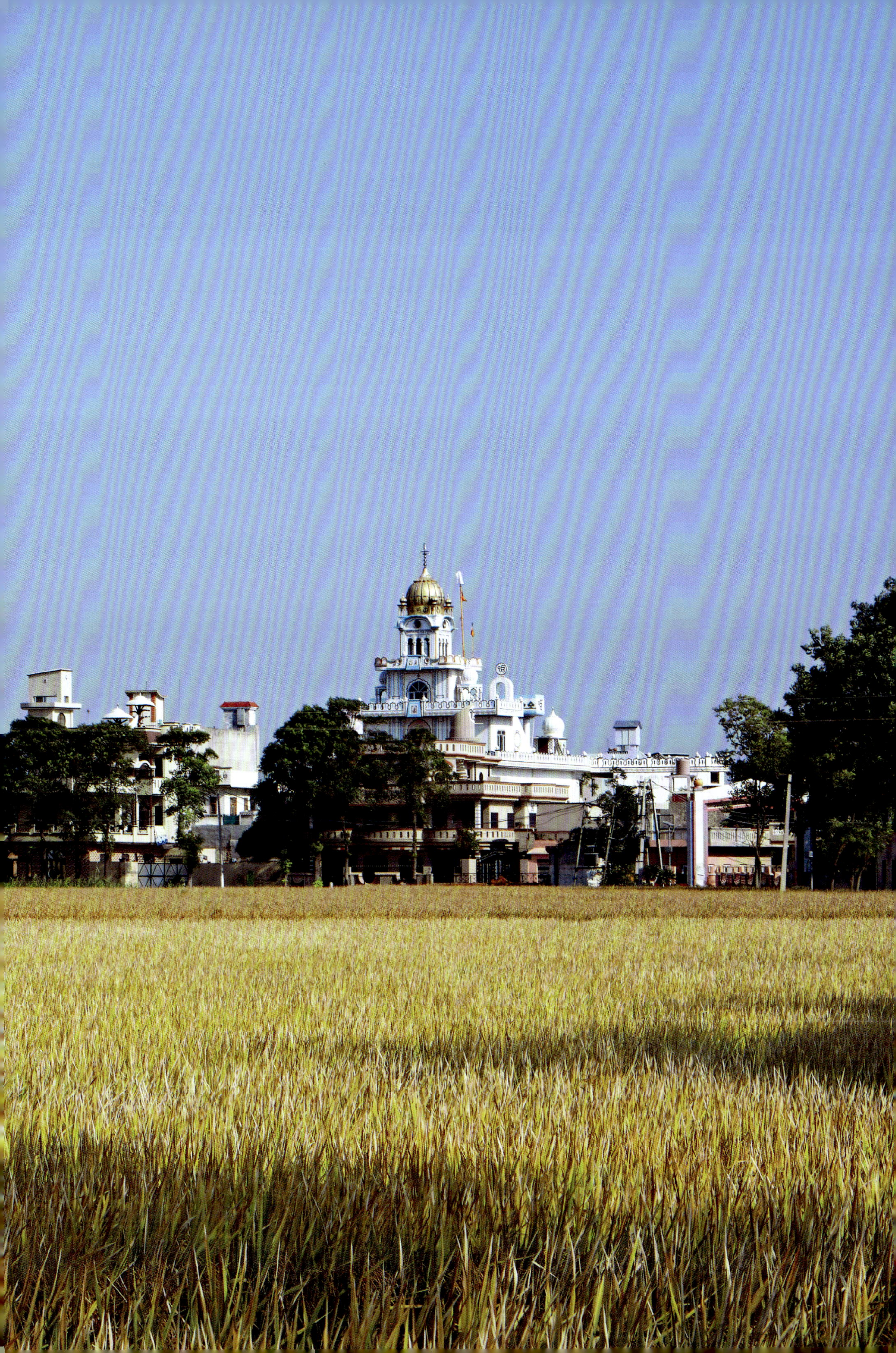

# REPRODUCTIVE ROOFTOPS

SAJDEEP SOOMAL

IT WAS A BRIGHT winter morning in my grandparent's bungalow in southwestern Ontario, Canada; the cold stuck to the glass of the windows. I was looking at photographs of the gated two-storey mansion that had been erected on our ancestral property in rural Punjab, while my *dadi ji* [paternal grandmother] distractedly walked in and out of the living room with *pakoras*, *chai*, *besan* [gram sweets], and her one-a-day energy balls. In the late 2000s, my *baba* [grandfather] and his brothers had contributed large sums of money to build an extended family home in Paddi Khalsa, the small village where he was born and raised in the Jalandhar district of central Punjab. The handful of documentary photographs that my *dadi ji* kept on file captured the new build in its early days. Typically stored away in a small white envelope in her filing cabinet alongside her registration documents, tax returns, and mortgage information, these photographs were far from the family portraits that she had placed on her bookshelf or tucked away into albums. My *dadi ji* had cared for these photographs as if they were addenda to the property deed itself, official documents proving our hereditary right to that plot of land and house sitting near the Grand Trunk (GT) Road in central Punjab.

Nestled between the Beas and Sutlej rivers, the Jalandhar area is named for its geographical location: *jal*, meaning "water," and *andhar*, meaning "inside." Due to its proximity to the melting Himalayas, it is one of the most fertile regions of Punjab. Archaeological evidence tells us that the region was first settled by the Harappan peoples during the third millennium BCE after aridification in the southwest led them to move upward along the Indus River basin in search of heavier monsoon rains.[1] Agrarian life has continued in the sparsely wooded, continuous flat plains of Jalandhar into the present day, even as successive waves of imperial rulers took hold of the region and introduced their own vernacular systems of social hierarchy, property rights, and revenue collection.[2] The settlement of Paddi Khalsa likely first appeared in the mid-eighteenth century, when emerging Sikh chiefs in the region wrested control of the Jalandhar region away from the Mughal administration.[3] After conquering central Punjab, the Sikh leadership redistributed the double-cropped fields of wheat and maize around Jalandhar among their subordinate adherents (largely from the Jat Sikh community), until each soldier had taken his share of land. That is likely how my warring ancestors laid claim to a tract of agriculturally rich land in central Punjab and pursued the idyllic promises of sedentary farming in Paddi Khalsa, a new settlement named for its commitment to the Khalsa form of Sikhism.

When the British took control of the region following the Second Anglo-Sikh War (1848–49), colonial ethnographers devised racial theories that imagined the Jats as a martial race, biologically ideal for agrarian and military labour yet intellectually incapable of its strategic organization.[4] In exchange for their cooperation in the colonial agricultural and military schemes to settle western Punjab and consolidate imperial rule in India, the British Raj upheld and legally sanctified the land claims of the Jat Sikh peasantry of central Punjab. As drought and famine decimated India in the late nineteenth century, Jat agriculturalists started mortgaging and selling off their land.[5] Concerned with the political instability that would result from waning agrarian power in the region, the British introduced the Punjab Alienation of Land Act, 1900 to further lock society into place. The new system of classification divided the Punjabi people along an agricultural axis of caste, preventing "traditional agricultural tribes" (Jats, Rajputs, etc.) from alienating their land or mortgaging it for extended periods to "traditional non-agricultural tribes" (Chamars, Chuhras/Bhangis, Dalits, etc.). This laid the foundation for an emergent agricultural, landowning tribe of Jat Sikhs to culturally tie themselves to the soil and lands of central Punjab while solidifying economic and political power across the region during the twentieth century, including in the village of Paddi Khalsa.

Despite the colonial infrastructure supporting Jat Sikh hegemony in Punjab, the economic viability of agriculture in the Jalandhar district was further called into question as the already small family holdings were parcelled along multiplying lines of patrilineal descent. Inheriting shrinking plots of land, the progeny of Jat Sikh landowning families left agricultural life to seek fortunes elsewhere during the early twentieth century. As these migrants settled into military, agricultural, or industrial life abroad, familial remittances started flowing back to the Jalandhar district to supplement the variable income of agrarian life, leading to an uneven accumulation of monies in the hands of the Jat Sikhs living there. The influx of capital was used to pay off mortgages, secure lower interest rates, buy adjacent land, and build *pucca* brick houses, upholding the fantasy of an abundant yeoman way of life in central Punjab.[6] The monies that my *baba* remitted after leaving India in the early 1960s were used like this to help with mortgage payments, as well as to pay for food, clothing, household items, wedding ceremonies, and other necessities. Those remittances continued until his final visit to India in 1974, when he sponsored the last of his siblings and parents to come and work in the textile industries of southwestern Ontario. It wasn't until the 2000s that my grandfather sent monies back again, when his brothers proposed building the new two-storey house on the family property.

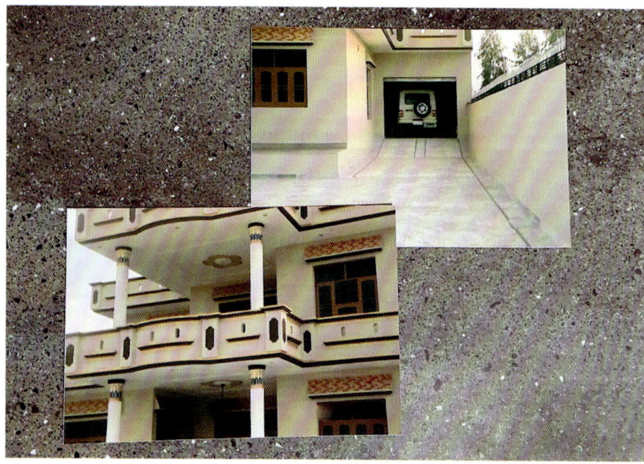

Soomal house, village of Paddi Khalsa.
Photos courtesy of Soomal family

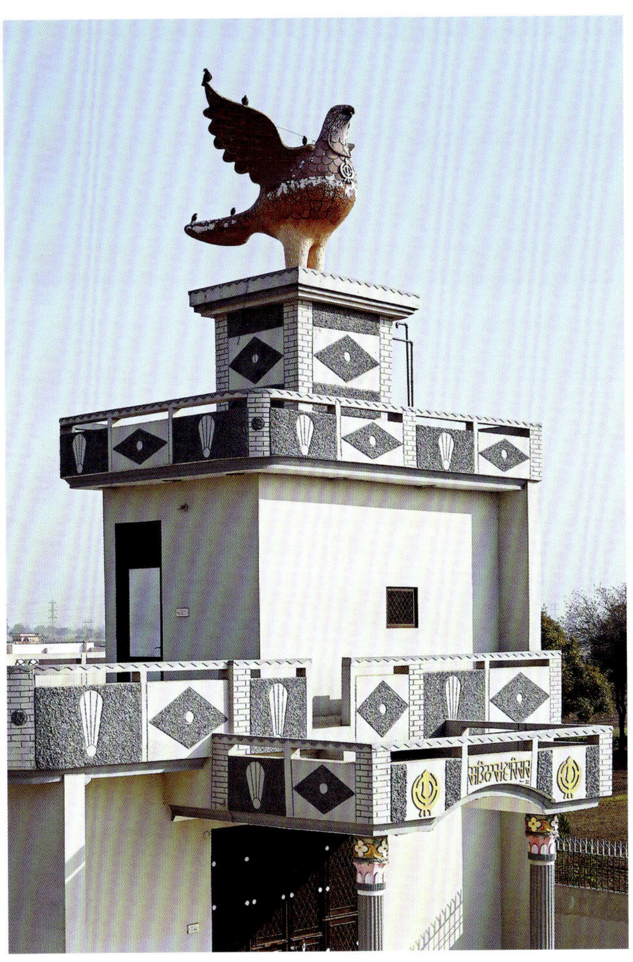

Falcon (*baaz*) on top of water tank, village of Paddi Khalsa, 2014.

As I took the two photographs out of the envelope and placed them on the marbled coffee table, my *dadi ji* returned to her filing cabinet. It was hard to get a clear picture of what the front elevation of the house looked like; each photograph narrowed into disparate architectural details of the new build. I noticed that the house was a bit of an outlier, lacking the ostentatious character of the two-storey mansions that had started appearing across the Punjabi countryside in the 1970s. Its simplified white Corinthian columns, sand-coloured marble tiled floors, wood-encased windows and doors, and black and gold art deco colour scheme evoke a more subdued vision of wealth than its neighbours. In the early 1990s, architectural historian Gautam Bhatia described the emergence of this modern vernacular architectural style as Punjabi Baroque.[7] The new builds were typically an extravagant and fanciful mix of the Bavarian castles, French châteaus, Italian villas, and American antebellum plantation houses that Punjabi people were encountering in popular films, television shows, and magazines as the epitome of wealth and power. The ongoing flow of remittances through the late twentieth century—paired with the financial bubble of the Green Revolution (the short-lived benefits of new agricultural technologies in India), the endless supply of cheap labour made available by the durability of caste inequality, and the liberalization of the Indian economy in the 1990s—all propelled the nouveau riche Jat Sikhs to build these vernacular McMansions on their small plots of land, consecrating themselves as the kings of rural Punjab by the turn of the twenty-first century.

Despite brazenly imitating the gated estates of the landed gentry who once ruled Western Europe and its colonies, these mimetic structures often lack the architectural foundations of the originals. Like many other modernist buildings erected in post-independence India, our two-storey bungalow is made not of traditional *pucca* brick, classical stone, or timber, but primarily out of concrete and steel.[8] After reinforced concrete was developed at the turn of the twentieth century, it was adopted in the late 1920s as the key building block for modern architecture in Western Europe.[9] After the partition of Punjab in 1947, Le Corbusier fashioned the buildings in the planned capital of Chandigarh with reinforced concrete, materializing a postcolonial vision of modernity that has underlined the rapid urban development of agrarian Punjab over the past fifty years.[10] The demand for reinforced concrete has led to the further development of carbon-intensive industrial steelworks, along with the unabated and unsustainable dredging of sand from the riverbeds of Punjab. While the provincial government has started regulating sand-mining practices and heavy metal pollution from the steel industry, the new standards are rarely and unevenly enforced.[11] And even though some vernacular architects in India are recommending local and less-processed building alternatives, such as timber, clay, and other soils, reinforced concrete remains the building material of choice across contemporary eastern Punjab.[12]

Towering walls and steel gates often surround the small-holding farms of central Punjab. The securitization of domestic life at the familial level is a long-standing phenomenon in the subcontinent; the persistence of this practice reveals the material insecurities underlying life in rural Punjab, where memories of partition and civil war—paired with ongoing corruption and crime—have led some residents to further securitize private property by not only building gated walls but hiring personal security who carry military-grade weapons. This sense of uneasiness about the permanence of settlement and life undergirds the McMansion builds of rural Punjab.

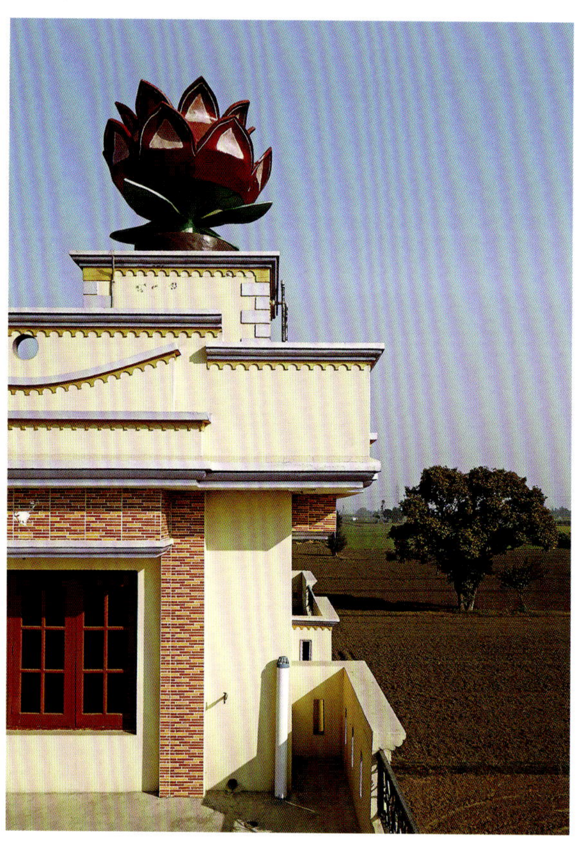

Lotus on top of water tank, village of Paddi Khalsa, 2014.

Towering over the traditional single-storey courtyard dwellings made of brick and mud, these luxury estate homes now dominate the landscape of rural Punjab. Since 2014, Rajesh Vora has been tracking across the hinterlands of Punjab to document one of the more idiosyncratic architectural features of the vernacular McMansions: the larger-than-life sculptures affixed to their rooftops. Ranging from militaristic monuments of army tanks, warrior falcons, and musclemen to domestic and recreational artifacts such as soccer balls, pressure cookers, and compact cars, the rooftop sculptures speak to the personal stories, desires, and anxieties of the families that have commissioned them.

When the sculptures first emerged in the late 1970s, they were manufactured to surround and hide water tanks that engineers placed on rural rooftops to improve household water supply through increased hydrostatic pressure. Starting in the early 1970s, the central government began providing grants for states to implement rural water supply and sanitation programs.[13] As water and sewage piping was laid down across the villages of Jalandhar district, residents started installing water storage tanks on the rooftops of their newly built homes and commissioning sculptures to surround them. Now often installed independently from the water tanks, these idiosyncratic sculptures have emerged as a favoured regional genre of retrofitted architectural decoration, permanently altering the skylines of rural Punjab.

Driving along the GT Road, Vora was astonished as he saw the numerous sculptures covering the roofs of the nearby village of Paddi Khalsa. For Vora, the village quickly turned into a "gold mine" that would supply a considerable number of photographs for his documentary project. After capturing the roofscape of the village on camera, Vora went door to door, asking residents for the stories behind the sculptures standing atop their houses. He learned that rooftops are not only protective architectural elements designed to provide shelter from inclement weather but cultural spaces of everyday domestic life in rural Punjab. Punjabi cinema is replete with rooftop scenes depicting elderly women fastening clothing to washing lines, extended families sitting on casually arranged *manjaas* [traditional Indian woven beds], and love-struck couples gazing up at the moon.

When I got a chance to look through Vora's photographs of my ancestral hometown, I was struck by the lotus flower statue in the centre of the village. The lotus is the ultimate symbol of creation and divine fertility in the Indian subcontinent. In Vedic thought, the lotus flower is the generative organ of the maternal procreative water that not only gives birth to

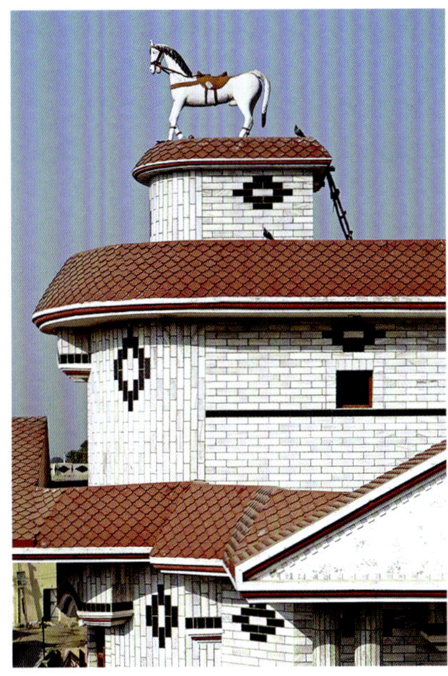
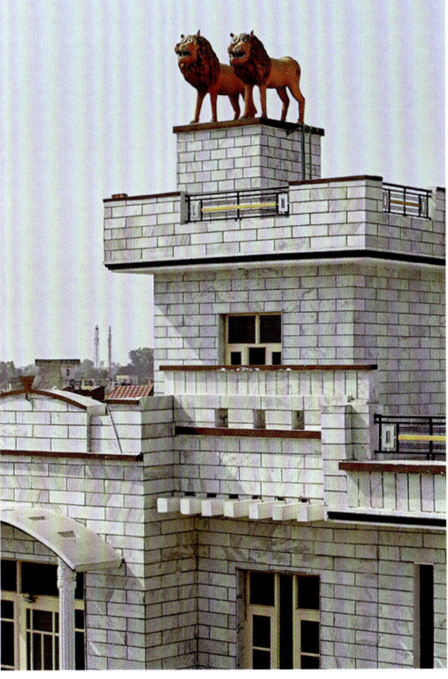
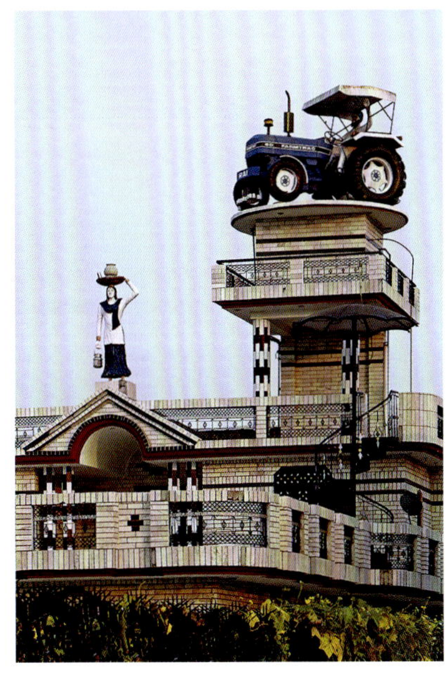

Horse on top of water tank, village of Paddi Khalsa, 2014.

Lions on top of water tank, village of Paddi Khalsa, 2015.

Farmer and wife, village of Bara Pind, 2015.

the gods but produces the phenomenal world entirely. During his travels, Vora found and documented several other lotus-shaped water tanks atop the mansions of rural Punjab. In a way, these blooming lotuses symbolically transfigure the rooftops of Punjab into maternal reproductive organs for the familial households that they enwomb.

This vision of the rooftop as a site for reproductive speculation and manifestation is rooted in local calculative practices. Some families use the rooftop to predict whether newly married brides will bear boys or girls. Young children are asked if there is a *kaavan* [large masculine crow] or a *chidi* [small feminine sparrow] sitting on the rooftop. If they see a crow, then the house will be blessed with a son, but if the child looks upon a sparrow, then the family will be cursed with a daughter. Under this allegorical tradition, wildlife creatures are transformed into technologies of reproductive speculation as they visit the rooftops of Punjab, indicating the sex of the baby on the way and the corollary economic privileges or struggles awaiting its family. The eugenic world of sex prediction—and in some cases sex selection—in Punjab is not only the provenance of the biologically inscribed body but extends outward to the architectural domain.

Once speculative sites for handling the uncertain future, the reproductive rooftops of rural Punjab now openly enunciate the dreams of technological modernity, Khalsa rule, and idyllic agrarian life incubating within its wombs. On the rooftops of Paddi Khalsa, there is a warrior falcon about to take flight, a muscular bodybuilder performing an overhead press, a white horse saddled for war, a pair of twin lions standing guard shoulder to shoulder, and the revolutionary Bhagat Singh himself wearing the colours of the Sikh Khalsa as he holds up an Indian flag. These are the ideal progeny of rural Punjabi society. These moulds are the product of overlapping histories and idealistic political projects rooted in masculine, militaristic agrarian power, flagrantly displayed in this rooftop scene that depicts a rather colonial vision of the martial Jat Sikh man with his menagerie of warrior animals. It is these Lions of Punjab who, sometimes with rifles in hand, continue to exercise control over the means of (re)production in rural Punjabi society, from the wombs of its daughters to the hands of its landless labourers.

Placed alongside the antagonist Lions of Punjab, many of the other sculptural works appear more benign. It feels much harder to indict the statues of Indian-branded tractors, commercial airliners, sewing machines, pressure cookers, and small motor vehicles that

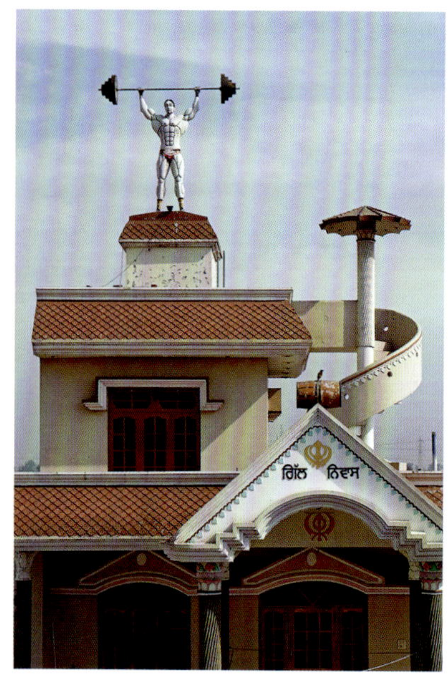


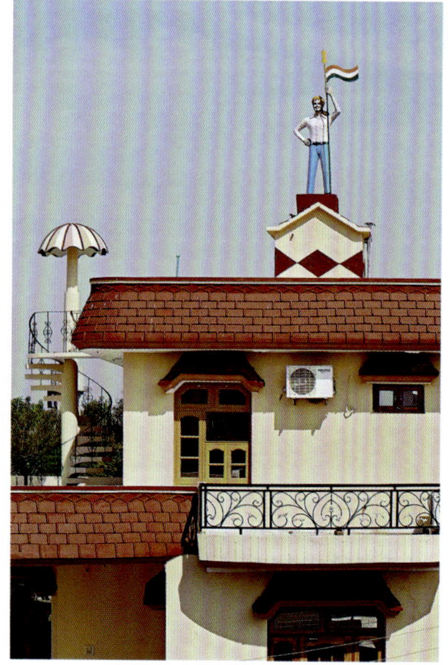

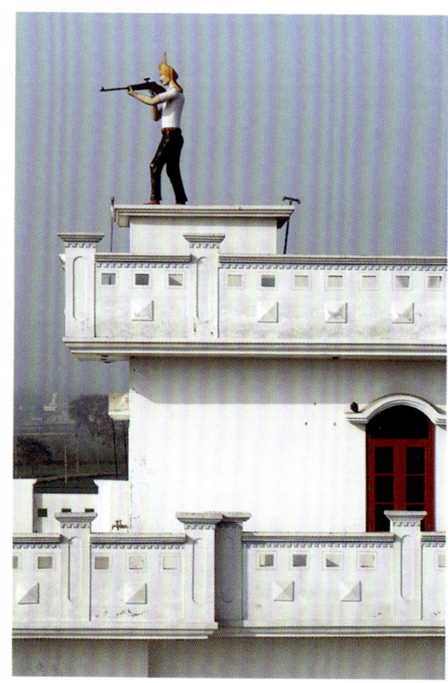

Weightlifter on top of water tank, village of Paddi Khalsa, 2015.

Freedom fighter Bhagat Singh on top of water tank, village of Paddi Khalsa, 2019.

A young man on top of water tank aiming his rifle, village of Kandola Kalan, 2015.

dot the houses of rural Punjab in equal proportion. Production of these consumer items of technological modernity ramped up in India during the post-war period, improving domestic life by reducing the time required for cooking and transportation. Unfolding alongside the mechanization of agriculture, these technological changes laid the foundations for an expanded economy of leisure in the agrarian countryside. How could one play recreational sports if they were busy working the fields? The statues of soccer players, bodybuilders, and tug-of-war games reveal the places where younger generations of Jat Sikh men in rural Punjab are spending their newly available leisure time. While the playful worlds of Punjabi masculinity flourish on the rooftops of rural Punjab, the feminine is largely absent and only appears in the constricting form of the dutiful wife bound into traditional agrarian life.

A handful of the everyday monuments are one of a kind. There is a golden kangaroo wearing red boxing gloves; a miniature Statue of Liberty; a fluffy white bunny. These anomalies in the manufactured world of rooftop sculptures provide unlikely visions for the future of rural Punjabi life. They remind us of the complex, uncontainable, and open-ended possibilities incubating within and beyond its securitized Jat Sikh households.

There is no sculpture atop our house in Paddi Khalsa. The reasons are manifold: partly the logistical difficulties in building consensus among all the family members with a stake in the house, and partly the lack of interest that my late grandfather had in retrofitting the newly built house. When I asked my *dadi ji* whether she would like to commission a rooftop statue that holds an alternative vision for Punjabi life, she started sternly lecturing me on my spending habits. “You and your father are always spending my money,” she said temperamentally. “We are not going to have anything left when you are done.” For my *dadi ji*, there are better ways to spend money than on architectural decoration.

The monies that my *dadi ji* does send back to Paddi Khalsa take the form of annual donations to upkeep a small shrine known colloquially in our family as the *juggah*, or “the place.” In the early 1970s, my grandparents sent remittances to build a big concrete canopy to encase the shrine, outfitting it with a large dome roof and a finial made of solid gold. They infused the sacred shrine to Guru Nanak with concrete modernity to expand its lifespan, hoping that it would continue to serve as a quiet place of reflection for future generations.

Surrounded by securitized private bungalows that are topped by warrior animals, the *juggah* holds onto an open-doors architectural vision for the Punjab that is premised on inviting *gharibi lokh* [the poor, the estranged, the homeless] inside rather than turning them away. Unlike the architectural photographs of the two-storey house that my *dadi ji* has neatly filed away as addenda to the property deed, our photograph of the *juggah*, taken shortly after it was architecturally retrofitted in the 1970s, is prominently displayed on my *dadi ji*'s bedroom dresser. It is an architectural photograph of a religious kind; one that I grew up bowing my head toward. Imbued with the sacredness and open-ended visions of its architectural object, the *juggah* photograph might function as a sort of alternative philosophical guide to architectural practice, urging us to build an open world without religious borders, vernacular McMansions, or securitized gates.

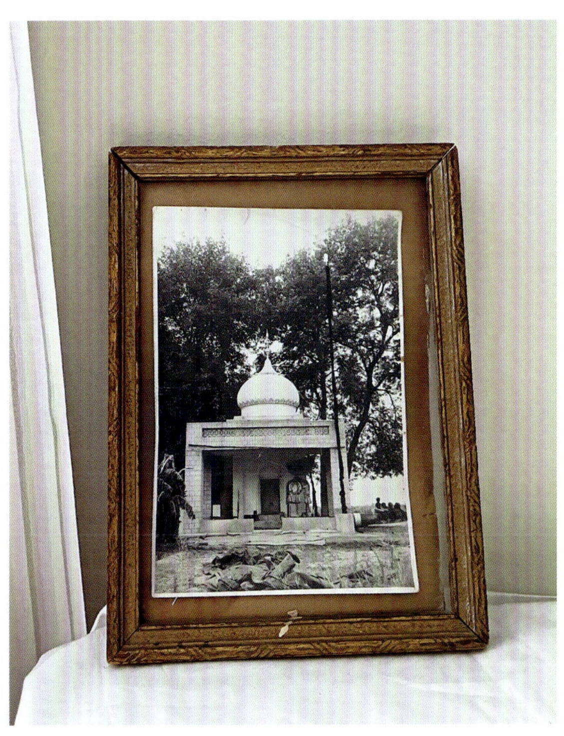

This photo, displayed in the Soomal house in Cambridge, Ontario, Canada, depicts the shrine in Paddi Khalsa.
Photo courtesy of Soomal family

## NOTES

1 For further details on the migration of the Harappan peoples, see Liviu Giosan, Peter D. Clift, Mark G. Macklin, Dorian Q. Fuller, Stefan Constantinescu, Julie A. Durcan, Thomas Stevens, et al., "Fluvial Landscapes of the Harappan Civilization," *Proceedings of the National Academy of Sciences* 109, no. 26 (2012): E1688–E1694; and Liviu Giosan, William D. Orsi, Marco Coolen, Cornelia Wuchter, Ann G. Dunlea, Kaustubh Thirumalai, Samuel E. Munoz, et al., "Neoglacial Climate Anomalies and the Harappan Metamorphosis," *Climate of the Past* 14, no. 11 (2018): 1669–86.

2 For more on the history of settlement following the Harappan era and into the Mughal period, see David Ludden, *An Agrarian History of South Asia* (Cambridge: Cambridge University Press, 2011). For later periods, see David Gilmartin, *Blood and Water: The Indus River Basin in Modern History* (Oakland: University of California Press, 2015); and Neeladri Bhattacharya, *The Great Agrarian Conquest: The Colonial Reshaping of a Rural World* (Albany: State University of New York Press, 2019).

3 For a history of this world-in-transition, read Chetan Singh, *Region and Empire: Panjab in the Seventeenth Century* (Delhi: Oxford University Press, 1991); and Indu Banga, *Agrarian System of the Sikh: Late Eighteenth and Early Nineteenth Century* (New Delhi: Manohar, 1978).

4 For more on the martial race theory in Punjab, see Heather Streets, *Martial Races: The Military, Race and Masculinity in British Imperial Culture, 1857–1914* (Manchester, UK: Manchester University Press, 2004).

5 Pervaiz Nazir, "Origins of Debt, Mortgage and Alienation of Land in Early Modern Punjab," *Journal of Peasant Studies* 27, no. 3 (2000): 55–91.

6 For details on the uneven accumulation of capital in the region during the early twentieth century, see Mridula Mukherjee, *Colonializing Agriculture: The Myth of Punjab Exceptionalism* (New Delhi: SAGE, 2005).

7 Gautam Bhatia, *Punjabi Baroque and Other Memories of Architecture* (New Delhi: Penguin Books India, 1994).

8 For more on the emergence of the bungalow in twentieth-century Punjab, see Madhavi Desai, Miki Desai, and Jon Lang, *The Bungalow in Twentieth-Century India: The Cultural Expression of Changing Ways of Life and Aspirations in the Domestic Architecture of Colonial and Post-colonial Society* (Farnham, UK: Ashgate, 2016).

9 Adrian Forty, *Concrete and Culture: A Material History* (London: Reaktion Books, 2013).

10 Vikramaditya Prakash, *Chandigarh's Le Corbusier: The Struggle for Modernity in Postcolonial India* (Seattle: University of Washington Press, 2002).

11 Shreekant Gupta, Shalini Saksena, and Omer F. Baris, "Environmental Enforcement and Compliance in Developing Countries: Evidence from India," *World Development* 117 (2019): 313–27.

12 Ciara Nugent, "Western Architecture Is Making India's Heatwaves Worse," *Time*, May 16, 2022.

13 Shamsher Samra, Julia Crowley, and Mary C. Smith Fawzi, "The Right to Water in Rural Punjab: Assessing Equitable Access to Water through the Punjab Rural Water Supply and Sanitation Project," *Health and Human Rights* 13, no. 2 (2011): 36–49.

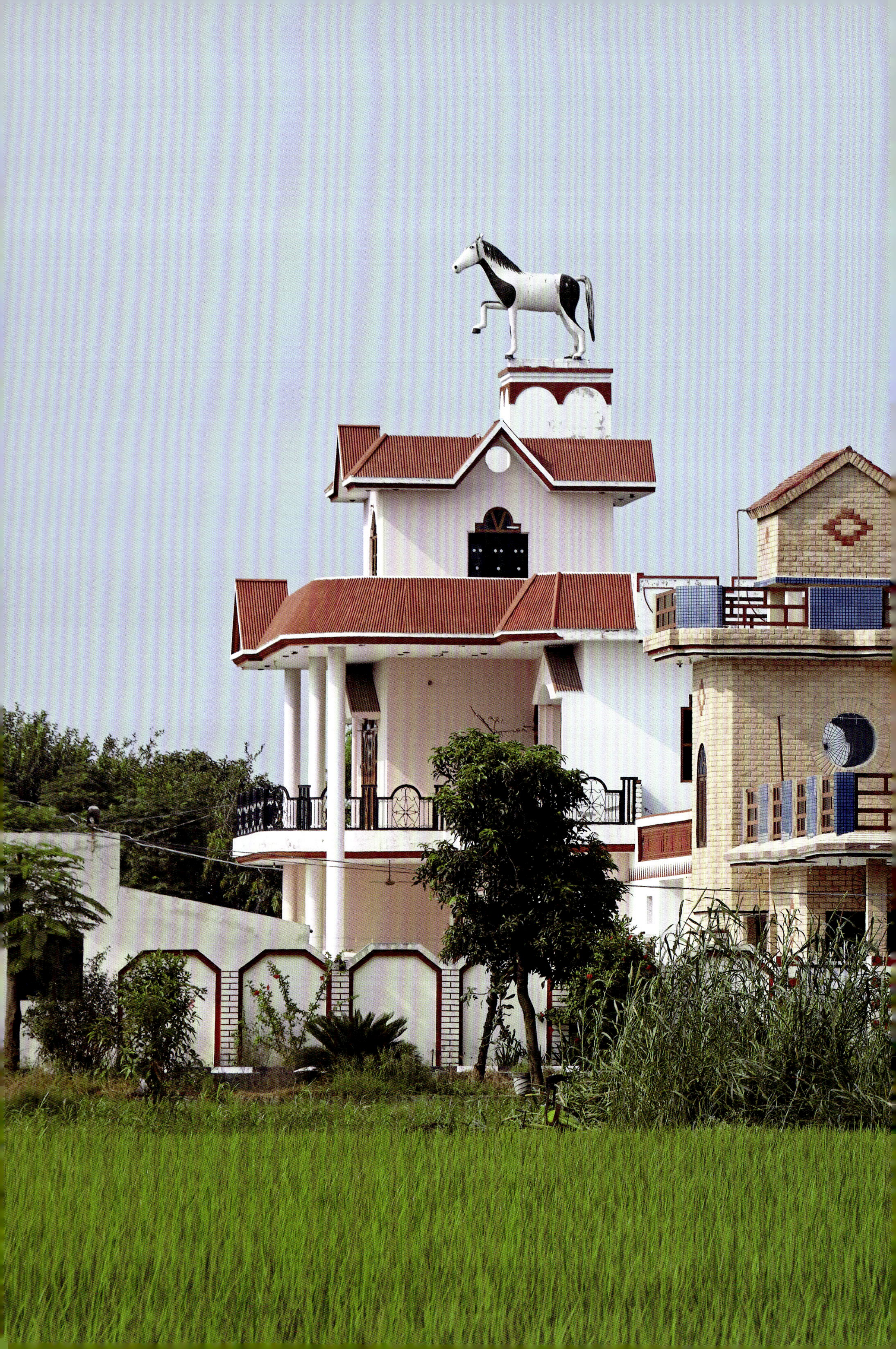

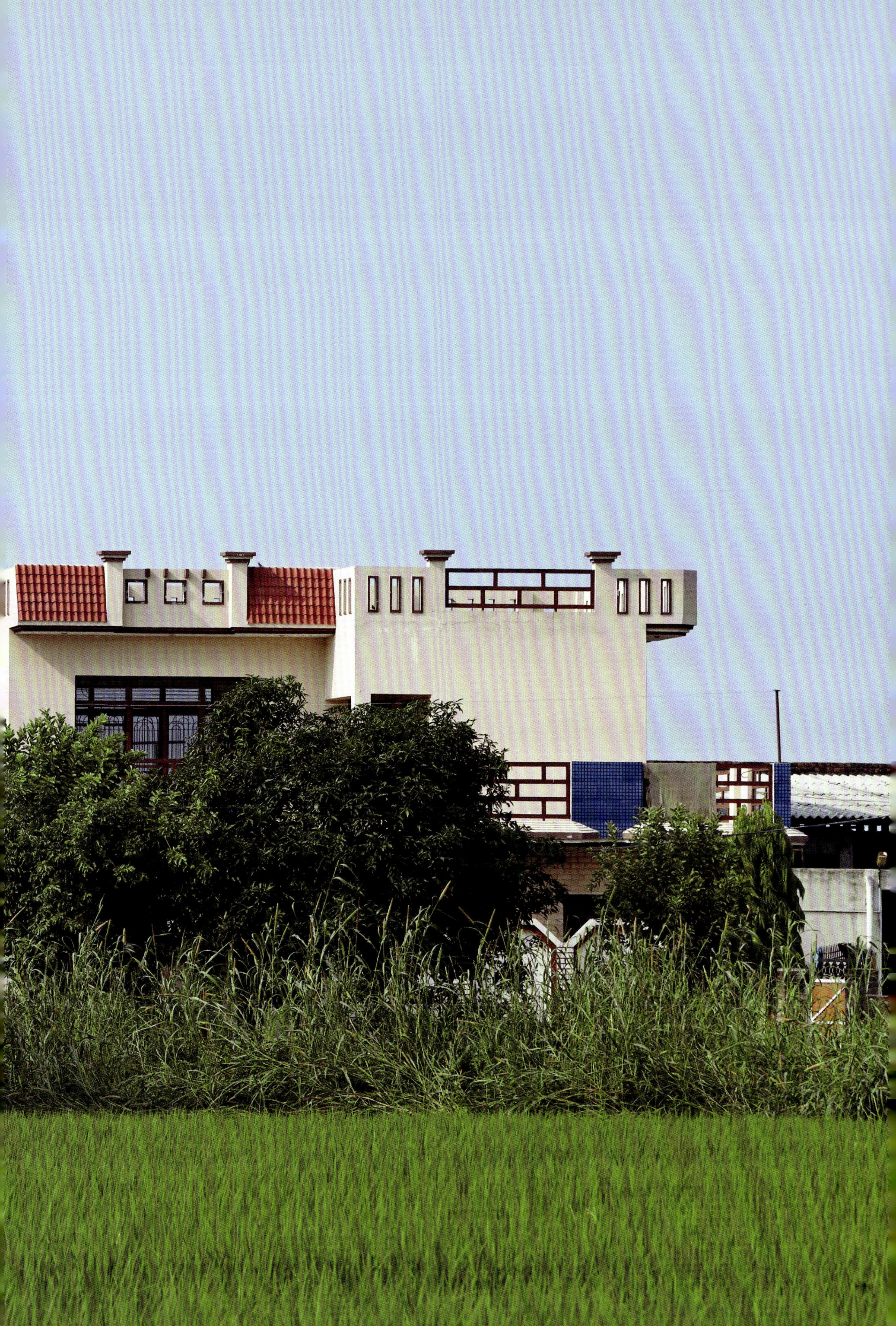

# (RE)MAKING HOME AWAY FROM HOME: MEMORY, BRAVADO, AND BELONGING

SATWINDER KAUR BAINS

**The landscape of rural Punjab is now punctuated, and in some areas of Doaba dominated, by huge brick, and often marble, built NRI (Non-Resident Indian) houses. Some of these are built on the site of an original or existing family farm, others on newly purchased land. Such sites constitute what [sociologist Avtar] Brah terms "diaspora spaces" within Punjab, and "the transnational Jat Sikh Punjabi pursuit of home has been directly shaped by the shifting economic, cultural and social context of Punjab, South Asia, and processes of social inclusion and exclusion therein."**

STEVE TAYLOR

I ARRIVED IN Vancouver, Canada, on November 15, 1975, as a young impressionable Punjabi Indian woman. Following the colonial notion engrained in my Indian education that the "West is best," I had rose-coloured glasses firmly planted on my nose. My acculturation and adaptation were swift, out of sheer necessity, and unbelievably painful at times because of the overt racism I experienced almost from day one. My first year was filled with the excitement of a new world—and also with tears that sprang from the melancholy of being separated from my home, family, and friends; hurt from the ignorant barbs and practices of Canadians; and the constant and relentless push to be a model minority on a trajectory of upward mobility at all costs. I learned soon enough that not giving up the identity markers that make me who I am was going to be a painful and uphill battle as Canada and Canadians tried to assimilate me into a similitude of Whiteness. Assimilating into Whiteness and giving up cultural identity markers (like clothes, accent, language, religion, etc.) was hardly my goal, especially as I got my bearings and the lay of the new land, but it would take many long and arduous years to find and be content with my own hybrid sense of self.

The landscapes I previously experienced—Punjab's vast fields of mustard, wheat, and rice—have slowly been superimposed by magnificent mountains, lush valleys, and the endless ocean. But for a long time the longing and yearning for my birth home did not subside, even while Canadian manifestations of home found room in my mind as I adapted to my new circumstances.

Since 1975 I have travelled back to Punjab frequently, and the familiarity of its streets, its people, its cities, its vistas, its landscapes always rushes up to me like a crashing wave of the ocean I temporarily leave behind in the Canadian west. The imagination I took with me of the land-left-behind is fully ignited and once more becomes real, albeit for a short time, while I visit relatives, work to restore heritage, marvel at the vast changes, and find quiet moments of reverie and contemplation. Visiting Punjab is inescapably a full-on sensory experience, with experiences that are larger than life and that evoke for me as a non-resident Indian myriad emotions.

My sense of voluntary displacement from India is sharpened by poignant memories that cling to my mind and resurrect themselves at the very hint of anything to do with Punjab or Punjabiyat, the movement to regenerate a shared cultural heritage. In Canada for the last forty-seven years, I have found many personal and professional pathways to ensure my active engagement with Punjab in my diasporic life. When I viewed and interacted with Rajesh Vora's photographic exhibition *Everyday Monuments*, I again tuned into the keen sense of nostalgia that lives in my bones and is a wellspring of reflection and introspection. His photographs flooded my visual senses with evocations of the idea of "home"; I felt the heart-wrenching ache of longing and belonging in my body. Along with that came this intimate, warm, and prideful sense of "knowing" what the monuments in the photographs mean to me and many Punjabis like me who have made new homes in the Canadian diaspora and elsewhere in the world.

The idea of home is fraught with much nostegia (a mix of nostalgia and amnesia) for most immigrants and refugees, and takes on poignant, often traumatic emotional meaning. If as an immigrant I see my first home (India) in terms of home-as-identity, speaking to the part of my self that affiliates with place, then Punjab and Punjabiyat (the ethos) certainly have shaped my identity. However, the memory of Punjab as a physical space has been both blurred and intensified by my transnational travels and what I now embrace as my Canadian identity. I have slowly but surely replaced those physical spaces of my past with tightly woven and easily recovered memories that I aim to protect from the unavoidable deterioration of the mind as I age. The new home (Canada) now fills my daily social, physical, and cultural spaces, and this spatial attachment has invaded my old spaces (India) with great alacrity. However, both hold prime space in my memory bank—one from my youth and one from my current life. Do they meet and collide at times, or are they on distinctly separate yet parallel tracks?

When I encountered Vora's photographs, my old and new homes collided but the train of my thoughts and memories chugged along. The emotional meanings rooted in his photos at times made me stand still: the idiosyncratic forms of self-expression, of joyful identity construction, of pride in diasporic contributions to the homeland and showing off success, sometimes in far-off lands. I moved slowly through his exhibition to savour it. Each photograph tells a story of the meaning held in the sculpture, in its artistry and crafting, and in its final position on a rooftop—there for all to see, not requiring a formal invitation into the home—where it contributes to a landscape that reaches for the skies. My memories of home came rushing back as I unravelled the stories of migration, healthy comradery and competition, home and hearth, personal agency, and cultural crafts that are embedded in these sculptures. I came to realize that the temporal dimension of the idea of home has left an imprint on my mind that is triggered by the senses, no matter how far I have come from that home. And I have to ask myself—does the utopian-nostalgic character of my memories somehow romanticize these memories?

Critically important for me is to understand the tug of memories from a previous home when I am now so ensconced within my home in Canada, where I have lived longer than in India. But I realize that space and time do not dull the keen sense of belonging and the multi-dimensional experience of home even when one is away from it for long periods. Canada and India are halfway across the globe from each other, but the two countries claim parts of my heart, spirit, and soul in ways that are complementary and supportive. This merger of identities brings into sharp relief that which formed me as a youth and that

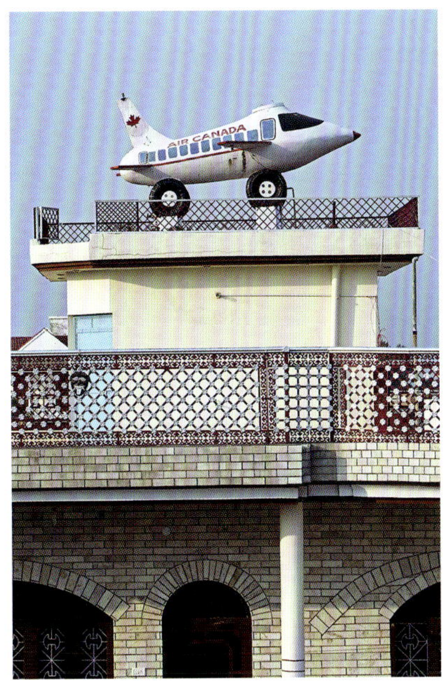
AIR CANADA

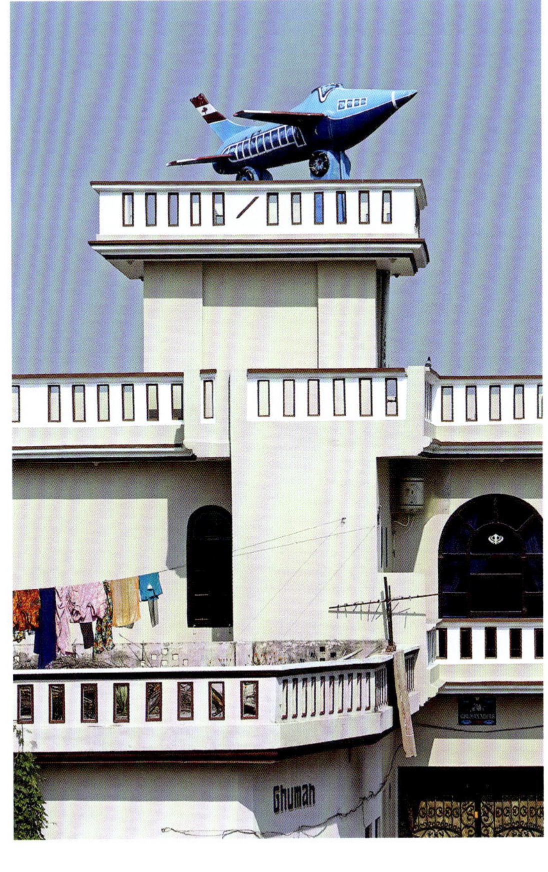
Ghumah

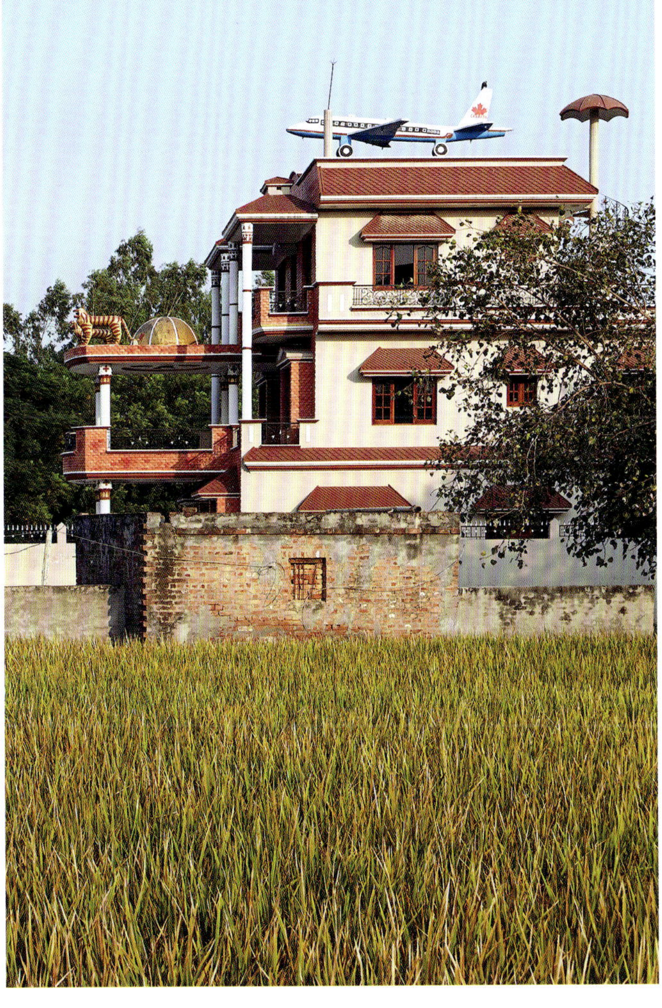

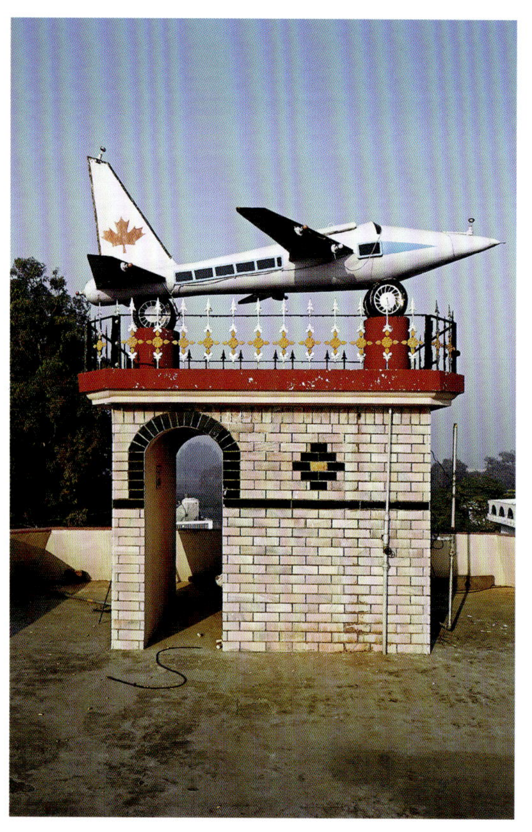

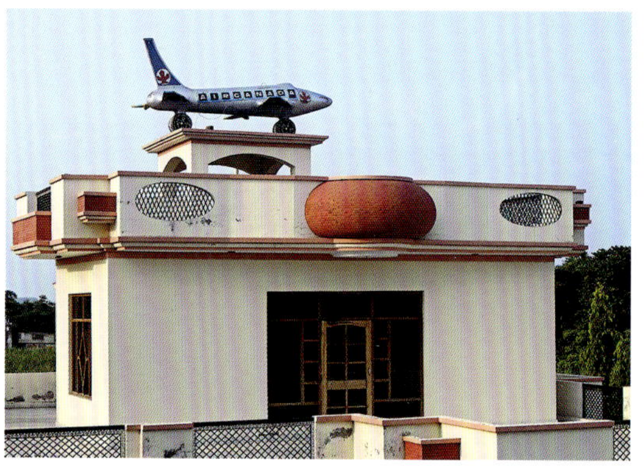

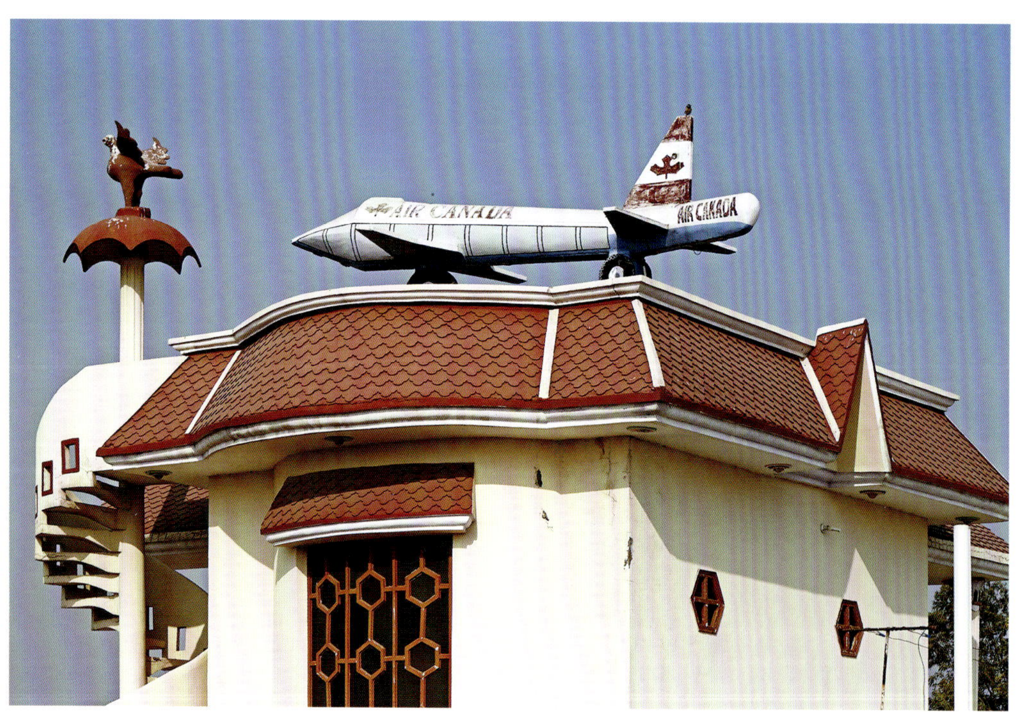
AIR CANADA
AIR CANADA

which contributed as I matured. It is clear that Canada has a place in Punjab's reality and imagination as the land and its people have created a fertile plain for migration to Canada for more than one hundred years. With our agrarian roots providing the means (land as disposable income), Punjabis have travelled to Canada since the late 1800s, arriving to a land that was considered raw and unsettled, waiting to be explored by colonists. No mention was made at the time of the devastating effects of creating a new nation: the displacement of Indigenous Peoples and appropriation of their land, the efforts to annihilate their cultures and languages, the erosion of the heritages of civilizations. Neither did the migrant/settler Punjabis ask whose land they were stepping upon and settling within. The irreparable legacies of the British Raj in India are also written on the bodies of Punjabis, but here in Canada the truth of Indigenous Peoples' colonial experiences is yet to be fully understood and reconciled.

Longing for the past is a common inclination of immigrant groups. Actively keeping nostalgic memories of the past alive through ritual, custom, tradition, art, music, language, religion, food, and so on is commonplace among non-Indigenous Canadians, and I am no exception. While nostalgia may be seen as a sentimental barrier to full participation in a new country, it provides a kind of solace to the soul, one that nourishes well-being and uplifts the spirit. Giving up one's home, as the cost of gaining a new one, is hardly a desired state as the experiences of home(s) create social bonds that generate a sense of security and warmth from any inclemently negative elements.

Rajesh Vora's *Everyday Monuments* speaks to a kind of storytelling that otherwise may remain locked in the family home and the circles that have access to it. The significant and beckoning monuments on the rooftops of Punjabi homes tell of effort, sacrifice, and joy in a way that is borderless, boldly encouraging, and not shy of judgment. It begs the question, why are Punjabis so keen to tell their story to their communities in such a unique and extravagant manner? Especially when the homes are empty part of the year because of global migration, with snowbirds from the West spending only the winter in their Punjab homes. I believe that the inner home within the Punjabi mind is never closed to exploration and that design and community have meaning beyond the criss-crossing of homes in narrow village alleys. Punjabis carry the idea of home with them wherever they go and bring back their migration story for others to partake in and take courage from. The monuments seem to say, you too can go far away and come back and tell us what you hold dear. The monuments speak to the transcending of cultural boundaries, where Punjabis experience home within Canada by transculturally sharing their journeys with others in India who might aspire to do the same. The social capital they bring back with them is paralleled by their economic capital (and its clout)—so evident in the larger-than-life water tanks and monuments that "adorn" their rooftops.

*Everyday Monuments* is testament to those who migrated in the 1960s and '70s following the liberalization of immigration policies and amid the promulgation of multiculturalism in Canada. They have traversed the oceans to (re)build their homes, and now find pride of place for monuments that speak to their journeys in myriad ways. No singular monument is completely protected from imitation, as collectively they speak to the upward mobility of families and individuals in a bold, graphic, and intricate mix of time periods, genres, and styles. As time, the great divider, goes on, newer generations of Canadian-born Punjabis may never have the same nostalgic drive to feel and memorialize the connection between two homes, separated as they are by distance, memory, experience, and ancestry. The part of the idea of home that depends on lived experience of the place will slowly ebb and die as the transcultural mingling of experiences dwindles with each generation, forcing a further separation between the parents' past and the present.

For Punjabis experiencing Vora's photographs of Punjab landscapes in the context of Canada, their two homes are suddenly thrown together in one place, stepping into and out of at the same time. The photos prove that migration is not a neutral act; that new, improved mobility has made the home-left-behind accessible like never before and that this allows a continuous unabashed claim to "home." That claim is loudly exhibited for all to see, in a form of swagger that holds within it the Punjabiyat that Punjabis continue to hold so dear. The ostentatious home and the various monuments that serve as water tanks are not intended to be viewed with derision by visitors; rather, their form is to be accepted as functional and decorative, filled with expression, and excused for their size by their success-oriented messaging. And herein lies the weight of the matter: as a largely agrarian state, Punjab's access to clean potable water provides the wealth for this agricultural community. The tanks symbolize a wealth beyond the capital that migration has produced; they further symbolize the diasporic pursuit of home and belonging—by looking back and memorializing a past, present, and future. There continues to be an attachment to the "people, places and … imagined home[s] of Punjab."[1]

While Vora is a photographer of architecture and cultural subject matter, here he has lovingly created a collection of photographs that defy simple analysis. Exhibiting at Surrey Art Gallery in British Columbia, with local curator Keith Wallace, was a stroke of genius because the site provided a valuable backdrop of the diaspora in the region and beyond. This critically important backdrop is steeped in cultural pride, nostegia, and understanding of longing, which provided Vora and Wallace with a user experience that cannot be duplicated elsewhere.

## NOTES

EPIGRAPH: Steve Taylor, "'Home Is Never Fully Achieved … Even When We Are in It': Migration, Belonging and Social Exclusion within Punjabi Transnational Mobility," *Mobilities* 10, no. 2 (2015): 199, https://doi.org/10.1080/17450101.2013.848606; citing Avtar Brah, *Cartographies of Diaspora: Contesting Identities* (London: Routledge, 1996), chapter 8, 175–207.

1 Taylor, 208–9.

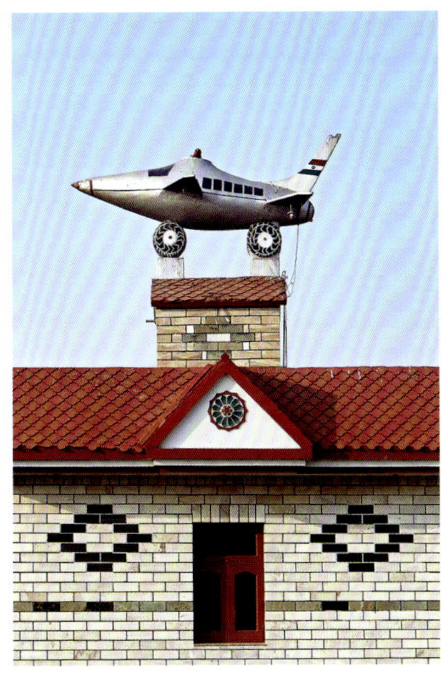

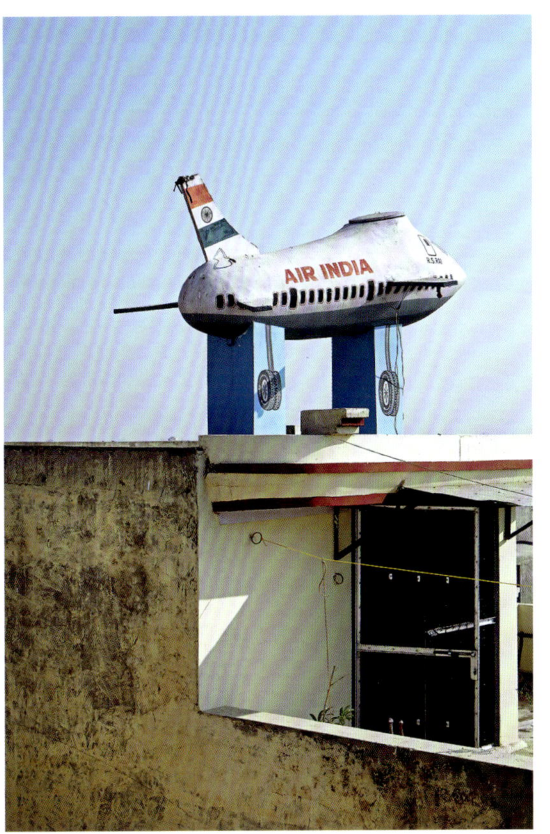
AIR INDIA

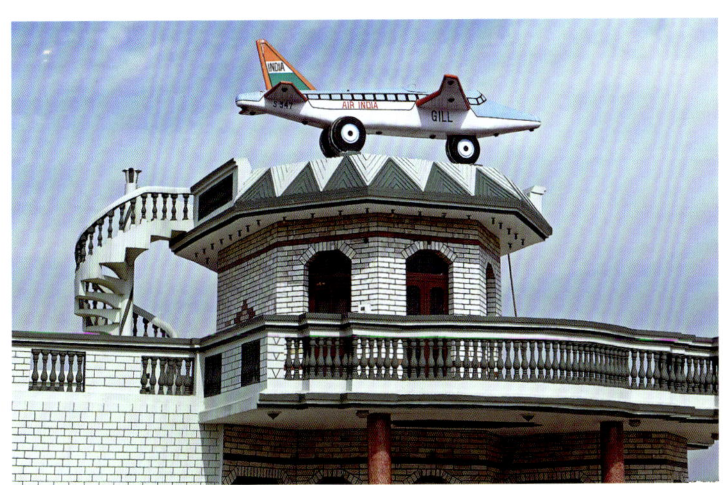
INDIA
AIR INDIA
GILL

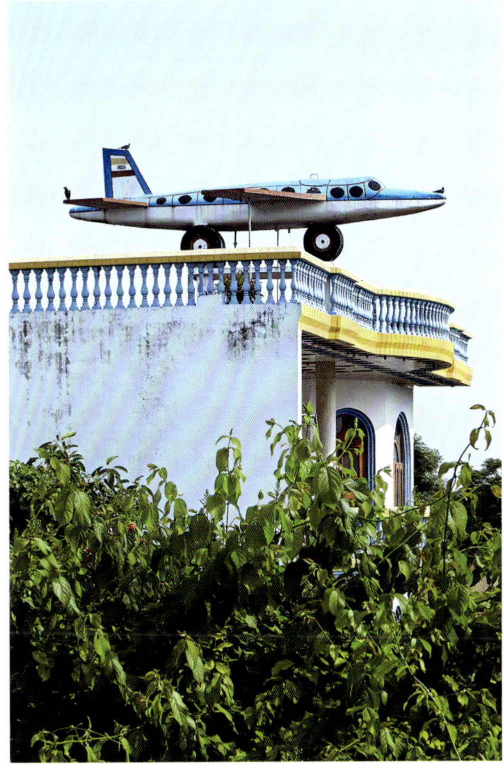

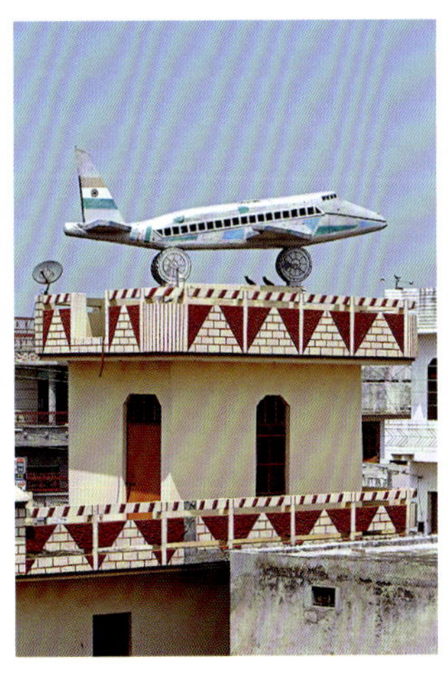

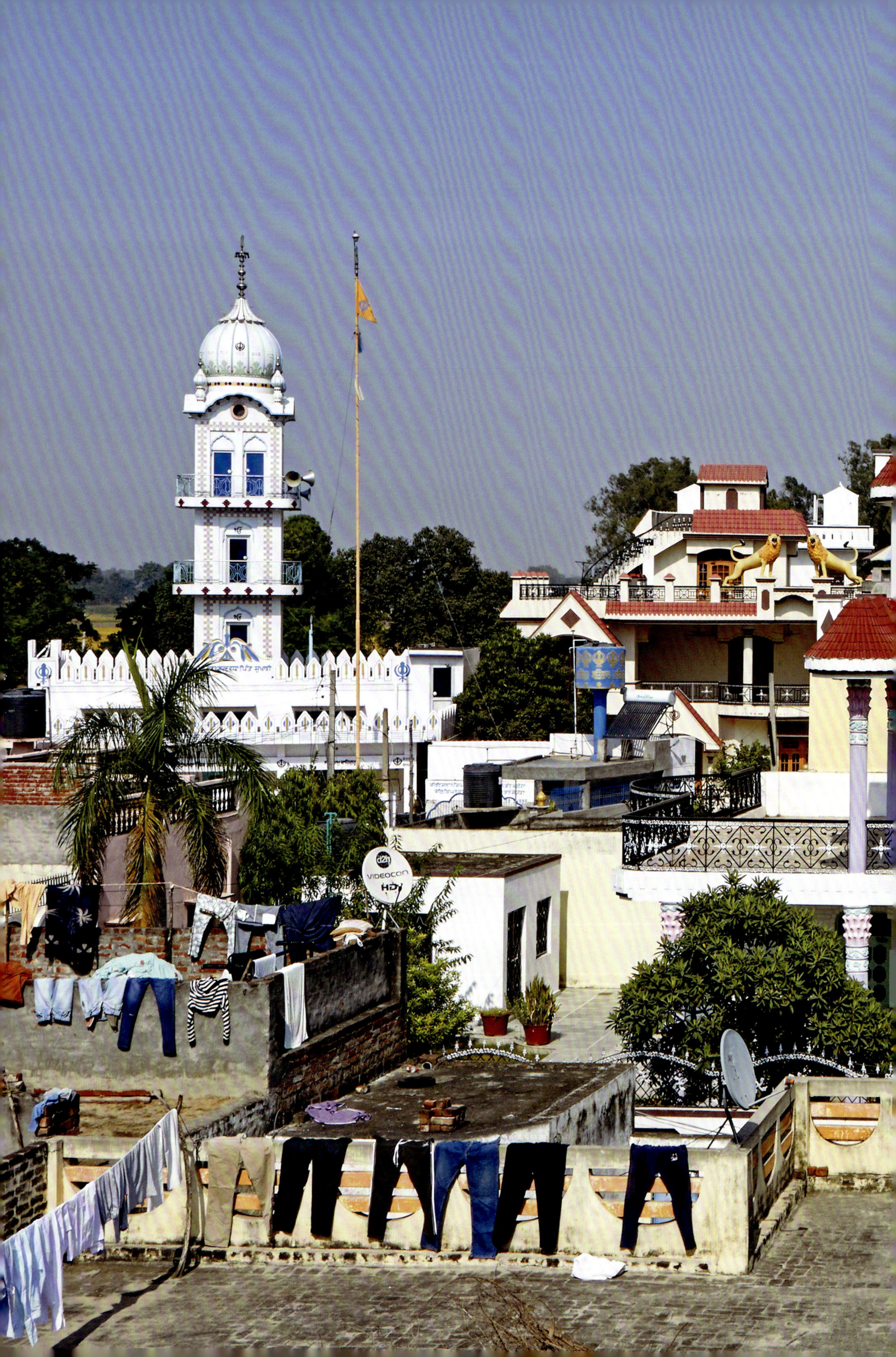
d2h
VIDEOCON
HD

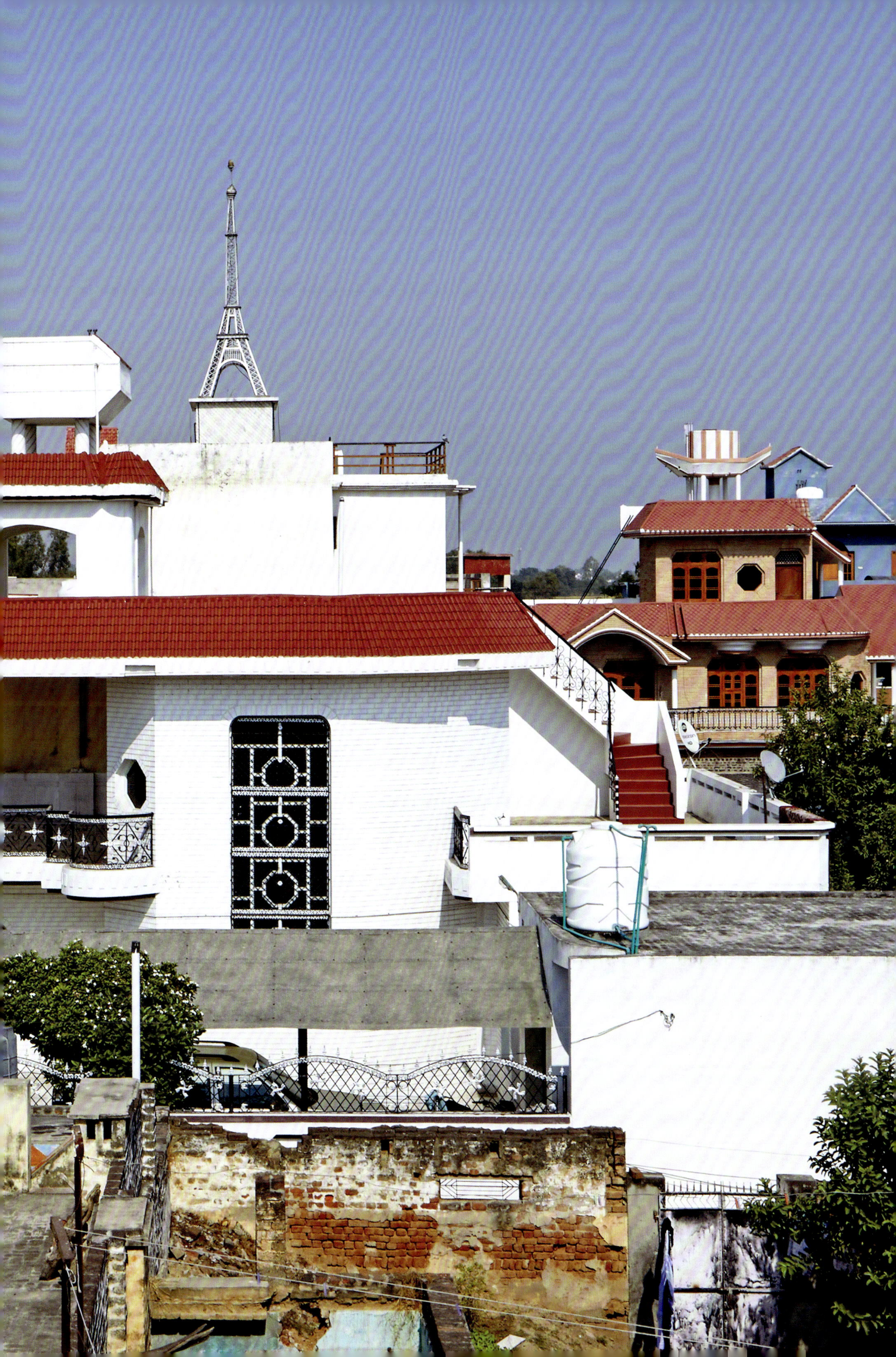

# ACKNOWLEDGMENTS

**RAJESH VORA** I am deeply grateful to the villagers of Punjab who warmly welcomed and opened their doors for me to photograph their homes. Without their hospitality, this project would not have been accomplished.

I am thankful to Devika Daulet-Singh for her support from the start of the project and for exhibiting my early photographs from this series at PHOTOINK, New Delhi. A special thanks to Keith Wallace, who understood and believed in my work, travelled with me to Punjab, and worked tirelessly to see that my photographs were shared with the Punjabi population in Surrey, BC. I was delighted to be part of his journey.

I am indebted to Surrey Art Gallery for inviting me to exhibit my project, and sponsoring a publication, and valuably enabling the exhibition to travel to other venues. I can't forget each individual at the gallery who contributed so eloquently and expertly that I have no words to express. The publishing team at Figure 1 were wonderful collaborators in helping me realize this substantive book.

Many friends were there to help me when I was down and had doubts about my project—thank you to Jon Alff, Pradeep Dalal, Aashna Jhaveri, Sanjay Kothari, Savia Mahajan, Rahul Mehrotra, Swapan Parekh, Aurobind Patel, Amandeep Sandhu, Ketki Seth, Paulomi Shah, Mahendra Sinh, Isha Vora, and Ram Pratap Yadav.

Lastly, I would like to thank artist-fabricators Sonu Lobhiya and Davinder Kumar and other artists of Doaba, Punjab, whom I couldn't meet during my trips.

**KEITH WALLACE** I would like to thank Surrey Art Gallery and its staff for their support in making this exhibition and book possible, and Rajesh Vora whose work is the inspiration. Thanks also to Mohamed Ahmed, Dr. Satwinder Kaur Bains, John Bass, Balwinder Bassi, Dinesh Bhagat, Dr. Rajinder Bhandari, Jo-Anne Birnie Danzker, British Columbia Arts Council Project Assistance for Visual Artists, Devika Daulet-Singh, Herb Dhaliwal, Sukhwant Singh Dhillon, Diana Freundl, Dr. Gurdev Gill, Harbhajan S. Gill, Gurnam Hundel, Thamilini Jothilingam, Kulvinder Lehal, Diwan Manna, Priya Ramesh Mehta, Helga Pakasaar, Sadira Rodrigues, Dharminder Sharma, J.P. Singh, Gayatri Sinha, and Rajnish Wattas.

# VILLAGES VISITED AND PHOTOGRAPHED

During several trips to the Doaba region of Punjab between 2014 and 2019, Rajesh Vora photographed rooftop sculptures in over 150 villages.

**HOSHIARPUR DISTRICT**

Basiala
Dansiwal
Datta
Gujarpur
Hoshiarpur (city)
Kot Fatuhi
Kotli
Mahilpur (town)
Mananhana
Mandhali
Mohanwal
Tanda
Thinda
Tuto Mazara

**KAPURTHALA DISTRICT**

Baler Khanpur
Bhandal Dona
Bhanoki
Chachoki
Chaheru
Dhapai
Fattu Chak
Jallowal
Khaira
Khangura
Kheri (Sapror)
Kotla (Kotllay)
Mehat
Nangal Majja (Sapror)
Nangal Sapror
Narur
Nathu Chahal
Pader
Palahi
Paroo Majra
Phagwara
Prempur
Rampur Khalian
Sahni
Sukhani
Tashpur
Thakarki

**JALANDHAR DISTRICT**

Athoula
Attowal
Bara Pind
Bath Kalan
Bhogpur
Bir Bansian
Bir Pind
Boparai
Budhiana
Chak Khurd
Chak Vendal
Chamiara
Dhaliwal
Dhapli
Dhuleta
Doshanj Kalan
Gakhal
Garhi Mahan Singh
Goraya
Haripur
Jamsher Khera
Jand
Jandiala Manjki
Johal
Kabulpur
Kandola Kalan
Kang Araian
Khaira
Khaira Majja
Khaira Patian
Khela
Kot Kalan
Kotli Khakhian
Kular
Littran
Madhopur
Mallian Kalan
Mathda Khurd
Mehatpur
Mohem
Muradpur
Nagar
Nakodar (town)
Nangal Fateh Khan
Nauli
Pachranga
Paddi Khalsa
Pandori Khas
Patara
Pawar Pind
Pratab Pura
Rama Mandi
Rurka Kalan
Safipur
Sangha Jagir
Talhan
Thabalke
Umarpur
Uppal Bhupa
Uppal Khalsa
Virk (Birka)

**NAWANSHAHR DISTRICT**

Bahua
Banga
Barnala Kalan
Barwa
Bisla-Behram
Chahal Khurd
Chak Guru
Chak Mander
Chuharpur
Daulatapur
Garcha
Hapowal
Jhander Kalan
Jhikka (Ladhana)
Jhingran
Kamachon
Karnana
Kultham
Mahal Khurd
Mandhali
Mehrampur
Mubarakpur
Nai Mazara
Nano Mazara
Nawanshahr (town)
Punnu Mazara
Saloh
Sandhwan
Sarhala Ranuan
Soondh

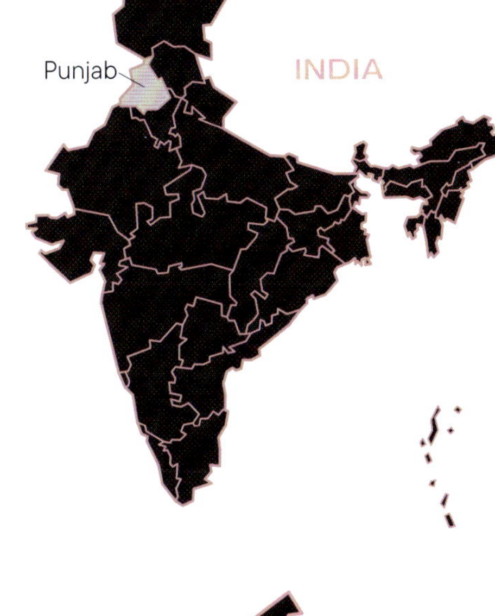


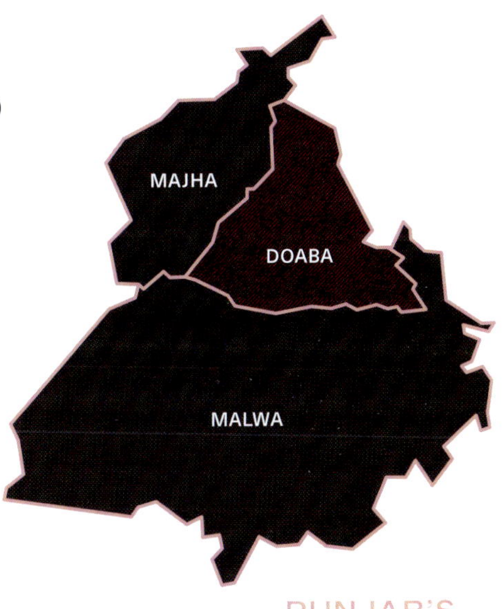


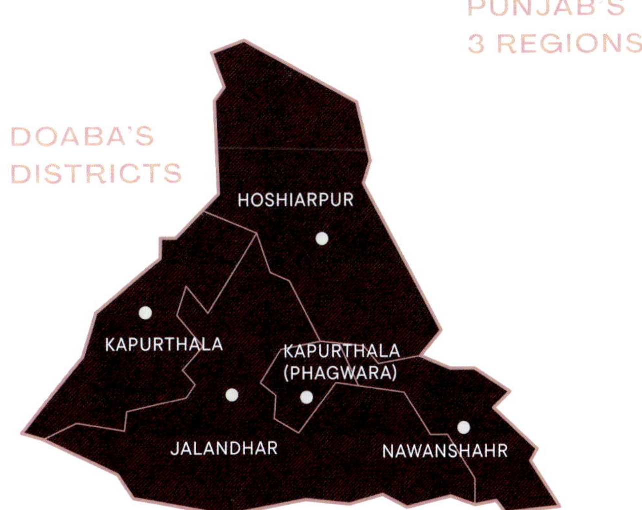

# EXHIBITION VIEWS

*Rajesh Vora: Everyday Monuments*, Surrey Art Gallery, April 9 to May 29, 2022, Guest Curator Keith Wallace.

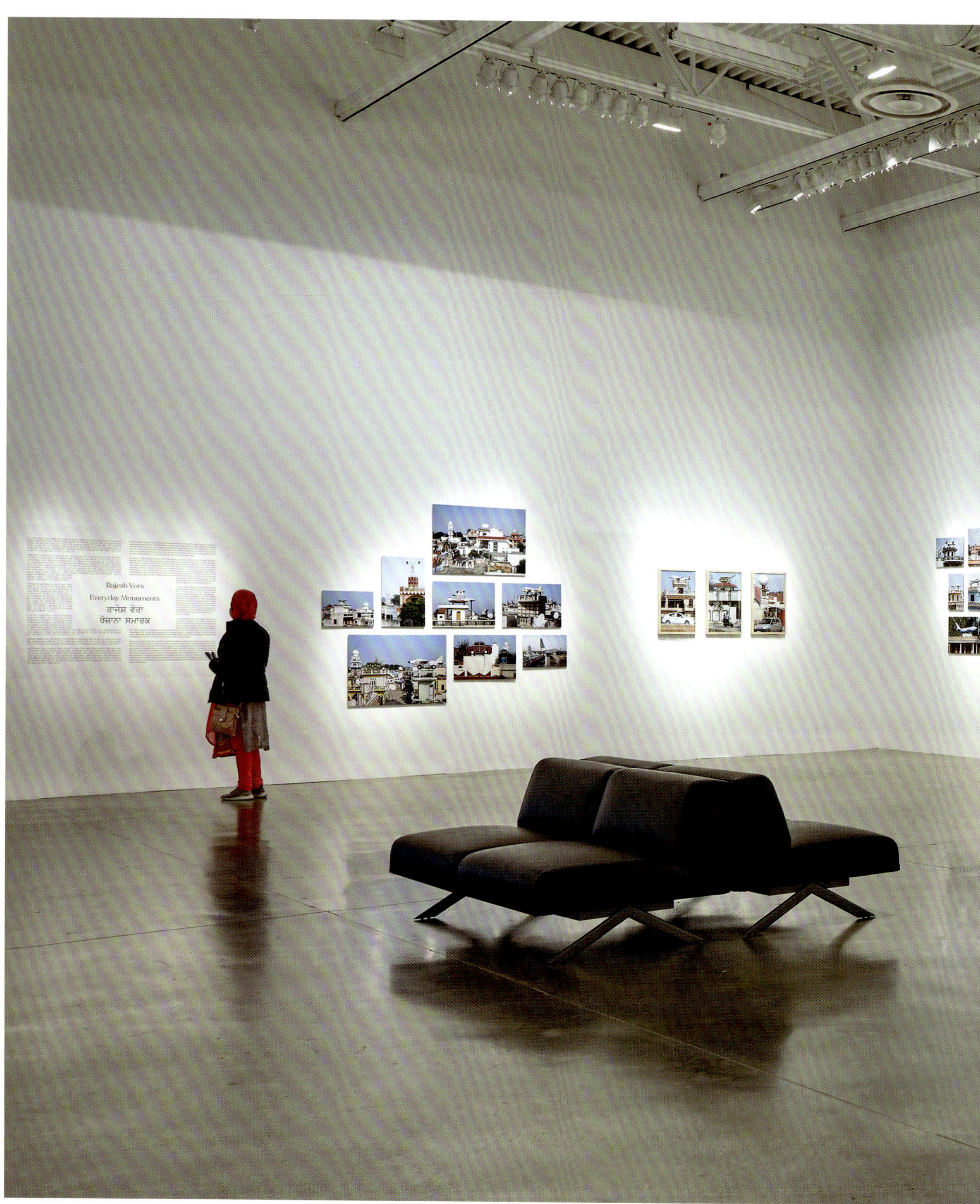


East and south gallery walls

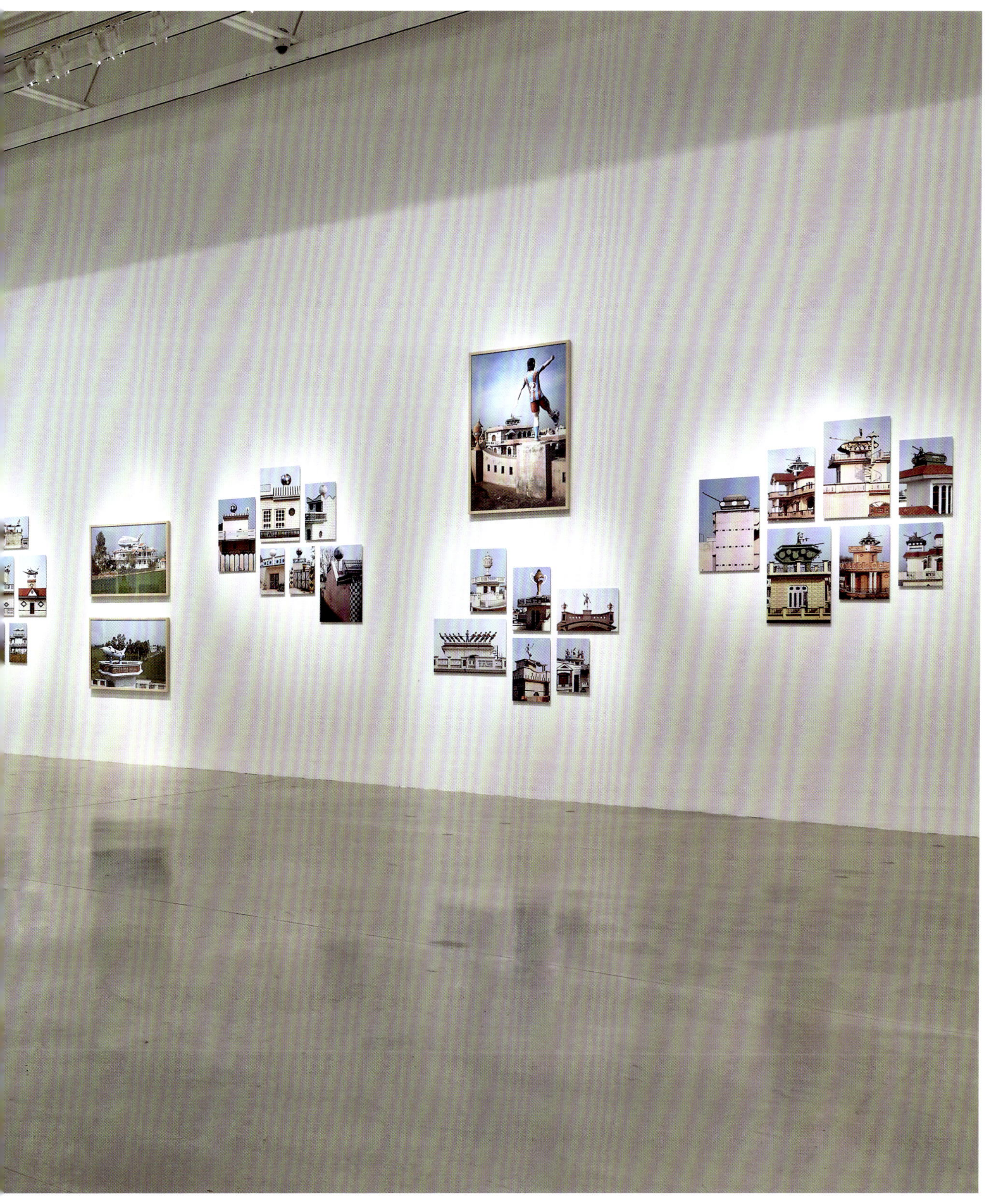

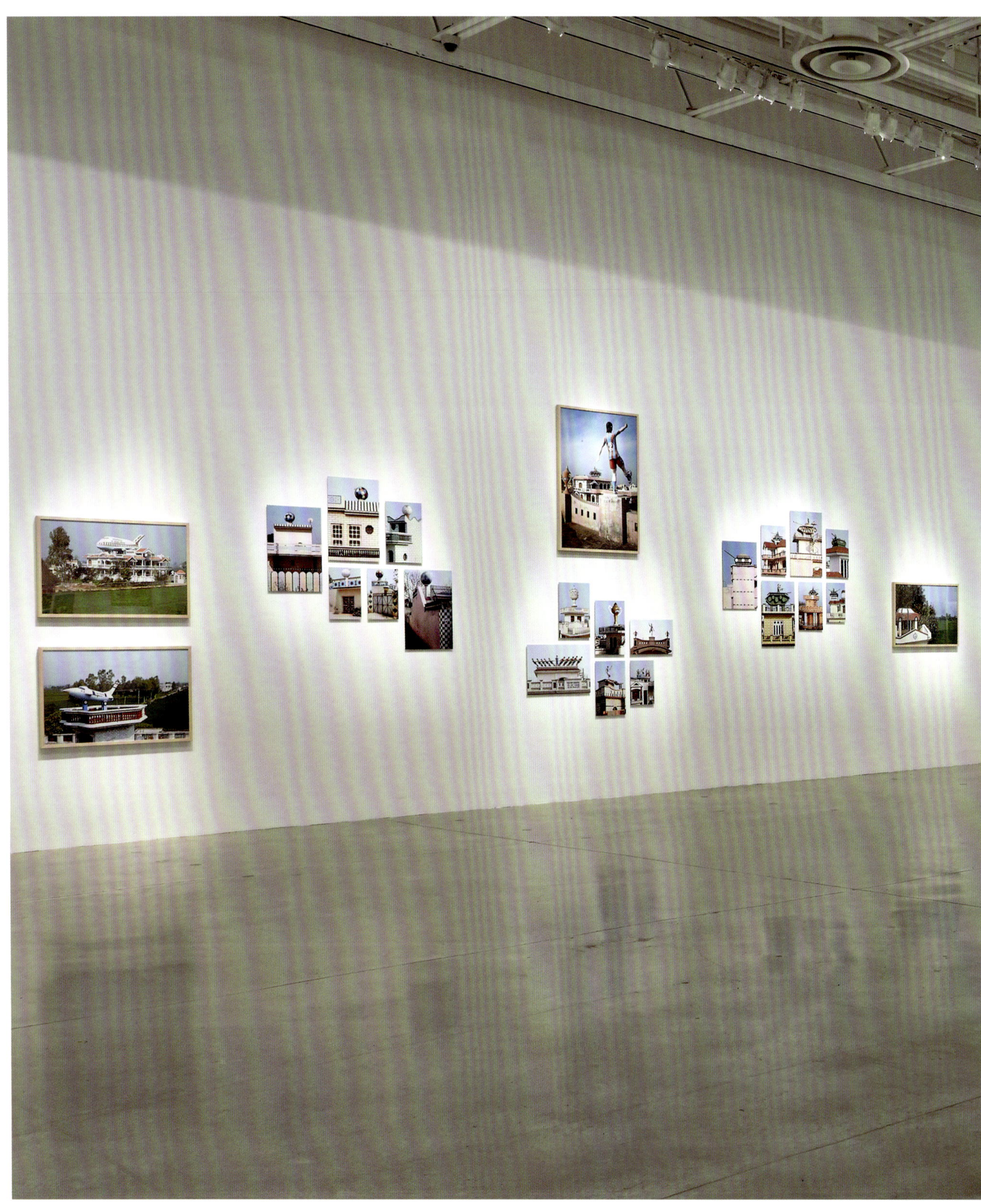

South and west gallery walls

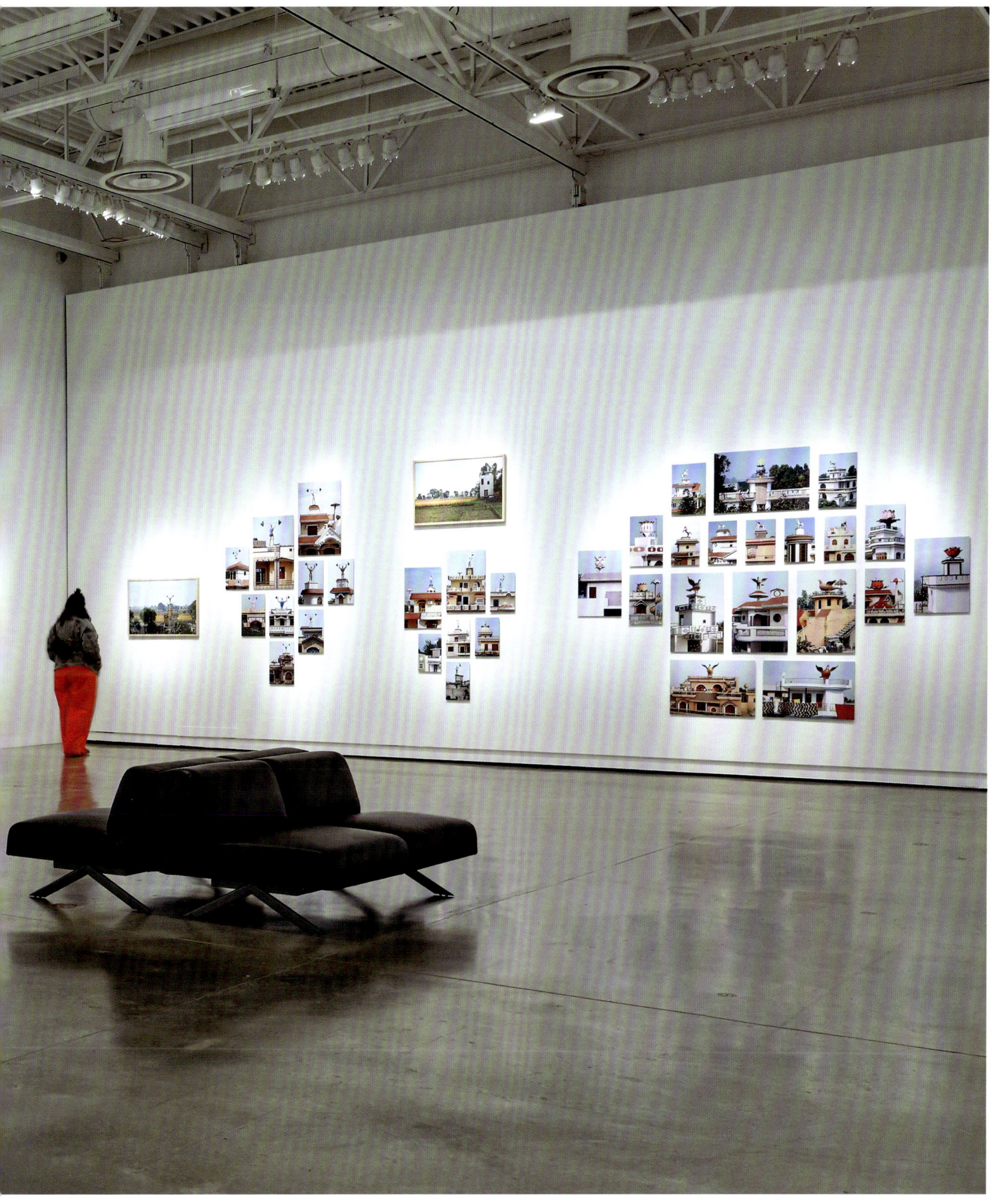

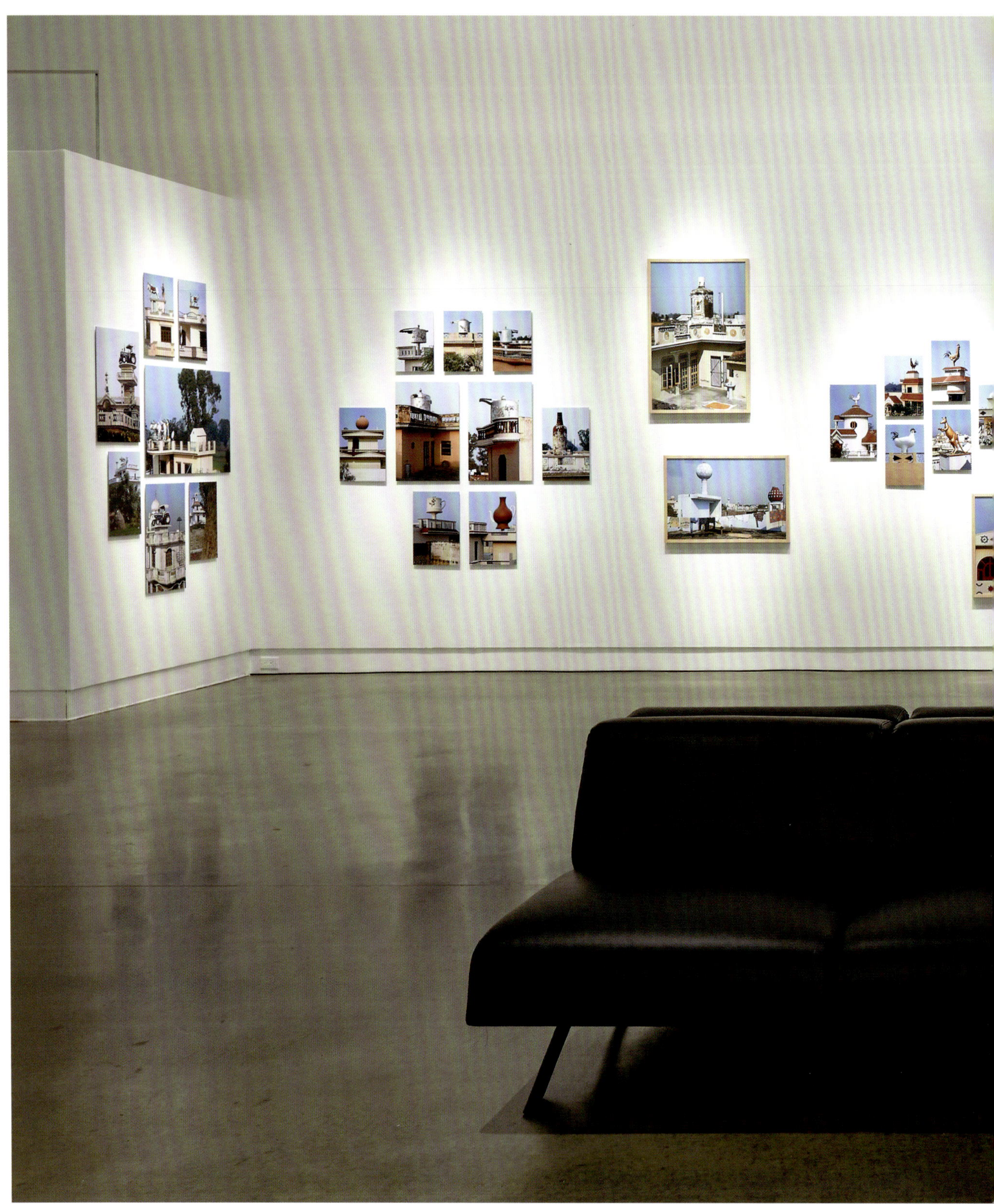

North gallery wall

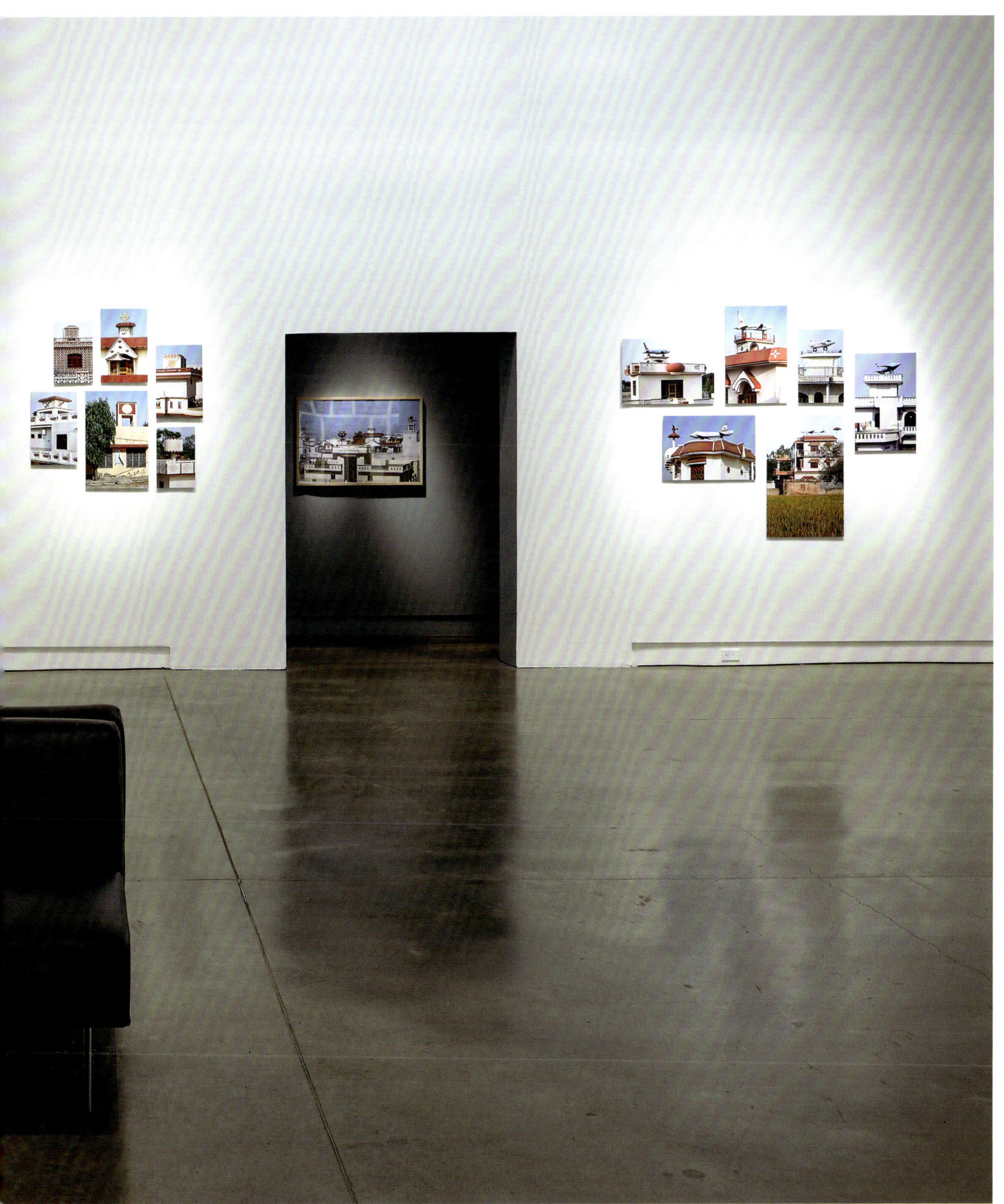

# LIST OF WORKS

Works that were not included in the *Everyday Monuments* exhibition are indicated with an *asterisk. Dates refer to the creation of the photographs, not the sculptures. All photographs are inkjet prints, dimensions variable.

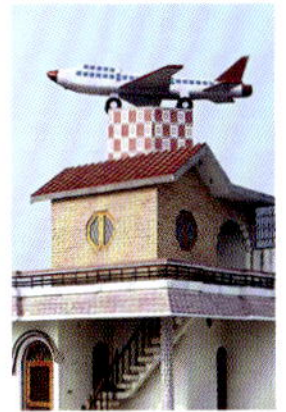

Cover, airplane,
village unknown, 2014

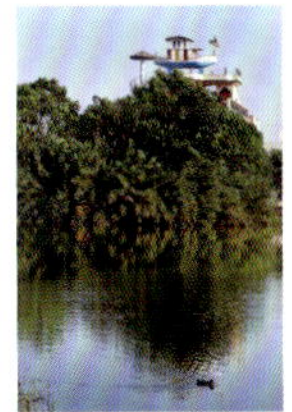

Endsheet/flyleaf, *ship,
village of Bir Bansian, 2019

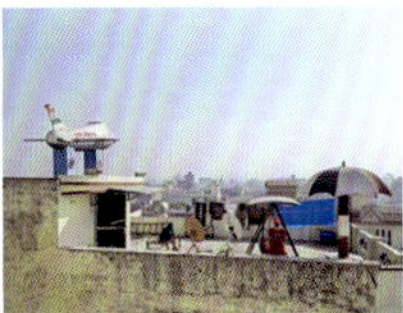

pp. 4–5, *village of
Boparai, 2015

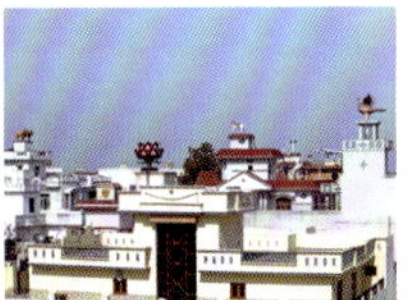

pp. 8–9, village of
Paddi Khalsa, 2015

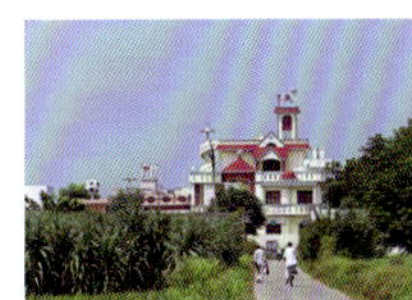

pp. 14–15, *town of
Nawanshahr, 2015

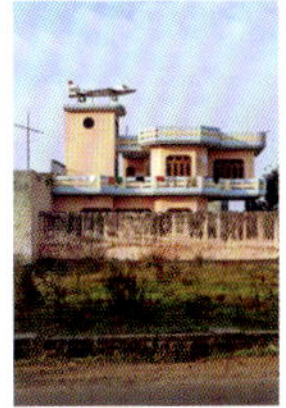

p. 19, *airplane,
village of Banga, 2015

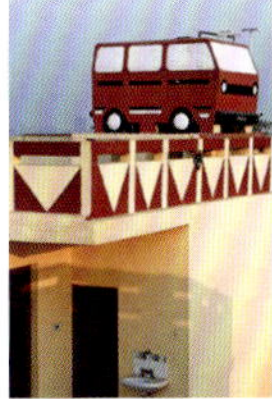

p. 20, *Maruti van,
village of Mehat, 2014

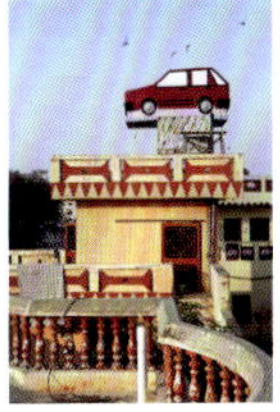

p. 21, *Maruti car,
village of Khaira, 2014

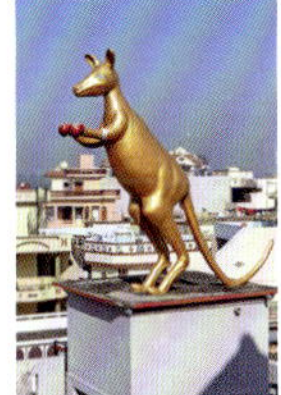

p. 23, kangaroo,
village of Chaheru, 2019

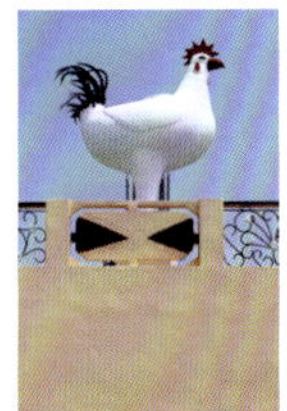

p. 24, rooster,
village of Soondh, 2015

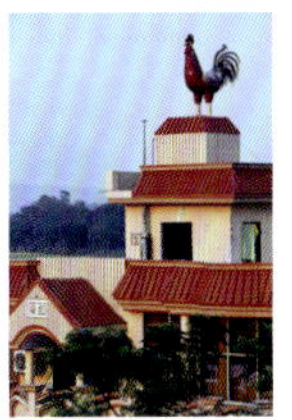

p. 25, rooster,
village of Basiala, 2019

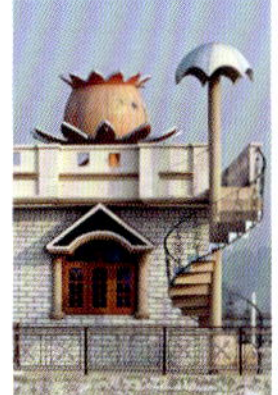

p. 26, lotus flower,
town of Nakodar, 2015

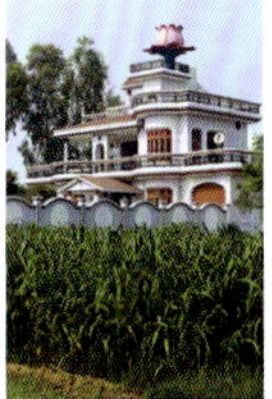

p. 27, *lotus flower,
village of Mehatpur, 2015

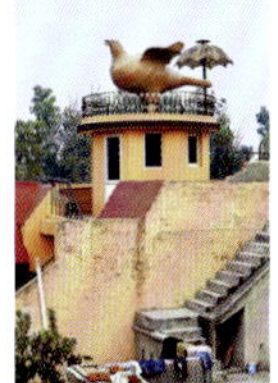

p. 29, falcon,
village of Hapowal, 2019

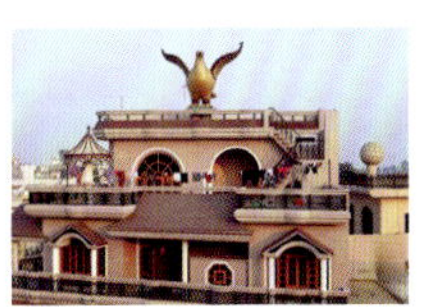

pp. 30–31, falcon,
village of Mehatpur, 2014

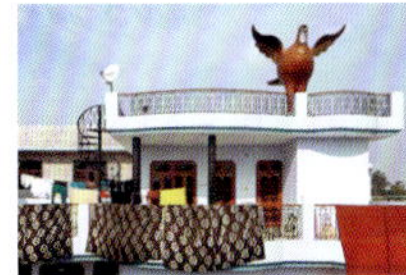

pp. 32–33, falcon,
village of Mathda Khurd, 2015

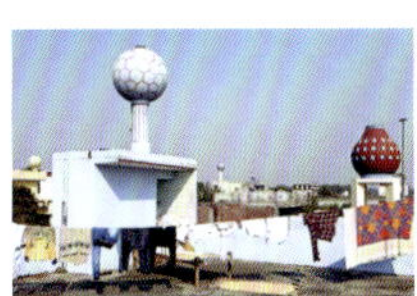

pp. 34–35, footballs and
water pot, village of
Garhi Mahan Singh, 2015

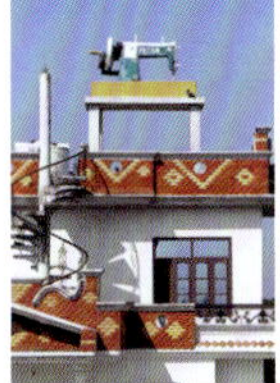

p. 36, *sewing machine,
village of Gujarpur, 2019

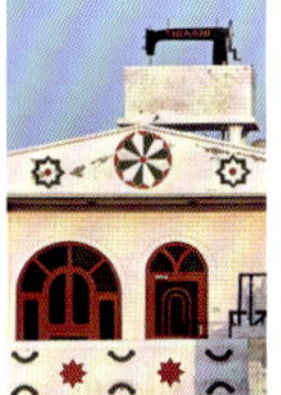

p. 37, sewing machine,
village of Kular, 2015

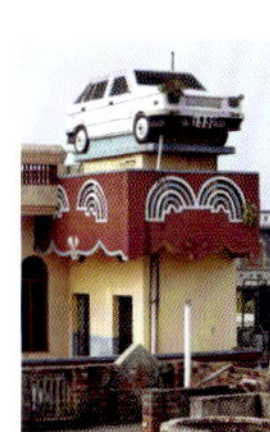

p. 39, Maruti car,
village of Chak Guru, 2014

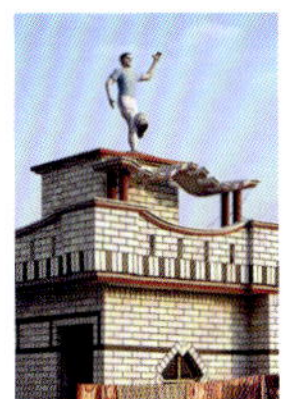

p. 40, football player,
village of Palahi, 2014

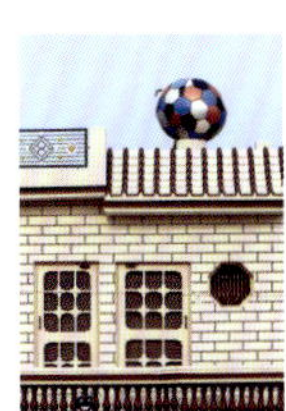

p. 41, football,
village of Barnala Kalan, 2015

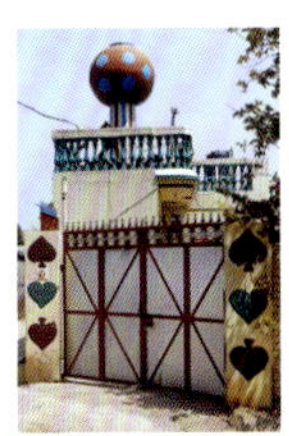

p. 42, football,
village of Bhandal Dona, 2015

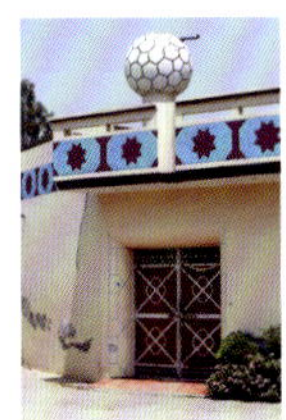

p. 43, football,
village of Kular, 2015

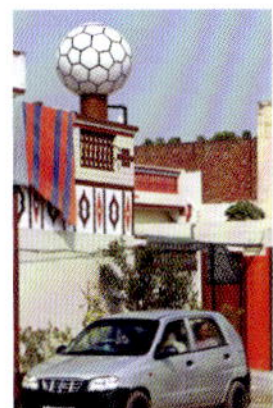

p. 45, football,
village of Bath Kalan, 2015

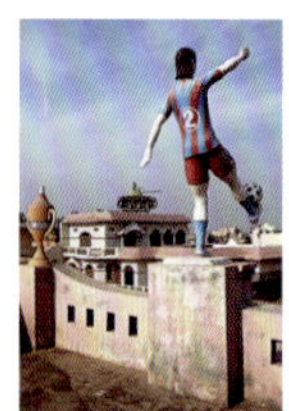
p. 46, football player, village of Jandiala Manjki, 2014

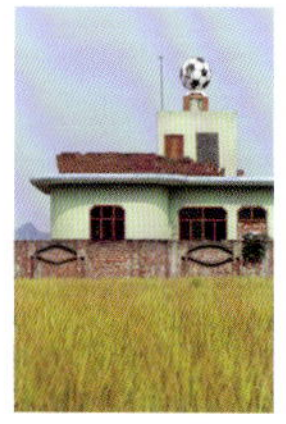
p. 48, *football, village of Tanda, 2015

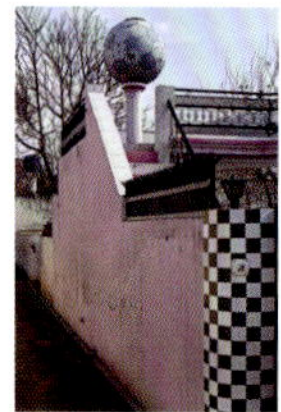
p. 49, football, village of Datta, 2015

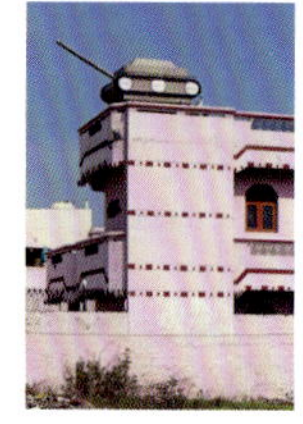
p. 51, *army tank, village of Virk (Birka), 2015

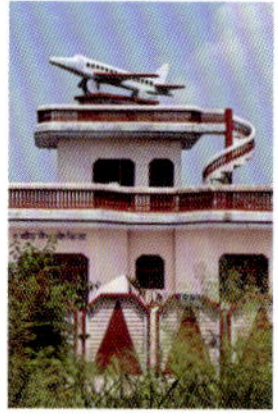
p. 53, airplane, village of Sandhwan, 2015

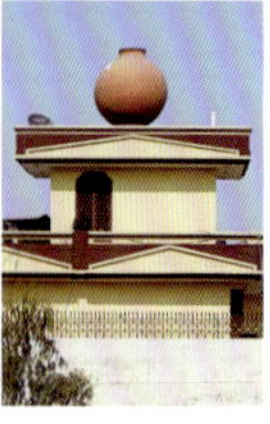
p. 54, water pot, village of Virk (Birka), 2015

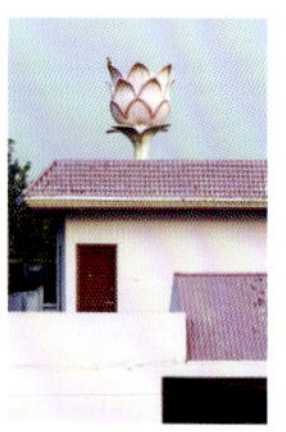
p. 55, lotus flower, village of Chak Vendal, 2015

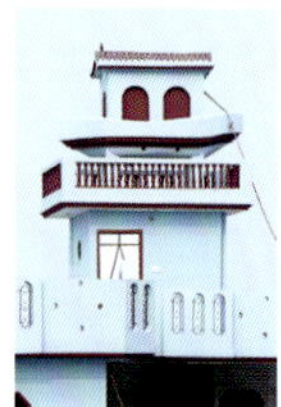
p. 56, ship, village of Dhaliwal, 2015

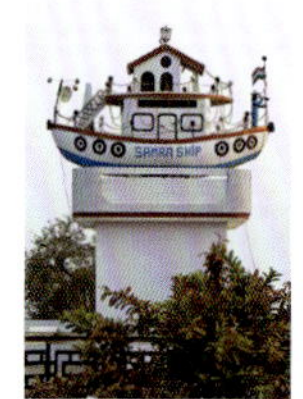
p. 59, ship, village of Mehatpur, 2015

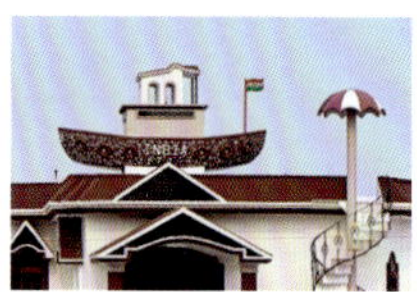
p. 60, ship, village of Bir Pind, 2015

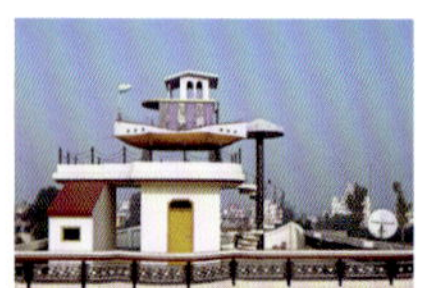
p. 61, ship, village of Bir Bansian, 2014

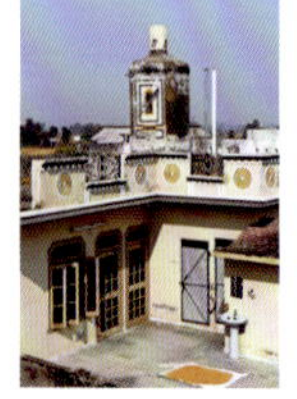
p. 62, whisky bottle, village of Jhander Kalan, 2015

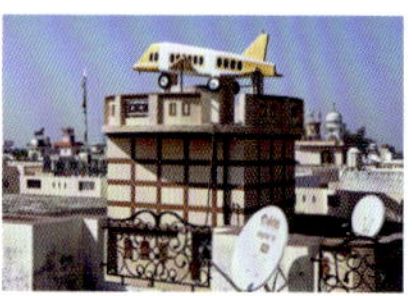
p. 62–63, airplane, village of Chamiara, 2019

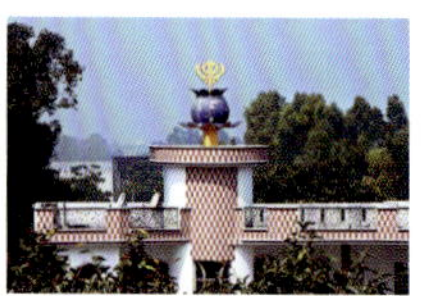
pp. 64–65, lotus flower with khanda, village of Nathu Chahal, 2015

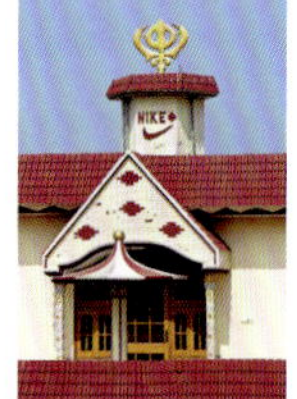
p. 65, khanda, village of Bhandal Dona, 2015

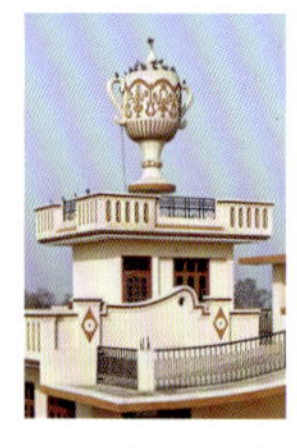
p. 66, cricket trophy, village of Kandola Kalan, 2015

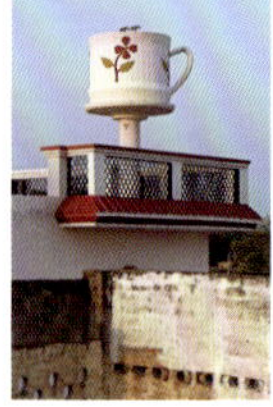
p. 67, tea cup, village of Kot Kalan, 2015

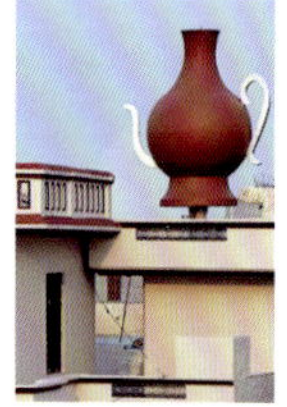
p. 68, water jug, village of Jhander Kalan, 2015

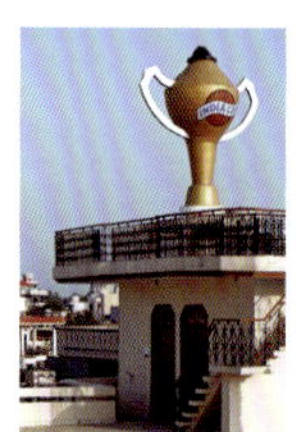
p. 69, cricket trophy, village of Kular, 2015

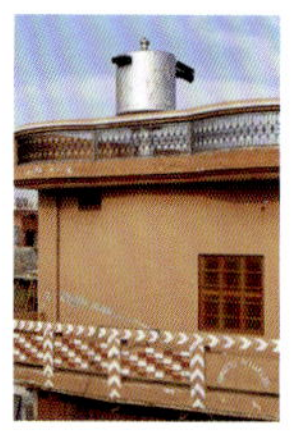
p. 71, *pressure cooker, village of Jhander Kalan, 2019

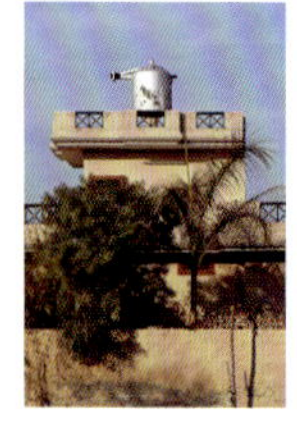
p. 72, pressure cooker, village of Karnana, 2015

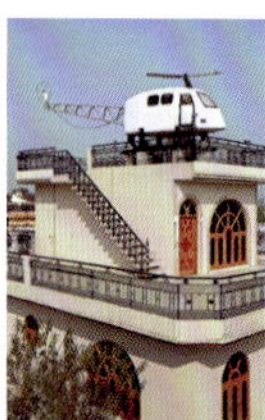
p. 74, helicopter, village unknown, 2014

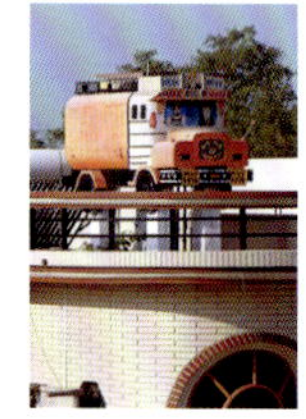
p. 75, *oil tanker, village of Kotla (Kotlay), 2015

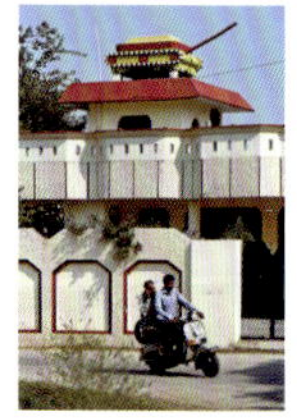
p. 77, army tank, village of Sarhala Ranuan, 2015

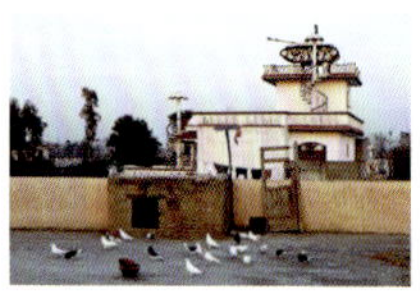
pp. 78–79, *army tank, village of Thinda, 2015

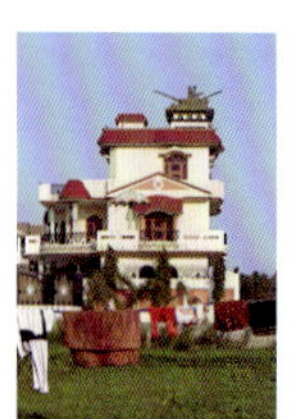
p. 80, *army tank, village of Kheri (Sapror), 2015

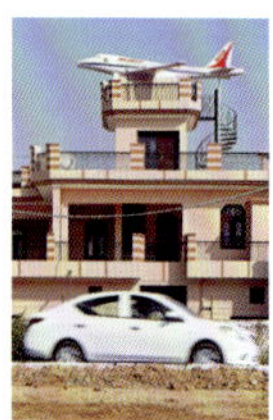
p. 83, airplane, village of Bahua, 2019

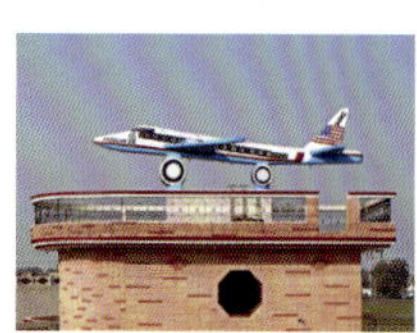
p. 84, airplane, village of Paddi Khalsa, 2014

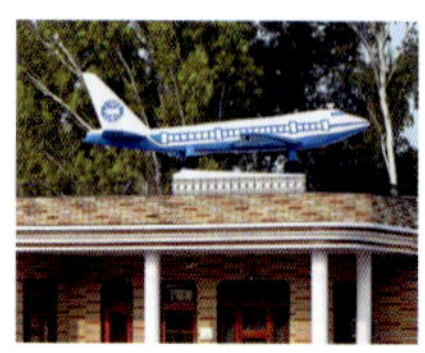
p. 85, airplane, city of Hoshiarpur, 2015

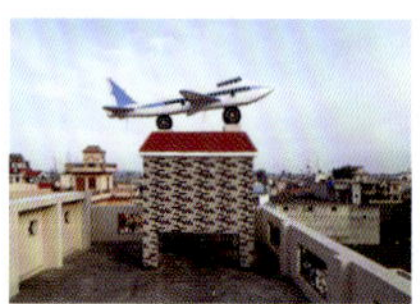
pp. 86–87, *airplane, village of Chak Mander, 2014

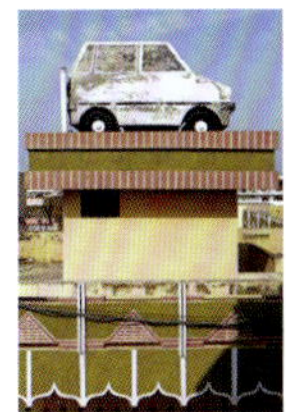
p. 88, Maruti car,
village of Khela, 2015

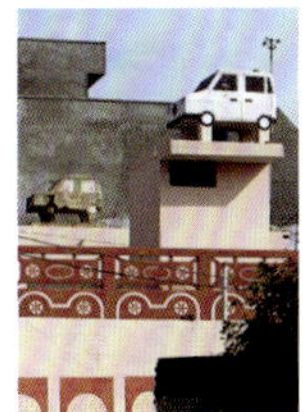
p. 89, *Maruti cars,
village of Goraya, 2015

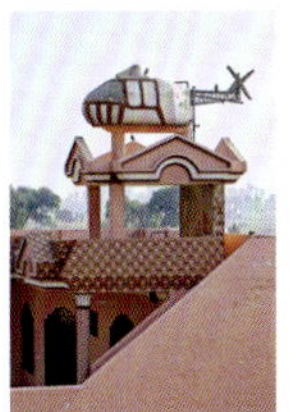
p. 90, *helicopter,
village of Hapowal, 2014

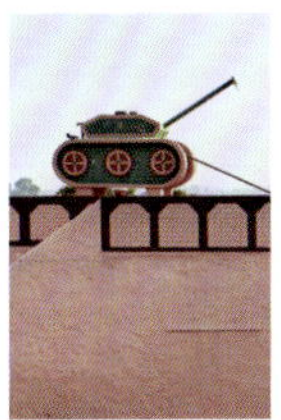
p. 91, *army tank,
village of Hapowal, 2014

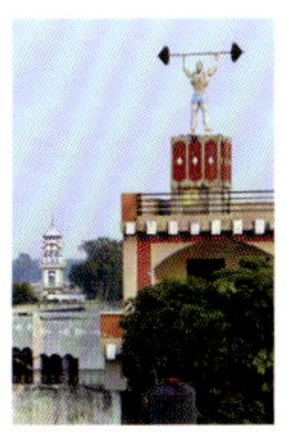
p. 93, weightlifter,
village of Dhuleta, 2015

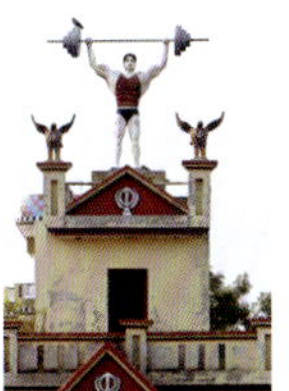
p. 94, *weightlifter,
village of Pachranga, 2015

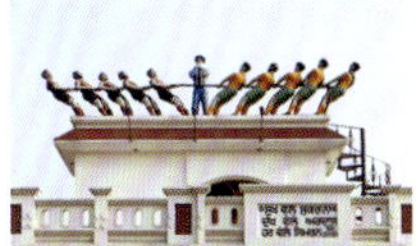
pp. 96–97, tug-of-war,
village of Haripur, 2014

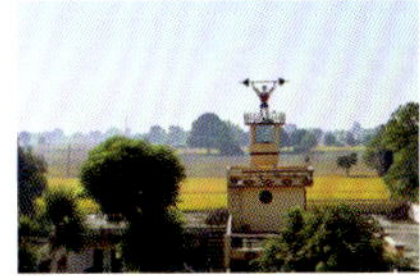
pp. 98–99, weightlifter,
village of Chamiara, 2019

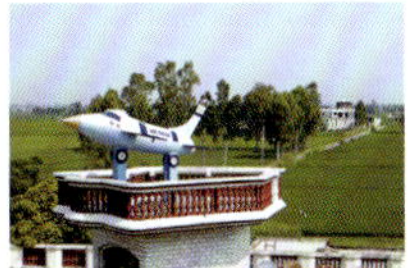
p. 100, airplane,
village of Rampur Khalian,
2015

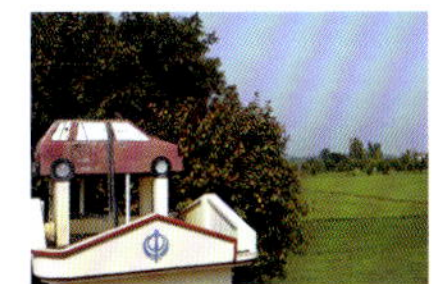
p. 101, Maruti car,
village of Sahni, 2015

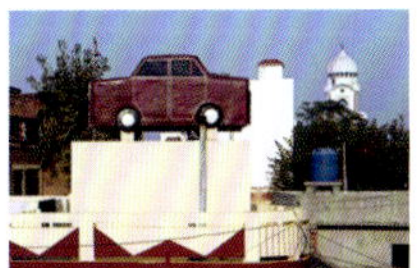
pp. 102–3, Maruti car,
village of Bir Bansian, 2014

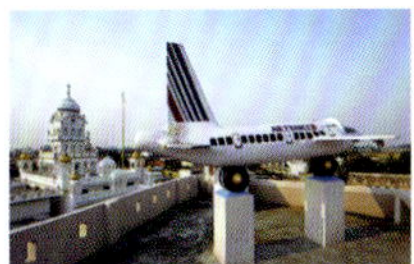
pp. 104–5, airplane,
village of Khaira, 2015

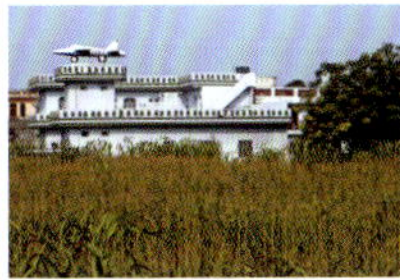
pp. 106–7, *airplane,
village of Mubarakpur, 2015

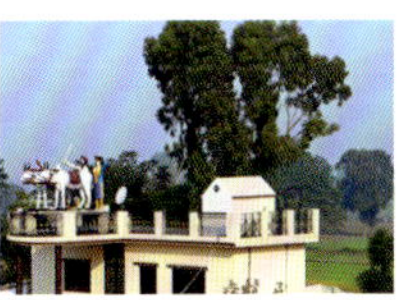
pp. 108–9, farm bullocks,
village of Safipur, 2015

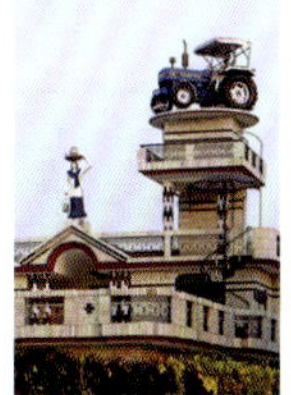
p. 111, farm tractor,
village of Bara Pind, 2015

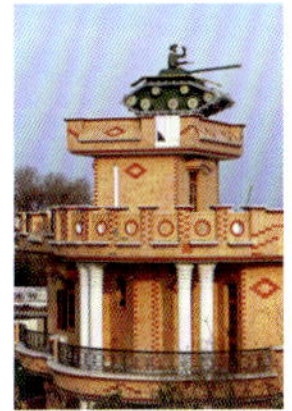
p. 112, army tank,
village of Jamsher Khera, 2015

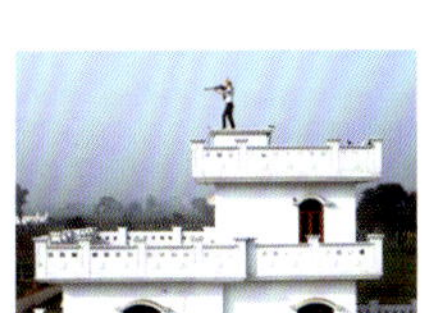
pp. 114–15, *man with rifle,
village of Kandola Kalan, 2015

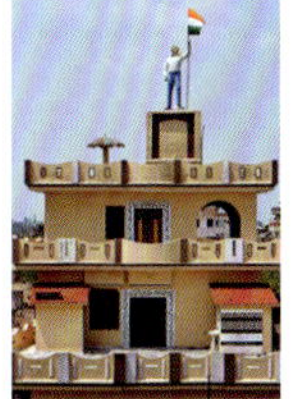
p. 116, freedom fighter
Shaheed Bhagat Singh,
village of Mahal Khurd, 2015

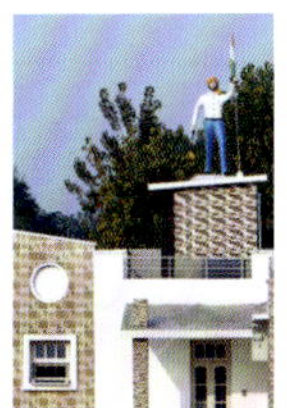
p. 117, freedom fighter
Shaheed Bhagat Singh,
village of Banga, 2015

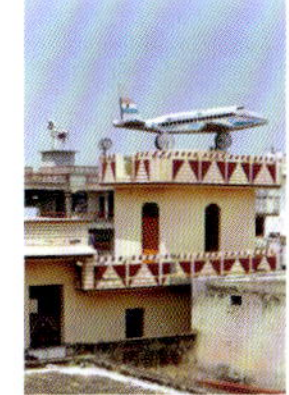
p. 118, *airplane,
village of Garcha, 2015

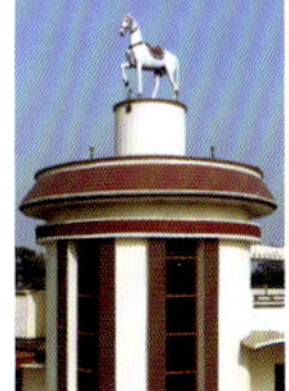
p. 119, horse,
village of Bir Pind, 2014

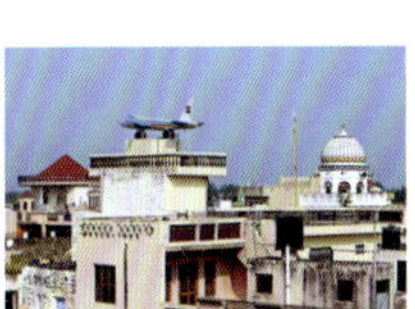
pp. 120–21, airplane,
village of Sahni, 2015

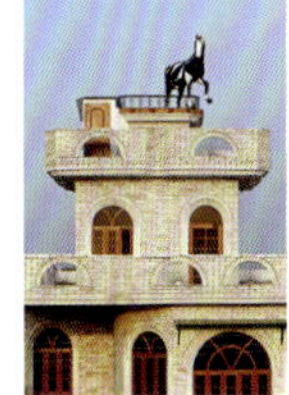
p. 123, horse,
village of Kot Kalan, 2015

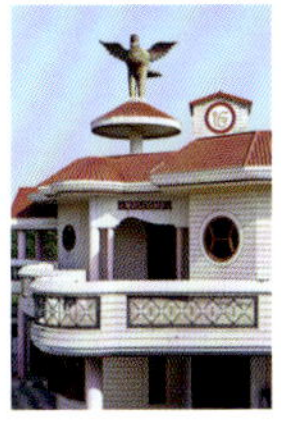
p. 124, falcon,
village of Umarpur, 2019

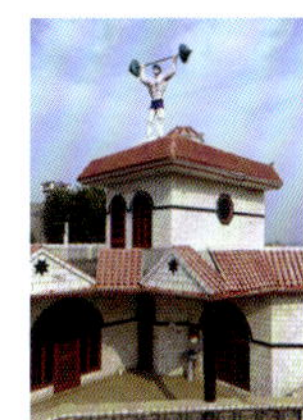
p. 125, *weightlifter,
village of Mandhali, 2014

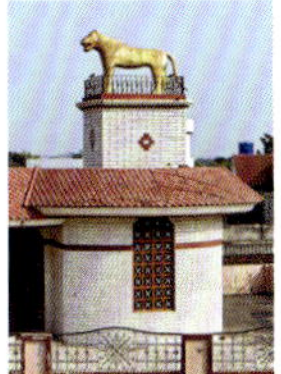
p. 127, *lion,
village of Hapowal, 2015

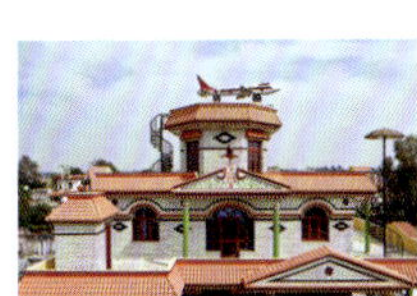
pp. 128–29, airplane,
village of Kotli Khakhian, 2019

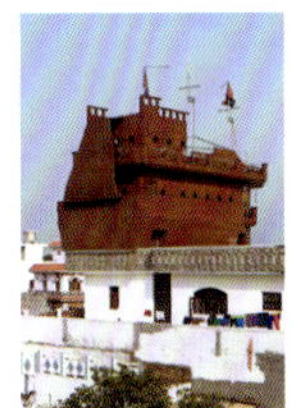
p. 130, *ship,
village of Pandori Khas, 2015

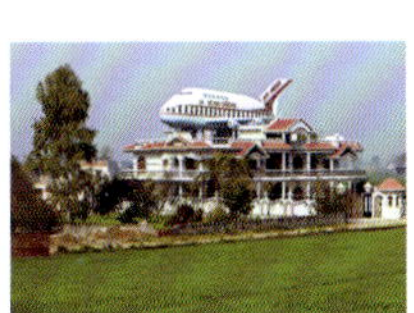
pp. 130–31, airplane,
village of Uppal Bhupa, 2015

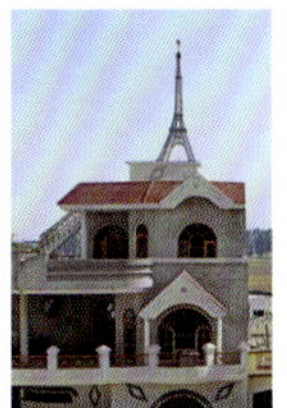
p. 132, *Eiffel Tower,
village of Sukhani, 2019

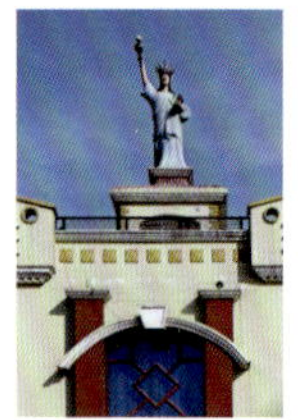
p. 133, *Statue of Liberty, village of Kultham, 2015

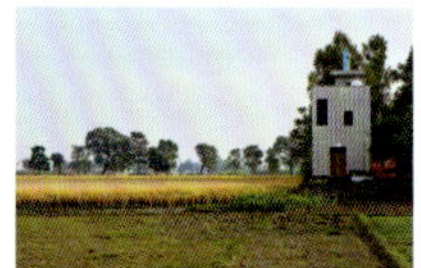
pp. 134–35, Statue of Liberty, village of Jhander Kalan, 2019

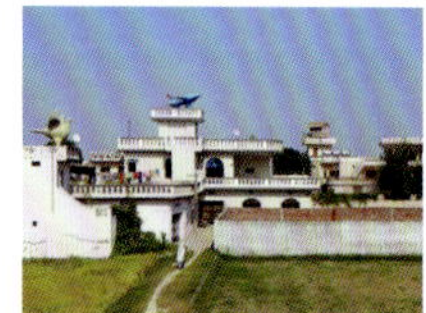
pp. 136–37, *village of Jhander Kalan, 2015

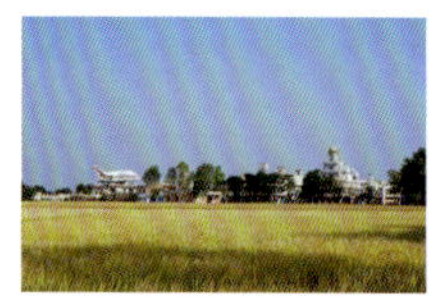
pp. 152–53, *village of Uppal Bhupa, 2015

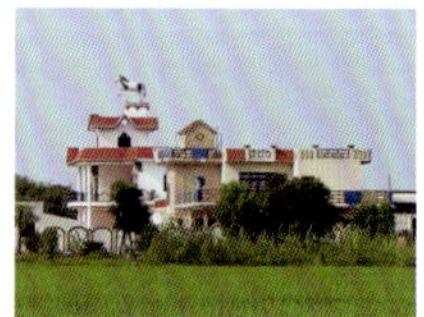
pp. 162–63, *horse, village of Johal, 2015

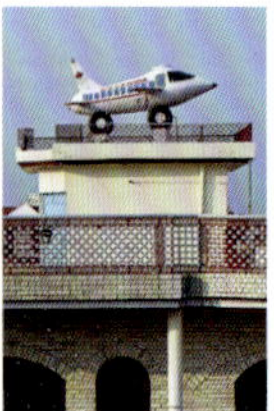
p. 167, airplane, village of Talhan, 2019

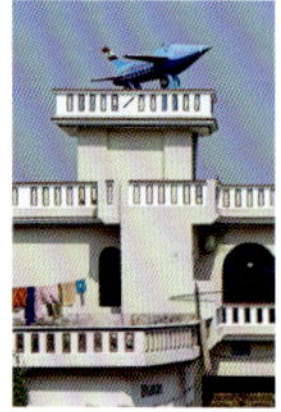
p. 167, airplane, village of Jhander Kalan, 2015

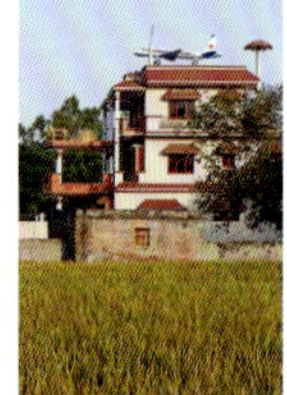
p. 167, airplane, village of Bir Bansian, 2019

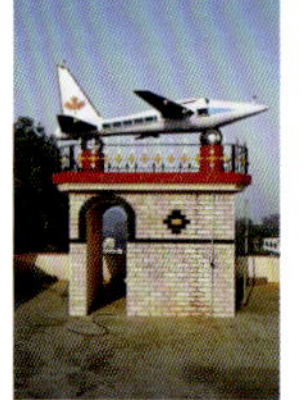
p. 168, *airplane, village of Rurka Kalan, 2014

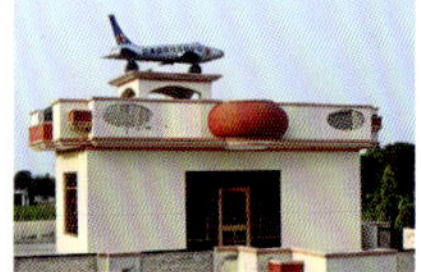
p. 168, airplane, village of Nangal Fateh Khan, 2015

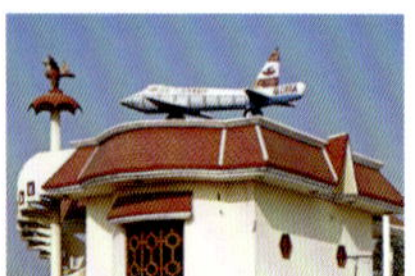
p. 168, village of Bisla-Behram, 2014

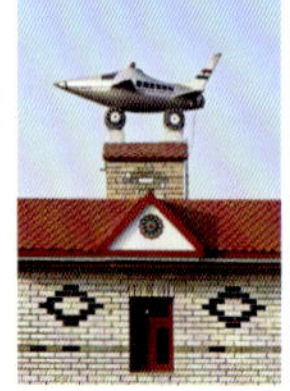
p. 171, airplane, village of Palahi, 2014

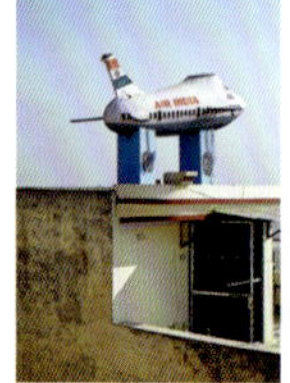
p. 171, *airplane, village of Boparai, 2015

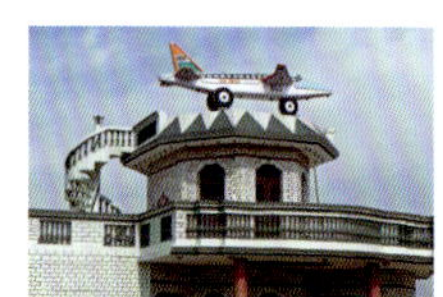
p. 171, airplane, village of Datta, 2015

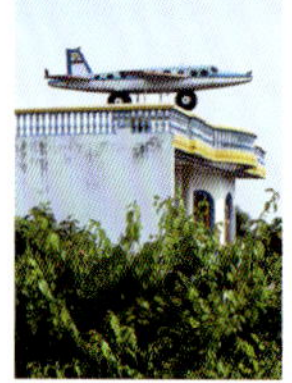
p. 171, *airplane, village of Sandhwan, 2015

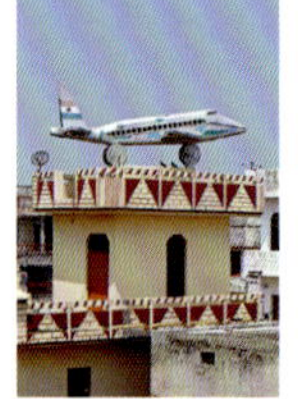
p. 171, airplane, village of Garcha, 2015

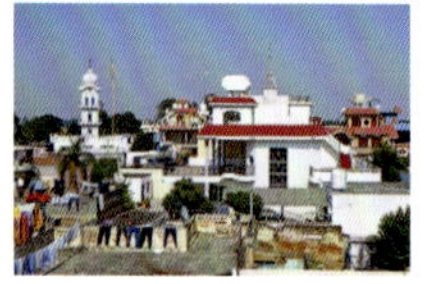
pp. 172–73, village of Sukhani, 2019

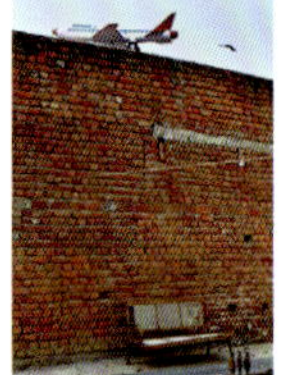
Endsheet/flyleaf, *airplane, village unknown, 2014

# ADDITIONAL WORKS SHOWN IN THE EXHIBITION

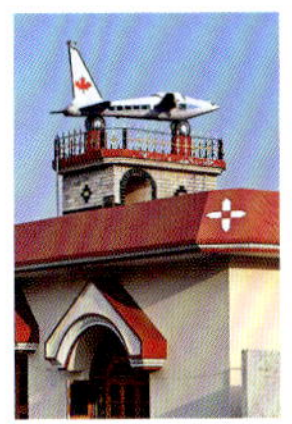
Airplane, village of Rurka Kalan, 2015

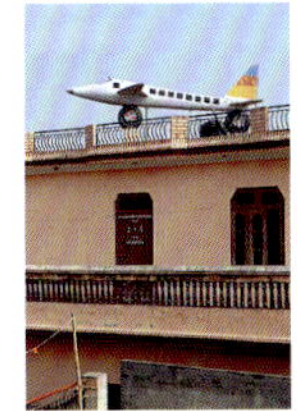
Airplane, village of Nano Mazara, 2014

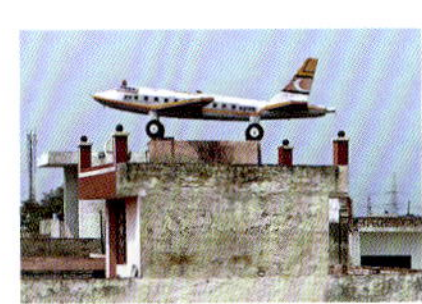
Airplane, village of Rama Mandi, 2015

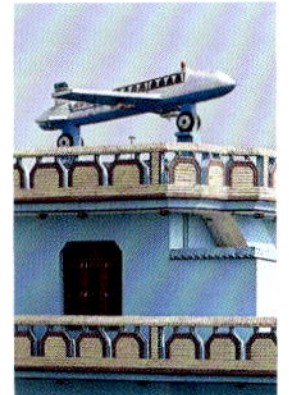
Airplane, village of Kultham, 2015

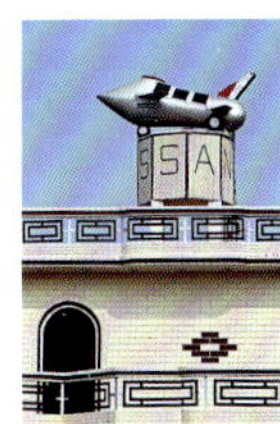
Airplane, village of Mohem, 2015

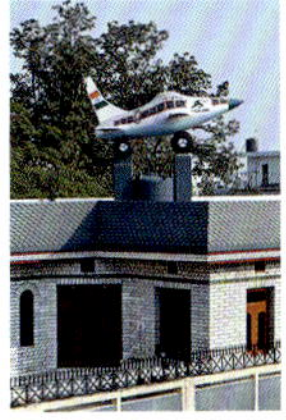
Airplane, village of Palahi, 2014

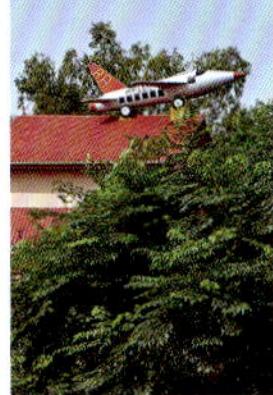
Airplane, village of Baler Khanpur, 2015

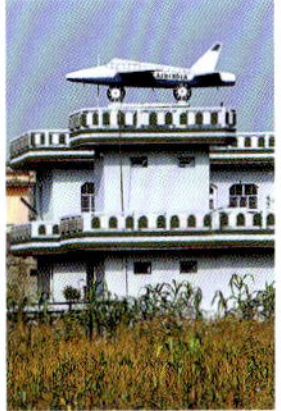
Airplane, village of Mubarakpur, 2015

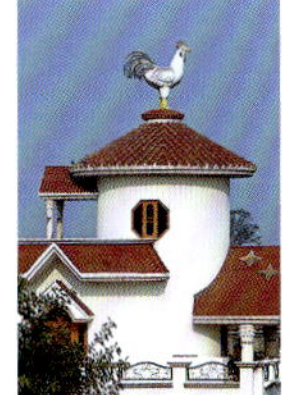
Rooster, village of Nai Mazara, 2015

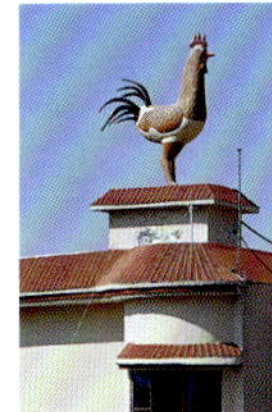
Rooster, village of Gujarpur, 2019

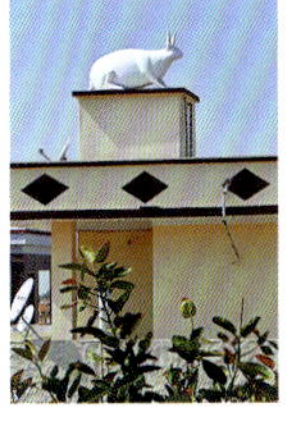
Rabbit, village of Littran, 2019

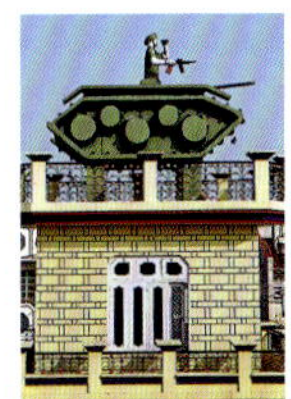
Army tank, village of Daulatapur, 2015

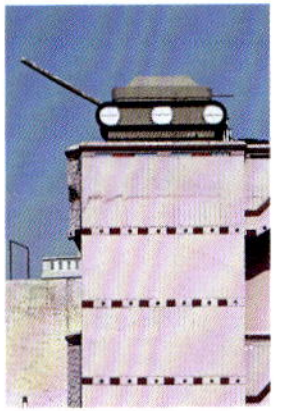
Army tank, village of Virk (Birka), 2015

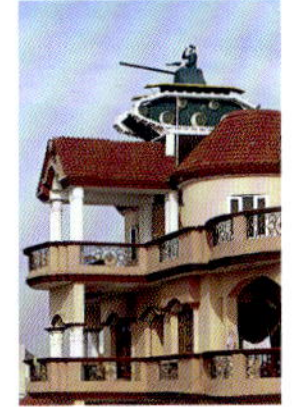
Army tank, village of Chaheru, 2015

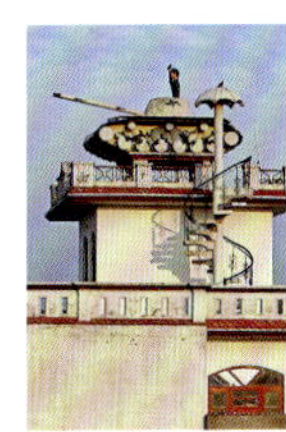
Army tank, village of Thinda, 2015

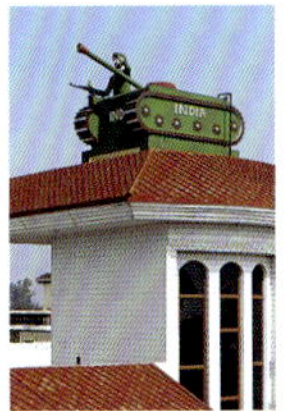
Army tank, village of Khela, 2015

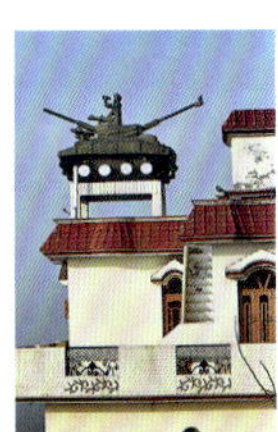
Army tank, village of Kheri (Sapror), 2015

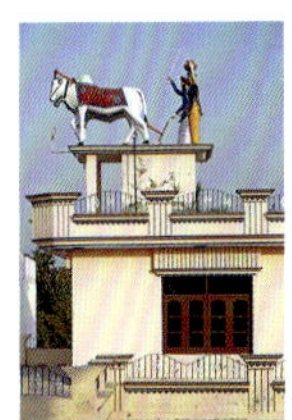
Farm bullocks, village of Jhikka (Ladhana), 2014

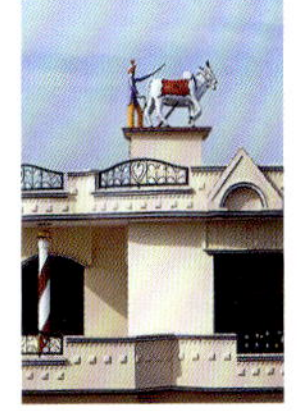
Farm bullocks, village of Chuharpur 2015

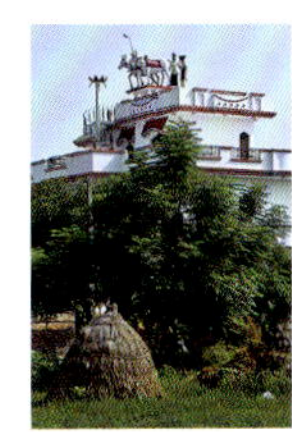
Farm bullocks, village of Prempur, 2015

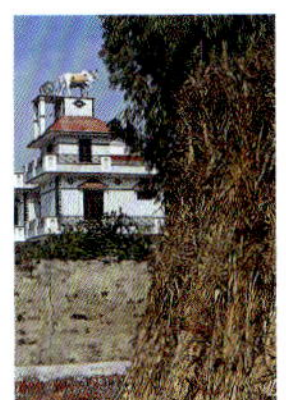
Farm bullocks, village of Datta, 2015

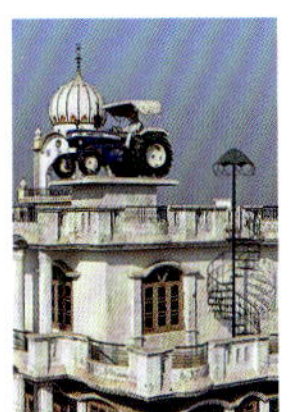
Tractor, village of Kang Araian, 2014

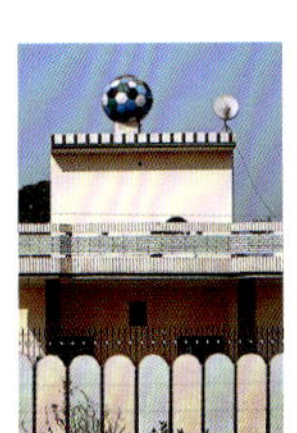
Football, village of Nagar, 2014

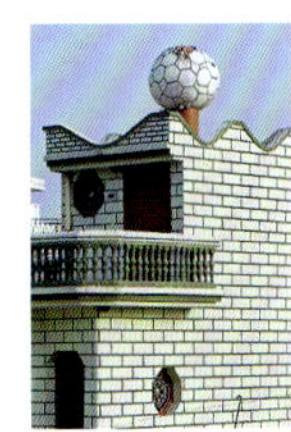
Football, village of Barnala Kalan, 2015

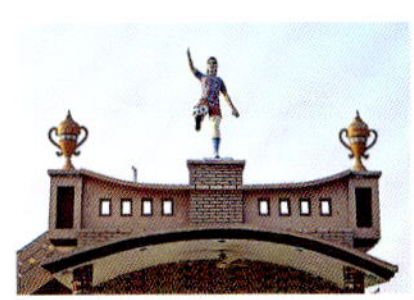
Football player and trophies, village of Jandiala Manjki, 2014

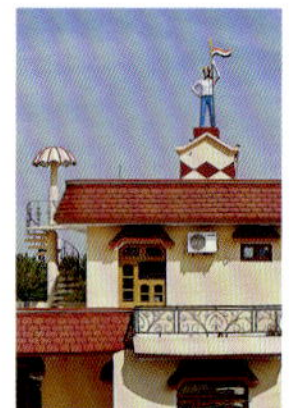

Freedom fighter Shaheed Bhagat Singh, village of Paddi Khalsa, 2019

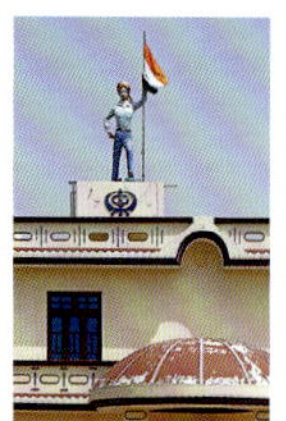

Freedom fighter Shaheed Bhagat Singh, village of Mehrampur, 2015

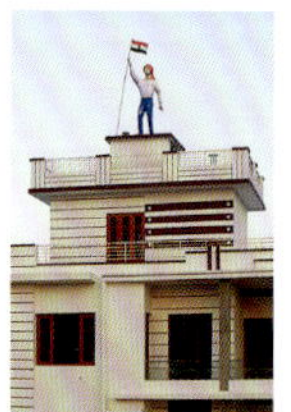

Freedom fighter Shaheed Bhagat Singh, village of Basiala, 2019

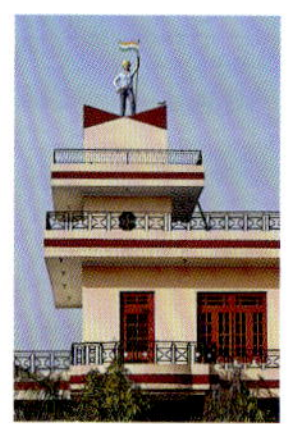

Freedom fighter Shaheed Bhagat Singh, village of Boparai, 2015

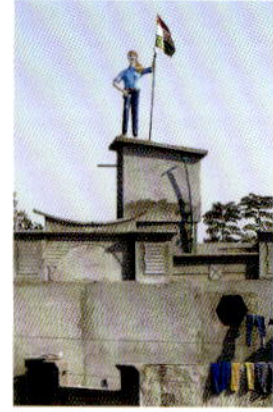

Freedom fighter Shaheed Bhagat Singh, village unknown, 2014

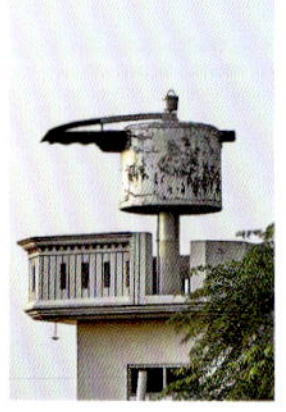

Pressure cooker, village of Saloh, 2015

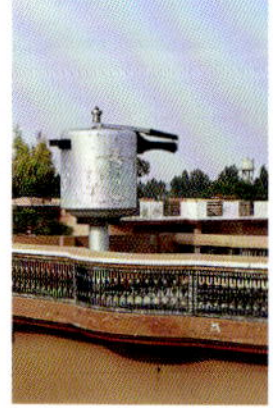

Pressure cooker, village of Jhander Kalan, 2019

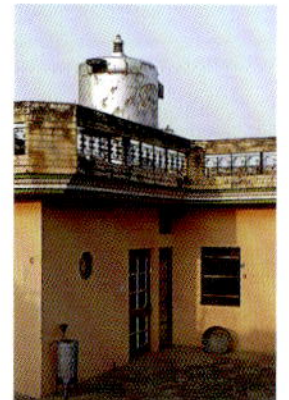

Pressure cooker, village of Saloh, 2015

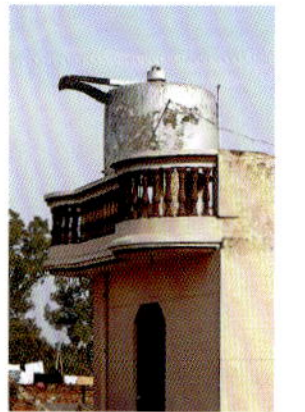

Pressure cooker, village of Hapowal, 2014

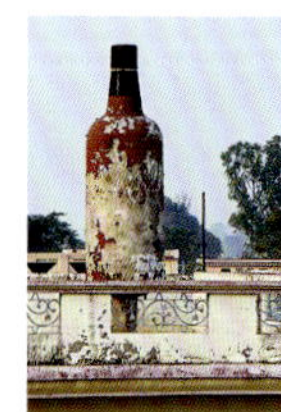

Liquor bottle, village of Jhander Kalan, 2015

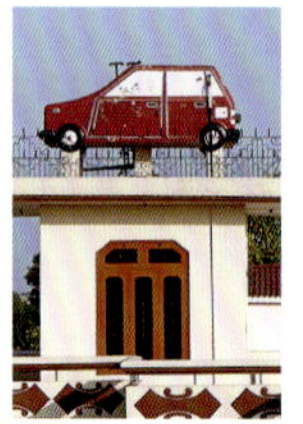

Maruti car, village of Kular, 2015

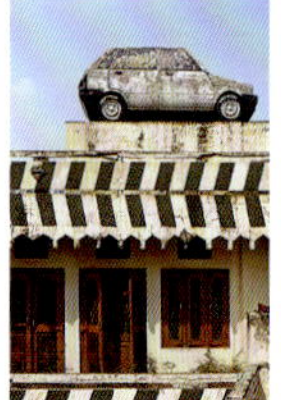

Maruti car, village of Paroo Majra, 2015

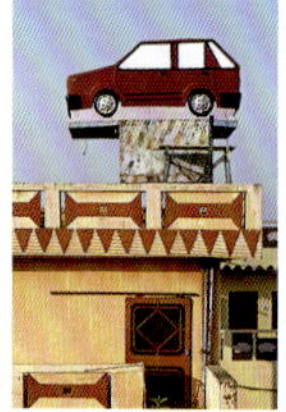

Maruti car, village of Khaira, 2014

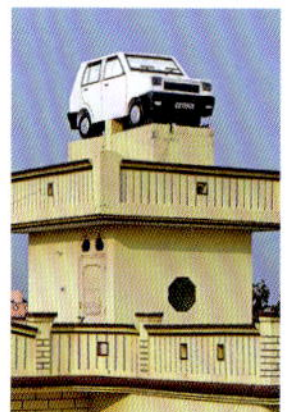

Maruti car, village of Nai Mazara, 2015

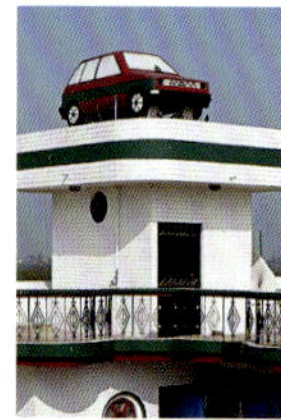

Maruti car, village unknown, 2014

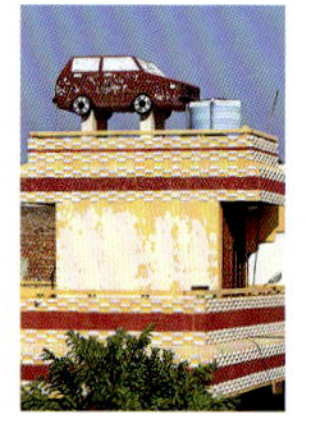

Maruti car, town of Mahilpur, 2019

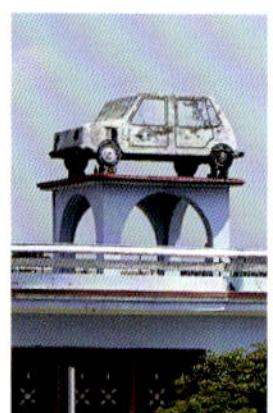

Maruti car, village of Tashpur, 2015

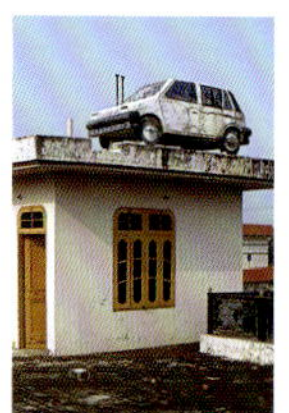

Maruti car, village of Dhapai, 2015

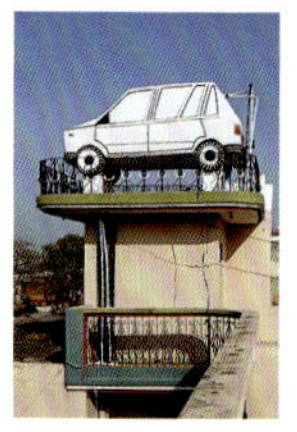

Maruti car, village unknown, 2014

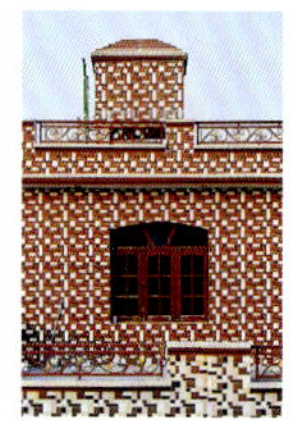

Decorated water tank, village of Bir Bansian, 2019

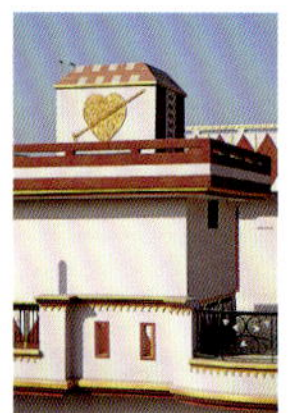

Decorated water tank, village of Paddi Khalsa, 2014

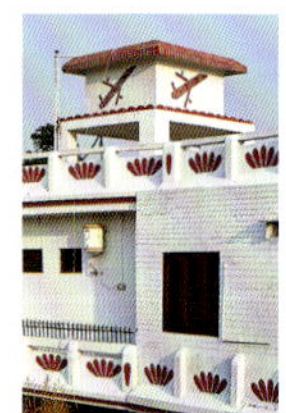

Decorated water tank, village of Bir Bansian, 2019

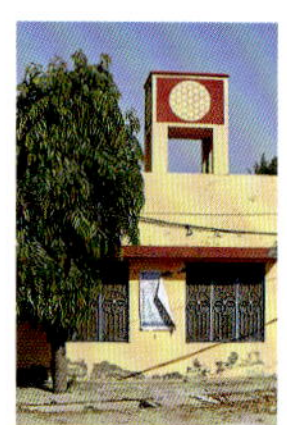

Decorated water tank, village of Soondh, 2019

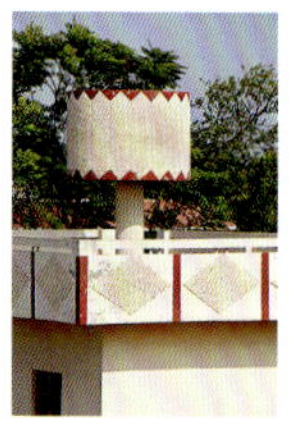

Decorated water tank, village of Sukhani, 2019

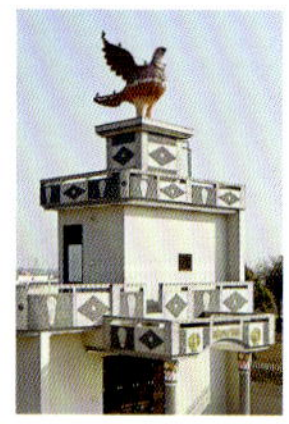

Falcon, village of Paddi Khalsa, 2014

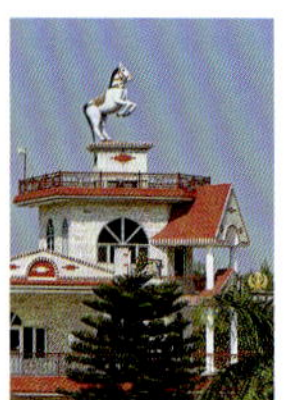

Horse, village of Kandola Kalan, 2019

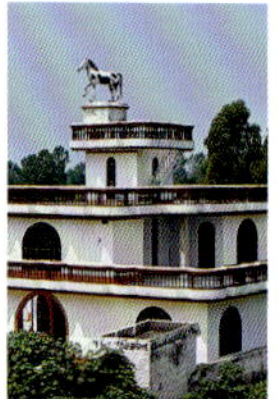

Horse, village of Budhiana, 2015

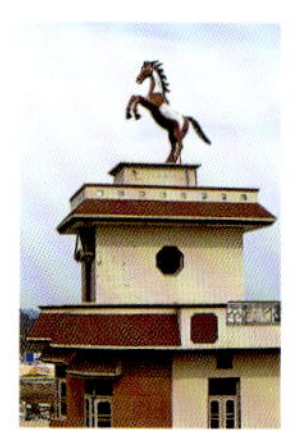

Horse, village of Soondh, 2015

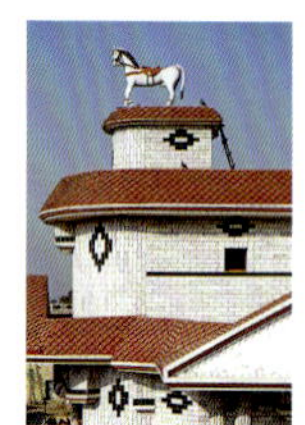

Horse, village of Paddi Khalsa, 2014

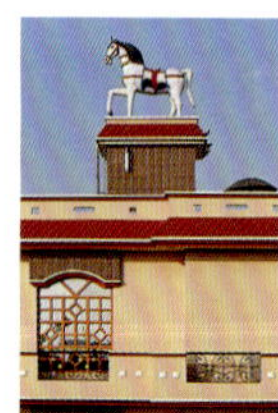

Horse, village of Madhopur, 2015

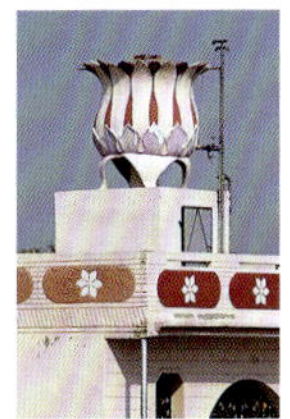
Lotus flower, village of Mathda Khurd, 2015

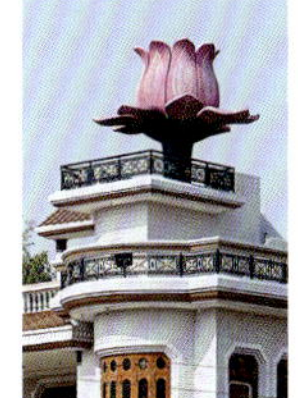
Lotus flower, village of Mehatpur, 2015

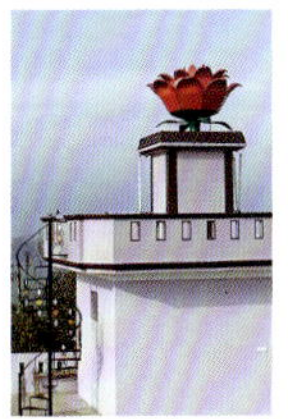
Lotus flower, village of Palahi, 2015

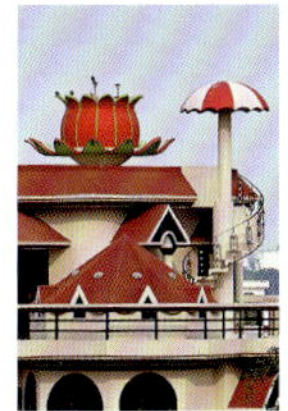
Lotus flower, town of Nakodar, 2015

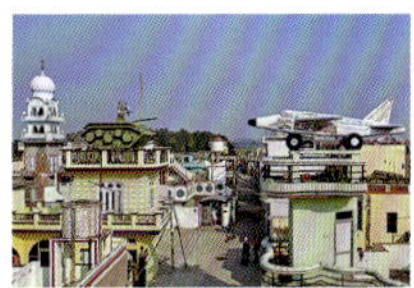
Village of Daulatapur, 2015

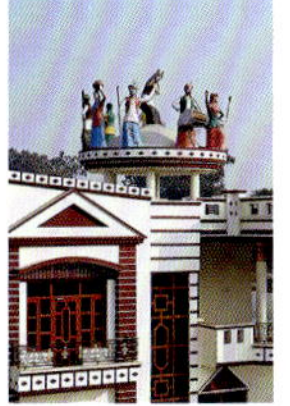
Bhangra group, village of Bath Kalan, 2014

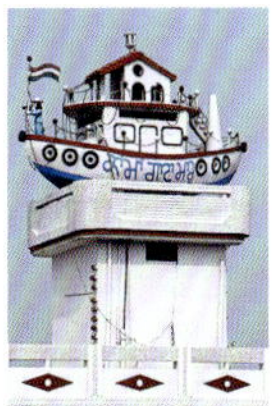
Ship, village of Mehatpur, 2015

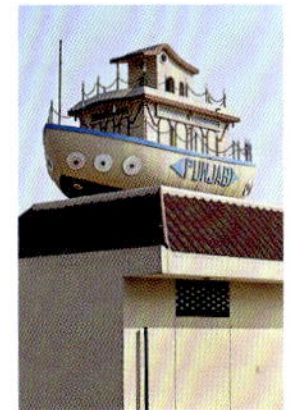
Ship, village of Kandola Kalan, 2015

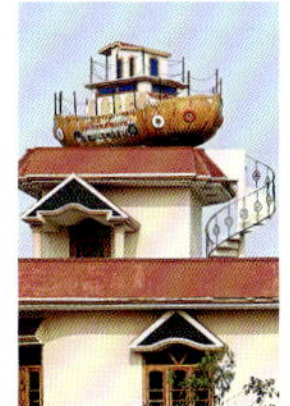
Ship, village of Bir Pind, 2015

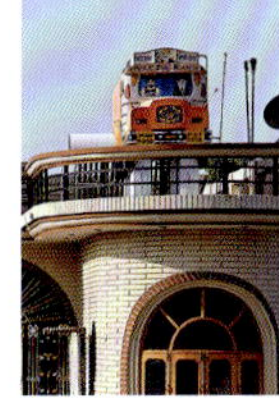
Oil tanker, village of Kotla (Kotlay), 2015

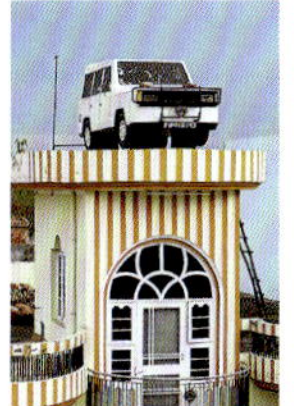
SUV, village of Nangal Sapror, 2014

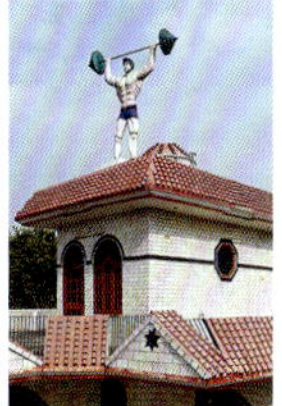
Weightlifter, village of Mandhali, 2014

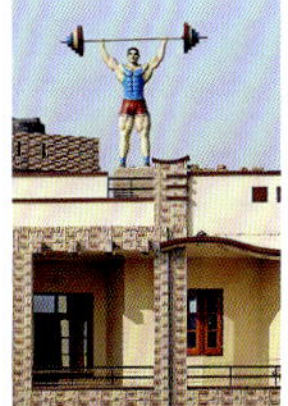
Weightlifter, village of Palahi, 2014

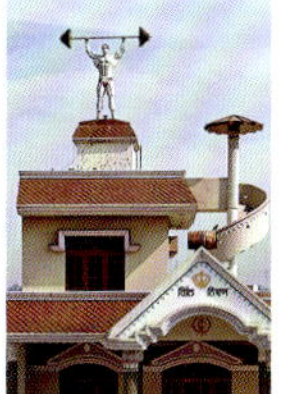
Weightlifter, village of Paddi Khalsa, 2015

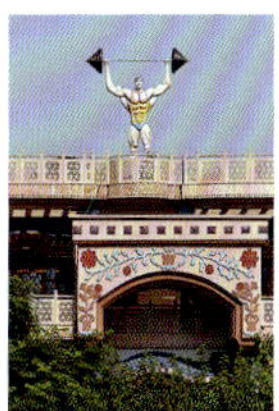
Weightlifter, village of Jallowal, 2015

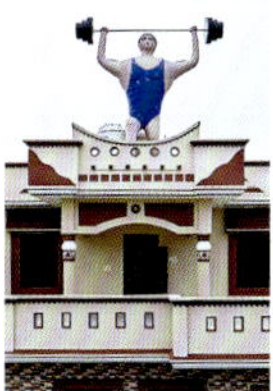
Weightlifter, village of Khaira Patian, 2019

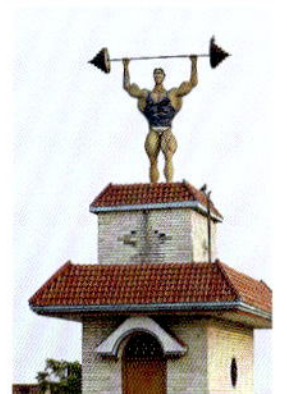
Weightlifter, village of Chak Vendal, 2015

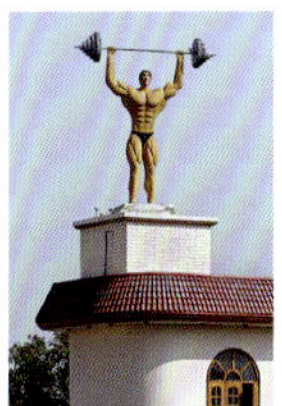
Weightlifter, village of Mallian Kalan, 2015

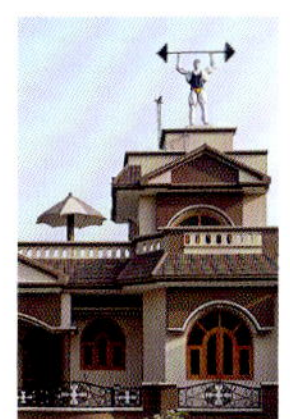
Weightlifter, village of Nauli, 2015

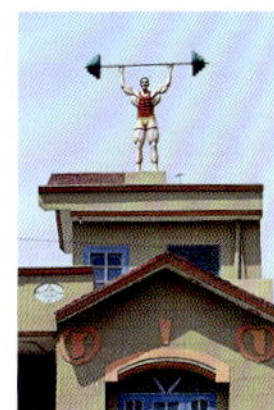
Weightlifter, village of Narur, 2015

# CONTRIBUTORS

**DR. SATWINDER KAUR BAINS** is Director of the South Asian Studies Institute and an associate professor of Culture, Media, and Society Studies at the University of the Fraser Valley in Abbotsford, British Columbia, Canada. Her critical analysis of India's multilingual policy and planning has fuelled her interest in studying the Impact of language, culture, and identity on South Asian Canadian migration, settlement, and integration. Her widely published research includes and intersects cross-cultural education with a focus on anti-racist curriculum implementation; race, racism, and ethnicity; identity politics; Sikh feminist ideology; migration and the South Asian Canadian diaspora; and Punjabi Canadian cultural historiography. She has served on numerous boards locally, nationally, and internationally, and as a commissioner on the BC Provincial Agricultural Land Commission, director of the Fraser Basin Council, bencher of the Law Society of British Columbia, and member of the BC Farm Industry Review Board. She currently sits on the boards of the Knowledge Network and the Abbotsford Community Foundation. Her scholarship, extensive community service, and work with various organizations have earned her numerous awards for her commitment to social justice, preservation of histories and cultural knowledge, and women's rights.

**RAHUL MEHROTRA** is the principal founder of RMA Architects in Mumbai, as well as professor of Urban Design and Planning and the John T. Dunlop Professor in Housing and Urbanization at the Graduate School of Design at Harvard University in Cambridge, Massachusetts. Since 2014, Mehrotra has been a member of the International Committee of Architectural Critics, and he is a member of the steering committee of the Lakshmi Mittal and Family South Asia Institute at Harvard. Since 1990, RMA Architects has completed numerous major private and public projects, including a Hewlett-Packard campus in Bangalore, a conservation master plan for the Taj Mahal, a social housing project for elephants in Jaipur, and buildings for three postsecondary institutions in Ahmedabad. In 2018, RMA Architects received a special mention from the jury at the Venice Biennale. Mehrotra's many publications and exhibitions include, most recently, *The Kinetic City & Other Essays* (2021); *Working in Mumbai: RMA Architects* (2020); *The State of Housing: Realities, Aspirations and Imaginaries in India* (Gallery MMB, 2018; co-curated with Ranjit Hoskote and Kaiwan Mehta); *Ephemeral Urbanism: Does Permanence Matter?* (2017; with Felipe Vera); and *The State of Architecture: Practices and Processes in India* (2016; co-edited with Ranjit Hoskote and Kaiwan Mehta).

**SAJDEEP SOOMAL** is a PhD student in the Department of History at the University of Toronto, where he is working through science and technology studies, histories of political consciousness and madness, and contemporary art practices within and beyond South Asia. Soomal currently works as a research assistant at the Montreal Museum of Fine Arts, where he helps coordinate acquisitions, conduct collections research, and organize public programming for the Kapany Collection of Sikh Art. He serves as the chairperson of the Canadian Filmmakers Distribution Centre (CFMDC), a collective member of Sanghum Film, and a programming committee member of InterAccess. Soomal has previously conducted oral historical research and digital archiving projects for the South Asian Visual Arts Centre (SAVAC), The ArQuives, and the Family Camera Network. He holds a BA in History from McGill University and an MA in History from the University of Toronto.

**RAJESH VORA** is a Mumbai-based photographer focused primarily on architectural and cultural subject matter. He graduated in 1979 from the National Institute of Design in Ahmedabad, India, where he developed an interest in documenting peoples and regions that are threatened by change. His architectural photography has appeared in *Domus* (India), *Architectural Design* (India), *Inside Outside*, *Dezeen*, *ArchDaily*, and COLORS, where he contributed for fifteen years as a photographer, researcher, and writer. He photographed architecture projects for The Aga Khan Award for Architecture Foundation in 2001, 2007, 2010, and 2016. His documentary photos have appeared in numerous publications, most recently *The Kinetic City & Other Essays* (2021), *Working in Mumbai: RMA Architects* (2020), and *The Architecture of I.M. Kadri* (2016). He has exhibited photographs in group shows in New Delhi, the Canary Islands, the Netherlands, France, and the United States. His ongoing personal project, *Everyday Baroque*, first appeared as a solo exhibition in 2016 at PHOTOINK, New Delhi. This project was reconceived as *Everyday Monuments* in 2022 for Surrey Art Gallery, British Columbia, Canada.

**KEITH WALLACE** has been a curator of contemporary art since 1979. For ten years he was curator, then director/curator, of the Contemporary Art Gallery in Vancouver, where he developed a program of regional, national, and international exhibitions. As an independent curator, he organized exhibitions for the National Gallery of Canada in Ottawa (*Reality Check*); the Vancouver International Centre for Contemporary Asian Art (*Resonance: Contemporary Art from New Delhi*, with Anita Dube and Subodh Gupta); and The Power Plant Contemporary Art Gallery in Toronto (*Stretch*, co-curated with Eugenio Valdés Figueroa). For seven years he was associate director/curator at the Morris and Helen Belkin Art Gallery at the University of British Columbia in Vancouver. He has contributed to numerous publications, including *Vancouver Anthology* (1991), *Whispered Art History* (1993), *Action–Camera: Beijing Performance Photography* (2009), *Jayce Salloum: History of the Present* (2009), *Sunil Gupta: Queer* (2011), *The Spaces Between: Contemporary Art from Havana* (2014), and *Anna Wong: Traveller on Two Roads* (2018). His long-time support of artist-run centres led him to organize InFest: International Artist–Run Culture, a 2004 conference in Vancouver. From 2004 to 2020, Wallace was editor-in-chief of *Yishu: Journal of Contemporary Chinese Art* published by ARTCO, Taipei.

23 24 25 26 27   5 4 3 2 1



Cataloguing data is available from Library and Archives Canada
ISBN 978-1-77327-201-6 (hbk.)

Design by Naomi MacDougall
Production coordination by Keith Wallace
Editing by Michael Leyne
Copy editing by Stephanie Fysh
Proofreading by Renate Preuss
Maps by Satwinder Dhillon / Metabrand

Maps are used for general representational purposes only.

All photos by Rajesh Vora, unless otherwise noted.
Rajesh Vora is represented by PHOTOINK, New Delhi (www.photoink.net).

Printed and bound in China by C&C Offset Printing Co.
Distributed internationally by Publishers Group West

We acknowledge the support of the Canada Council for the Arts.

Figure 1 Publishing Inc.
Vancouver BC Canada
www.figure1publishing.com

This book was published in conjunction with the exhibition *Rajesh Vora: Everyday Monuments* at Surrey Art Gallery, April 9 to May 29, 2022.

Surrey Art Gallery
Surrey BC Canada
www.surrey.ca/arts-culture/surrey-art-gallery

Alison Rajah, Director
Jordan Strom, Curator of Exhibitions and Collections
Rhys Edwards, Assistant Curator
Suvi Bains, Assistant Curator
Zoe Yang, Curatorial Assistant
Lindsay McArthur, Visual Arts Programmer
Jinsil Haveliwalla, Learning Coordinator
Alanna Edwards, Education and Engagement Coordinator
Avishka Lakwijaya, Engagement Facilitator
Opal McLean, Engagement Facilitator
Chris Dawson-Murphy, Volunteer Coordinator
Charlene Back, Communications Coordinator
Chris Dean, Lead Preparator
Scot Keefer, Preparator
Claire Chupik, Assistant Preparator

Figure 1 Publishing works in the traditional, unceded territory of the xʷməθkʷəy̓əm (Musqueam), Sk̲wx̲wú7mesh (Squamish), and səlilwətaɬ (Tsleil-Waututh) peoples.

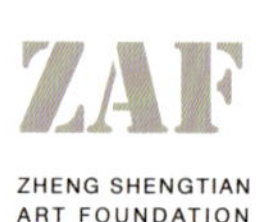


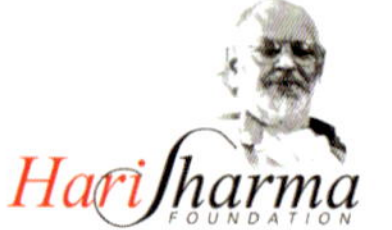


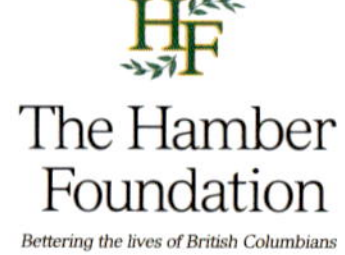


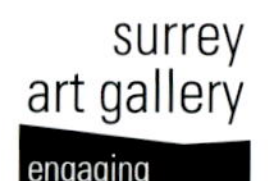


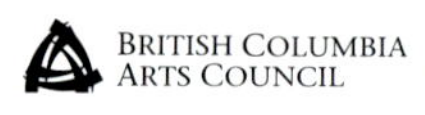


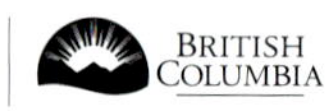


Supported by the Province of British Columbia

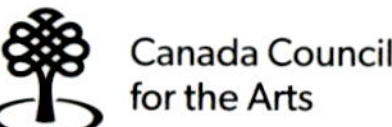

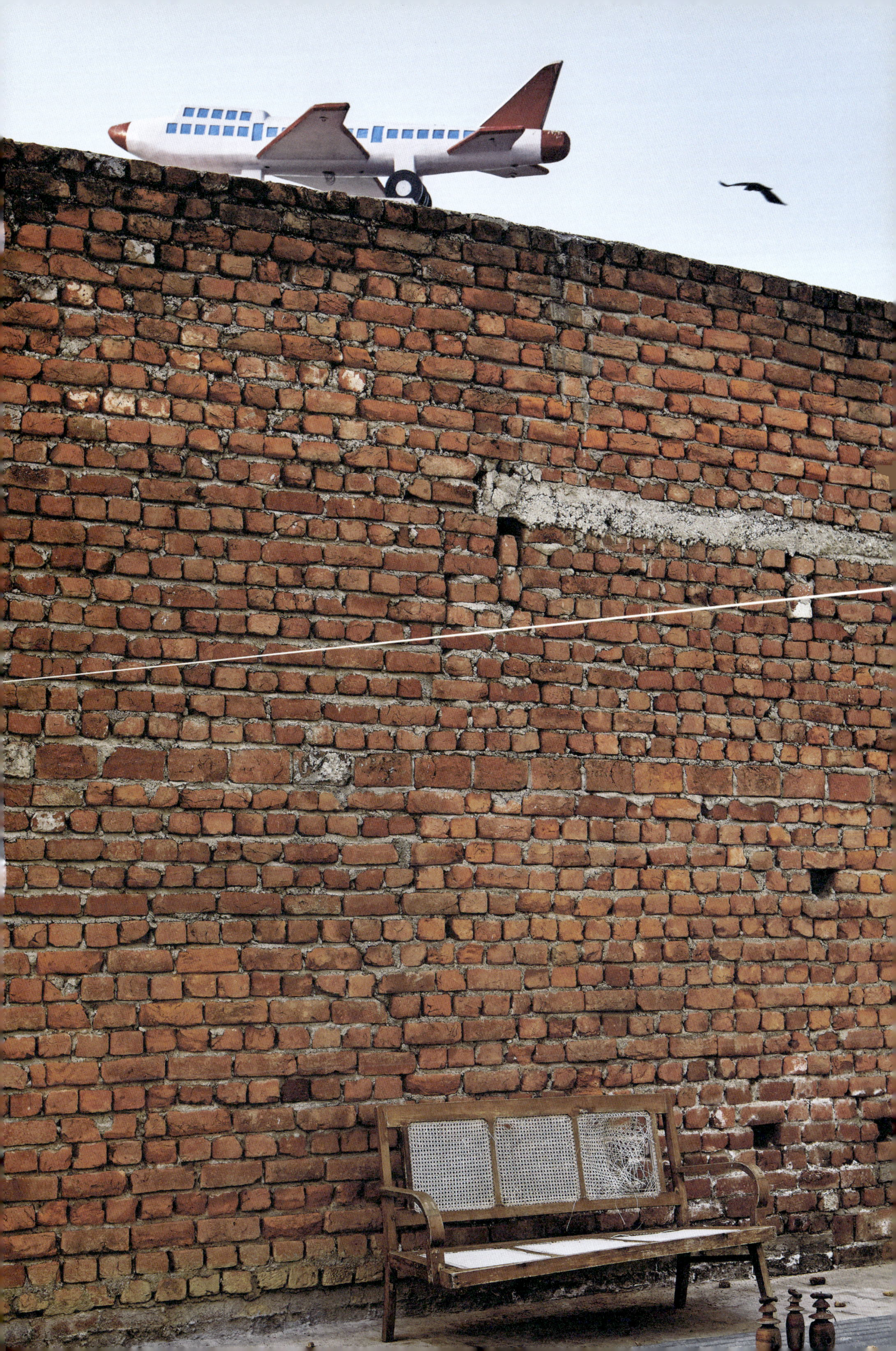